THE CIVIL WARS

A MILITARY HISTORY OF ENGLAND, SCOTLAND,
AND IRELAND 1638–1660

Portrait of Charles I and family
by Van Dyck

Shortly after he arrived in London in 1632 Anthony Van Dyck, one of the most accomplished artists in Europe, painted this delightful family scene. Charles I, with Charles, prince of Wales (born 29 May 1630) at his knee, is seated next to Queen Henrietta Maria who holds the infant Princess Mary (born 4 November 1631) on her lap. In the background is a view of the Thames at Westminster. The remote grandeur of the king is striking, as is the sense of intimacy between the royal couple. These were years of peace and prosperity in England: in the countryside, despite political discontent, there was no major economic crisis; while at court the royal family grew in numbers — the queen was pregnant almost every year. Charles's devotion to his Catholic wife and his love of culture and art, combined with his ecclesiastical policies, left him open to charges of being pro-papist.

THE
CIVIL
WARS

A MILITARY HISTORY OF
ENGLAND, SCOTLAND, AND
IRELAND 1638–1660

EDITED BY

JOHN KENYON AND JANE OHLMEYER

Consultant Editor

JOHN MORRILL

Oxford · New York

OXFORD UNIVERSITY PRESS

1998

Oxford University Press, Great Clarendon Street, Oxford OX2 6DP

Oxford New York

Athens Auckland Bangkok Bogotá Buenos Aires Calcutta
Cape Town Chennai Dar es Salaam Delhi Florence Hong Kong Istanbul
Karachi Kuala Lumpur Madrid Melbourne Mexico City Mumbai
Nairobi Paris São Paolo Singapore Taipei Tokyo Toronto Warsaw
and associated companies in Berlin Ibadan

Oxford is a trade mark of Oxford University Press

Published in the United States
by Oxford University Press Inc., New York

British Library Cataloguing in Publication Data
Data available

Library of Congress Cataloging in Publication Data
The civil wars : a military history of England, Scotland, and Ireland 1638–1660/
edited by John Kenyon and Jane Ohlmeyer;
consultant editor, John Morrill.
Includes bibliographical references and index.
1. Great Britain—History—Puritan Revolution, 1642–1660.
2. Great Britain—History—Civil War, 1642–1649.
3. Great Britain—History, Military—1603–1714.
4. Scotland—History—17th century.
5. Ireland—History—17th century.
6. Scotland—History, Military.
7. Ireland—History, Military.
I. Kenyon, J. P. (John Philipps), 1927–1996
II. Ohlmeyer, Jane H.
III. Morrill, J. S. (John Stephen)
DA405.C58 1998 941.06—dc21 98–19829

ISBN 0–19–866222–X

1 3 5 7 9 10 8 6 4 2

Typeset by Alliance Phototypesetters, Pondicherry
Printed in Great Britain
on acid-free paper by
Biddles Ltd
Guildford and King's Lynn

DEDICATED TO THE MEMORY OF

JOHN PHILIPPS KENYON

(1927–1996)

PREFACE

I became co-editor of this book under very sad circumstances. On 6 January 1996 John Philipps Kenyon died suddenly after a short illness. While John commissioned the essays for this volume and read two of them, his untimely death denied him the opportunity to edit them. Since I had known John as a student (he was my Head of Department while I was an undergraduate at St Andrews University), as a mentor and increasingly as a friend, I felt especially honoured when Oxford University Press invited me to complete the task.

However, this book would never have been finished without the help and support of many people. I would like to thank the editorial staff at Oxford University Press—especially Michael Cox, Alysoun Owen, Alison Jones, and Rowena Anketell—and John's widow, Angela, for their co-operation and commitment to this project. I owe a special debt of gratitude to my fellow contributors, especially Edward Furgol who answered seemingly endless queries about seventeenth-century Scotland; to Geoffrey Parker and Ian Gentles, who read the manuscript and made many helpful suggestions for improvement; and to John Morrill, who served as an exemplary general editor and kindly agreed to write the Introduction and Postlude. I would also like to thank my colleague Frederick Pedersen for answering my computer queries; the secretaries in the History Department at the University of Aberdeen, especially Sandra Williams; and the staff of Glucksman Ireland House at New York University—Bernie Burke, Pat King, Eliza O'Grady, and Bob Scally—for their hospitality and tolerance as I finalized this volume. As always I greatly appreciate the continued support of my family, Shirley Ohlmeyer, Alex Green, Dagmar Heyer, and my sons Jamie and Richard. Finally, I would like to acknowledge the enormous debt which I owe to John Kenyon. This volume is dedicated to his memory.

J.O.

Glucksman Ireland House, March 1997

Spellings from contemporary sources have been modernized and for proper names modern spellings have been preferred.

CONTENTS

PART I
Civil Wars in the Stuart Kingdoms

PART 2
The British and Irish Experiences of War

LIST OF MAPS

J. P. KENYON
1927–1996
A Personal Appreciation

GEOFFREY PARKER

I first met John Kenyon in December 1961 when he interviewed me during 'Scholarship Entrance' for a place to read History at Christ's College, Cambridge. All I can remember of that occasion, apart from the terror of being inside a don's room for the first time, was the interviewer's penetrating sidelong gaze, delivered from a huge red chair surrounded by piles of exam papers. John left nine months later to become head of the History Department at Hull (a remarkable accolade for a man of 35), just as I came up to Christ's and so he never taught me. For the next twenty years I saw him only when he came to give a lecture to the Seeley Society or to dine at High Table and 'combine' in The Room.

All that changed in 1981 when he moved to the university of St Andrews (where I had taught since 1972) and became my Head of Department. Not only was I the only historian he knew there; for his first term, while Angela Kenyon sold their home in Hull and I was waiting to move into a new house, we both lived on the same floor of Dean's Court, a university residence for graduate students and faculty. For the next five years, until I left St Andrews, I saw 'JPK' (as his colleagues always called him) almost daily, and grew to admire greatly his historical and his administrative skills. By the time he came to St Andrews he had of course perfected both: his first book, *Sunderland*, came out in 1958 and half-a-dozen more seminal works had appeared since then; he had also been a professor and department head for eighteen years. Nevertheless the speed with which John took stock of both the department and the university impressed all his colleagues (no mean feat, since John's predecessor was Norman Gash, another prolific scholar and experienced administrator). Time after time, although apparently acting on the spur of the moment, he displayed an uncanny ability to anticipate both his colleagues' reaction and the solution to each problem.

On meeting JPK, one first noticed the style: authoritative, clear, and concise. John never used two words when one would serve, and he showed a keen interest in how others used language. Once, when I mentioned having received a letter from Hugh Trevor-Roper, he sent me an admonitory note: 'I hope you're collecting and preserving such things; I am. He [Trevor-Roper] and Elton are much better value in the epistolary line than vaunted litterateurs like Firth and Trevelyan.'

Next one relished John's ability, through a remarkable blend of irony, understatement, and wit, to make people laugh. He was the master of the sardonic one-liner but he also deployed three 'devices' to accentuate these gifts: a deep sigh or groan when someone made a particularly silly or obvious point; a drift into 'Yorkshire' (both accent and vocabulary) when he felt combative; and, most memorably, an emphatic sniff which served almost as punctuation following epigrams or put-downs.

John matched his efficient use of language with a remarkable energy. He worked hard and he worked fast. He seemed to produce his limpid prose almost effortlessly; he certainly produced it prolifically. Apart from the impressive corpus of books and articles, he reviewed extensively—most prominently for the *Observer*, both under his own name as their principal history reviewer and as 'Kelvin Johnson' for science fiction (which he read voraciously). When he stopped reviewing for the *Observer*, after his departure to a chair at the university of Kansas in 1987, he noted (with characteristic ambiguity) that although no one seemed to note the absence of John Kenyon's reviews a number of readers complained about the disappearance of Kelvin Johnson. Although his reviews generally praised and accentuated the positive, he had no time for loose writing, narrow horizons, or sloppy scholarship. ('This is a very disappointing book' he began one review, and it went downhill from there.)

On top of this professional output, as department head JPK always led from the front, firing off innumerable letters and memoranda. One of his longer and more acerbic missives berated the Dean of Graduate Studies at St Andrews for agreeing to admit to the History department an American academic on the eve of retirement who wished to study early modern Scots law. 'It would no doubt be stimulating to have a senior professor in his late 50s as a Ph.D. student in the department', he began, 'but it is an experience I and my staff are very willing to forego.' Three cogent 'considerations which seriously limit, indeed, prohibit, his admission' followed; but John then (characteristically) ended on a more helpful note: 'I am advised that the Department of Scots Law at Edinburgh is running an SSRC project on the social history of law in seventeenth-century Scotland into which [the American Professor] would fit like a weevil in a biscuit.'

John also devoted much time to advancing the interests of his colleagues—advising them how to get their research into print, supporting them for outside awards and honours, striving to secure them recognition and promotion within the university as well as showing great personal kindness and consideration. I shall never forget coming into the Mill Lane Lecture Rooms in 1984, full of trepidation, to give my first Lees-Knowles Lecture on 'The Military Revolution':

there, on the edge of one of the rows, I saw Kenyon's broad back, clad in its distinctive houndstooth jacket. He had driven down from St Andrews specially to provide support, and I felt immensely reassured. When the lectures were published, I thanked him again for this, but he turned the matter into a joke: 'I am amazed that you should thank me for attending your first Lees-Knowles lecture; as I told a thin-lipped [department secretary] when I raided the Class Grant for my expenses, it was my duty as your then chairman to attend.'

Finally John also proved tireless in helping his students, whether with advice on style, with letters of recommendation, or with a sympathetic ear for their problems. John always seemed ready to listen to other people's difficulties and he possessed the knack of gaining and retaining almost anyone's confidence when he chose. He also maintained a voluminous correspondence in which he managed to unlock many a secret, thanks to his remarkable insights and inferences.

For much of his last eight years, John Kenyon wrestled with serious health problems. In 1988–9 he underwent a debilitating round of surgery, discomfort, and chemotherapy for cancer, but he fought back and made a total recovery. Not long afterwards, however, he suffered a mild heart attack which caused an aneurysm, forcing him to confront the possibility that he might—quite literally—drop dead at any moment. Yet I never once heard him complain about any of these setbacks, nor did it affect his voracious appetite for news and gossip, his love of history, or his ability to laugh. Amid these setbacks he showed a fortitude that I, like many others, found inspiring; and he always remained great fun to be with.

At all times I valued his support and enjoyed his humorous, penetrating, and acerbic commentary on both the past and the present. His writings will serve as his public monument, but those who met him will also cherish the memory of his deep, assured voice; his loud, infectious laugh; and that distinctive, dismissive sniff.

LIST OF CONTRIBUTORS

BERNARD CAPP is Professor of History at the University of Warwick, where he has taught since 1968. His publications include *Cromwell's Navy: The Fleet and the English Revolution, 1648–1660* (Oxford, 1992); *The World of John Taylor the Water-Poet, 1578–1653* (Oxford, 1994); *The Fifth Monarchy Men* (London, 1972); and *Astrology and the Popular Press* (Ithaca, NY, 1979). He is currently writing a book on female autonomy and networks in early modern England (*When Gossips Meet*) and a reassessment of the English revolution.

CHARLES CARLTON is Professor of History at North Carolina State University. His books include *Charles I, the Personal Monarch* (London, 1983); *Royal Childhood* (London, 1986); *Archbishop William Laud* (London, 1987); *Royal Mistresses* (London, 1990), and *Going to the Wars: The Experience of the British Civil Wars 1638–1651* (London, 1994). He is currently working on a book on the concept of monarchy in the seventeenth century.

PETER EDWARDS is Reader in History at the Roehampton Institute, London. He is the author of *The Horse Trade of Tudor and Stuart England* (Cambridge, 1988) and of articles on the supply of horses and arms during the English Civil Wars. He is currently writing a book on the arms trade and the British Civil Wars, 1638–51.

EDWARD M. FURGOL, a graduate of the College of Wooster and the University of Oxford (Pembroke and St Cross Colleges), has a strong interest in early modern military history. *The Regimental History of the Covenanting Armies, 1639–1651* (Edinburgh, 1990) is his major work on the subject. After working for the Pendle Heritage Centre and Historic Scotland, he became the curator of The Navy Museum, Washington, DC, in 1990. His professional duties include co-ordinating the internship and offsite exhibits program of the US Navy's Naval Historical Center. In addition to his new expertise in American naval history, he has continued to write and speak on British history.

IAN GENTLES is the author of *The New Model Army in England, Ireland and Scotland, 1645–1653* (Oxford, 1992), and numerous articles on the English Civil Wars. He is presently at work on a three-kingdoms history of the civil wars. He is Professor of History at Glendon College, York University (Toronto).

RONALD HUTTON is Professor of British History at the University of Bristol. He has written seven books, of which the first was *The Royalist War Effort, 1642–1646* (London, 1982) and subsequent examples include *Charles II: King of England, Scotland, and Ireland* (Oxford, 1989); *The Pagan Religions of the Ancient British Isles* (Oxford, 1991); and *The Rise and Fall of Merry England* (Oxford, 1994).

JOHN KENYON, prior to his unexpected death in January 1996, had recently retired from his position as the Joyce & Elizabeth Hall Distinguished Professor in Early Modern British History at the University of Kansas. His books include *Robert Spencer, Earl of Sunderland 1641–1702* (London, 1958; further edns. 1975 and 1992); *The Stuart Constitution: Documents and Commentary* (Cambridge 1966; rev. 1986); *The Popish Plot* (London 1972; 2nd edn., 1984); *Revolution Principles: the Politics of Party 1689–1720* (Cambridge, 1977; rev. 1990); *Stuart England* (London, 1977; rev. 1985); *The History Men: The Historical Profession in England since the Renaissance* (London, 1983; rev. 1993); and *The Civil Wars of England* (London, 1986). He also contributed numerous articles to scholarly journals on various aspects of seventeenth-century English History. In 1981 he was elected a Fellow of the British Academy.

JOHN MORRILL is a Fellow and Vice-Master and Reader in Early Modern History at Selwyn College, University of Cambridge. His books include *The Revolt of the Provinces* (London, 1976; rev. 1980); *The Nature of the English Revolution* (London, 1993); and *Revolution and Restoration* (London, 1993). He has also edited *Reactions to the English Civil War 1642–1649* (London, 1982); *Oliver Cromwell and the English Revolution* (London, 1990); *The Scottish National Covenant in its British Context* (Edinburgh, 1990); *The Impact of the English Civil War* (London, 1991); and *The Oxford Illustrated History of Tudor and Stuart Britain* (Oxford, 1996). He has recently been elected a Fellow of the British Academy and has been at the forefront of the recent debates on the British and Irish Civil Wars.

JANE OHLMEYER, author of *Civil War and Restoration in the Three Stuart Kingdoms: The Career of Randal MacDonnell, Marquis of Antrim 1609–1683* (Cambridge, 1993) and editor of *Ireland from Occupation to Independence 1641–1660* (Cambridge, 1995), has also contributed articles on various aspects of the Confederate Wars to scholarly journals and anthologies. She lectures in Irish and British History at the University of Aberdeen and is currently working on aristocratic indebtedness in early modern Ireland.

WYLIE E. REEVES secured a BA at Texas Lutheran College, an MA at North-Eastern University, and an M.Phil. on siegecraft in the English Civil Wars from Bristol University.

INTRODUCTION

JOHN MORRILL

This book explores the greatest concentration of armed violence to take place in the recorded history of the islands of Britain and Ireland. More men died of wounds sustained in battle within these islands in the decade of the 1640s than in any other of our history. It has been calculated that between 1642 and 1651 there were at least 463 military clashes in which one or more persons was killed; the same period witnessed more than half the battles involving above 10,000 men ever fought on English soil; it is likely that as many as one in three or one in four of all the male population between the ages of 16 and 50 bore arms for part or all of the war; and a majority of the incorporated towns of the kingdoms of Britain and Ireland were both garrisoned and besieged for days, weeks, or months. The biggest and bloodiest single battle ever fought on English soil was the battle of Towton which took place in a blizzard in North Yorkshire in 1461 (it was the battle that gave Edward IV the throne); but the next five in size were fought in the 1640s at Marston Moor, Newbury, Edgehill, Lansdown, and Naseby.

This extraordinary military history was accompanied by extraordinary political events in each of the kingdoms of England, Scotland, and Ireland. Since the beginning of the fourteenth century, reigning English monarchs had been deposed on eight occasions (1327, 1399, 1461, 1470, 1471, 1484, 1485, 1553) and most accessions had been contested. However, with the anomalous exception of Lady Jane Grey in 1555, no monarch had hitherto been put on trial and executed; nor had the institution of monarchy itself ever been at serious risk before it was abolished in the late winter of 1649, to be replaced first by a Commonwealth and then by the Protectorate of Oliver Cromwell. The House of Lords was abolished along with the monarchy, and so was the Established Church—from 1647 to 1660 men and women had an obligation to attend worship every Sunday, but not worship in a parish church. They could gather in any religious assembly which the regime of the moment deemed to be no threat to the civil peace. As a direct result of these changes, all the land belonging to the crown, to the bishops, and to the cathedral chapters and the estates of almost one thousand prominent royalists were sold off. It was the greatest redistribution of land in English history after the Norman Conquest and the dissolution of the monasteries.

In Scotland, too, the violent death of monarchs was nothing new—a majority of the Stewart dynasty had died at the hands of others—but again, the abolition of monarchy had not been on the agenda; nor had the abolition of the Scottish Parliament and the rude incorporation of the Scottish kingdom into an enhanced English state by military occupation, followed by a unilateral act of union. The all-conquering English then sought to emasculate the power of the Scottish nobility by removing all their legal authority over their tenants.

Similarly in Ireland, the English destroyed the semi-autonomous legislative and executive institutions of that satellite kingdom, and incorporated Ireland into a pan-British state. More dramatically, almost half the land mass of Ireland was confiscated from its existing (Catholic) owners and redistributed to demobilized English soldiers and to men of property in England who had put venture capital into the Irish 'Adventure' with that express aim in view. In 1641 around sixty per cent of Ireland was owned by Catholic families settled there for centuries; by 1662 that percentage had shrunk to around twenty. It was possibly the greatest act of ethnic cleansing in European history. The military events described and discussed in this book are thus both dramatic and harrowing of themselves and in their consequences.

The traditional terms used to describe the conflicts which engulfed Ireland and Britain during the 1640s have included 'the English Revolution', 'the Puritan Revolution', 'the Great Civil War', and more recently 'the British Civil Wars'. Yet none of these reflect the fact that the conflict engulfed all three Stuart kingdoms; or that, in addition to the war possessing a pan-archipelagic dimension, each kingdom fought its own civil war and its own series of local and regional wars. The tension is caught in the fact that some historians speak of the 'War of the Three Kingdoms' and others of the 'Wars of the Three Kingdoms'.[1] Even that fails to reflect the extent to which the European superpowers—the Spanish Habsburgs, the French Bourbons, and to a lesser extent the mercantile Republic of Holland—were active participants in one or more theatres of these internal wars. Their ambassadors promised more than they ever delivered in military and financial aid, but their promises affected the decisions made by the king, his representatives, and his enemies. Furthermore, foreign powers released mercenaries for service back home, they and their financiers were willing to grant favourable credit or to allow the purchase of military equipment, and they all offered their services as negotiators and brokers. Too busy and too exhausted to make Britain and Ireland a major theatre of their operations, they still saw the outcome of the British and Irish wars as vital to their own long-term self-interest. The 'Wars of the Three Kingdoms' are a peripheral but actual part of the Thirty Years War, the greatest of all continental European wars before the era of Bonaparte.[2]

More generally, indeed, there was a complexity to the conflicts within the Stuart dynastic conglomerate which bears comparison with the Thirty Years War which had engulfed the whole of continental Europe in so many interlocking regional conflicts since the 1610s and which was somehow a great deal more than the sum of its parts. It was at once a series of internal wars within the composite or multiple kingdoms—or dynastic conglomerates—that made up much of western, central, and northern Europe and it was a conflict between rival dynasties and rival confessional groupings (Protestant and Catholic). The Austrian Habsburgs sought to strengthen their hold both on the Habsburg ancestral lands of Austria, Hungary, and the Balkans and within the Holy Roman Empire; the Spanish Habsburgs to strengthen their grip on the peripheral parts of their Mediterranean and North Sea Empire; the Poles and the Swedes to resolve long-standing disputes of rival dynasties. The war *began* with internal wars within Germany, the Baltic region, Italy, and the Low Countries. Those internal wars became enmeshed one with another and, as France, Denmark, and (more fitfully) Charles I's Britain became drawn into one or more of those theatres, became a truly international conflict. But the war also *caused* a further round of internal wars, creating what was once fashionably known as the 'General Crisis of the Seventeenth Century'. The military costs of the conflicts led to unprecedented attempts of governments to increase levels of taxation and military supply; to develop institutions which could levy and deploy those massively increased resources; and to impose central and centralizing structures to supervise the new institutions. The result was a wave of rebellions in the peripheries of the French, Spanish, Polish, Austrian, and Russian conglomerates; and also revolts by élites who felt disproportionately mulcted or inadequately consulted. The relationship of the crisis of the British monarchies to this wider crisis of governance through-out Europe in the second quarter of the seventeenth century is ripe for re-evaluation. It is quite clear that the rebellions of 1638, 1640, 1641, and even 1642 were not a part of that European-wide phenomenon. The Stuarts had not overextended themselves militarily in the decades down to 1639 and the problem of managing their dynastic conglomerate—difficult though that was proving—was not essentially a problem of sustaining a militarized state. However, the internal wars of the 1640s did cause a crisis with precisely the lineaments of the continental crises of the early 1640s. The Wars of the Three Kingdoms may not have begun as part of the European General Crisis, but they very possibly developed into the epitome of it.

I hope that this is the kind of context John Kenyon had in mind when he designed this book. Although all his archivally researched books were concerned with the last quarter of the seventeenth century and the first quarter of the eighteenth century, he was endlessly fascinated by the period of the British Civil Wars, and between 1958 and 1988 he offered no less than five synoptic accounts of the period. In 1958 he published *The Stuarts: A Study in English Kingship*, a series of interpretative essays on the lives of the seven monarchs who reigned between 1603 and 1714. This addressed the personal responsibility of James VI and I and

Charles I for the collapse of royal authority and it found Charles far more wanting than James. His discussion of the 1620s and 1630s is strong and startling even now; but it has to be said that it becomes very desultory for the years of fighting and of Charles's defeat and death. In 1966 Kenyon published *The Stuart Constitution: Documents and Commentary*, wondrously supple and clever in its structure and again full of polemic against the prevailing view that England slid inexorably into civil war or experienced a revolution. There is a very strong chapter on the constitutional and institutional aspects of civil war; but while the book was iconoclastic in its many confrontations with Whiggish and *marxistante* historiography, in ways which anticipated revisionism by more than a decade, it remained resolutely Anglocentric. The first edition (1978) of *Stuart England* in the Pelican History of England had been too rapidly written and was riddled with factual errors; but it was always a clever and observant study, and the tidied-up second edition (1985) is one of the best surveys currently available. It contains an exceptional forty-five-page review of the historiography relating to the origins and nature of what he by then recognized as a three-kingdom crisis. In 1986 he published a thoroughly revised second edition of *The Stuart Constitution*, much stronger on the lack of ideological polarization about law and/or religion in the early seventeenth century than the first edition had been. The intuitions of 1966 were now turned into firm demonstrations. Finally, in 1988 he published *The Civil Wars of England* which succeeded in telling the story of the war within its political and institutional context.

If Kenyon's view remained remarkably stable, that was because it took the rest of the historical profession thirty years to catch up with him. He remained implacably opposed to the use of the word 'revolution' to describe the events of the 1640s and 1650s (he said that S. R. Gardiner's persistence in calling the Great Rebellion 'the Puritan Revolution' was 'his greatest disservice to scholarship').[3] He himself reserved the word 'revolution' for the title of one chapter of *The Stuart Constitution*: 'The Laudian Revolution'. He was equally consistent and forthright in seeing the crown and its agencies as the dynamic, progressive element in the early seventeenth century, and he came to take this view further than anyone else.[4] Conversely Parliament and parliamentarians were shown to have been conservative, reactionary, and incompetently self-defeating (as early as 1958 he could refer to 'the first part of Charles I's reign ending in the suicide of the House of Commons').[5] He suggested that the Stuarts were opposed not so much by an ever-strengthening body of Puritan fanatics as by self-interested congeries of anticlerical landowners.[6] The intellectuals were on the side of (royal) progress; Parliament had its share of intemperate hotheads, but they were more dogs-in-mangers than visionaries;[7] while men complained about the application and use of royal powers, they did not question the existence of those powers. Kenyon was the first historian to plead for an essentially consensual view of the early Stuart constitution: 'Wild claims were made by wild men on both sides, by Sir John

Eliot as well as Roger Manwaring, but these were ignored, just as the theories of philosophers were [later] rejected. In the sphere of practical politics the disagreement essentially lay in how to operate a constitution of whose nature few had any doubt.'[8]

Kenyon resolutely refused to find long-term economic and social causes of the great events of the British and Irish Civil Wars; and while he found much complaining and the articulation of much prejudice on matters of law, government, and religion, he did not find an escalation of conflict and anything remotely inevitable or predestined about the descent into violence.

Almost every historian from S. R. Gardiner [i.e. from the 1880s] down to Lawrence Stone [in 1972] traces the causes of these events back to 1603, to 1558, even to 1529. They are, in fact, devotees of the theory of historical inevitability, which has been called, in less reverent terms, the 'rolling stone' theory. According to this hypothesis, a stone dropped on the mountain heights (say, in 1558) rolls irresistibly down the slopes, gathering momentum as it goes, dislodging larger boulders, scree and snow, creating a cumulative movement which bursts on the unsuspecting villages below as an avalanche.

In its place, Kenyon offered a foreshortened chronology:

it is impossible not to turn to a tactical or political explanation, and find causes of the Civil War in the state of the monarchy: first its general weakness, which unbalanced the working constitution—as many contemporaries realized—and secondly the perverse ineptitude of Charles I and some of his advisers, which triggered off a series of crises, beginning with the Scottish National Covenant of 1638, which made civil war inevitable. The 'rolling stone' in fact started rolling when that celebrated maidservant Jenny Geddes threw her stool at the dean of St Giles, Edinburgh, on 23 July 1637.[9]

The perverse ineptitude of Charles I was a constant theme of his writing, never more memorably caught than in his first account published in 1958:

his eyes did not dwell on those around him but looked through them and beyond, finding no point of rest. He was intellectual without being intelligent, and he lacked entirely the common touch so obvious in his father and his eldest son, Charles II. His was never a masculine character and his feminine delicacy of feature, his *tristesse*, that Pre-Raphaelite droop so attractive to the old ladies of Anglo-Catholicism, had a limited appeal to contemporaries ... Not only was he ill-equipped for kingship, he never enjoyed the act of ruling as his father and his sons so clearly did. The duties imposed on him by God he fulfilled with a kind of petulant distaste that struck a chill into those around him. He expected nothing from politics but a crown of thorns; he anticipated betrayal and neglected to reward loyalty, taking it as his due.[10]

This is wonderful writing; and it expresses his deep conviction that while there were many frailties about the early Stuart state, there was only one real cause of its collapse. However, if Kenyon believed there were no great causes of the English Civil Wars, he recognized that there were mighty consequences. He was never persuaded that the social order came close to collapse, and he refused to get excited about the antics of the sects in the late 1640s and 1650s; but he recognized that there was a functional radicalism to the war itself, that the frightened re-actionaries who began it found they had unleashed forces beyond their control. The effortless interweaving of the military and the political and institutional history of the 1640s which is the hallmark of his *The Civil Wars of England*, was also the inspiration behind the design of this book. He was not fascinated by the technology of war, or the antiquarian recovery of the precise locations of particu-lar manœuvres of particular battles. He was interested in those who sought to ride the tigers of war, in those who succeeded—often briefly—and in those broken by it. He was matter-of-fact about the suffering of war, dry-eyed in his accounts of military triumph and catastrophe, but he was drawn always to the passions to be found in accounts of the councils of war and peace and in the private exchanges of letters. He was asked to edit a military history; and he planned it as a book about the war that raged within men's minds as much as in their arms. This book, his last book, is a tribute to his passion to understand a mental world we have lost as well as a physical world we have lost. Few of his words are to be found in it; but it is his book none the less.

PART ONE

CIVIL WARS IN THE STUART KINGDOMS

I

THE BACKGROUND TO THE CIVIL WARS IN THE STUART KINGDOMS

JOHN KENYON WITH JANE OHLMEYER

The Demilitarization of England

By the end of the sixteenth century the English nobility had lost one of the main functions of an aristocracy, which was leadership in war, and in the classes below them knowledge of the art and practice of war had also suffered a decline. Noblemen like Robert Dudley, earl of Leicester and Robert Devereux, 2nd earl of Essex, habitually kept large retinues of liveried (uniformed) retainers, which they could readily mobilize for war, but Leicester's unhappy record in the Netherlands in the 1580s, and Essex's in Normandy and Ireland in the 1590s exposed their deficiencies. Conversely, as the seventeenth century dawned the English crown was defended by a force which the lowliest German margrave would have held derisory: the picturesque Yeomen of the Guard at the Tower of London, and a personal bodyguard of about forty gentlemen pensioners.

However, it is a truism that the English monarchy at this stage needed no stronger defences. Despite innovations in ship design and maritime weaponry, the Channel still posed an almost insuperable barrier. Internally, the governing classes were constrained by a national legal system which was usually accepted as equitable and just, strictly administered by the king. In parliament they also enjoyed a system of representation which allowed them to initiate changes in the law and monitor the government's execution of it. This gave them a grip on government finance, and increasingly the power to assess and criticize policy. In turn they kept a firm hold over the classes below them, that 'many-headed monster' with an enormous potentiality for unrest and revolt, which (it was thought) could only be held down in co-operation with the monarchy. This 'powder keg' mentality reaffirmed the autocratic power of the crown, and the Church of England was preaching the Divine Right of Kings long before James VI and I set his seal on it. The king was the keystone in an arch of government which held together a rigid social system.

ENGLISH MILITIAS

True, the nobility and gentry still commanded the only nationwide military force available, in the shape of the county militia. Ever since Anglo-Saxon times every adult Englishman was enjoined to be ready, suitable arms in hand, to defend the homeland, an obligation codified by Edward I in the Statute of Winchester in 1285. A major reform completed in 1558 had provided for annual militia rates to be levied throughout the country, for regular training and for the establishment of county arsenals. However, the complexities of the system and the many inequities built into it had made it hard to enforce and the administrative will to make it work was lacking. Under the threat of Spanish invasion in the 1590s, Elizabeth I had done her best to overhaul the militia, strengthening the practice of appointing a senior nobleman in each county to command it, with the title of lord lieutenant. Each of them was now able to choose his own deputies to assist him. However, like her father and grandfather, she did not relish the idea of her subjects having arms in their hands. Moreover, central government, ever short of money, always tried to shunt the cost of training and equipment on to the localities, which sought to pass it back. In any case, to mobilize this militia on a large scale against the monarchy called for a degree of co-operation between magnates which it was impossible to achieve except in times of crisis, and not always then. They were violent enough; in fact, in the words of one historian, 'the behaviour of the propertied classes . . . was characterised by the ferocity, childishness and lack of self-control of the Homeric age'; but the exercise of interpersonal violence was probably a salutary outlet for deeper frustrations, and it rarely extended into politics.[1] Meanwhile the Tudors were always mean with patents of nobility, and one in five peerage families continued to die out in the male line every generation, with the result that the English aristocracy, traditionally the leaders of opposition to the crown, were proportionately one of the smallest in Europe. Finally—and most important—until the 1640s there was lacking any issue, dynastic or confessional, which might have divided the English governing classes into distinct factions, still less united them against the government. England remained preeminently a court society, dominated by a struggle between the ins and the outs. Thus even on the death of Edward VI in 1553, potentially the most serious crisis the Tudors ever faced, when his ministers set up a Protestant claimant against his half-sister Mary, the governing classes spontaneously rallied to the Catholic princess, notwithstanding the serious implications for the future of Protestantism.

Certainly the monarchy was subject to increasing stress over the sixteenth century, an anxiety only partly disguised by Elizabeth I's carefully nurtured charisma, and her public role as the champion of English Protestantism and nationalism against Catholic Spain. The theoretical or ideological ascendancy of the crown was thus enhanced, but the nuts and bolts which held together the structure of the crown were showing signs of wear. In particular, in a period of rampant inflation the real value of the crown's income from fixed sources steadily declined, and only unrelenting parsimony and a degree of sharp practice, plus regular requests to parliament for extra money, enabled Elizabeth to maintain her government and play any part at all in the affairs of Europe. The Parliaments of the 1590s did vote unprecedented sums in direct taxation, grumbling prodigiously and congratulating themselves on their generosity, but the antiquated 'subsidy', based on assessments not reviewed since 1547, brought in less and less with every passing decade, a double handicap when the real value of money was in steep decline. Elizabeth's greatest failure was her unwillingness to use her almost unique prestige to effect a wholesale reform of the fiscal system. Had she done so she would have transformed England's ability to wage war both abroad and at home.

Militarized Scotland and Ireland

Yet England's riches far exceeded those of Scotland and before acceding to the throne of England in 1603, James VI of Scotland proved even more poverty-stricken than his English cousin. Moreover he ruled over a country plagued by endemic lawlessness, feuds, and inter-baronial wars. In particular the Western Isles had, by the late sixteenth century, become more militarized than elsewhere in Scotland, with 6,000 fighting men, or 'buannachan', allegedly ready to serve in Ireland or raid neighbouring clans. To the south, feuding proved 'the great cancer of the Borders' and one English official noted with horror how reivers 'will subject themselves to no justice but in an inhumane and barbarous manner fight and kill one another'.[2] For example, in 1597 on the West March (the heavily defended parts of Cumberland bordering Scotland), the damage allegedly done by the Scots in England during the previous ten years was assessed at £12,000 and that by the English in Scotland at £13,000. Similarly in Ireland, despite English attempts to pacify the country, local lords continued to raid for cattle while rebellions, which erupted with alarming regularity throughout the sixteenth century, thwarted English colonial initiatives and fostered a culture of fighting. During the later stages of the Nine Years War (1594–1603), the rebellious earl of Tyrone and his Ulster allies allegedly mustered 2,000 'buannachts' (or native mercenary soldiers) and 4,000 to 6,000 ordinary swordsmen regularly enlisted for service. Scottish mercenaries supplemented these native soldiers and between the 1560s and 1590s some 25,000 warriors found employment in militarized Ulster.

At least the warlike nature of these outlying regions afforded inexperienced English and Lowland armies with a rare opportunity to fight in an active theatre of war. During the later decades of the sixteenth century a number of costly English campaigns completed the military conquest of Ireland. In Scotland James VI defeated the earls of Huntly, Errol, and Angus in a series of royal campaigns in the north-east (1589–95) and launched five 'fire and sword' expeditions along the western seaboard between 1596 and 1608, expropriating where possible lands belonging to the insubordinate MacGregors, MacLeods, Maclains, and MacDonalds. However, the fact that the Stuart kingdoms enjoyed nearly four decades of years of peace during the early seventeenth century deprived the king's troops of opportunities to flex their military muscle at home.

While peace, together with a range of government policies, facilitated the de-militarization of some troublesome regions, especially the Anglo-Scottish borders, military might continued to articulate the political order in other regions, particularly parts of Gaeldom. By 1630, according to the Scottish Privy Council, the Highlands swarmed with a 'number of broken and lawless lymmars [thieves] . . . who . . . were some years bygone reduced to the obedience of law and justice, [and] have now begun to renew their . . . wicked trade' and on the eve of the Bishops' Wars (1638–40) lawlessness in the Highlands had reached levels characteristic of the 1590s.[3] The fact that nobles maintained their monopoly over the administration of justice in the localities, largely through baronial and regality courts, frustrated attempts by the crown to replace their private authority and to introduce Justices of the Peace into Scotland. Ironically, however, with the onset of civil war in Scotland after 1638 it was to these regional power-brokers on both sides of the North Channel that both the covenanters and Charles I turned as they prepared for war.

Military Migration

While Scottish and Irish warlords could raise considerable numbers of fighting men, they often lacked the expertise needed to train them in the latest military techniques. This task fell instead to the English, Irish, and Scottish mercenary soldiers who served in the continental armies during the later sixteenth and seventeenth centuries and who returned to fight in the Stuart kingdoms after 1638.

Military migration to Europe during these years was often involuntary. From the 1570s the crown exported considerable numbers of convicts, troublemakers, and unemployed swordsmen on the assumption that 'more than three parts of the four of these countrymen do never return'.[4] Shortly after he assumed the throne of England, James VI and I sent 2,000 troublesome Grahams from Eskdale in Cumbria to fight in the Netherlands. In the wake of the plantation of Ulster Lord Deputy Chichester tried to transport nearly 6,000 ferine Irish swordsmen to Sweden. During the 1620s the crown allowed the Lord of Spynie from Elgin to impress all 'strong and sturdy beggars and vagabonds, masterless men and idle loiterers'.[5]

Others left more readily. From 1572 onwards contingents of English volunteers crossed the Channel to support the Protestant cause in the Netherlands and in 1585, after the assassination of the Dutch leader William the Silent, Elizabeth

IRISH SOLDIERS IN SERVICE OF GUSTAVUS ADOLPHUS, 1631.
Contemporary German Broadside in British Museum.

Scottish mercenaries

During the course of the Thirty Years' War roughly 25,000 Scots served in the Danish, German, Swedish, Dutch, and Russian armies while a similar number of Irishmen fought in the French and Spanish forces. This contemporary German print depicts Scottish mercenaries in Highland (or Irish) dress arriving to take up arms on behalf of the Swedish king, Gustavus Adolphus in 1631. The accompanying caption describes them as 'a strong, rugged people which gets by with little to eat. If they lack bread, they eat roots or even bugs if necessary. They can run twenty German miles in a single day, and use bows and arrows and long knives as well as muskets.' Mercenaries such as these flooded back to Britain and Ireland during the later 1630s, exposing the native soldiers to the latest ideas about military technology and practices.

herself assumed the title of Protector of the Netherlands, and dispatched an expeditionary force under the earl of Leicester; she also sent contingents to the aid of Henry IV of France after 1588. When she relinquished the Dutch commitment in 1598 she left behind an 'English' brigade of about 8,000 (one-third of them Scots) under Sir Francis Vere which formed a valued element in the Dutch army, distinguishing itself at the battle of Nieuport in 1600 and the epic defence of Ostend 1601–4. Other English mercenaries followed and during the early decades of the seventeenth century a further 10,000 to 15,000 saw active service in the Thirty Years War (1618–48). Irishmen also fought abroad. A regiment of Irish troops, originally recruited in the early 1580s to help the Dutch in their war against Spain, later defected—together with their English colonel, William Stanley—across the border to serve with the forces of Philip II. In the wake of their defeat in the Nine Years War increasing numbers of Irish swordsmen sought service abroad and it has been recently estimated that between 1586 and 1621 6,300 Irishmen served at any one time in the Army of Flanders; by the mid-1630s the figure hovered around seven thousand, dropping to roughly a thousand by the later 1630s largely because six of these regiments defected to the service of France. (In 1623 they were joined by a regiment of Catholic Scots, under the command of the 7th earl of Argyll, who had fled to Flanders to escape his creditors.)

Throughout the early seventeenth century both France and Spain vied to recruit Irish mercenaries. 'There lives not a people more hardy', the staunchly Protestant William III of Orange later wrote, 'neither is there any will endure the miseries of war . . . so naturally, and with such facility and courage that they do.' He added that 'the Irish are soldiers the first day of their birth'.[6] Another contemporary condemned the Irish as a 'sordid, lazy, heartless people . . . yet it is well known, that in foreign parts . . . after once they have been trained in strict discipline, and come to understand themselves, the world hath not a better soldier'.[7] Many examples can be found to support this. For instance, Thomas Preston, a captain in the Army of Flanders and later the Irish Catholic confederate commander in Leinster, distinguished himself during the defence of Louvain (1635) and in 1641 became governor of Genappe; while in 1640 Owen Roe O'Neill, who later commanded the confederate Army of Ulster, and his force of 1,500 fought bravely at Arras despite being heavily outnumbered. Just as the Catholic powers coveted Irish cannon-fodder, so the Scandinavian and German princelings sought Scottish mercenaries who, like their Irish counterparts, were regarded as 'strong enduring people . . . when they have no bread, they can endure hunger for 3 or 4 days, feeding instead on water, cress, roots and grass; when necessary they can walk more than 20 miles a day'.[8] Though the Scots formed a small proportion of the Dutch army (roughly seven per cent by the early seventeenth century), they enjoyed a formidable reputation. By 1629 one contemporary had dubbed them 'the bulwark of the Republic' while another asserted that 'These are sure men, hardy and resolute, and, their example holds up the Dutch'.[9] Between 1624 and

1637 the Stuarts allowed recruiters to export roughly 41,400 Scots to serve in the Dutch, French, Danish, Swedish, and Russian armies. Whether these levy quotas were met in full remains unclear; certainly, 25,000 men—or roughly ten per cent of the adult male population—left Scotland to serve in the Danish, Swedish, and Russian armies between 1625 and 1632. These included a substantial force raised by the royal favourite James, marquis of Hamilton, for service in Sweden, and by members of the Leslie family from Aberdeenshire who fought in Germany and Russia during the 1630s.

These mercenaries, whether of English, Irish, or Scottish provenance, quickly gained military training and combat experience in the most advanced practices of warfare. Little wonder that the covenanting government immediately recalled the Scottish veterans from foreign service and late in 1638 insisted that out of every regiment's seventy officers not fewer than thirty-two (the two field officers and thirty for the ten companies) were to be skilled in warfare. These experienced troops arrived home in sufficient numbers to train the covenanters' Lowland forces for the 1639 campaign. They included Alexander Leslie (see picture on p. 47), formerly one of Gustavus Adolphus's most trusted field marshals and his second-in-command, David Leslie; Sir James Turner, who fought for both Denmark and Sweden before returning home to serve in the convenanting armies between 1640 and 1648; and Robert Munro, author of the first regimental history in the English language, who served in Germany before taking effective command after 1642 of the Scottish troops based in Ulster. Similarly with the outbreak of war against the Scots numerous English veterans rallied to the king's cause. Jacob Astley, who had enjoyed a distinguished career in Flanders and Germany, served as major-general of foot between 1639 and 1640; the unfortunate English Catholic commander of Drogheda in 1649, Sir Arthur Aston, had fought in the Russian, Polish, and Swedish armies, before joining the king's army in 1640; and the Flemish veteran Sir Charles Lucas, who fought with distinction during the Bishops' Wars and at Marston Moor (1644). Others—including Lawrence Crawford, a veteran of Danish and Swedish armies; Sir John Hotham, who had served in Germany; or Sydenham Poynts, a major-general in the imperial army —offered their services to Parliament. In a poem dedicated to the parliamentary commander Lord Thomas Fairfax (see picture on p. 125), the English poet Andrew Marvell drew particular attention to his military training on the continent:

> From that blest bed the hero came,
> Whom France and Poland yet does fame:
> Who when retired here to peace,
> His warlike studies could not cease;
> But laid these gardens out in sport
> In the just figure of a fort;
> And with five bastions it did fence,
> As aiming one at every sense.[10]

After the outbreak of rebellion in 1641, the Irish confederates, who now ruled most of the country, urged their compatriots serving in Germany, France, Flanders, and Spain to fight in Ireland. The English ambassador in France noted early in 1642 that 'the common men come from their winter quarters by twenties and thirties . . . and hasten towards Ireland as fast as they can'.[11] The trickle soon turned into a flood. By 1645 there was only one Irish regiment serving in Spain. The returning veterans included Owen Roe O'Neill, Thomas Preston, and John Burke and many of their officers—James Preston, Hugh Dubh O'Neill, Garret Wall, Con and Brian O'Neill—who were all career soldiers well versed in the ways of continental warfare. These professional soldiers, like their fellow practitioners in Scotland and England, transmitted the latest developments in continental warfare back to Ireland and exposed the county to the various facets of the 'Military Revolution' (discussed in Chapters 2, 3, 4, and 6).

The Origins of the Civil Wars in the Stuart Kingdoms

ENGLAND'S MILITARY IMPOTENCE

England's inability to wage war effectively abroad during the 1620s soured relations between the king and the political nation. James VI and I's intervention in the Thirty Years War on behalf of his ill-fated son-in-law achieved little, as did the overambitious schemes hatched by his successor. An amphibious expedition against Cadiz in August 1625 proved a total disaster; particularly galling for a nation which ever since the repulse of the Armada in 1588 had prided itself on its proficiency in maritime warfare. Meanwhile an attempt to organize a conscript expeditionary force for the German war under the unsavoury *condottiere* Count Mansfeld was an even greater fiasco, and a volunteer force sent to the aid of Christian IV of Denmark was swept away with him at the battle of Lutter in 1626. And so it went on. The duke of Buckingham's inept diplomacy after 1626 propelled England into war with France, as well as Spain, and from then on his efforts were exclusively directed to relieving the Huguenots, besieged by the French government in La Rochelle. But this only served to expose England's military inadequacy once more and, of course, it made no contribution whatsoever to the resolution of the German crisis.

Charles's attempts to sustain the war-effort in 1626 and 1627 by the levy of forced loans only exacerbated the government's unpopularity, especially when he took to coercing prominent taxpayers by imprisoning them without trial. A major confrontation ensued in 1628 and 1629 when a new parliament forced Charles to accept a Petition of Right, which declared illegal many forms of prerogative revenue-raising and outlawed imprisonment without due process. This, combined with the death of Buckingham at the hand of a deranged assassin in August 1628 and the end of the war with France in 1629 and with Spain the following year, began to heal the divisions within the political nation. Natural courtiers like the earls of Bristol and Pembroke, and Sir Thomas Wentworth, one of the chief architects of the Petition of Right, were taken back into favour, and Wentworth was granted a viscountcy and appointed lord president of the Council of the North, before becoming lord deputy of Ireland. The birth of a son, the future Charles II, to Henrietta Maria in 1630, and another, the future James II, three years later, put the succession beyond all doubt.

THE PERSONAL RULE

England's withdrawal from the continental theatre of war, however, enabled Charles I to rule without recourse to parliament. Instead he resorted to dubious fiscal devices—distraint of knighthood, enforcement of the antique forest laws, the issue of monopolies in defiance of an Act of 1624—which evaded the terms of the Petition of Right. This, combined with his heavy-handed use of the prerogative courts of Star Chamber and High Commission, has led some inflamed historians to dub this period the 'Eleven Years Tyranny' rather than the 'Personal Rule' (as the decade prior to the outbreak of the civil wars is now more commonly known). The most notorious of these fiscal devices was ship-money, an annual levy, first on the coastal counties in 1634, then extended inland in 1635, for the reform and enhancement of the navy. In view of the squadrons of Dutch, French, and Spanish privateers, not to mention North African corsairs, which now roamed the Channel and the Western Approaches, this was a sensible and patriotic aim, which also pandered to English illusions of their all-conquering sea power. It caused a bad-tempered flurry in most counties, but this was largely because of the tactics employed rather than any principle involved. The government simply named the sum of money required from each county and ordered the sheriffs to collect it as best they could. This necessitated a strict and fair assessment, with no favour shown and few evasions allowed, and it was a principle unblushingly adopted by the Long Parliament in 1642. Whether because of this unwonted efficiency, or because of a general indifference to the question of principle, more than ninety per cent of the sums assessed were collected over the years between 1634 and 1638, a startling improvement on any previous direct tax. John Hampden mounted a celebrated legal challenge in 1637, but failed in the High Court. Payments fell off while taxpayers awaited the judges' ruling, but they caught up later.

LAUDIANISM

Just as Charles's foreign policy had led to conflict in Parliament during the later 1620s, so too his attachment to the High Church movement alarmed many. His deep involvement with William Laud, bishop of London from 1628, and archbishop of Canterbury from 1633, committed him to strengthening the ceremonialist aspects of worship, and upholding episcopal oversight and enforcement of uniformity, and thus barring for ever the kind of piecemeal reform over time on which the Puritans within the Church rested their hopes. Moreover, against the ministry of the word, by sermons, extempore prayer, and intense Bible study, which was integral to the Puritans' concept of the Church, Charles and Laud stressed the ministry of the sacrament, by communion, set prayers, and formal worship, hedged about by ritual offensive to Puritan susceptibilities. From early in the reign a determined effort was made to ensure that everyone used and confined themselves to the Book of Common Prayer, and adhered to all its rubrics. Worse still, Laud and many of his supporters were darkly suspected of Arminianism, that Protestant heresy, denounced at the Synod of Doort in 1618, which denied the doctrine of predestination and reprobation central to Calvinist theology. Indeed, a royal proclamation now forbade preaching on this issue by either side. Fury at these developments boiled over in the Commons in 1629, after a fortuitous series of deaths the previous year had allowed Laud to pack the episcopal bench with his own nominees. The suspension of parliament thereafter, and tight control of the press, forced the controversy into the background, but discontent rumbled on. In an atmosphere in which the least deviation from strict Protestant orthodoxy was deemed 'popery'—a term of infinite gradations—it did seem that the king was in the popish rather than the Protestant camp. Laud's noisy prominence in the king's councils, secular as well as ecclesiastical, and the appointment of one of his bishops, Juxon of London, as lord treasurer in 1635, fuelled the anticlericalism endemic amongst the upper classes; and the conspicuous role assumed by Henrietta Maria and her Catholic cronies at court, her obvious ascendancy over her husband, and the presence at Whitehall of thinly disguised envoys from Rome, caused understandable anger and alarm. The very self-confidence of Charles I and Laud in their own Protestantism, their refusal to explain or excuse themselves, proved their undoing in the long run.

By the later 1630s, Charles's regime was clearly unpopular across a broad front, but the depth of that unpopularity is difficult to measure, and cannot be projected backwards from the hysterical atmosphere of 1640 and 1641, and he certainly never faced the same opposition as his son James II. There is little doubt that had Charles managed to control his other dominions as he controlled England his peaceful reign could have been extended indefinitely. First Scotland, then Ireland proved his undoing.

Ireland

From the middle of the twelfth century England ruled Ireland as a feudal fief (Henry VIII only became 'king' rather than 'lord' of Ireland in 1541) and while successive English monarchs occasionally toyed with the idea of completing the conquest they lacked the money and manpower to do so. Instead the crown subordinated the Irish parliament to the English Privy Council, strove to preserve and promote the English political system which existed, in a basic form, in Dublin and the surrounding area, known as the Pale, and in parts of Munster and south Leinster, and sought to civilize the Gaelic-speaking 'native Irish' population. Prior to the onset of the Protestant Reformation in Ireland, the English interest was defended and promoted by colonists of Norman extraction (the 'Old English'). This colonial, English-speaking élite was largely confined to the Pale, to the towns and to the river valleys of the south-east and included families such as the FitzGerald, earls of Kildare, the Butlers, earl of Ormond, and the Clanricard Burkes. From the 1530s English Protestant settlers, known as the 'New English' or 'Old Protestants', effectively replaced the Catholic Old English as Ireland's colonial élite as they settled on vast tracts of land confiscated from the native Irish.

PLANTATION

Demands for colonial enterprise and expropriation of native lands dated from the later Middle Ages. However, only after the Desmond rebellion of the 1570s did wholesale plantation win widespread acceptance. Edmund Spenser, in *A view of the Present State of Ireland* (1596), called for the destruction of the existing Gaelic order and the systematic colonization of Ireland with English settlers who were to be made responsible for the erection of the political, economic, and social framework that was considered the necessary support of a civil life and the Protestant faith. During the sixteenth century the government attempted, with varying degrees of success, to plant parts of Laois, Offaly, Down, and Antrim together with the earl of Desmond's patrimony in Munster. Then, in the wake of English victory at the end of the Nine Years War, Ulster met a similar fate. The unexpected flight of leading Ulster lords to the continent (1607) and the revolt of Sir Chair O'Dogherty (1608), enabled the state to confiscate and redistribute to Protestant colonists much of Ulster in order to create a British type of rural society. In an attempt to inculcate a vested interest in the settlement 300 'deserving' Irishmen also received estates, albeit outside their traditional lordships. Predictably the Catholic population, deprived of their lands, felt aggrieved and became increasingly frustrated with the newcomers who exploited their holdings for a quick return. From the crown's perspective the settlement did not generate much revenue and during the reign of Charles I the wranglings over how the plantation in County Londonderry should be administered alienated the City of London which had invested £100,000 in the scheme between 1609 and 1635, without reaping any tangible reward. Hardly surprisingly, the City refused to lend Charles the money he needed to fight the Scots after 1638 and later sided with Parliament.

In addition to confiscating Irish acres, the crown interfered in land titles. In 1606 James VI and I established the Commission for the Remedy of Defective Titles which, on pain of fine or forfeiture, required all Irish landowners to prove their title to their estates. Many failed and this resulted in the redistribution of land in Counties Wexford, Leitrim, Longford, and other areas in the Midlands between 1610 and 1620. Just as the tenurial policies of the Stuarts in Scotland (discussed below) unnerved Scottish landowners, James's eagerness to interfere in land titles provoked disquiet among Irish landowners. Taking advantage of the domestic crisis caused by the prospect of war with Catholic Europe, especially with Spain, they presented Charles I (who succeeded to the throne in 1625) with a list of grievances, known as the 'Graces' (1628), which articulated their concerns for the security of land tenure and requested that the crown not only guarantee existing rights of ownership but end its policy of plantation. The king finally accepted most of the Graces (though he refused to suspend recusancy fines or to allow Catholics to hold office) and gave an undertaking that they would be passed in the next Irish parliament. Ultimately this never happened and Thomas Wentworth later refused to enforce them.

THOMAS WENTWORTH, EARL OF STRAFFORD

In 1633 Sir Thomas Wentworth became lord deputy of Ireland and set out to govern the country without any regard to any interest but that of the crown. His 'thorough' policies aimed to make Ireland financially self-sufficient; to enforce religious conformity with the Church of England as defined by his close friend and ally Laud; to 'civilize' further the Irish; and to extend royal control through the policy of plantation. He believed that the settlement of English colonists remained the best means of enriching the English government and for 'civilizing . . . this people, or securing this kingdom under the dominion of your imperial Crown'. He continued that 'plantations must be the only means under God and your majesty to reform this subject as well in religion as manners'.[12] To this end Wentworth challenged the legitimacy of land titles wherever he could and after 1635 attempted to plant with English colonists parts of Clare, Connacht, and the lordship of Ormond. Ultimately the earl of Clanricard skilfully torpedoed this initiative by persuading the king to exclude County Galway from the settlement. However, Wentworth's eagerness to meddle in land titles fostered an uneasy alliance amongst his Catholic and Protestant opponents and this anti-Wentworth interest, which joined forces with the king's adversaries in the Long Parliament and with the Scottish covenanters, played a prominent role in orchestrating his ultimate downfall after November 1640.

Scotland

JAMES VI AND I

Throughout his reign as king of Scotland, James VI, like his predecessors, had endeavoured with some success to increase his financial base, to enhance the prestige and authority of the crown, and, where possible, to tame his nobles. For example, he skilfully twisted traditional Scottish baronial rivalries to his own advantage. In the north-east he favoured the Gordons; while in the Western Isles royal power rested with the Mackenzies of Kintail (who replaced the troublesome MacLeods) and with the Campbells, earls of Argyll, who, in the wake of the collapse of the lordship of the Isles after 1493, acquired vast estates stretching from Kintyre through the central Highlands to Cawdor in the north-east and acted as an effective (albeit self-interested) bulwark against the rebellious Clan Donald South. James also sought to make local lords directly responsible for the action of their kin and in 1587 extended the 'General Band' to the Highlands, requiring chiefs to find sureties for the peaceful conduct of their followers. The Statutes of Iona (1609), brokered by Andrew Knox, bishop of the Isles, aimed to make the Highland chieftains agents of 'civilization' by requiring them to obey the king and to observe the laws and Acts of the Scottish parliament and to demilitarize the clans by ridding them of the 'buannachan' or 'idle men' and outlawing the exaction of 'conyie' or tribute.[13]

Closely linked to this the crown interfered, where it could, in land titles. In 1598 James ordered leading Highland landowners to produce a legal deed to their holdings and to find sureties for the payment of royal dues. He also set out to tame the Isles by planting 'colonies among them of answerable inland subjects, that within short time may reform and civilize the best inclined among them: rooting out or transporting the barbarous and stubborn sort, and planting civility in their rooms'.[14] (Ultimately his plans came to nothing and local hostility to the venture frustrated three attempts (1595–1602, 1605, 1609) to settle the forfeited Isles of Lewis and Harris with adventurers from Fife.) Where possible his anglicized son Charles I continued these initiatives often with disastrous consequences. In particular, the comprehensive nature of the 1625 Act of Revocation aimed at renegotiating the terms on which those who had acquired secularized Church lands held them so as to ensure an enhanced revenue for the clergy and a regular rent for the crown. This thoroughly rattled Scottish landowners who, in the words of the Privy Council, felt that 'nothing has at any time heretofore occurred which has so far disquieted the minds of your good subjects'.[15] While the king's willingness to tamper with land titles alienated landowners, his ecclesiastical policies triggered a rebellion which involved all elements of Scottish society.

THE KIRK

The major issue in Scotland was the future of the Presbyterian Kirk, then as now the Established Church. James VI and I had never relented in a thirty-year campaign to bring the Kirk under crown control, culminating in the 'Black Articles' of Perth in 1618, which had not only ruled on such matters as kneeling to receive communion but had also reintroduced the office of bishop, though with less power and a lower status than in England. Charles wholeheartedly embraced and then extended his father's policies. In 1633, when he paid a brief visit to Scotland for his coronation, Archbishop Laud, who accompanied him, staged an elaborately ritualistic coronation service, offensive to Scottish tastes, and foregathered for deep discussion with the bishops, who were anxious to exalt their own status at almost any cost. (It was later thought that the lords of the council had held off because they wanted to see the bishops humiliated; they got more than they bargained for.) Soon after his return to England it became known that Charles had ordered the preparation of a modified version of the English prayer-book for use in Scotland, which was to be imposed on the Kirk, until now without any regular, generally accepted form of worship. Whether he had the right to do this—whether he was Supreme Governor of the Church in Scotland as in England—remained a moot point, but in any case Scottish nationalism and religious prejudice were deeply affronted, and the attempt to introduce the new prayer-book in 1637 provoked a wave of riots, beginning at St Giles's, Edinburgh. The nobility and gentry stood for the most part squarely behind their ministers in rejecting the prayer-book, and simply because of the less developed state of Scottish society, the looseness of its legal system, they were capable of mounting a direct challenge to the king's government, outside legal norms, which was quite unthinkable in England. The new prayer-book also offered them a tightly focused, easily understood issue on which to rally public opinion.

A National Covenant calling for the immediate withdrawal of the prayer-book was speedily drawn up in January 1638. Despite its moderate tone and conservative format the National Covenant was a radical manifesto against the Personal Rule of Charles I which justified a revolt against the interfering sovereign. It called 'for the maintenance of religion and the King's Majesty's authority, and for the preservation of the laws and liberties of the kingdom, against all troubles and sedition'. One of its co-authors, Sir Archibald Johnstone of Wariston, hailed the signing of the National Covenant as 'that glorious marriage day of the kingdom with God'.[16] The leading nobility, gentry, ministers, and burghers all signed the National Covenant at a ceremony in the Greyfriars church at Edinburgh and copies for signature were circulated far and wide throughout Scotland. *Ad hoc* assemblies in the provinces manfully supported a provisional government of 'The Tables' in Edinburgh which had no legal status but soon began recruiting an army. It called Alexander Leslie, the Swedish veteran, out of retirement to lead it, and officers from the continental armies began to return home (see above).

The First Bishops' War

ROYALIST GRAND STRATEGY

The turn of events in Scotland horrified Charles I who determined in June 1638 to 'reduce that people [the Scots] to their obedience . . . [since] not only now my crown but my reputation, forever, lies at stake'. He added ominously, 'I will rather die, than yield to those impertinent and damnable demands'.[17] Although the king lacked a standing army he still possessed considerable advantages (see map on p. 21). First, he controlled Edinburgh and Dumbarton Castles: the former dominated the kingdom's capital; while the latter provided a secure anchorage and landing place for troops shipped in from Ireland or western England. Second, he enjoyed considerable support among the Gordons in the north-east, led by George, marquis of Huntly; among the small Catholic pockets in the western borders; among the north-east and western Highlands; and among the anti-Campbell clans who included the Irish followers of Randal Macdonnell, 2nd earl of Antrim. Third, control of the Royal Navy enabled him to assault Scotland by sea, to hinder imports of continental arms, and to disrupt the burghs' trade. Charles's grand strategy for subduing the covenanters drew on these strengths: Huntly planned to rise in the north-east; Antrim, together with an army of 5,000 raised from amongst his Irish and Scottish dependants, aimed to wrest control of the western Highlands and Islands; James, marquis of Hamilton, was to land a force in the Firth of Forth; while the king would rally an English army at Berwick-upon-Tweed (whether Charles intended to smash his way to Edinburgh with the main field army, or merely wait for the inevitable collapse of the covenanters and then make an impressive triumphal entry into the capital remains unclear). Between his allies inside Scotland and the concentric blows from the forces outside the country, the king felt confident of victory.

Mustering an army in England was not easy, however, except on paper. Since the beginning of his reign Charles had been trying to improve the militia. In 1626 he had recalled a number of veteran non-commissioned officers from Dutch service to supervise its training in the counties, but when he tried to extend the system into the years of peace he provoked a series of squabbles over who was to pay these 'muster masters', an issue which caused as much aggravation as ship-money. Nevertheless, the drive for a 'Perfect Militia' had gone on, and efforts had been made to re-equip it with modern weapons, though understandably these weapons were not kept in militiamen's homes, but locked in county armouries except when needed. The eagerness with which both sides moved to seize these magazines in 1642 highlights their importance.

In 1639 Charles ordered the mobilization of the militia in the northern counties, plus a special levy of about 6,000 volunteers; he also invoked half-forgotten feudal custom by calling upon his tenants-in-chief to provide additional cavalry. By March he had a notional army of about 20,000. But money was desperately short, and Sir Jacob Astley, another continental veteran appointed to lead the infantry, was shocked by their poor condition and the inadequacy of their weapons when he arrived at York to take over. The militia regiments, the core of the army, should have consisted of trained yeomanry and minor gentry, but for the most part these worthies had taken advantage of a 'substitution' clause in the Militia

Randal MacDonnell, second earl and first marquis of Antrim (1609–83)
by Michael Wright

A Gaelic warlord of Scottish descent and a leading Caroline courtier, Antrim owned estates and enjoyed extensive contacts throughout the three Stuart kingdoms. After 1638 he played a leading role in rallying support for the king in Ireland and Scotland. In 1644 he dispatched 2,000–3,000 Irish veterans to serve in Scotland where, under the command of Montrose, they won a string of important victories. As the Civil Wars dragged on Antrim became increasingly involved in confederate affairs in Ireland and briefly served as President of the Supreme Council. Despite collaborating with Cromwell during the 1650s he was restored to his extensive patrimony in County Antrim after the Restoration.

Act to send instead the dregs of the lower classes. It might have been different if the army had been stiffened by a corps of mercenaries, or led by a committed, warlike nobility, but Charles could not afford mercenaries, and such noblemen as assembled at York proved far from martial. There were also serious dissensions in the high command, where the earl of Essex (see picture on p. 109), a veteran of the war in the Low Countries, was suddenly displaced as lieutenant-general of horse by the earl of Holland, one of the queen's shadier favourites. Charles had no experience of war, and nor had his overall commander, the earl of North-umberland.

Since the English nobility proved unable to provide him with large numbers of troops, Charles called upon his Irish lords. Late in 1638 he ordered Antrim, an influential courtier and a Gaelic warlord, to raise an army of 5,000 men from among his Catholic kin and followers in Ireland and in the Western Isles of Scotland. By the spring of 1639, Antrim had rallied the leading Irish families in Ulster: the O'Neills, O'Haras, O'Lurgans, Magennises, MacGuires, MacMahons, MacDonnells, MacHenrys; or, as the lord deputy maliciously phrased it, 'as many Oe's and Macs's as would startle a whole council board' and 'in a great part the sons of habituated traitors'.[18] However, Antrim needed experienced officers not only to train and discipline his recruits, but also to lead them, 'for there are no principal commanders in these parts' and he himself had 'no experience in war'.[19] In the absence of veteran officers in Ulster, Antrim's first instinct was to import from the continent men—such as his cousins Owen Roe O'Neill and Daniel O'Neill, or his half-brother Captain Maurice MacDonnell—well versed in the ways of modern warfare. The very idea horrified Wentworth and so the earl was forced to make do with 100 relatively inexperienced drill sergeants from the king's army with 'one or two able old soldiers to be commanders'.[20] Ultimately a breakdown of communications between Antrim and the king combined with a total lack of support, financial or otherwise, from the administration in Dublin, ensured that these soldiers never left Ireland. However, the abortive expedition was not without its significance since it further destabilized affairs in Scotland by alienating support for the king and forcing Antrim's great rival Archibald Campbell, 8th earl of Argyll and his followers into the covenanting camp.

COVENANTING STRATEGY

Despite the array of forces against them, the covenanters remained hopeful. Many, particularly the clergy and burgesses, drew inspiration from the linking of God and the Scots in a National Covenant which maintained that 'Religion and Righteousness may flourish in the Land, to the glory of God, the honour of our King, and peace and comfort of us all'.[21] That document also provided assurance for those less inclined to think of Scotland as the new Israel, because it contracted the opponents to Charles's policies to each other. Furthermore the spectre of defeat threatened dire punishment to the covenanters, enhancing their mood of resistance. The first signing of the National Covenant enjoyed near-unanimous support from western Galloway to the Mearns and from Berwickshire to Argyll. Consequently the Tables could rely upon an enthusiastic and large pool of manpower with which to resist the king. In addition the covenanters possessed the advantage of interior lines against projected attacks from England and Ireland. However, their domestic foes jeopardized control of Scotland itself. The covenanters therefore aimed to control the royal castles; to suppress the king's supporters in the Gordon territory, the south-west borders, and the central and western Highlands; and to guard against landings by an Irish army.

CONFRONTATION IN SCOTLAND

Military activity by the covenanters began in February 1639 with the seizure of Inverness burgh and castle. The proud, arrogant, and intensely loyal marquis of Huntly responded by mustering the Aberdeenshire and Banffshire royalists on 13 February but failed to win control over the north-east. The following month a combined army of north-eastern covenanters, under the command of James Graham, 5th earl (and after 1644 marquis) of Montrose and Alexander Leslie, entered the royalist burgh of Aberdeen and captured Huntly. In return for his freedom, Montrose persuaded Huntly to sign a modified form of the National Covenant; however, Leslie promptly seized him and carried him to Edinburgh. In March the covenanters also occupied Dunglas and Tantallon Castles (in the south-east), and captured Edinburgh and Dumbarton Castles, thereby securing the capital and reducing the possibility of an Irish landing in the west; while 3,000 horse accompanied by 2,000 foot under Major-General Sir Robert Munro, another veteran of the Thirty Years War, established a watch on the eastern border. In the west Argyll's forces dealt with supporters of the anti-Campbell conspiracy led by Antrim, and constructed an artillery fort at Lochhead, Kintyre. The covenanters also took steps to secure the south-western and Forth coasts. Along the former, men under John Kennedy, 6th earl of Cassillis and Alexander Montgomery, 6th earl of Eglinton, guarded against an invasion by Irish forces; while units patrolled the shores of the Forth in anticipation of Hamilton's landing. His mother—the only woman to command a covenanter unit—rode with her horse troop and a pistol loaded to shoot her son should he land. Yet, divisions within the royalist camp eliminated the possibility of an amphibious assault. Wentworth, regarding Antrim's operation as the foundation for the revival of a destabilizing McDonnell-MacDonald hegemony in Ulster and Argyll, sabotaged the effort by withholding weapons and shipping. In the Forth Hamilton, fearing the covenanters would confiscate his estates, dallied.

Back in the north-east the Gordons, now under the leadership of James, Viscount Aboyne, Huntly's second son, stirred again. Assisted by a professional soldier and a shipment of arms, Aboyne's royalists entered Aberdeen on 6 June. Apparently, the viscount lacked a clear plan, for on 15 June his men had only

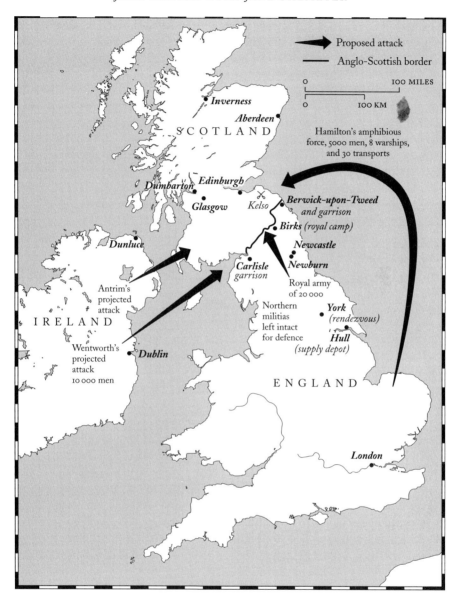

Proposed attack
Anglo-Scottish border

100 MILES
100 KM

Hamilton's amphibious
force, 5000 men, 8 warships,
and 30 transports

Inverness

Aberdeen

SCOTLAND

Dumbarton
Edinburgh
Glasgow
Kelso
Berwick-upon-Tweed
and garrison

Birks (royal camp)

Dunluce

Newcastle
Newburn

Carlisle
garrison

Royal army
of 20 000

Antrim's
projected
attack

Northern
militias
left intact
for defence

IRELAND

York
(rendezvous)

Hull
(supply depot)

Wentworth's
projected
attack
10 000 men

Dublin

ENGLAND

London

First Bishops' War 1639

reached the outskirts of Stonehaven—just fifteen miles south of Aberdeen. The day before, Marischal mustered 1,200 men from the Mearns to face the royalists. The two forces collided at Megra Hill, near Stonehaven, where Marischal's cannon-fire routed Aboyne's Highlanders. The royalists retired to Aberdeen, where they fortified the southern end of the Bridge of Dee in anticipation of the covenanters' arrival. On 17 June Montrose united with Marischal, increasing their forces to 4,000–4,600 men. Aboyne had only 2,000 foot and 300 horse, but the Dee provided them with security. The next day, the covenanters attacked with artillery (two twenty-three-pounders plus some light pieces) but the gunners fired too high to affect either the royalists or their works. An evening onslaught by the foot-soldiers of the burgh of Dundee failed to carry the bridge. However, on 19 June, after a further covenanting offensive, the royalist army retreated, leaving Montrose free to enter Aberdeen. His interventions in the north-east had brought glory to the covenanting war-effort, but had earned him the undying enmity of the Gordons.

CONFRONTATION IN ENGLAND

Meanwhile back in England the confrontation of the two main field armies had already produced a temporary respite to hostilities. On 20 May Alexander Leslie concentrated between 12,000 and 20,000 troops in the eastern borders on Duns Law, which he extensively fortified. The covenanters spent their time preparing for action: the officers continued drilling the regiments, while the chaplains held daily prayer-meetings and gave sermons to heighten the men's trust in God and to bolster their morale. For his part, Charles brought his host north from York, settling into a fortified camp at Birks, west of the border fortress at Berwick. It quickly became clear that his grand strategy for the subjugation of Scotland had misfired, leaving Charles no alternative but to negotiate. The king and covenanter nobles signed the Treaty of Berwick on 18 June, which stipulated a return to the *status quo ante bellum*, and the armies disbanded. It represented an unsatisfactory compromise: while the covenanters had preserved their position in Scotland, they had failed to gain royal approval for their policies; at the same time the king's forces had endured one humiliation after another, and he stood no closer to being master of Scotland.

The Second Bishops' War

An uneasy truce descended between the two sides. The covenanters, wary of the king's intentions, retained their mercenary officers and kept them training men in the Lowlands. Meanwhile, Charles planned a fresh offensive which involved an Irish army, led by Wentworth, now elevated to the earldom of Strafford, invading the west, while royalists tied down the covenanters in the Highlands, the south-west borders, and the north-east. The formation of Wentworth's 'New

Army' (as it was known) of 8,000 foot and 1,000 horse marked a daring departure in that, unlike previous forces which had been raised in England, with the exception of the senior officers, it was a predominately Catholic body. (However, just as Antrim's plans had been fraught with delay the previous year so too were Strafford's and his army did not even assemble until July 1640.)

THE SHORT PARLIAMENT

By the spring of 1640 the payment of ship-money had virtually ceased, but whether this was simply a reaction to the large sums now being levied for the recruitment of troops, no one can say. There is some evidence that men were beginning to draw the obvious inference: that if the king could fund an army, as he was already financing the navy, without parliamentary grants, and if he then conquered Scotland, then there would be no further restraint on his authority. However this may be, Strafford, now in charge of the king's war-effort, at once called for a parliament, as the only way of raising money quickly, and it assembled in April 1640. It only lasted three weeks (hence its name the 'Short Parliament'). The Commons were willing to vote the huge sum of twelve subsidies, but first they demanded statutory action to ensure a permanent end to their major grievances with the king's policy in Church and State, a process which at the very least would have postponed the next campaign into 1641. The king, hoping to get money on less stringent conditions from Philip IV of Spain (hopes quickly dashed as Philip's regime faced a forest fire of provincial revolts) precipitately dissolved the Short Parliament, and plans went ahead to mobilize the militia again, but this time from south of the Trent. However, these southern counties, well out of the Scots immediate reach, proved even less willing to give of their best, though they were probably more skilled and better equipped than their poorer brethren in the north. An untrained, ill-armed crew of misfits and drop-outs trailed north, some of them mutinying on the way, and for all Strafford's efforts little money was forthcoming to pay them.

CONFRONTATION IN SCOTLAND

From the spring of 1640 the covenanters again seized the initiative in Scotland. The north-eastern royalists felt the first blows. Munro occupied Aberdeen from 5 to 8 May before he headed inland, capturing and pillaging the homes of royalist lairds, especially the Gordons. With a determined covenanter general in their midst the royalists failed to rise for Charles. Unlike the previous year strongholds loyal to the king in the Lowlands held out for months. Thus the covenanters besieged Edinburgh Castle (see picture on p. 223) from late May until its surrender, due to lack of food, on 19 September; while Argyll assaulted Dumbarton Castle for about three weeks, taking it on 27 August.[22] Increasingly Argyll became the key player in the covenanting war-effort. He received two commissions from the Committee of Estates (an executive body of the Estates): one authorized him to defend the west against the Irish; while the other ordered him to proceed with fire and sword against the royalists of central Scotland. Both commands enabled the earl to satisfy his loyalty to the covenant and to enhance his clan's position of hegemony in the western and central Highlands. On 18 June 1640 Argyll mustered his men at Inverary, Argyll, and at Clachandysert and Glenorchy, Perthshire. Between 4,000 and 5,000 of his kinsmen, allies, tenants, and servants appeared, forming three regiments, two under the earl and one under Sir Robert Campbell of Glenorchy. His troops ravaged the lands of the MacDonalds of Keppoch in Lochaber and pillaged and burned in Badenoch and the Braes of Mar before entering Atholl where they encountered a force under the earl of Atholl and the local lairds. Under the pretence of negotiations Argyll lured the leaders to his camp and forced them to disband their men. Subsequently he compelled the Athollmen to pay for quartering his army; he also bound Atholl to raise a regiment for Leslie's army. Argyll next marched against the royalist Ogilvies in the Braes of Angus. Despite a protection from Montrose, he razed the house of Airlie and destroyed Airlie's house at Forter. After ravaging Ogilvy lands for a week, Argyll marched into Rannoch, home of the royalist Robertsons, which his men plundered and wasted. After six weeks, on 2 August, the devastating expedition against the enemies of the Campbells and the Covenant ended.

CONFRONTATION IN ENGLAND

The most dramatic campaign of the war, indeed one of the most impressive of the seventeenth century, began a few weeks later when Montrose led Leslie's army across the Tweed. Having initially mustered his forces on the Leith Links, Leslie moved to Choicelee Wood, Berwickshire. For three weeks (until mid-August) more regiments arrived, while Leslie completed his plans, and the covenanters received assurances of help from factions within England fed up with the Personal Rule of Charles I. Mustering between 17,000 and 22,000 foot and horse, plus a train of over sixty artillery pieces, Leslie's army gathered supplies for the campaign. Meanwhile in England the royal army had contrived to follow courses of action that played into the covenanters' hands. Rather than concentrating the fresh levies in one place, the king had allowed two centres of assembly to emerge: one in central Yorkshire, the other in Northumberland. This proved a tactical error for a united royal force would have at least equalled Leslie's in size, if not possessed outright superiority in numbers. Furthermore, the theatre commanders, especially Viscount Conway, and the council in London discounted all news of possible covenanter invasion plans. Conway spent his scarce financial resources on fortifying Berwick, neglecting the far more important town of Newcastle, source of London's coal supply. Indiscipline and disrespect for the royal cause among the English troops coupled with shortages of weapons and ammunition further complicated the king's task. Consequently, his officers led a force hardly prepared for Leslie's bold move.

Disregarding the standard practices of early modern warfare Leslie determined upon an offensive strategy while leaving uncaptured enemy strongholds in his rear. With units besieging Edinburgh Castle and masking the fortress town of Berwick, Leslie elected to invade England aiming from the start for Newcastle. Even though he was negotiating secretly with the king, Montrose marched the main body of the army across the Tweed at Coldstream on 20 August. Lieutenant-General James Livingstone, Lord Almond, led a another group from Kelso. In eight days Leslie pushed his men to the outskirts of Newcastle. He used an inland route, preventing the royal navy from observing his movements, from firing on the Scots, or from landing parties of the royal army to oppose the covenanters. The Berwick garrison made several ineffectual sorties against the Scots. In that area of operations the most important English triumph occurred when an indignant English servant of Major-General Thomas Hamilton, 2nd earl of Haddington, exploded the powder supply in Dunglass Castle on 30 August, killing his master and several other officers. Conway failed to impede Leslie's advance by any means, and often lacked knowledge of his whereabouts. Meanwhile the other royal army began a leisurely advance through Yorkshire, ensuring that Conway would be outnumbered by about two to one. English incompetence and the covenanters' skill had placed Leslie's army in a very advantageous position.

ENGLISH DEFEAT

The campaign climaxed on 28 to 30 August. Conway, worried about the unprepared state of Newcastle, left 7,500 men to guard the town, while he brought 3,000 foot, 2,000 horse, and eight guns west to guard the nearest ford of the Tyne opposite Newburn. Leslie had 17,000 more men and an overwhelming superiority in artillery. General of Artillery Alexander Hamilton skilfully placed the guns on ground higher than the English fieldworks, even using the village's church tower for some pieces. On the afternoon of the 28th an overwhelming force of covenanter infantry and cavalry supported by artillery fire crossed the river, panicking the royal foot and driving the cavalry away. About 10,000 of Leslie's men made it over the river before the high tide prevented use of the ford. Conway fell back to Newcastle with part of his forces, while others fled south. Leslie worried unnecessarily about his divided force, because Conway and Sir Jacob Astley elected to abandon Newcastle and to retreat with utmost speed. While the English rushed south at a much faster pace (they covered forty-one miles in two days) than their comrades in Yorkshire, the covenanters completed crossing the Tyne. On 30 August they entered Newcastle, cutting London's coal supply. By 10 September logistical problems began to affect Leslie's army, and it started requisitioning food from the Northumbrians. Meanwhile a force of Scots advanced into Durham, reaching the Tees where they halted. With a minimum of losses to both sides Leslie had removed the threat of invasion, seized a strategic prize, demoralized the English army, and heartened the opponents to royal policy.

In desperation Charles summoned a Great Council of the peerage to York on 24 September, but they only advised him to call a further truce and summon another parliament. Shortly thereafter he began negotiations to suspend hostilities and concluded treaties of armistice on 16 and 26 October. The main provisions of the agreement, known as the Treaty of Ripon, ensured a military *status quo*, but pledged to pay the Scots £850 per day for their quarter. As the two north-eastern counties could not afford that level of exaction, the king had to recall parliament.

The Long Parliament

When a new parliament assembled at Westminster on 3 November 1640 no one dreamt that it would become the 'Long Parliament', persisting until it was thrown out by the army in April 1653 and experiencing a cryogenic resurrection in 1659–60. Nor was there the least expectation of rebellion or civil war in even the most radical Member's mind. No, Charles must be restrained by the removal of his present advisers, wrongs must be righted and grievances met in the usual legislative way, the Church must be reformed, and the Scots bought off. This done, they could disperse, perhaps with some proviso for the summons of parliaments regularly in the future. The king's supporters had been decimated at the polls and imprisonment of Strafford and Laud removed his most feared advisers, a reform programme was to hand, and Charles agreed, though no doubt with mental reservations, to go along with it. With a bare handful of supporters left in the Commons, and not many more in the Lords, and an empty exchequer, he had little choice. However, the military pressure which had forced Charles into line and held him there generated new tensions. The need to pay off the Scots called for the floating of huge loans, which could only be had on the assurance that this Parliament would not be abruptly dissolved, like its predecessors. A Triennial Act passed in February 1641 decreed that parliaments be held every three years, but it only applied to future parliaments; much more effective was a revolutionary Act of May 1641 which forbade the prorogation or dissolution of the present Parliament without its own consent. Charles naturally regarded this as a blatant invasion of his prerogative, and he only passed it under extreme pressure and with considerable resentment.

DEATH OF STRAFFORD

Meanwhile, the suspicion that Strafford was negotiating for military aid from Spain, even from the Tower, and Charles's stubborn refusal to disband the New Army served as a prime incentive for Parliament to get rid of the great earl once and for all. But his impeachment and attainder, which brought him to the block in May 1641, widened the gap between Parliament and the king, who had staked

Trial of Thomas Wentworth, earl of Strafford (1593–1641)

In 1633 Wentworth became lord deputy of Ireland and set out to govern the country without regard to any interest but that of the crown. His 'thorough' policies, which aimed to make Ireland financially self-sufficient, to enforce religious conformity with the Church of England, and to 'civilize' the Irish, merely served to alienate both the Catholic and Protestant communities throughout Ireland. With the outbreak of the Bishops' Wars Strafford, who became the king's principal adviser, urged him to use Irish troops against his enemies. Determined to rid Charles of his evil counsellors the Long Parliament, which assembled on 3 November 1640, immediately called for Strafford's impeachment. The lengthy trial at Westminster (March–April 1641)—orchestrated by Protestants and Catholics from Ireland, Scottish covenanters, and the king's English opponents—highlights the importance of the interconnections between the Stuart kingdoms. On 10 May Charles reluctantly agreed to Strafford's execution and he was beheaded the following day on Tower Hill before a vast and cheering crowd.

his honour on Strafford's safety. Moreover, the volunteer nucleus of the English army of 1640 was still camped in Yorkshire, resentful that its claims for back pay had been shelved in favour of the Scots, and in May 1641 an abortive plot was discovered to march it south to join with the strong Portsmouth garrison in coercing Parliament. At the same time the overwhelming presence of the Scots in the north, and the influence exerted by their commissioners in London, was palpably hindering the conclusion of a Church settlement, which was emerging as the most contentious item on Parliament's agenda. Meanwhile, political confusion resulted in economic depression and widespread unemployment, bringing huge mobs out on to the London streets to agitate in favour of Parliament. In response Charles strengthened the garrison at the Tower, and his guards at Whitehall.

In these circumstances the programme of reform legislation, finally implemented in June and July 1641, which settled almost all the opposition's grievances except in religion, and would almost certainly have satisfied the Short Parliament of 1640, fell miserably flat. Charles seemed uninterested in forming a new government, as he was expected to do, taking on board some of the opposition leaders; since Strafford's death he seemed unremittingly hostile to Parliament, and he and the queen were profoundly mistrusted, but it was difficult to see what further curbs could be placed on his future conduct. The announcement that he intended to visit Edinburgh in August galvanized Parliament into completing its payments to the Scots, who finally departed across the Tweed on 7 September, and paying off the Army of the North. In the event Charles's stay at Edinburgh, though it was extended into November, brought him little joy; in fact it put him further at odds with the Scottish provisional government, who over the summer and autumn of 1641 became increasingly suspicious of the king. To begin with, Charles's clandestine relationship with Montrose, which culminated in the latter being arrested and tried after the fall of Newcastle, created friction within the movement. Second, during Charles's sojourn in Edinburgh, a plot, known as 'The Incident', was uncovered. According to an informer, a well-regarded professional soldier, Sir John Cochrane of that Ilk, planned to murder Argyll, Hamilton, and Hamilton's brother, the earl of Lanark, and to reimpose royal control. Finally, news of the Irish rising of October 1641, with the rebels' claims of royal approval, further strained relations between the covenanters and their king. Just as Scotland had provoked the initial crisis, so Ireland drove England into civil war.

Rebellion in Ireland

THE ANTRIM PLOT

The Irish Parliament, which had been summoned in March 1640 to pay for the New Army, supported its English counterpart by adopting a petition of remonstrance which condemned every aspect of Strafford's government in Ireland. It also provided evidence against him at Westminster in the lengthy trial which followed. Horrified by these developments, Charles plotted to save his disgraced lord lieutenant. Towards the end of April 1641, according to an account later related by the earl of Antrim, the king had insisted that 'those eight thousand men, raised by the earl of Strafford in Ireland, should be continued without disbanding, and that they should be made up to twenty thousand, and that they should be armed out of the store of Dublin, and employed against the parliament'.[23] When it became clear that Strafford's case was lost, the king reluctantly agreed on 8 May to disband the New Army but then in the late summer he issued fresh royal orders 'that all possible endeavours should be used for getting together again those 8,000 men so disbanded; and that an army should immediately be raised in Ireland, that should declare for him [the king] against the Parliament in England'. According to Antrim, these instructions were qualified with the important proviso that this Irish army should only be used against the Parliament 'if occasion should be for so doing'. That occasion never arose. The political climate in England and Scotland appeared to shift in the king's favour so that by the early autumn it no longer suited Charles 'to use Irish troops against his parliamentary opponents'. Nevertheless Antrim 'imparted the design to the lord of Gormanstown, and to the lord of Slane, and after to many others in Leinster, and after going into Ulster, he communicated the same to many there'.[24] In the event the 'Antrim plot' came to nothing and it was the 'O'More–Maguire plot' which eventually gave rise to the insurrection. From February 1641, various designs were hatched—by Rory O'More, Lord Maguire, Colonel Hugh MacMahon, Sir Phleim O'Neill, and others—which planned to overthrow the Ulster plantation by capturing key strongholds in the north. Sometime late in the summer of 1641 the northern conspirators learnt from Antrim of the king's wishes to use—'if occasion be for so doing'—an Irish army against his recalcitrant English Parliament. This delighted them for it threw a cloak of quasi-legality over their own plot; but 'the Fools', Antrim later related, 'well liking the business, would not expect [i.e. await] our time or manner for ordering the work, but fell upon it without us, and sooner, and otherwise than we should have done, taking to themselves, and in their own way, the managing of the work, and so spoiled it'.[25]

CAUSES OF REBELLION

The 1641 rebellion is one of the central military events in Irish history and played an important role in shaping the fate of the triple Stuart monarchy during the seventeenth century. Yet according to accounts left by Protestant officials it came as a total surprise: Audley Mervin, Member of Parliament for County Tyrone, was amazed that it was 'conceived among us, and yet never felt to kick in the womb, nor struggle in the birth'.[26] In reality it derived, on the one hand, from 'long-term' social, religious, and economic causes (namely tenurial insecurity, economic instability, indebtedness, and a desire to have the Catholic Church re-stored to its pre-Reformation position) and, on the other, from 'short-term' polit-ical factors which triggered the outbreak of violence. The plantation of Ulster (discussed above), combined with government attempts to replace the existing redistributive economic order with one centred on markets and the exchange of money, had alienated many members of the Catholic population and resulted in widespread indebtedness and in a dramatic increase in mortgages throughout Ireland. Particularly in Ulster a large number of Catholic landowners alienated vast portions of their estates to speculators and sank deeply into debt. For ex-ample, Sir Phelim O'Neill, one of the leaders of the Irish rebellion, mortgaged land in County Tyrone to cover debts in excess of £12,000; little wonder, perhaps, that one of his creditors, Mr Fullerton of Loughgall, to whom Sir Phelim owed £600 'upon mortgages', was one of the first to be murdered in the rebellion! A chronic shortage of specie, combined with a run of poor harvests between 1636 and 1639, exacerbated the economic crisis and helps to explain the willingness of many to contemplate rebellion. Political and military developments in Scotland and England offered them an opportunity.

To begin with, the Scottish example of successful rebellion had a profound im-pact on Ireland and according to one pamphleteer filled the Irish 'with thoughts of emulation'.[27] On the one hand, Charles I sought aid from Ireland—from Antrim during the First Bishops' War and from Strafford during the Second—and thereby involved the kingdom directly in his struggle with the covenanters. On the other, the Scots not only offered the Irish a model for resistance against royal authority but created circumstances favourable for the fomenting of rebel-lion. For as the royalist historian and statesman Edward Hyde, earl of Clarendon, perceptively noted in his *History*:

if this scottish [*sic*] people had not, without any provocation, but of their own folly and barbarity, with that bloody prologue engaged again the three kingdoms in a raging and devouring war; so that though Scotland blew the first trumpet, it was Ireland that drew the first blood; and if they had not at that time rebelled, and in that manner, it is very prob-able all the miseries which afterwards befell the King and his dominions had been pre-vented.[28]

IMPACT IN ENGLAND AND SCOTLAND

Whether 'all the miseries' which later befell Charles I could have been avoided remains open to debate. Certainly the Irish standing army—a poorly supplied and armed Protestant force of 2,297 foot and 943 horse—failed to crush the in-surrection which broke out in October 1641 and this resulted in a struggle be-tween Charles I and his Westminster Parliament over who should control the army to be raised to quell the Irish insurgents. Had the English king accepted the 'Grand Remonstrance' (December 1641) and somehow reconciled his differences with Parliament, there can be little doubt that the revolt in Ireland could have been quashed with relative ease. As it was, rumours circulated that Charles (and his queen) had somehow been involved in the Irish rebellion. Parliamentary propagandists repeatedly asserted that Henrietta Maria 'hath countenanced and maintained that horrid and execrable rebellion'.[29] Sir Phelim O'Neill's claim in November 1641 that he held a royal commission fuelled these suspicions. Certainly the Irish insurgents themselves, like the Scottish covenanters, maintained that they had risen 'only for the preservation of his majesty, and his rightful government over them . . . the defence of their religion, laws, and liberties'.[30] These both confirmed and inflamed fears of a great Catholic conspiracy, which parliamentary leaders—especially John Pym—exploited ruthlessly, claiming that England was on the verge of being reduced to popery. Hyde later acknowledged the damage caused by 'the imputation raised by parliament upon the king, of an intention to bring in, or . . . of conniving at and tolerating, Popery'.[31]

The outbreak of rebellion in Ireland not only helped to trigger the onset of the First English Civil War, but also presented the covenanters with considerable concerns and opportunities. First, they feared for the safety of the thousands of largely Presbyterian Scottish settlers (and for that of their Protestant English counterparts). Second, as a direct result of the rebellion, Scotland became the host for hundreds of refugees, straining the country's charitable resources. Finally, the covenanters worried about the spectre of a total Catholic Irish victory, which would provide the king with a ready ally against his recalcitrant Scottish subjects and would threaten to subvert their repression of native Catholics. The opportunities came in several guises: in the short term a treaty for a Scottish army in Ulster maintained the covenanters' military power at the expense of the English Parliament, while in the long term the army's presence there provided Scotland with the leverage to claim a role in the territorial redistribution following the rebels' defeat and would legitimize Scottish involvement in a previously English-dominated part of the three kingdoms. Thus within days of learning of the insurrection the Scottish Parliament offered to send an army of 10,000 to Ulster to crush it on the grounds that 'unless we do fully vindicate these malicious papists [in Ireland], these two kingdoms both Scotland and England, cannot sleep long in security.'[32] The 'Wars of the Three Kingdoms' had begun.

Civil Wars in the Stuart Kingdoms

THE WARS OF THE THREE KINGDOMS

Charles I saw the events of the 1640s as a single war, and he constantly sought to deploy the resources of each of his kingdoms in the struggles in the others. Many of his advisers, most notably the marquis of Hamilton and George Lord Digby, thought likewise; as did many of his principal supporters in Ireland, headed by the marquis of Ormond, and many of the leading confederates, including the earl of Antrim. Perhaps the group most passionately committed to the view that there could be no settlement in any kingdom without an imposed settlement through-out all the kingdoms was that around the earl of Argyll and the proponents of the Solemn League and Covenant (1643) which formalized the role of the Scots army in Ireland, committed 20,000 Scottish troops to the English theatre, and provided for a fundamental postwar change in the constitutional relationships between all three kingdoms and for religious uniformity throughout the archipelago.[33]

With so many leading figures committed to a holistic view of the conflict it is not surprising to find that at the height of the war in 1644, there were Scottish and Irish troops in England, English and Scottish troops in Ireland, and Irish (but not English) troops in Scotland—altogether perhaps 40,000 troops 'out of theatre'. Furthermore, after the autumn of 1645, *all* the major battles involving more than 5,000 men—at least ten of them—were fought either outside England or between English and Scottish armies. In 1648 the Second Civil War was in fact a badly co-ordinated attempt by an imprisoned king to destabilize England by regional revolts in preparation for a Scottish invasion which would overthrow the Long Parliament; and after Charles I's execution, his son spent five years concentrating on regaining his thrones via Ireland and Scotland, and he was indeed crowned (significantly as king of Great Britain and Ireland and not just as king of Scotland) at Scone on New Years Day 1651. The first battle of the *English Civil Wars* took place at Powicke Bridge on the outskirts of Worcester on 23 September 1642. The final battle of the *British* Civil Wars occurred in the fields around Worcester in 3 September 1651.

WARS IN THE THREE KINGDOMS

Yet three very different civil wars, each fought according to different codes and in different ways, also occurred in the Stuart kingdoms.

In England in each of the campaigning seasons of 1643, 1644, and 1645 there were between 120,000 and 150,000 under military discipline in the 'marching armies', the regional army corps, local militias, and in official garrisons. That represented about one in ten of the male population between the ages of 16 and 50 and it seems probable that something like one in three or one in four adult males actually bore arms at some point, an astonishing proportion for any pre-industrial economy. In the four years of the First English Civil War, there were five battles in which the number of combatants exceeded 25,000 men (Edgehill, the 1st and 2nd battles of Newbury, Marston Moor, and Naseby); another seven in which the total number of combatants comfortably exceeded 10,000; and between fifteen and twenty in which the numbers surpassed 5,000.[34] In the same period there were at least thirty-eight major and prolonged sieges of walled towns or medieval castles, and several hundred lesser sieges[35]—the New Model Army alone undertook forty-six sieges in the last phases of the first war.[36] The

A true and exact Relation of the

manner of his Maiesties setting up of His
Standard at *Nottingham*, on Munday the
22. of August 1642.

First, The forme of the Standard, as it is here figured, and who were present at the advancing of it

Secondly, The danger of setting up of former Standards, and the damage which ensued thereon.

Thirdly, A relation of all the Standards that ever were set up by any King.

Fourthly, the names of those Knights who are appointed to be the Kings Standard-bearers. With the forces that are appoynted to guard it.

Fifthly, The manner of the Kings comming first to *Coventry*.

Sixtly, The *Cavalieres* resolution and dangerous threats which they have uttered, if the King concludes a peace without them. or hearkens unto his great Councell the Parliament : Moreover how they have shared and divided *London* amongst themselves already.

Nottingham.

London, printed for *F. Coles.* 1642,

The King raises his standard at Nottingham

The First English Civil War formally began at Nottingham when the king raised his standard on 22 August 1642. This is an example of one of the many thousands of pamphlets, newspapers, declarations and broadsheets published during the 1640s. The protagonists, especially in England, used the press as a means of rallying support for their own side while provoking hatred for the other. The royalists denounced their opponents as religious schismatics while the parliamentarians responded by lambasting the king's supporters as foreigners and papists. In addition to being works of propaganda, these publications reported military action and political events thereby increasing the political awareness of society and exposing the people—often for the first time—to unorthodox, radical, and revolutionary ideas.

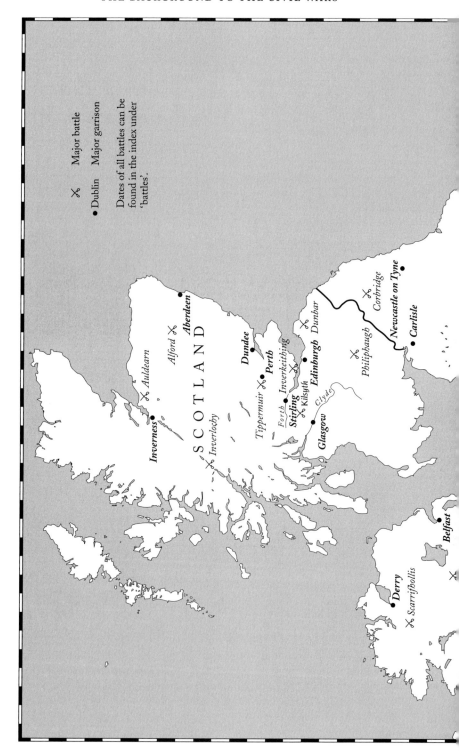

✗ Major battle

● Dublin Major garrison

Dates of all battles can be found in the index under 'battles'.

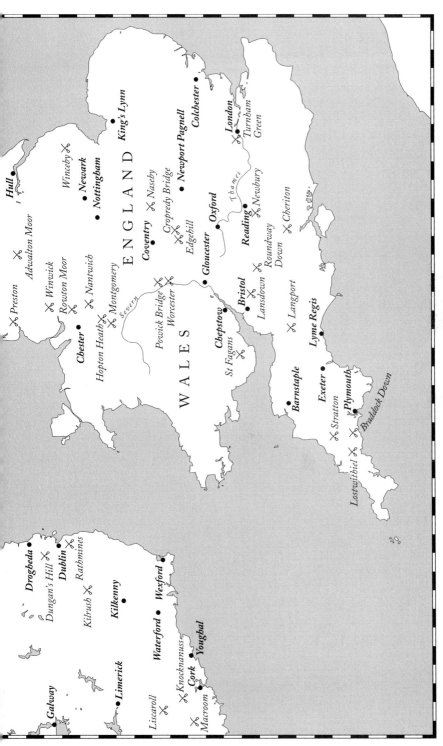

Civil wars in the three kingdoms

resulting loss of life has been compared proportionately to British casualty figures in the First World War.[37]

Yet it was a war of striking contrasts. Some counties—Kent, Cambridgeshire, and much of mid-Wales for example—saw much troop movement but not significant battles, skirmishes, or sieges. Other areas—notably the Severn Valley as far north as Shrewsbury and the Thames Valley from Maidenhead to Cricklade, and much of the west Midlands and south-west—saw more or less continuous fighting[38] and there were at least six counties where there was one or more sieges in progress throughout the war.

Both sides initially created a series of associations for military and fiscal purposes—Parliament's included a Northern Association made up of the counties previously under the jurisdiction of the Council of the North; an Eastern Association made up of Essex, Hertfordshire, Norfolk, Suffolk, Cambridgeshire, and Huntingdonshire (with Lincolnshire briefly added to it); a Southern Association made up of Kent, Surrey, and Sussex; and so on. Many of these associations included territory to be defended and territory to be occupied. Thus there were a series of regional wars. However, the king and the two Houses were constantly seeking to deploy regional armies outside their own theatre or to recruit from particular armies to the main marching armies, and this created tensions within the royalist and parliamentarian movements and occasionally led to fighting between men supposedly on the same side (the same phenomenon was even more marked and more debilitating within Ireland).

The basic *shape* of the civil war was of royalist advance in 1643 and then of steady parliamentarian attrition and expansion. In late 1642 there was a phoney war. Neutrality pacts kept many areas out of the war as both the king and the two Houses gathered armies expecting the conflict to be settled by a knock-out blow. The drawn battle of Edgehill (October 1642) and the king's decision not to storm London after he came as close as Turnham Green (Brentford) in mid-November 1642 transformed the situation. It was only then that both sides sought to create regional armies, county and regional civilian organizations, national war taxation. By the spring of 1643 the nation was in arms, with the king controlling most of the territory north of the Trent and the Severn, plus a tongue of land stretching through the south Midlands to Oxford, and Parliament more of the territory to the south of the Trent–Severn line. In the course of 1643 Charles consolidated his hold throughout the north and west, and made significant gains in the south-west counties and in the south Midlands. However, his failure to take Gloucester or to defeat the earl of Essex at the first battle of Newbury (20 September 1643) brought his advances to an end. By the end of the year the arrival of 20,000 Scottish troops in the north began the process of his defeat. It was always likely that the resources of London (especially the lines of credit extended by the merchant community), the more compact and defensible parliamentarian heartland, and control of the navy (see Chapter 5) would lead to a parliamentarian victory at the greatest of all the battles of the war, fought at Marston Moor on 2 July 1644. Thereafter, despite setbacks which seemed greater at the time than they were, the parliamentarians ground down the royalists, first in the north, then in the west, and finally in the Midlands and Wales. By the spring of 1646 the king had run out of options and of hope. He fled from Oxford to Southwell in Nottinghamshire and surrendered himself to the Scots in the hope of securing a better deal from them.

The presence of large Scottish armies in England during the 1640s should not detract from the fact that Scots experienced their own domestic conflict after 1638. In Scotland loyalty to the covenant, to the king, and to the house of Argyll resulted in a lengthy and, at times, bloody civil war which began in February 1639 when the covenanters seized Inverness and ended with the surrender of Dunnotter castle, near Aberdeen, in May 1652 (see Chapter 2). External factors—whether in the form of armed intervention from Ireland (1644–5) or from England after July 1650—exacerbated domestic divisions within Scotland, especially over religion, and heightened traditional baronial rivalries. In the case of the ancient feud between the Campbells and MacDonalds the onset of war after 1639 elevated what had previously been an 'Irish Sea World' struggle into a major international conflict. Hatred of the House of Argyll underpinned the eagerness with which Antrim rallied to the king's cause during the Bishops' Wars; while a determination to prevent Clan Donald from reasserting its authority in Scotland drove Argyll deep into the covenanting camp. Similarly, in June 1644 Antrim sent nearly 2,000 Irish veterans to serve in Scotland under the marquis of Montrose in the hope that he would not only rid his County Antrim estates of a Scottish army of occupation, which included a significant Campbell component, but would also recover his patrimonial lands in the Western Isles. Hardly surprisingly, he and his kin hailed Montrose's victories at Tippermuir (1 September 1644), Aberdeen (13 September), Inverlochy (2 February 1645), Auldearn (9 May), Alford (2 July), and Kilsyth (15 August) as victories for the MacDonalds over the Campbells. One leading Gaelic poet, Iain Lom, commemorated the bloody rout of the 'wry-mouthed Campbells' at Inverlochy as 'a victory for Clan Donald'.[39] These royalist successes also had an immediate and dramatic impact on developments in Scotland and England. On the one hand, the covenanters sent an army of 6,000—led by Argyll—to counter the Irish invasion; while, on the other, Montrose's continued victories in the north prevented a third Scottish army of invasion from crossing the border. The Campbell–MacDonald feud impacted again on national affairs when in June 1646 Antrim and his allies in the Western Isles not only refused to surrender at the end of the First English Civil War but, in conjunction with Scottish and English royalists and Irish confederates, threatened to raise an army of 20,000 men which, after reducing Scotland, would march into England and free Charles I. Though it came to nothing, Antrim's design seriously threatened any chance of securing a peace between the king and the

English and Scottish Parliaments and it highlights the extent to which the vortex of the Wars of the Three Kingdoms lay, at certain key moments, along the Western seaboard.

A bitter and lengthy civil war also engulfed Ireland between the outbreak of the Irish rebellion in October 1641 and the surrender of Galway in April 1652 (see Chapter 3). It began as a series of regional popular risings which quickly spread from Ulster to engulf most of the country by the end of 1641. Yet without the intervention of the leading Catholic lords in December 1641 and the clergy the following May, these disparate insurrections would have achieved little. However, with the establishment of an alternative form of government, known as the Confederation of Kilkenny, in the spring of 1642—combined with the outbreak of civil war in England shortly afterwards—the Irish rebellion posed a real threat to the security of the Irish Protestants. Initially religion divided the protagonists fighting in Ireland. However, as the 1640s passed, loyalty to the king became the key factor in deciding allegiances. Thus the king's decision to sign a cease-fire with the confederates in September 1643 shattered the anti-Catholic coalition into those who supported Charles I (these Irish royalists were led by Ormond) and those who favoured Parliament (the British settlers in Ulster and Munster and the Scottish Army stationed in Ulster). After 1646 debates over whether the Irish confederates should conclude a peace with the king also undermined Catholic unity and during the summer and autumn of 1648 hard-line Catholics actually declared war on their former compatriots within the Confederation of Kilkenny for allying with Charles I. Ultimately these internal divisions facilitated the Cromwellian conquest of Ireland and frustrated confederate efforts to restore the supremacy of the Catholic Church in Ireland and to secure political authonomy within the context of the Stuart monarchies. They also ensured that that Ireland's contribution to the royalist cause after 1648 remain limited.

THE BRITISH CIVIL WARS

While the Scots had made a significant contribution to the First English Civil War, the Second and Third English Civil Wars enjoyed an important pan-British and Irish dimension. Without securing the support of the Scots the king would have been unable to continue his war-effort (they signed the 'Engagement' on 26 December 1647). Hard-line policies in England which aroused fears that Parliament was intent on reasserting English dominance throughout the Stuart kingdoms not only pushed many covenanters into the royalist camp but alienated key parliamentarians in Ireland. This resulted in the formation of pan-archipelagic coalition involving English royalists, Scottish covenanters, former Irish parliamentarians (led by Lord Inchiquin), Irish royalists (led by Ormond), and a significant number of Irish confederates. Only speedy action by the English army frustrated this anti-parliamentary alliance. However, the execution of Charles I in January 1649 merely served to galvinize Irish and Scottish support for his son,

Charles II in armour: 'The Theatre of English Misery'

A satirical engraving printed in Amsterdam in 1651 shows Charles II—'King of England, Scotland and Ireland'—ready to slay a gruesome, seven-headed dragon (the 'scum of the House of Commons'). A kneeling figure, representing Ireland, fastens Charles's armour while another, representing Scotland, presents him with a pistol. 'Drunk with the blood of the martyrs', the monster claws the heads of Strafford and Laud (having just discarded that of Charles I) and tramples on a document which symbolizes the House of Lords. According to the accompanying caption God showed his wrath at the execution of the king on 30 January 1649 (in the background) by setting off flashes of lightning and turning the sun purple and blue.

who was crowned king of 'Great Britain, France and Ireland' on 1 January 1651. Ultimately the defeat of the combined forces of the Irish royalists and the disbanded confederates at the hands of the English parliamentarians after August 1649, prevented them from fighting alongside their Scottish and English allies in the Third English Civil War. Cromwell's resounding victory at Worcester on 3 September 1651, not only gave him control over England but also facilitated the reassertion of English power over Ireland and Scotland. Though the embers of revolt in Ireland and Scotland smouldered for another four years, the Wars of the Three Kingdoms were finally over.

2

THE CIVIL WARS IN SCOTLAND

EDWARD FURGOL

The covenanters quickly mastered the elements of the Military Revolution and created a successful war machine. However, internal conflicts and political divisions, combined with external interference from a capable foreign foe, ensured that none of their efforts lasted beyond 1651. Indeed not until the revival of the Presbyterians after 1688 would Scotland again possess significant military prowess, and even then only as an ally of England. Thus in many respects the story of the covenanters' activities in warfare seems an anomaly in the country's military history, albeit a vital one for the Wars of the Three Kingdoms.

Given that the last Scottish war had ended over sixty years previously, how prepared for conflict were the covenanters in 1638? The inadequate state of Scotland's fortifications is discussed below in Chapter 6. Her populace was equally unprepared for war (see Chapter 1). After the Union of the Crowns, the traditional enemy became a friendly neighbour, thus diminishing the requirement of constant training for imminent warfare. Between 1603 and 1638 the Privy Council authorized few musters, and while Edinburgh held annual musters after 1607 (and some other burghs may have followed suit), the majority of men had little or no military experience. Yet, while the covenanters did not have a large body of disciplined forces at hand, some Scots had seen active service at home—in the western Islands and Highlands, in the northern Isles, and the central and northeastern Highlands—during the early decades of the seventeenth century. However, these campaigns occurred sporadically and involved relatively few Lowlanders. Only the clans possessed reserves of trained manpower, since military education remained an essential part of a Highland man's upbringing. Consequently, the importance of the decision taken by the 8th earl of Argyll, chief of the Campbells, to join the covenanters can be appreciated in military terms for, in addition to his own vast following, he brought with him a formidable array of allies, who included the MacAulays, Lamonts, Malcolms, MacDougalls, Macleans, and Camerons. Nevertheless, these Gaelic-speaking covenanters could have done little to impart their military knowledge (which may have been antiquated and unsuitable for resisting men trained in the Swedish and Dutch methods of warfare) to Lowland Scots-speakers.

This task fell to the Scottish mercenary veterans of the continental wars (see Chapter 1). The covenanting government immediately recalled them from foreign service and these experienced troops arrived home in sufficient numbers to train the covenanters' Lowland forces for the 1639 campaign. Despite this, the military neglect of the previous decades ensured that the covenanting forces remained unprepared for a large-scale action such as Lützen or Rocroi. Fortunately for them, their opponents were in a similar predicament.

The Military Machine

SWEDISH INFLUENCES

How did these veterans hope to levy an army in Scotland? Under the direction of Alexander Leslie the covenanting forces adopted the Swedish model of recruitment. In the early seventeenth century only Sweden possessed a functioning system of national conscription whereby the Vasa kings merged feudal obligation with the ancient duty of general military service. By 1620 one out of every ten eligible males was called up annually for twenty years of service (nobles, clergymen, only sons of widows, miners, arms workers, and dwellers of certain towns received exemptions). To facilitate this level of recruitment the crown split the country into eight military districts. The localities then selected the recruits and paid the taxes necessary to sustain the army. Even though the annual number of recruits varied from as many as 13,500 in 1627 to as few as 6,600 in 1646, by this method Sweden fielded three per cent of her population for war.

RECRUITING

As in Sweden, the Scottish central government established military districts (approximately twenty), nominated colonels, authorized the levying of troops, and established quotas by shire. (However, unlike the Swedish system, the covenanters set rigid quotas, not ones that reflected annual demographic changes.) To ensure co-ordination between national and local bodies, the covenanters created committees of war or committees of the shire, which consisted of men nominated by—and responsible to—the central government. These committees set the numbers of soldiers that each burgh or rural parish would raise to meet the shire quota, determined quarterings, and supervised the collection of 'cess' or taxation. In the burghs the councils functioned as the recruiting agencies; while in the rural parishes, the clergy and church elders listed men eligible for service and selected them with the assistance of local landowners. In town and countryside alike, the clergy publicized the levies and encouraged men to join up. For example, in September 1643 the session clerk of Carnock, Fife, urged the local men 'to go into

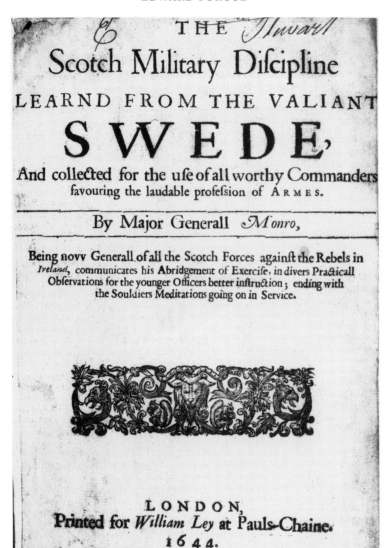

Title-page of 'The Scotch Military Discipline learnd from the valiant Swede'

From 1626 to 1633 Robert Munro (d. ?1680) served with Scottish regiments in the Danish and Swedish armies. His memoirs, reissued with a new title-page in 1644, encouraged prospective officers to serve in defence of Protestantism, offered eulogies to the Swedish king Gustavus Adolphus, and explained the elements of Swedish military practices. With the outbreak of the Bishops' War Munro joined the covenanting armies and in 1642 became the effective commander of the Scottish forces serving in Ulster. Throughout the early 1640s he launched numerous successful raids against the Irish insurgents until the Army of Ulster, led by Owen Roe O'Neill, routed his army at the battle of Benburb (5 June 1646). While Munro's conscientiousness and military skill probably appealed to the covenanter leaders, his pedantic and melancholy nature inhibited his role as an architect of the Military Revolution in Scotland.

England to withstand the violence of the Papists army that was engaged to invade us and take away the gospel from us'.[1]

The support of landowners, who could bring out their kinsmen, tenantry, and servants, proved central to the success of covenanter levies. For this reason the government chose nobles or lairds for regimental colonelcies, while captains of foot-companies or horse troops often came from the same classes. The commissioning of men from these social groups not only strengthened their ties with the covenanting cause but stimulated the recruiting process in areas where they held land or had kinship ties. One such regiment, that of Hugh, Viscount Montgomery, who raised his infantry from Renfrewshire, Cunningham, Paisley, and Glasgow, won acclaim from Robert Baillie, a covenanting chaplain:

> my Lord Montgomery's regiment [was] among the strongest; both the piety and military discipline of his people were commended above all the rest; yea none did doubt but in all our camp [Duns Law] those of the West were the most worthy. They came readily and in the greatest numbers; they made most conscience of the cause and their behaviour; the fear of them made others stand in awe, who else were near whiles to mutinous insolences.[2]

Over the course of the decade, soldiers raised in this manner campaigned as far south as Gloucester, north to the Orkneys, west to the shores of Lough Foyle, and east along the North Sea in England. The sheer number of soldiers mobilized by the covenanters is remarkable: in 1640 the Scots fielded approximately 24,000 men and by 1644 this figure had risen to 30,000. Although it was small in size, it equalled the magnitude of the comparable 1630 Swedish army—a remarkable achievement for a country which had only experienced the Military Revolution in 1639.[3]

In addition the covenanters recruited cannon-fodder outside this three-tiered system, especially in the Highlands and the north-eastern Lowlands (the shires of Aberdeen, Banff, and the Mearns). There, initially in response to royalist threats, heads of families and their cadets raised forces spontaneously which served for short periods, and usually remained within the region in which they originated. Of more questionable military value were the militia units, usually made up of farmers or tradesmen, fielded against Montrose in 1644–45. Lacking military training they generally responded to combat, as the battle of Tippermuir (1 September 1644) highlights, by flight.

COMPOSITION

In composition the covenanting units enjoyed much in common with other early modern armies. Following continental practice, the backbone of all covenanting armies, save that of the Western Association in 1650, was the foot or infantry regiment, comprising ten companies but varying enormously in size from 300 men to over 1,400. The weapons of foot-regiments remained fairly standard (see Chapter 7). The covenanters also followed the continental trend by increasing their firepower. Initially their infantry regiments had twenty per cent more musketeers than the Swedish or Dutch armies, which had one musketeer per pikeman. In 1640 and 1642 evidence from musters and arms importation indicates the foot had three musketeers for every two pikemen. In April 1644, if not before, the Estates allocated new regiments with two muskets for each pike. Only in the midst of a financial crisis and a stringent naval blockade by the Commonwealth in December 1650, did pikemen outnumber musketeers. Foot-regiments raised in 1651 were to have two musketeers for every three pikemen. The reliance of the covenanter foot-regiments upon firepower was tactically sound, except against the Highland charge, where counter-shock, whether by pikemen or cavalry, was the only suitable response.

Horse units in the covenanting armies existed from 1639, but took on greater importance with the raising of the Army of the Solemn League and Covenant in 1643. Their enhanced stature coincided with the arrival of David Leslie, a cavalry officer in the Swedish army who became one of the covenanters' best generals. Previously, horse units fought with the foot or served as independent troops; only rarely did they form regiments. Horse regiments (commanded by colonels) and troops (led by routmasters, ex-Reitermeister), varied greatly in strength. The first standard horse regiments of 1643 should have contained eight troops of seventy-five men each or 600 men, but many lacked one or two troops. The covenanters often armed a portion of men with lances to compensate for the poor quality of their horses. In 1648 the Estates dropped the cavalry regiment's strength to 180 men. Two years later they increased the numbers to 450 men (in six troops of seventy-five men), but authorized two regiments to levy 685 men in nine troops and one to raise 375 in five troops. In 1643 Leslie introduced a new type of horse regiment—dragoons who travelled to the battlefield by horse but fought on foot with carbines or muskets. Usually, a covenanter army contained only one or two dragoon regiments. The precise tactical arrangements (depth of ranks and whether troops formed individually or in squadrons) of the cavalry remains unknown; yet they appear to have charged in the Swedish manner with swords and pistols.

The last type of regular unit in the armies was the artillery. Once again the covenanters followed the Swedish example and regular officers and gunners (not civilian contractors, as occurred in some armies) transported and manned the cannon. Each regiment probably deployed lighter field guns together with larger cannon, generally mounted in fortifications or siegeworks. While the covenanting armies fielded a respectable number (twenty-two to sixty pieces) of artillery, the Scottish royalist forces possessed few, if any, cannon.

In addition to these regular Swedish-style units, the covenanters fielded clan forces and family retinues which represented continuity with Scotland's medieval military tradition. The records rarely mention the numbers serving under a clan leader, noble, or laird. However, when units boasted several hundred men one may assume the existence of some sort of company organization. In clan regiments, for instance, the chief and his close relatives served as the staff officers and the cadets acted as captains of the men from their districts. Companies varied in size in both clan and other informal units; the numbers reflected the men levied from a specific area or by an individual instead of meeting a standard goal. With the exception of the Gordons, Highland units consisted of infantry. A well-armed clansman carried a musket, sword, targe, dirk, and skean-dhu. Some might have only had polearms—a pike, Lochaber axe, or halberd—and others, probably officers, carried pistols and swords. The retinues fielded from the north-east Lowlands probably contained some cavalry. Perhaps the mounted leaders had some armour, a sword, and pistols. The better-armed infantry would have had muskets or pikes, but certainly others took the field with only sharpened agricultural implements. The non-regular units of both covenanters and royalists varied from men who fought to the last gasp to those who ran at the first sign of serious action; from war-hardened Highlanders to semi-drilled Lowland militia.

MORALE AND DISCIPLINE

Whatever their origin, Alexander Leslie's efforts to foster and maintain military and religious discipline among his forces provided cohesion and fostered an *esprit de corps*. Again following Swedish practice Leslie issued his army with printed copies of *The Articles and Ordinances of War* (which first appeared in 1639 and was reprinted regularly throughout the 1640s). These regulations specified the correct behaviour for soldiers in their relations with their comrades, the enemy, and civilians, including the punishments for offences. A unit was not considered a part of the army (and thus eligible for pay), until it had heard the *Articles* read and sworn the required oath. Thereby every soldier promised:

to be true and faithful in my service to the Kingdom of Scotland, according to the heads sworn by me in the Covenant: To honour and obey my Lord General, and all my Superior Officers and Commanders, and by all means to hinder their dishonour and hurt; To observe carefully all the Articles of War and camp discipline; never to leave the defence of this cause, nor flee from my colours so long as I can follow them: To be ready to watching and warding and working so far as I have strength: To endure and suffer all distresses, and to fight manfully to the uttermost, as I shall answer to GOD, and as GOD shall help me.[4]

To bolster the officers' control of their men and to ensure obedience to his code, Leslie authorized the establishment of an ecclesiastical system for the army. While the Swedes provided ministers for the regiments, presided over by a bishop, the covenanters created something new in an army, but traditional for Scottish society. They ordered that each regiment should have not only a chaplain (usually a beneficed minister from the same region as the men, as opposed to a man newly ordained for the unit), but also a Kirk session of elders selected from the officers. The army as a whole formed a presbytery (to assist the sessions with maintaining discipline, to ensure orthodoxy, and to deal with the more serious cases of immorality), to which each regiment contributed a minister and an elder.

General Leslie.

Alexander Leslie, first earl of Leven (c.1580–1661)

In 1605 this very model of an early modern general began a military career that spanned six decades. After serving in the Dutch army for three years, he joined the Swedish forces where he imbibed the military innovations which he later introduced into Scotland. Leslie gained fame as the defender of Stralsund against Wallenstein in 1628 and the Swedes later elevated him to the rank of field marshal. In October 1638 Leslie, together with 'many other' Scottish officers, retired home to fight in the Bishops' Wars. With the exception of the Engager Army, Leslie held at least titular command of the national covenanter forces, which were closely modelled on the Swedish example. Leslie played a key role in the campaigns of 1639, 1640, and 1644 and returned from active military service upon the return of the Army of the Solemn League and Covenant from England in 1647.

Consequently, the covenanter units drew cohesion from several sources: adherence to the covenant, a common geographical origin, similar standards of behaviour, and the same system of ecclesiastical discipline as existed in civilian society.

Wars in the Three Kingdoms, 1641–1644

THE ARMY IN ULSTER, 1641–1642

Over the winter of 1641 to 1642 the covenanters organized for military action in Ulster (see Chapter 1). Alexander Leslie, now earl of Leven, received the title of lord general; Major-General Sir Robert Munro, another veteran of the Thirty Years War, became the army's lieutenant-general. General of Artillery Alexander ('Sandy') Hamilton had his ordnance responsibilities extended to Ulster. In addition to the three regiments already in existence, the Scots authorized the raising of seven additional infantry regiments (including one under the command of Argyll). In March Munro embarked the three standing regiments at Ayr, but contrary winds detained them at Aran for three weeks. They reached Carrickfergus on 3 April. Throughout the year reinforcements arrived, bringing the army to a maximum strength of 11,371 officers and men.

Munro faced the challenges of providing the settlers with security and defeating the Irish insurgents. His first campaign, south-westward through Down to Newry (27 April–12 May 1642), began the pacification process and secured a southern anchor for the Scots. During the occupation of Newry his men drove most of the Irish from the town, and ordered the massacre of over eighty others. In the north-east, the Irish insurgents, largely tenants and kinsmen of the Catholic earl of Antrim, threatened the well-being of British Protestants who had settled along the coastal plains of Counties Antrim and Down. However, the massacre, by Argyll's foot, of the inhabitants of Rathlin Island off the Antrim coast and Munro's second expedition in May and June cleared this region of insurgents. Irish control of the stronghold of Charlemont in mid-Armagh, which served as a refuge for the forces of the confederate commander Owen Roe O'Neill, constantly vexed the Ulster Army and throughout the summer and autumn Munro attempted to capture it in order to rid Counties Armagh and Tyrone of the enemy and the cattle herders, or 'creaghts', who supplied them. The details of one such foray, made in the early summer of 1642 by a force under the command of Sir John Clotworthy into County Tyrone, was immediately published in London. On 25 June, as Clotworthy's force approached Mountjoy, the insurgents, after burning the castle and nearby houses, fled into the woods and 'made up some fortification about them'. After 'raising some works for their defence against the enemy', the British troops attempted to draw their opponents, who outnumbered them, from their refuge into open battle. When this failed they chased them from the woods to the nearby town of Moneymore, capturing

100 of their cattle in the process and killing 'many of their best men'. The enemy, however, remained undefeated and the two sides skirmished until 7 July when Clotworthy and his men retreated to their garrison in Antrim on the grounds that the insurgents had received fresh supplies of men and arms while they had 'a great and sore sickness amongst us which is much occasionen [*sic*] through want of good diet'.[5]

Thus by the end of 1642 Scottish operations in Ireland had assumed a rather repetitive character. Typically units of the Scottish Ulster Army, combined with infantry regiments and horse troops of the British settlers, would set forth on sweeps into the Irish-controlled countryside. O'Neill's forces would sometimes skirmish, but would more often melt away in the face of overwhelming force. The Scots massacred any 'creaghts', seized their charges, destroyed dwellings, and either captured or burned supplies of grain. Terror and economic warfare became the keynotes of covenanter-British operations in Ulster and while this strategy failed to defeat the Irish, it ensured the safety of the settlers.

THE ARMY IN ENGLAND

Meanwhile in England, over the course of 1642 and 1643 a growing unease developed among the covenanters' political leaders. Although they reacted with disappointment to the English failure to develop a British governmental structure and to promote a national Presbyterian establishment in the southern kingdom, they basked in the sunlight of security that the king's acceptance of the Scottish revolution provided. The bitter confrontation between Charles and his English subjects certainly benefited the covenanters by constraining the monarch from laying new plans for revenge against the Scots. However, when the English controversies burst the bonds of political discourse into the fields of conflict, the covenanters had cause for anxiety. A royal victory in England would provide Charles with what he had lacked during the Bishops' Wars—trained troops and a secure source of revenue. Consequently, the military stalemate which developed in England in 1642 suppressed the covenanters' fears for their own safety. Equally the royalist military successes of mid-1643, combined with rumours of aid for the king from Ireland, terrified the Scots quite as much as they did the parliamentarians. The arrival of the latter's commissioners on 7 August in Edinburgh found a highly receptive audience. Within ten days the covenanters, drawing on personnel from the General Assembly and the Convention of Estates, agreed to an alliance with the parliamentarians: the Solemn League and Covenant.

THE SOLEMN LEAGUE AND COVENANT

The document targeted the king and his supporters as the disturbers of international amity, and bound the covenanters and parliamentarians to oppose them as a divinely sanctioned obligation. In their continual efforts to achieve security within Great Britain the covenanters insisted upon the establishment of a Presbyterianism in England as a clause of the treaty; the parliamentarians had merely wanted a civil league against the royalists. Military preparations accompanied the treaty negotiations: on 28 July the convention ordered the raising of the 'Levied Regiment' or 'College of Justice Foot' and three troops of horse. Three weeks later the convention placed all fencible (able-bodied) men on forty-eight-hour stand-by and called upon them to defend 'the true protestant religion the liberties of the kingdom his majesty's honour and the peace and safety of this their native country'.[6] From 22 to 26 August the government nominated commanders for the new army and selected Leven to serve as lord general. On 16 September the troops authorized in July met on Leith Links. About four days later they occupied the open town of Berwick. As the summer ended it appeared that a major upheaval would occur in the military situation in England.

The panic which accelerated the Edinburgh negotiations and preparations subsided just as the treaty reached London. Quite literally the three-pronged royalist drive on the capital halted. Consequently, the parliamentarians methodically dealt with the treaty, modifying one celebrated clause, regarding the new Church government for England, before ratifying it in September. A military settlement followed on 29 November, which authorized the Scots to raise an army at Parliament's expense. Only in mid-December, however, did the levies for the new force (the Army of the Solemn League and Covenant) enter the south-eastern Lowlands, rendezvousing at Harlaw, Berwickshire, on 1 January 1644. Within two weeks Leven had massed 18,000 foot, 3,000 horse (including 400 dragoons), eighteen heavy and medium guns, forty-two three-pounders, and eighty-eight cases of frames at Berwick. The covenanters entered England full of hope in their military ability; the unfolding of events would show they were overly sanguine.

CAMPAIGNS IN ENGLAND, 1644

The covenanter campaigns in the three kingdoms in 1644 marked a change from their previous initiatives. The year saw the Scots enter into in an ever-accelerating vortex of death and destruction, particularly at home. The successes of 1639–43 against ill-led, poorly trained forces had inflated the reputation of the covenanters. Consequently, many expected Leven's army to reduce rapidly the English royalist presence in northern England. Equally, the covenanters and their parliamentarian allies doubted the Scots royalists would offer a serious threat to the covenanting regime. That events followed an entirely different pattern diminished the weight of the covenanters' councils in the political and ecclesiastical decision-making in London. Furthermore the brilliant successes of royalist forces in Scotland from August 1644 severely tested the covenanters' very ability to survive. However, when Leven stood poised to cross the Tweed in January, no one suspected the possibly malevolent repercussions of involvement in England's civil war.

In some respects Leven's 1644 march into Northumberland resembled that of 1640. His men crossed the border at Berwick on 19 January. Initially the royalists responded with little opposition until the covenanters reached the Tyne Valley. However, William Cavendish, earl of Newcastle, possessed a cool head and devoted, veteran troops, which enabled him to prevent Leven from repeating his successes during the Second Bishops' War. He had prepared Newcastle to withstand a siege, and had mustered a field army (by stripping southern Yorkshire of most of the royalist forces) to oppose the Scots. At Corbridge on 19 February the royalist horse had the better of an encounter with their opposite numbers. Leaving six foot regiments north of the Tyne to watch the town of Newcastle, Leven led fifteen infantry and six cavalry regiments across the river on the 28th. A week later, on 7–8 March, the two armies skirmished outside Sunderland at Boldon Hills. Newcastle temporarily withdrew, allowing the Scots to undertake operations against South Shields Fort at the mouth of the Tyne. An assault on the 15th failed, but after fasting on the 19th Leven's men successfully stormed the fortification on the 20th. The Scots headed back to Sunderland, where they again had an inconclusive encounter with Newcastle's army at Hilton on 24–5 March. The covenanters' failure to take Newcastle or defeat the royalist army dismayed their supporters: however, the Scottish presence resulted in a significant shift in the strategic picture of northern England.

Newcastle's decision to oppose Leven in the field had greatly reduced the size of the royalist force in the East Riding, creating an opportunity for the parliamentarian troops under Ferdinando Lord Fairfax and his son Sir Thomas. On 11 April they stormed the royalist town of Selby, recovering the region they had lost in the 1643 campaign. A significant danger now existed to York, the other major northern town under Newcastle's control. (Simultaneously Leven threatened Durham—a centre of Laudian Church polity as well as a strategic block on the main north–south route.) Newcastle hurried to reinforce York, leaving the allies to manœuvre freely. On 20 April the covenanters rendezvoused at Tadcaster with Fairfax's men. Two days later the allies besieged York, threatening to deprive the king not only of a prestigious town, but also of an entire army.

MONTROSE AND THE SCOTTISH ROYALISTS

Meanwhile royalists struck the covenanters in the north-east and the western borders. On 19 March Sir John Gordon of Haddo raided Aberdeen and seized some of the burgh's leading covenanters. Later in the month Huntly mustered 1,200 men at Aboyne, then captured Aberdeen. Between Deeside and Banff the royalists came out *en masse*, forcing the covenanters to remain in their tower houses. On 21 April Huntly took the town of Montrose. Further south the earl of Montrose, now a staunch royalist, and Viscount Aboyne, captured Dumfries. The covenanters in the borders quickly reacted, mustering a force at Selkirk. In the face of an advance by the growing covenanter force, Montrose abandoned the

James Graham, first marquis and fifth earl of Montrose (1612–50)

Montrose was a man full of contradictions who enjoyed a complex career. He remained a Presbyterian while relying on Episcopalians and Catholics to man his armies; a proud noble who valued the royal prerogative; and a lover of peaceful pursuits who is remembered as a warrior. Spurned by Charles I in 1636, Montrose found himself socially and theologically inclined towards the anti-prayer-book movement. However the covenanters' rejection of royal authority and the elevation of Argyll to pre-eminence in their councils led him to embrace the king's cause in the summer of 1640. On the battlefield he showed great versatility, tactical genius, and bravery, but frequently underestimated the importance of reconnaissance. Following his remarkable campaigns of 1644–5, Montrose became a political embarrassment to the crown until the future Charles II used him as a bargaining chip in the 1650 negotiations with the Kirk party. Executed in 1650 for a loyalty that neither royal master deserved, the marquis symbolized the triumph of the Scottish royalists at the Restoration when they reburied him in the high kirk of St Giles, Edinburgh.

burgh on 19 April. His former allies pursued him to the border, before returning to Teviotdale. Years later, Major James Turner, an officer in Sinclair's Foot, claimed that the officers of that and Lothian's Foot had plotted to join forces with Montrose, had he moved north from Dumfries. Perhaps this was true, but equally Turner may have wished to find a means of excusing his covenanter past.

In any case Montrose's first attempt against the covenanters had failed utterly, leaving the Gordons alone to bear the brunt of the covenanters' fury at the rising. Argyll received command of an army, which he mustered in central and eastern Scotland. On 26 April his 4,700 infantry reached the Earl Marischal's home, Dunnottar Castle, where retinues of north-eastern covenanters joined them. With Argyll's army one day's march from Aberdeen, Huntly disbanded. On 2 May the covenanters entered the burgh, then marched against royalist castles in the region. On the 14th Argyll set out for Elgin, then returned through Strathbogie to Aberdeen, where he arrived ten days later, marking his route with the destruction of royalist property. In the face of overwhelming covenanter forces Huntly fled to Strathnaver, where he sheltered with the royalist Lord Reay for the next two years. Having garrisoned castles in Deeside, Argyll led his men south on 1 July. Seemingly the royalist threat to Scotland had ended.

THE ARMY IN ULSTER, 1644

Despite the withdrawal of three regiments to fight in England, the situation in Ulster had also taken a positive turn for the Scots. In the spring the British units in the province had sworn the Solemn League and Covenant, which effectively placed them under Scottish control. Munro then planned a major raid into the northern territory of the confederate Irish. The first units gathered at Lisnagarvey, near Lisburn in County Antrim, on 27 June. Four days later he had 12,000 foot and 1,000 horse poised to strike south from Armagh. Between 2 and 11 July Munro's force marched through Counties Monaghan, Cavan, Meath, and Louth destroying Irish supplies and encountering no serious opposition. His force disbanded on the 15th, but ten days later Munro prepared another expedition. Gathering troops from western and eastern Ulster, he marched into Armagh to encounter the earl of Castlehaven's confederate Army of Ulster. On 16 August Munro's men fortified a camp in the county, where they remained for a month. Castlehaven's men skirmished with the Protestant force, but the earl avoided a major confrontation. After the Irish retreated southward in mid-September, Munro again raided County Cavan. He stayed in south-western Armagh until 28 September, going into winter quarters on 7 October. Despite the loss of three regiments and the ability of the Irish to concentrate their forces against Ulster due to the cease-fire concluded between the king and the confederates in September 1643, Munro had kept his enemy at bay during the campaigning season.

COVENANTER OFFENSIVE IN NORTHERN ENGLAND

More dramatic events transpired in northern England, where the royalists' stout efforts eventually proved futile. In the wake of Leven's lack of progress and Montrose's seizure of Dumfries, the covenanters created a new army under Lieutenant-General James, earl of Callander. In May the earl's men raided royalist Cumberland. However, Montrose with a mixed Anglo-Scottish royalist force won the laurels north of the Tyne. His campaign resulted in the recapture of Morpeth and Stockton Castles, South Shields Fort, Stockton, and Hartlepool. News of the royalist successes stung Callander into action. On 25 June his army entered England, retook the lost strongholds, then commenced the siege of Newcastle on 28 July. The contentions in the north-east paled before those in Yorkshire.

MARSTON MOOR (2 JULY 1644)

Ensconced in York, the earl of Newcastle withstood the armies of the covenanters, the Yorkshire parliamentarians, and the Eastern Association until Prince Rupert's arrival changed the strategic balance. The allies lifted the siege to engage the new royalist force, but the prince outmanœuvred them and reached York by a different route. Worried about a royalist advance southward the Scottish and parliamentarian armies withdrew toward Tadcaster on 2 July. Rupert, desperate to smash the enemy in a pitched battle, slowly mustered on the north side of Marston Moor (see map on p. 139). In response, Leven marshalled his combined forces. Rupert lost his initial advantage due to difficulties in marching Newcastle's army on to the moor. In the wake of a thunderstorm the allies charged forward. Action in the centre soon reached a stalemate. The royalists swept the right wing of the allied cavalry from the field. With the exception of three foot-regiments of the infantry's right centre, the covenanter foot broke and Leven fled. Lieutenant-General William Baillie and Major-General James Lumsden rallied the broken men, sending them to reinforce the three hard-pressed regiments. With the cavalry gone from the right, these units anchored the allied line. Meanwhile, Lieutenant-General David Leslie and three covenanter cavalry regiments ably seconded Cromwell's right wing of horse. At a critical moment in the action Leslie even replaced a wounded Cromwell. The Scots played a crucial role in the last phase of the battle when Colonel Hugh Fraser's Dragoons blasted a gap in the ranks of Newcastle's white-coated infantry immured in White Sike Close. The victory deprived Charles of two field armies; two weeks later York surrendered, reducing the royalist presence in the north to several isolated strongholds (also see Chapter 4).

Sieges occupied the attention of Leven's army for the remainder of the year. After a detour to southern Yorkshire his men joined forces with Callendar's army outside Newcastle on 15 August. Springing mines, the covenanters successfully assaulted the town on 19 October. Eight days later they commanded the castle, as well as the fortifications controlling access to the Tyne. Once again London could receive its coal supply unimpeded by royalist levies. To the west the royalist hold over Carlisle presented a constant threat to the south-western Lowlands. Using local parliamentarian forces and regiments from the Army of the Solemn League and Covenant Lieutenant-General Leslie besieged the city in December; it fell in June 1645. Although the covenanter forces failed to repeat the speedy victory of the 1640 campaign, they performed an important role in weakening royalist military might and swung the war decidedly in favour of Parliament.

Civil War in Scotland, 1644–1647

THE ANTI-COVENANTER ALLIANCE

From August 1644 the situation in Scotland turned topsy-turvy with the union of several anti-covenanter forces. In the spring the Campbells had successfully dealt with incursions by Alasdair MacColla MacDonald, an ally of Antrim and the son of a Highland adventurer. He returned in July accompanied by 2,000–3,000 troops who had been armed and supplied by the Irish confederates. The rank and file soldiers were almost exclusively native Irishmen from Ulster, many of them dependants of Antrim (see picture on p. 18); while their officers, many of whom had served in the Spanish Army of Flanders or in Ireland itself, also largely originated in Counties Antrim or Londonderry. An additional 800 Highlanders also followed MacColla. Though little is known of how these men were trained, their subsequent performance on the battlefield suggests that they were well disciplined. For example, at the battle of Tippermuir (1 September 1644), they held their ground following a charge by the cavalry and then annihilated their attackers; while at Auldearn (9 May 1645) they regrouped repeatedly after unsuccessful charges by the covenanters.

After landing in Ardnamurchan early in August, where they captured and garrisoned Argyll's new stronghold of Mingary Castle, MacColla's troops headed for Inverlochy, 'burning, killing, pillaging and spoiling all the way'. The Captain of Clan Ranald and other leading royalists quickly joined them and late in August they finally met up with Montrose at Blair Atholl. The combined forces of Montrose's Highland warriors and MacColla's Irish seasoned troops presented the covenanters with a formidable enemy. Furthermore both men possessed a tactical genius that few covenanting generals could match. The first army to fall victim to them consisted largely of Fife and Perthshire militia. On 1 September at Tippermuir an outnumbered Montrose and MacColla defeated David Wemyss, Lord Elcho, using the relatively new tactic of the Highland charge. The charge, which probably originated with the Irish confederate forces in Ulster, consisted of two phases: first the troops, armed with muskets, advanced to within

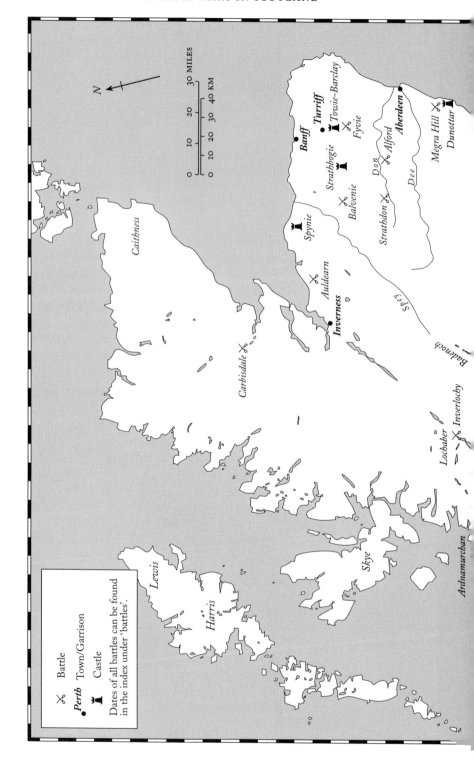

Civil wars in Scotland

Dundee
St Andrews
Perth
Tippermuir
Dunblane
Berwick
Coldstream
Dunbar
Dunglass
Duns
Kelso
Philiphaugh
Tweed
Burntisland
Leith
Edinburgh
Musselburgh
Inverkeithing
Stirling
Forth
Kilsyth
Glasgow
Hamilton
Dumbarton
Mauchline
Carlisle
Dumfries
Annan Moor
Caerlaverock
Threave
Greenock
Irvine
Ayr
Dunoon
Rhunahaorine
Dunaverty
Inveraray
Lagganmore
Craignish
Skipness
Jura
Mull
Islay
Loch Gorm
Dunyveg

Field of Battle

Dunbar
Broxmouth House
Pass over road
LAMBERT
CROMWELL
PRIDE
MONCK
LESLIE
Doon Hill
Spott Burn

0   1 MILE
0   1   2 KM

a hundred yards and fired a single volley; they then dropped their muskets and charged their opponents with broadswords. Following Tippermuir, the army occupied and pillaged Perth for two days. They pushed north, and on 13 September, outside Aberdeen, Montrose and MacColla with 1,500 men repeated their initial success against a covenanter army of 2,700 regulars, burgh militia, and retinues. With its defenders dispersed (800 troops allegedly lost their lives), the burgh fell and endured three days of sacking.

The Committee of Estates responded to the first defeat by making Argyll commander of a new army. The committee, underestimating the power of the new royalist war machine, withdrew troops from Leven's army. However, they detached insufficient numbers and far too few cavalry to alter the military balance in Scotland. For eight weeks Montrose's men outmarched Argyll's who contented themselves with ravaging and burning royalist lands. Late in October Argyll brought his adversary to bay at Fyvie Castle, but failed to press his advantage. Having accomplished nothing against the royalist army, Argyll none the less laid down his commission in mid-November. However, his enemies refused to acknowledge the difficulties of winter campaigning. Even the earl of Clarendon, never one to praise Irish Catholics needlessly, commented upon their stamina, courage, endurance, and the fact that 'neither the ill fare nor the ill lodging in the Highlands gave them any discouragement'.[7] Desperate to strike at his hereditary enemies the Campbells, MacColla persuaded Montrose to undertake a daring invasion of Argyll. In early December sympathetic guides led them through the passes into Campbell country. For several weeks they plundered and burned, killing 900 Campbells of military age in the process. Fearing a counter-attack, Montrose headed north toward the Great Glen leaving mourning, smoke, and destruction in his wake.

The new year brought further trials to the covenanter armies, especially at home where Montrose and MacColla threatened the regime's very existence and forced Munro to dispatch 1,400 foot back to Scotland to oppose Montrose. Despite this Munro continued his onslaught against the confederates and their supply lines, twice leading his men into southern Down, and making a unique foray into County Fermanagh. At harvest time Munro struck deeply into confederate territory with an expedition to County Longford. While the Ulster Army remained a potential source of troops for operations in Britain, perhaps its location across the North Channel and the covenanters' desire to maintain a presence in Ireland helped isolate it from the maelstrom to the east.

ROYALIST VICTORIES IN SCOTLAND

Continued royalist depredations in Argyll required an immediate covenanter response. The marquis of Argyll formed an army of his clansmen and some raw Lowland regulars, while George, 2nd earl of Seaforth gathered a force at Inverness to prevent Montrose's escape from the Great Glen. Argyll moved north to

Inverlochy with Montrose in retreat up the glen. However, the royalist general decided that his men's animosity to the Campbells would provide him with a battlefield advantage, so he led his force back down the glen in the teeth of a driving snowstorm. On 2 February 1645 Montrose and MacColla added to their tally of victories when another Highland charge swept the stationary covenanters from the field at the battle of Inverlochy. One Gaelic poet lauded this 'victory for Clan Donald' over the 'wry mouthed Campbell's' in the following terms:

> That was no faulted manœuvre
> Alasdair MacColla made to Scotland
> burning, killing, wreaking destruction,
> broken by him the cock of Strathbogie [Argyll].[8]

The destruction of Argyll's army, together with the military reputation of Clan Campbell, led Seaforth to disband his men; Montrose now held sway in the north-east. His army received an important reinforcement when Lord Gordon with a force of his clan's cavalry joined the royalists. In March Lieutenant-General William Baillie, the main covenanter commander in Scotland, blocked Montrose from moving south from Perthshire. Hoping to satisfy his men's demand for plunder, the marquis led them in storming Dundee on 4 April. News of the attack reached Baillie in Perth, who quickly set out to catch the royalists in disarray as they sacked the burgh. Baillie's men entered the town on the tail of Montrose's. The next day, with the royalists unready for action, the covenanter cavalry commander Major-General John Urry failed to press his pursuit to a decisive result. Receiving additional troops Urry marched north to Inverness, ravaging royalist territory *en route*. Gathering together a motley collection of 4,000 regulars, Moray militia, and Highlanders, Urry attempted a surprise attack on Montrose's camp at Auldearn, near Nairn, on 9 May. Musket-firing by the covenanters to clear potentially damp powder alerted the royalists who, under MacColla, offered a desperate resistance to superior forces, allowing Montrose to organize the army for a counter-attack in which the Gordon horse proved vital. Simultaneously the right wing of covenanter horse collided with their neighbouring foot which caused great disorder to the army's front line. At the end of the day Montrose's 1,700 men held the field upon which half the covenanter army lay dead. Throughout May and June Baillie and Montrose sparred like wary boxers. On 2 July 2,000 covenanters again attacked Montrose's 1,500 men at Alford. However, the failure of Balcarres's horse to take out the Gordon horse stemmed the covenanter advance and permitted Montrose to launch a charge that cleared the field. Montrose's victories —'those wonderful acts', as Clarendon dubbed them—eliminated serious opposition to the royalists north of the Tay.[9]

COVENANTER IMPOTENCE IN ENGLAND

Meanwhile news of the royalist triumphs in Scotland hampered Leven's operations in England. He eventually took the field in May, but disobeyed orders from the Committee of Both Kingdoms to head south of the Humber. Instead he hung back in Cumbria and Yorkshire manœuvring to prevent the king from sending Montrose reinforcements, an action that might have altered the entire strategic balance in Britain. As Lieutenant-General David Leslie's siege of Carlisle dragged on until 25 June, the royalists held an important staging point for such an initiative for the whole of the spring. Gradually Leven drew south as the king's army headed north. The resounding parliamentarian victory at Naseby persuaded Leven to obey the committee's orders to proceed against Hereford, which he commenced besieging on 30 July. Thirteen days later Lieutenant-General Leslie led 4,500–5,000 horse from Leven's army to oppose English royalist forces. The departure of his cavalry deprived Leven of his main source of intelligence and prevented him from offering battle to the king's relief expedition. Consequently, he lifted the siege of Hereford on 27 August and returned to Yorkshire without playing a significant part in the summer campaign.

Events in Scotland had reached cataclysmic proportions for the covenanters. Montrose managed to march into the central Lowlands with a greatly reinforced army of 5,000 men. William Baillie desperately needed men, but he could only hope for Lowland militia not seasoned troops. Having gathered 7,000 men (nearly half of whom were raw Fife militia), Baillie found his plans overruled. On 15 August at the battle of Kilsyth Montrose's men stalled the covenanter advance. His inevitable counter-attack panicked the militia who fled the field instead of assisting the hard-pressed front-line troops. In the following slaughter 3,000 covenanters died and Montrose won control of Scotland. Although he quickly gained submissions from the burghs, received promises of aid from royalists, and had MacColla disperse the south-western covenanter levies, his position lacked stability. Seizing the moment, MacColla marched off to Argyll with most of the Irish troops, who drove the Campbells into their castles and restored MacDonald hegemony in the western Highlands and Islands. Simultaneously Huntly recalled the Gordons under his son James, Viscount Aboyne. With news of the king's desperate situation after Naseby ringing in his ears, Montrose headed to the eastern borders to recruit an army for service in England. By 13 September he had 2,000 men and many promises of more with which to redress the balance across the border.

DEFEAT OF MONTROSE

Montrose's continued successes proved a catalyst to David Leslie. Hearing of Kilsyth and its aftermath Leslie led his cavalry force northwards, reaching Berwick on 6 September. A week later outside Selkirk Leslie's horsemen struck the Philiphaugh camp of a typically unprepared Montrose. The covenanters won a total victory, driving Montrose into flight to the Highlands, killing most of his army on the battlefield, and massacring the remaining Irish. The covenanters attributed their victory to divine intervention: 'God be praised, we have lost no

Noblemen, or chief Officer. [We tell you this] so you may join with them and us in giving God the praise, who hath wrought all this and all our works for us.'[10] Although Montrose raised a new force, he wasted it in a siege of Inverness. Similarly the Gordons took the field again, but they failed to mount a serious threat to the covenanters. Having left Major-General John Middleton to contain the royalists, Leslie and most of his horse had returned to England by December. The royalist *annus mirabilis* in Scotland ended with disappointment; ultimately Montrose's impressive victories neither toppled the covenanter state nor changed the strategic balance in Britain.

The last major covenanter operations of 1645 occurred against the English royalists. In late October Lord Digby and Sir Marmaduke Langdale invaded Scotland to assist Montrose with the remnant of the Northern horse. Heading north from the covenanter garrison at Carlisle Colonel Sir John Brown and his eight-troop-strong horse regiment stumbled across them on Annan Moor, Dumfriesshire. In the ensuring action the Northern horse was routed and its officers fled to the Isle of Man. In mid-November Leven led his army to join the parliamentarian siege of Newark and the Scots occupied the eastern side of the siegeworks until the town's fall. In comparison with the spectacular parliamentarian victories of 1645, the covenanters had little to show for the campaign; yet one should not disregard the grave threat they dealt with at home.

CHARLES I'S SURRENDER TO THE COVENANTERS

In 1646 the covenanters had decidedly mixed military fortunes in the three kingdoms. In England the siege of Newark (see picture on p. 213) ended after Charles I surprisingly entered the Scots camp on 5 May. Afterwards Leven's army decamped to the north-east, where protracted and futile negotiations occurred between the king and his Scottish and English subjects. Having failed to convert Charles to Presbyterianism, the Army of the Solemn League and Covenant, following a generous pay settlement, handed the king over to Parliament and evacuated England in early February 1647. Meanwhile in Ulster the covenanters suffered a great defeat when Major-General Munro encountered Owen Roe O'Neill's army at Benburb, Armagh, on 5 June. An exhausted Scottish-British force of 5,400 foot and 700–800 horse were deployed on a cramped piece of ground, preventing the second-line regiments from supporting those in front. Hemmed in, they fell victim to the attack by a similarly sized Irish army. Between 2,000 and 3,000 men lost their lives and Munro felt humiliated. He later wrote, 'The Lord of Hosts had a controversy with us to rub shame on our faces, as on other armies, till once we shall be humbled, for a greater confidence did I never see in any army that was amongst us, and we behoved to taste of bitterness as well as others of both nations; but praised be God, being now humbled before God, we increase in courage and resolution'.[11] For the time being, however, Ulster lay open to the Irish confederate forces. Yet O'Neill failed to exploit the victory, turning Benburb into a tactical embarrassment for the covenanters, instead of a strategic disaster (see Chapter 3).

COVENANTER OFFENSIVE AGAINST THE SCOTTISH ROYALISTS

In Scotland the covenanters balanced success and failure. MacColla and his allies continued to hold sway over the Campbells, who had suffered a rout at the battle of Callander (13 February) during a raid on royalist lands in Perthshire. Campbell fortunes revived in June when they captured the strongholds of the Lamonts on the Cowal peninsula and massacred over 130 prisoners at Dunoon in retaliation for the Lamonts' shift of allegiance to MacColla after Inverlochy. In the north-east royalist fortunes fluctuated. Montrose lifted the siege of Inverness at the approach of Major-General John Middleton's army in April. Shortly afterwards his allies, the Mackenzies, submitted to Middleton. Huntly briefly took the field in May–June, winning another royalist victory at Aberdeen before disbanding. However, following the king's order to cease hostilities, Montrose broke up his army on 30 July, then sailed for Norway on 3 September. The other leading Scottish royalists refused to disperse: MacColla entrenched himself in the Western Isles and the irrepressible Huntly raised the Gordons, seizing the burgh of Banff where he remained unchallenged throughout the winter. The covenanters feared that these forces would serve as a rallying-point for the renewal of the king's war-effort and Robert Baillie noted in June that if 'the king escape to them, it will be a woeful case'.[12] During the late summer and early autumn of 1646 Antrim, who joined MacColla in Kintyre, tried to raise an army of over 20,000 men from among the anti-Campbell clans which would march on Newcastle and release the king. The royalists in Scotland, encouraged by the court in exile, were no longer an embarrassment but rather a serious threat to any chance of securing a British peace.

In an attempt to crush these malignants once and for all the Estates authorized the levy of the Scottish New Model Army. In February 1647 Leven took command of this force of 6,000 foot (seven regiments) and 1,200 horse (fifteen horse troops and two dragoon companies). Although Leven held the title of general of the army, he never led it in a campaign. Age had debilitated the earl and the field command devolved upon Lieutenant-General David Leslie and Major-General John Middleton. In March the two generals attacked the north-eastern royalists, capturing garrisons and occupying Gordon territory. Leaving Middleton to overawe the royalists, Leslie campaigned against MacColla and his men in Argyll and the Isles in May. In a repeat of the victory at Philiphaugh, Leslie's horse drove 1,300 Irish and Highlanders from their position at Rhunanhaorine Point, Kintyre, clearing the way for the main body. The capture of Dunaverty Castle in June ended with the massacre of 300 defenders at the instigation of the covenanter chaplain; MacColla, however, managed to escape to Ireland with the rump of the force he had brought over in 1644 and a significant number of High-landers. Having purged Scotland, for the time being, of royalists, the army remained quartered in small units throughout the country.

The Engagement, 1647–1649

AN ALLIANCE WITH CHARLES I

In a series of political manœuvres Charles I's cousin James, duke of Hamilton; James's brother William, earl of Lanark; and John, earl of Lauderdale, made an alliance—known as the 'Engagement'—with Charles I on the Isle of Wight on 26 December 1647. The agreement—brokered by the earl of Ormond, who had recently handed Dublin over to the parliamentarians—stipulated that the Scots would join forces with the English royalists to restore Charles to power in return for the establishment of Presbyterianism in England for a period of three years. Hamilton found it politically inexpedient to ally with the recently defeated Scottish royalists. Instead the duke sought to create a pan-archipelagic coalition involving conservative and moderate covenanters, together with royalists and Presbyterians in both Ireland and England. The covenanters no longer believed the English parliamentarians could be trusted to build a Britain suitable for preserving the Scottish revolution of 1641 and, worse still, feared, as they had in the late 1630s, that 'our poor country [should be] made an English province'.[13] Despite his earlier duplicity, the king now offered them a viable means of securing their independence and the Engagement won widespread support among the covenanting nobles and lairds who, like Hamilton, vowed to make Charles 'as glorious a King as ever reigned in Europe, to settle Religion according to the Covenant, & to establish and preserve the peace of both Kingdoms, according to our Solemn League and Protestation'.[14] However, understandably, the Kirk and its allies balked at the conclusion of an alliance relating to religion without reference to the General Assembly, especially as it abandoned the policy of a permanent English Presbyterian settlement.

For the time being, the Engagers (as those who adhered to the Engagement were known) won the day; they took control of the Scottish Parliament in April 1648 and attempted to raise an army. The levy met with trouble from the start. On 5 May the commission of the General Assembly attacked Parliament for proceeding in matters of religion without consulting it. Following the commission's onslaught, the synods, presbyteries, and Kirk sessions petitioned the committees of war and Parliament to halt the levy until the commission was satisfied that the covenants had not been abandoned. Committees of war and burghs in the south-west Lowlands, along with the committees in Fife and Midlothian, supported the commission with petitions to Parliament; while local ministers assailed the Engagement in their sermons. These efforts successfully disrupted the levy and, as a result, Hamilton entered England early in July with a force of only 14,000 to 15,000 men, or forty per cent of the potential force he could have expected.

THE SECOND ENGLISH CIVIL WAR

Once inside England a northern royalist force of between 3,000 and 4,000 men under Sir Marmaduke Langdale joined Hamilton. A speedy march south was essential to divert Fairfax and Cromwell from crushing the royalist risings which had erupted in Wales and East Anglia. Hamilton, however, failed to move. He attempted to rally Lancastrian Presbyterians to his cause, but the opposition of the Scottish Church prevented that. Insubordination and a lack of artillery also plagued the duke's army. For instance, General George Munro, who commanded the forces sent from the Ulster Army, refused to obey orders from Hamilton's lieutenant-generals, William Baillie and the earl of Callendar. Thus, Munro's men hung back from the main army, merely protecting its supply line to Scotland. More seriously, Hamilton's senior officers argued with each other and refused to accept the duke's authority. Eventually, the Engagers headed south in appalling weather without supplies, plans, or effective leadership. The destruction of Hamilton's forces on 19 August at the battle of Winwick arose not only from Cromwell's skill as a military commander but also from Hamilton's lack of martial qualities. This disaster which left 1,000 Engagers dead and a further 2,000 in parliamentary hands (an additional 2,600 surrendered at Warrington that night), combined with the annihilation of the English royalists at the battle of Preston two days earlier, not only effectively ended the Second English Civil War but facilitated the disintegration of the covenanting movement.

POLITICAL DIVISIONS WITHIN THE COVENANTERS

Back in Scotland, the covenanters had fragmented into two groups: the Engagers, who continued to support the king despite their rout on the battlefield, and the Whiggamores (or 'Whigs'), supporters of the Kirk party. The latter had tried in June to stir up an anti-Engager rising but their most serious challenge came in September when Colonel Robert Montgomery, a son of the earl of Eglinton, attacked a troop of Lanark's horse. Other leading Lowland lairds and their tenants, together with the earl of Argyll, joined the Whiggamore revolt and converged on Edinburgh, as the Engagers moved to Stirling. Despite their military advantages, the Engagers quickly succumbed and by the Treaty of Stirling (27 September 1648) both armies agreed to disband. Shortly afterwards Oliver Cromwell, who had allied himself with Argyll and the Whigs, crossed the border with several thousand horse. The Kirk party gained control and set out both to establish a godly government and to levy a new godly force. They argued that since the Engagers had betrayed the covenant and incurred God's wrath (in the form of defeat on the battlefield), these 'malignants' should be purged from both the government and the army. The Act of Classes (January 1649) excluded all Engagers from holding civil office (those wishing to do so had to publicly repent in the Kirk and repudiate their involvement in the Second English Civil War). On 10 November 1648 the synod of Lothian and Tweeddale issued a resolution, which supported the General Assembly's desire for an army free of sinners:

That the commanders of the present forces or any other forces may happen to be raised may be persons faithful in the covenant free from any malignancy and sectarizme [sic] known to be no plunders nor oppressors but obedient both to civil and ecclesiastical laws and that the soldiers under their command may consist of such persons as has honest testimony that thereby profane persons and vagabonds may not be taken in the levies and that a solid course be taken that church discipline be used in the army.[15]

This Army of the Covenants, under the command of David Leslie, spent the spring of 1649 squashing royalist risings in Inverness, Stirling, and Atholl. Then at the battle of Balvenie on 9 May three troops of horse and twelve musketeers under Colonel Gilbert Ker routed the royalist force of over 1,000 men. That victory laid the basis in the minds of the most radical Kirk partymen for the concept of a small holy army that God would favour with victories. However, it did not eliminate the royalist threat. In March 1650 Montrose, together with 1,200 Danish and German mercenaries, landed in Orkney. The following month at the battle of Carbisdale, Archibald Strachan, a radical Kirk partyman, surprised and devastated Montrose's force. The royalists allegedly suffered over 1,000 casualties, while Montrose himself was captured, marched to Edinburgh, and executed (21 May). Strachan's tremendous victory provided excellent propaganda for the ministers and lairds who supported the theory that God would only favour an army free of malignants and sinners. On the eve of the battle he had impressed this upon his men: 'Gentleman, yonder are your enemies, and they are not only your enemies, they are the enemies of our Lord Jesus Christ; I have been dealing this last night with Almighty God, to know the event of this affair, and I have gotten it: as sure as God is in heaven, they are delivered into our hands and there not a man of us fall to the ground.'[16]

The Third Civil War, 1650–1652

Ironically as the Kirk party mopped up royalist resistance at home, they were also negotiating with Charles II and by the Treaty of Breda (1 May 1650) agreed to raise an army on his behalf. On 23 June the king arrived in Scotland and, despite personal reservations, took the covenant. For their part, the covenanters managed to muster 16,000 foot and 7,000 horse, free of Engagers and notorious sinners. The formidable task of defending Scotland from invasion from England by another godly army now fell to this Army of the Covenants, under the command of David Leslie.

DUNBAR CAMPAIGN

Undoubtedly the greatest challenge of Leslie's career was the Dunbar campaign (see map on p. 68). Following the example of the Roman general Fabius, Leslie stripped the counties in the path of the English army of food and fodder. Furthermore, he strengthened the fortifications of Leith and Edinburgh, and connected the seaport and capital with earthworks which ran along the present line of Leith Walk. With his left flank protected, Leslie forced Cromwell to drive inland over rough terrain. Lacking the numbers for a siege or assault of Leslie's fortifications, Cromwell needed to bring about a decisive action. Throughout July and August Leslie used his superior position to refuse a pitched battle. With his supplies dwindling and his men suffering from the rigours of the campaign, Cromwell withdrew to Dunbar with the intention of embarking for England. From Doon Hill, outside the burgh, Leslie looked down upon the invaders realizing he had won the campaign. Prodded by the clergy (particularly members of the Commission of the General Assembly), Leslie ordered the army down from the security of the open heights. Cromwell recognized that the opportunity of striking the Scots which had eluded him previously had arrived. Bad weather on the night of 2–3 September convinced many of the raw covenanting officers to shelter in buildings away from their troops. Furthermore, Major-General John Holborn ordered the infantry to extinguish the matches essential for firing their muskets (significantly the only foot-regiment to offer heavy resistance had firelocks which did not require matches). Leslie was so convinced of Cromwell's intention of departing from Dunbar that he failed to send out an adequate number of scouts. As a result the covenanter force lay totally unprepared for the English surprise attack which came a little before sunrise on the 3rd. This combination of covenanter errors cost them an army and control of Edinburgh. Four thousand Scots died in the battle, another 10,000 fell prisoner, while only 4,000 (mainly cavalry) escaped. Rather than bringing the Commonwealth regime to the brink of collapse, the actions of the Army of the Covenants had placed Scotland in danger of conquest. According to one historian, 'If Naseby ruined the Stuart monarchy in England and Rathmines blasted its hopes in Ireland, Dunbar not merely wrecked the covenanters but it weakened the forces of the king in Scotland and secured England for Independency.'[17] Little wonder Cromwell hailed the victory at Dunbar as 'a high act of the Lord's Providence to us' and as 'one of the most signal mercies God hath done for England and His people'.[18]

THE REMONSTRANTS

The more radical members of the Kirk party perceived the rout at Dunbar as further evidence of God's anger with Scotland for having betrayed the covenant and called for additional purges of the army. Other members of the Kirk party favoured sinking their differences with the royalists and Engagers in an attempt

'The Scots holding their young kinges nose to ye grinstone', 1651

A cartoon from a broadsheet of 1651 lampoons both Charles II and the Scots. While in Breda in the spring of 1650 Charles negotiated a settlement with a delegation of Scottish parliamentary commissioners. In return for the military aid he so desperately needed to recover his English throne he accepted the covenant and agreed that Parliament should determine all civil affairs in Scotland (at his coronation he also swore to uphold the Solemn League and Covenant of 1643 which would have made him a Presbyterian king on both sides of the Tweed). Shortly afterwards Charles travelled to Scotland where the Presbyterians immediately chastised him for his frivolous lifestyle and forced him to acknowledge his own sins, together with those of his parents.

Battle of Dunbar (3 September 1650)

Shortly after the Scottish defeat at Dunbar an English artist memorialized the event in a detailed print of the battle. The English camp, stretching inland from Dunbar Kirk and burgh, appears on the right. The shipping plainly indicates the invaders' dominant naval might. Broxburn, running diagonally across the view, served as the boundary between the two armies on the night of 2–3 September 1650. The parties of foot crossing the burn mark the routes of Cromwell's and Lambert's forces respectively. On the English left three to five cavalry regiments under Lambert received support from three more commanded by Cromwell in their confrontation with 4,500 Scottish horse. Although contemporary accounts mention only two Scottish foot regiments—resisting 7,500 English foot—the print shows seven arrayed for battle. Behind them the Scottish infantry try to form up as the right wing of the English cavalry overrun the Scottish camp. Within a few hours 11,000 English troops defeated 22,000 Scots, killing 4,000 and capturing an additional 10,000.

to pose a united front against the English. However, the more radical members of the Kirk party still refused to ally with the royalists and issued a Western Remonstrance (earning themselves the name Remonstrants). These extremists negotiated with Cromwell, hoping that the English would evacuate the country leaving the Remonstrants in command. Predictably ideological divisions resulted in military weakness. The Cromwellians rejected their advances and on 1 December 1650 destroyed their army at Hamilton, on the south bank of the Clyde. Then on Christmas Eve the royalist garrison in Edinburgh Castle was treacherously surrendered by Walter Dundas of Dundas the younger.

FORMATION OF A NATIONAL ARMY

Despite this, Charles II, based at Scone Castle where he was crowned king of Scotland in January 1651, managed to raise the only truly national Scottish army of the era, containing troops from nearly every shire in Scotland, members of clans previously absent from the covenanter armies together with royalists. The Scots took great care in raising the Army of the Kingdom. On 20 December 1650 Parliament issued a list of colonels, naming many royalists, Engagers, and Highland chiefs excluded not only by the Kirk party, but also by earlier covenanter regimes. The Act of Levy followed on the 23rd; however, the government continued to appoint new colonels throughout 1651. The danger to the kingdom forced Parliament to stipulate a *levée en masse*, with certain exceptions on political or moral grounds. Despite the dangers of English attack, the Scots only produced a sizeable fighting machine in the late spring of 1651.

Support for the defence of the kingdom came from many quarters. The Church strove to aid the levy from all levels of its authority. Probably of greater importance, because of their unity of purpose (with the obvious exception of the south-west Lowlands where the Remonstrants continued to enjoy support), were the nobles and lairds. The shire committees and the burghs, too, worked for the creation of a strong national army. Even then, in an enterprise where unity should have been paramount it was often lacking. The English threat failed to draw the Scots together. Instead Charles and the Estates faced many problems which even the Engagers had escaped: on several occasions in 1651 regiments in the army, often with official sanction, quartered on levy-quota delinquents; in Highland areas official recruiters had their levies disbanded by jealous chiefs or lairds; while elsewhere colonels quarrelled with the committees of war.

CROMWELL'S VICTORY AT WORCESTER

For much of the winter of 1650 and spring of 1651 a severe illness prevented Cromwell from taking the field. The respite ended with a vengeance in mid-July when Lambert landed in Fife, threatening the Scottish eastern flank. At the battle of Inverkeithing on 20 July a force of 4,000 to 5,000 men under Lieutenant-

General John Holburn and Major-General Sir John Brown suffered a disastrous defeat. The Lowland troops fled, leaving the foot of clans Buchanan and Maclean to be slaughtered by the English. Desperate, Charles led a spectacular dash south, reaching Worcester from Stirling in twenty-four days. This wild attempt to capture London proved futile; on 3 September, the anniversary of Dunbar, Cromwell, with a mixed force of 30,000 regulars and militia, approached the city and after a bitter day of fighting routed the king's army. Parliament took 10,000 prisoners; a further 3,000 died, while the remainder—including Charles II—fled. A Gaelic poet articulated his plight in 'A lament for the state of the country':

> Our king after his crowning,
> barely before he was adult,
> turned into a poor stripped vagrant
> without guard or parliament or court.
>
> Expelled from his rightful position
> without any of his friends with him,
> like a ship on the tip of the ocean
> without rudder or oar or port.[19]

Meanwhile in Scotland General George Monck's men stormed Dundee on 1 September, butchering 800 Scots in the fashion of Drogheda, then sacking the town. Just days before, his men had captured the Committee of Estates, Leven, and 800 troops in Alyth, north of Dundee. Opposition continued in Scotland from certain nobles—for instance Argyll, Huntly, and Balcarres—and isolated fortresses such as the Bass Rock, Dunnottar, and Dumbarton Castles held out into 1652. However, the English advanced north to Orkney without setbacks. The years of Scotland's most intensive military activity in the seventeenth century, if not in her history (save for the years between 1296 and 1329), had ended in defeat.

Having begun by raising troops to oppose an episcopalian royalist policy, the covenanters and royalists alike fell victim to the sectarian English parliamentarians and Cromwell's military genius. In little over a decade the Scots had gone from being the crown's firmest opponents to the monarchy's staunchest allies. The initial tension within the National Covenant had allowed such a change. After all they had risen, like the Irish confederates, in the name of the king and pledged to 'stand to the defence of our dread Sovereign, the Kings Majesty, his Person and Authority, in the defence and preservation of the foresaid true Religion, Liberties and Laws of the Kingdom'.[20] The military activities of the covenanters tell the story of a party which became accustomed to the use of force to secure political and religious ends. However, having achieved military successes, they failed to maintain stability in Britain and became enamoured of and committed to the use of the sword whether in the name of the Lord or of the

Coronation of Charles II

The earl of Argyll crowned Charles II at the traditional Scottish coronation place of Scone on 1 January 1651. He immediately took command of the Army of the Kingdom, the only national Scottish force of the era, which comprised former royalists and covenanters who fought under banners with the new motto 'For Religion, King and Kingdom'. In August 1651 the Scots invaded England for the fourth time since 1639 and made a spectacular dash for London. On 3 September, Cromwell routed them at the battle of Worcester and thereby won control over England and effectively ended the wars of, the wars in, and the wars for the three kingdoms. Prince Charles II narrowly escaped capture and fled to the continent where he remained until the restoration of the monarchy in 1660.

king. Thus the Scots confronted the prospect of continual military activity in order to secure victory or avoid defeat. That Cromwell and his army ultimately crushed them can be attributed in part to the divisions within the covenanting movement and in part to the quality of Cromwell's generalship and the fighting capabilities of his men.

THE CIVIL WARS
IN IRELAND

JANE OHLMEYER

The Irish Civil War—or the Eleven Years War—began in October 1641 with the outbreak of the rising and effectively ended with the surrender of Galway in April 1652. The conflict has also been dubbed the Confederate War since between 1642 and 1649 the Irish confederates, with their capital in Kilkenny, directed the Catholic war-effort against the various Protestant armies raised to crush them. As in covenanting Scotland, the thorny issue of loyalty to the Stuart crown confused and complicated the course of the war in Ireland. On the one land, the outbreak of the First English Civil War and the need to choose between the king and Parliament shattered the anti-Catholic alliance (with the Scottish covenanters and the British settlers in Ulster and in Munster allying with the parliamentarians until the end of 1647); while, on the other, the desire by some confederates to conclude a peace with Charles I eventually led to the outbreak of civil war within Catholic ranks after May 1648. As a result, Catholic Ireland failed to win lasting political autonomy within the context of a tripartite Stuart monarchy, but its rebellion nevertheless won legislative independence and freedom of worship for Irish Catholics in the 1640s.

Aftermath of the 1641 Rising

The rising (discussed in Chapter 1), which began in Ulster on 22 October 1641, quickly 'diffused through the veins of the whole kingdom'.[1] Even though an attempt on the 23rd to take Dublin Castle failed, the insurgents, led by Sir Phleim O'Neill, captured the key strongholds of Armagh, Charlemont, Mountjoy Castle, Tandragee, and Newry (only Derry, Coleraine, Enniskillen, Lisburn, and Carrickfergus escaped). From Ulster the insurrection quickly spread to Leinster. On 21 November the insurgents besieged Drogheda and skirmished with government forces in Counties Wicklow and Dublin. By December the rising had engulfed much of the country with the Catholics in Counties Roscommon, Mayo, Sligo, Kilkenny, and Tipperary joining the insurgents. The Catholics in

Counties Antrim, Limerick, Clare, Cork, and Kerry followed suit in the early spring of 1642.

1641 DEPOSITIONS

Inevitably bloodshed and unnecessary cruelty accompanied the insurrection but the extent of the 'massacre' of Protestants was exaggerated, especially in England where the wildest rumours were readily believed. Assessing the impact which the rebellion had on Irish society, however, is problematic since many of the contemporary accounts (known as the 1641 depositions) describing the insurrection were often inaccurate, biased, and misleading. There are two types of deposition: the statements taken down within a year or two of the events that allegedly occurred; and those collected during the 1650s. The earlier ones are more-or-less spontaneous reports; the later ones are largely works of propaganda. Yet for all their defects the depositions provide an abundance of information which cannot be ignored. That there was a collapse of authority can not be denied, and in the areas recovered by the Irish the Protestant settlers were evicted and the former owners resumed possession of their lands. Others lost their lives. For instance in County Antrim, during the various military encounters of 1642, fatalities occurred at Portnaw, Coleraine, Ballycastle, Ballintoy, and Dunluce; while at the battle of the Laney (February) nearly 600 men died. Estimating the precise number of deaths is almost impossible but, by and large, horror stories of massacres were gross exaggerations and more people seem to have perished in the famine and pestilence —'Colonel Hunger and Major Sickness'—which accompanied the disruption than by the sword. At Ballycastle, for instance, witnesses (albeit ones of Irish extraction) consistently deposed that only one or two individuals, rather than hundreds of Protestants, were murdered. Similarly evidence from the depositions collected in County Armagh, where some of the worst atrocities occurred, suggests that between 600 and 1,300 people (or between 10.5 and 25 per cent of a total settler population of 5,000) died as a result of the violence. In fact throughout Ireland perhaps 4,000 Protestants were murdered during the early months of the rising; a tragedy, to be sure, but a far cry from the figure of 154,000 which the lords justices, who now ruled Ireland, claimed in March 1642 had been butchered.

Much more common was the plundering and pillaging of Protestant property and the theft of livestock. According to one recent scholar, 'These attacks were usually associated with the economic tensions that had developed between the two communities in the years before 1641.'[2] They were anguished and spontaneous rural risings which lacked effective leadership and offered aggrieved Catholics an opportunity to settle old scores with their Protestant neighbours. The major towns and cities—Dublin, Cork, Waterford, Youghal, Limerick, Galway, Kilkenny, Wexford, Ross, Clonmel, Londonderry, Carrickfergus, and Belfast, where most of the Protestants resided—were not plundered; and when a town was attacked, most of the inhabitants were saved by their Irish neighbours.

However, refugees quickly descended upon these urban centres. By the spring of 1642 the lords justices estimated that 4,000 Protestant refugees had poured into Dublin, half of whom were classified as destitute and allegedly died at the rate of thirty a day. Other towns also attracted victims of the unrest. 'Miserable spectacles of wealthy men and women, utterly spoiled and undone, nay stripped stark naked', flooded into Drogheda in the immediate aftermath of the rising.[3] Thousands more fled to Scotland and England.

Civil War, 1642–1643

PROTESTANT RESPONSE

Despite the initial successes enjoyed by the insurgents, the Protestant community quickly rallied and began raising troops to supplement the Irish standing army (a Protestant force of 2,297 foot and 943 horse). In Munster Richard Boyle, earl of Cork, spent vast sums after the outbreak of the rebellion revamping local defences and buying guns and powder. He also lent considerable amounts of money to local commanders (usually his kinsmen) and raised and maintained at his own expense two companies of troops, including some veterans of the Nine Years War. The earl of Clanricard, although a Catholic, initially held Galway for the crown and the town—though not the fort—only declared for the insurgents in March 1642. In Ulster leading Protestant landlords—the Lord of the Ards, Sir James Montgomery, Sir Robert Stewart, Sir William Stewart, Sir William Cole, and Sir Ralph Gore—raised 9,900 foot and 750 horse by 1643. James Butler, earl and later marquis of Ormond, took charge in Dublin and, aided by commanders like Sir Charles Coote and Sir Henry Tichbourne, launched numerous forays against the insurgents in Leinster. In January 1642 Coote routed the Irish at Swords on the outskirts of Dublin; in February Ormond campaigned in County Kildare, capturing Naas and later winning a victory at Kilrush (15 April); in March Tichbourne raised the siege of Drogheda and went on to retake a number of key strongholds in County Louth (Ardee, Dundalk, and Carlingford). Despite the arrival of 2,600 foot from England over the winter of 1641 to 1642, the Protestant offensive throughout Leinster ground to a halt in May largely for want of supplies and Dublin merchants complained that Irish raiding parties came within half a mile of the capital. Elsewhere, the arrival of 10,000 Scots in Ulster under the effective command of Major-General Sir Robert Munro after April enabled the Protestants to clear much of east Ulster of insurgents during the spring and summer of 1642 (see Chapter 2); while the despatch of reinforcements from England to Munster in May helped to facilitate the victories of Murrough O'Brien, Lord Inchiquin, at Liscarroll (August) and Bandonbridge (November).

Despite logistical problems and the fact that the Irish controlled large chunks of the country, this anti-Catholic coalition which was loosely obedient to the

James Butler, twelfth earl and duke of Ormond (1610–88)
by Van Egmont

Raised as a Protestant at court, Ormond headed the predominantly Catholic and enormously powerful house of Butler and enjoyed an extensive patrimony in Counties Kilkenny, Tipperary, and Waterford. With the outbreak of the Irish rebellion he rallied to the king's cause and took command of the forces in Ireland loyal to Charles. He was involved in endless negotiations with the Irish Confederates throughout the 1640s but his refusal to make concessions over religion frustrated the conclusion of any permanent settlement with them. The consequences of this proved disastrous for Charles: the Irish manpower he had repeatedly requested and so desperately needed to win the First and Second English Civil Wars never arrived. As his campaigns during the late 1640s highlight, Ormond also proved a pedestrian and at times totally inept military commander who lacked strategic vision. He spent the 1650s in exile on the continent but returned to dominate Irish politics after the Restoration.

king, clearly enjoyed a tactical advantage. However, the outbreak of civil war in England in August 1642 had a destabilizing impact on their position. On the one hand, it reduced the amount of money and the number of supplies and soldiers available for the anti-Catholic war-effort and put pressure on the uneasy Protestant alliance. On the other, it gave a welcome boost to the Catholic insurgents which now enjoyed widespread support throughout the country.

FORMATION OF THE CONFEDERATION OF KILKENNY

As early as December 1641 the leading Old English lords concluded an alliance with the Ulster insurgents. Then in May 1642 the Catholic clergy, desperate to legitimize the rebellion, to control the popular uprising, and to restore law and order, met at Kilkenny. There they established an alternative form of government and drafted an Oath of Association which bound together the Catholic confederates, as they were now known. On 24 October the confederates held their first General Assembly at Kilkenny and elected a supreme council consisting of twenty-four members (six representatives from each province), twelve of whom were supposed to sit permanently and run the confederation. But as one historian has noted: 'extensive as the powers of the supreme council were, it was strictly subordinate to the assembly, a unicameral legislature composed partly of members elected on the normal parliamentary basis, and partly of temporal and spiritual peers who . . . were differentiated from commoners only by certain ceremonial marks of precedence.'[4]

Unlike the English parliamentarians and Scottish covenanters, the confederates never won control of the country's administrative structure and one of the first tasks of the newly formed confederation was to create a hierarchy of councils. The county councils (with two members from each barony) reported to provincial councils (with two members from each county) and these bodies in return answered to the general Assembly and its standing executive, the supreme council. In addition to creating a bureaucracy, the first General Assembly set up a judiciary, modelled on the pre-war system, and provided for the levy and maintenance of a standing force, composed of four provincial armies (together with a 'running army'). These administrative, legal, and military arrangements highlight the inherently conservative nature of the confederation and reflect its desire to promote unity. To this end, the General Assembly decreed that 'there shall be no distinction or comparison made betwixt old Irish, and old and new English, or betwixt septs or families, or betwixt citizens and townsmen and countrymen, joining in union, upon pain of the highest punishment'.[5]

A WAR OF RELIGION

From the outset religion played an important role in defining the confederate agenda. To begin with, religious grievances inspired many to take up arms 'for their own just and lawful defence against Puritans, and corrupt ministers of state' and 'for the restitution, and defence of that only true religion'.[6] Religious rancour on both sides also brutalized the struggle. One Protestant claimed in 1642 that the papists' cruelty was 'never used by the Turks to Christians . . . no quarter is given, no faith kept, all houses burnt and demolished, man, wife and child put to the sword'.[7] In the same year the Catholic General Owen Roe O'Neill noted that 'on both sides there is nothing but burning, robbery in cold blood, and cruelties such as are not usual even among the Moors and Arabs'.[8] In Britain captured Irish soldiers were immediately put to the sword or hanged; while in Ireland the royalists, Scots, and parliamentarian armies killed their prisoners unless they could be easily ransomed or exchanged. For instance, early in 1644 one parliamentary commander in Ulster allegedly killed 1,000 Irish soldiers and camp-followers in a single raid and later boasted that 'the reason why our prisoners were so few was because . . . [we] had no stomach to give such perfidious rogues any quarter'.[9]

Even though the clergy played no direct role in fomenting the rebellion, they seized the initiative after it broke out, calling for the immediate restoration of their churches and the overturn of all anti-Catholic measures. They also strove to harness the populist rising while at the same time legitimizing what had happened by promoting the Oath of Association (often in the Irish language) in their parishes in much they same way that members of the Kirk had done with the National Covenant in Scotland. Throughout the 1640s the bishops, who sat as spiritual peers in the general assemblies and were often elected to sit on the supreme councils, played a prominent role in governing the country (members of the clergy were also elected to the general assemblies). The arrival of a papal nuncio, Giovanni Battista Rinuccini, archbishop of Fermo, in late 1645 offered the native clergy decisive leadership and strengthened their resolve to resist a peace with the king which did not adequately address their concerns. The confederates also tried to turn their cause into a crusade by claiming that the Catholic religion was being threatened by an international Protestant conspiracy led by English Puritans. If Ireland fell, the confederate Supreme Council reminded their agent in Flanders, 'heresy will not only prevail but also extinguish the orthodox faith [in] all the north parts of the world. The Huguenots of France, Germany and Holland, and their correspondents, are not to be forgotten; and . . . the disunion of Catholic princes is too well known.' They added that, if only the Catholic princes would support their cause, Ireland 'might from thenceforth be a great bulwark against all the heretics of the Northern parts of Europe'.[10]

LOYALTY TO THE STUARTS

Despite the fact that the confederates (like the English parliamentarians and Scottish covenanters) blatantly violated the king's royal prerogatives and consistently refused to obey his instructions, they nevertheless referred to themselves as 'loyal subjects'. The confederate Oath of Association contained the phrase 'I further swear that I will bear faith and allegiance to our sovereign lord King Charles

Confederate seal

The seal shows a cross rising from a flaming heart, the Sacred Heart; while a traditional Irish harp and an imperial crown flank the cross. The image of the cross, crown, and harp adorned many banners and symbolized the confederate devotion to Catholicism and their genuine sense of loyalty to the crown. Hardly surprisingly, after Charles I's execution the majority of Irish Catholics, like the Scots, viewed Charles II as his legitimate successor and in 1660 joyously welcomed his return. 'There is nothing now to be seen or heard but joys and jubilees throughout the British Empire for the royal physician is come to heal the three bleeding nations' noted one contemporary of Charles's restoration.

. . . and that I will defend him . . . as far as I may, with my life, power and estate'; while the confederate seal of office bore the inscription 'Pro Deo, Rege et Patria, Hibernia Unanimis'—strikingly similar to the covenanter pledge of loyalty 'to God, to our king and country'.[11] The confederate battle flag displayed an Irish cross within a red circle; above the cross was the royal monogram 'CR' under an imperial crown and below the cross the motto 'Vivat Rex Carolus' ('Long live King Charles'). Clearly many confederates had no wish to wrest Ireland from Stuart control. As one Gaelic scholar has recently noted, for the majority of Irishmen 'Charles I was still their rightful king . . . [and they] were *sliocht Shéarlais*, "Charles' people" '.[12] However, reaching a political and religious arrangement acceptable to all parties proved predictably difficult.

The Military Machines

ARMY SIZE AND COMPOSITION

At the height of the Irish Civil War four separate armies—royalist, parliamentarian, covenanter, and confederate—served in the field. The absence of reliable quantitative data makes it impossible to estimate accurately the size of these forces; but the few surviving musters and the numerous qualitative sources (letters, ambassadorial despatches, intelligence reports, contemporary pamphlets, and newsheets) indicate that at least 45,000 men served in arms for much of the decade. It has been estimated that shortly after the outbreak of the rebellion between 33,000 and 60,000 men fought in the confederate, royalist, and Scottish armies; and that by 1649 this figure had risen to between 43,000 and 66,000 soldiers. The confederate standing armies reached a peak strength of 20,000 to 25,000 by 1646–7; while the levels of Protestant troops at least matched and often exceeded this level for much of the decade.

Extant musters provide further information on the composition and strength of these forces and on how well they were armed. On the confederate side the four provincial armies were supposed to consist of 6,000 foot and 400 horse, and the 'running army' of 2,000 foot and 200 horse. However, muster extracts suggest that the confederates were unable to maintain these levels of men and never had a sufficient number of cavalry. The Army of Leinster, when mustered in May 1646, numbered just over 5,000 men (with an average of eighty-four men, instead of the specified 100, in each company); but by 1649 this figure had dropped to just under 4,000 men (with an average of seventy-five men in each company). The Army of Munster, at a muster in April 1649, contained roughly 3,500 men (with an average of sixty men in each company). In 1643 the 10,000-strong Scottish army in Ulster counted roughly ninety-eight soldiers in each company; while the average size of the royalist companies varied from 108 in May 1642 to seventy-one in November 1642. Desertion was a problem which plagued the royalists in particular. During the early years of the war many of the troops garrisoned in Dublin fled to Wales and England, while others deserted to the confederates and, according to the lords justices, 'in some cases not above six or seven out of a company of forty remained on our side'.[13]

ARMS

Whatever the size of the unit, every effort was made to equip these troops with sufficient firearms and pikes.[14] For instance, during the First Bishops' War (discussed in Chapter 1) Antrim proposed to organize his army according to the most up-to-date European specifications and ordered that his three regiments of foot were to consist of two parts 'shot' (musketeers), and one-third pike; so too during the 1640s when the confederates decreed that in each company 'two parts [should be] armed with muskets well fixed and a third part with serviceable pike'.[15] An extant muster dating from 1649 suggests that these specifications were occasionally met, for nearly two-thirds of the Army of Leinster in that year were armed with muskets. The ratio of musket to pike among both the royalist and Scottish forces appears to have hovered around three muskets to every two pikes, but the musket did not reign supreme throughout Ireland. Barely half of the Army of Ulster was armed with muskets; while pikes predominated over muskets in the Army of Munster.

COMMANDERS

The musters further indicate the prevailing ratio of officers to the other ranks. For example, roughly eleven per cent of the Scottish army in 1642 were officers;

the percentage of officers in the Irish royalist forces nearly doubled from seven per cent in May 1642 to thirteen per cent in 1644, while the percentage of officers in the confederate armies varied from nine to nearly twenty per cent. With the exception of Ormond, who lacked military training and ability, many of the royalist commanders distinguished themselves in combat. In particular the Irish feared Sir Charles Coote, whom they dubbed 'the accursed scourge and per-secutor of the Gaels'.[16] A veteran of the Nine Years War, Coote held Dublin in the aftermath of the rising and launched many successful raids into enemy territ-ory before receiving his 'ticket to hell' (as the Irish termed it) at Trim on 7 May 1642. Similarly Inchiquin, who served both the king and Parliament, proved a formidable commander who quickly earned the respect both of his troops and his opponents. Thanks to his excellent intelligence networks and his well-trained forces, Inchiquin executed numerous successful, and often brutal, assaults throughout the 1640s despite being dogged by logistical problems. Many of the Catholic commanders were the heads of Gaelic septs or prominent noblemen: Lords Taaffe and Dillon, together with the earls of Westmeath, Castlehaven, and Antrim, all held confederate commands but lacked military experience. By and large the company officers, and especially their deputies, were all followers or kinsmen of these noblemen. An extant muster roll for Antrim's 1644 expedi-tionary force to Scotland lists the names of seventy-three officers who appear to have originated largely in Counties Antrim or Londonderry. The bulk of these names (fifty-six) were native Irish: MacAllesters, MacCormacks, MacDonnells, MacDermots, MacHenrys, MacQuillans, O'Cahans, O'Haras, and O'Neills, as one might expect, predominated. These men were supplemented by 'discon-tented officers'—particularly from Ulster and the Pale—who had been unable to find employment in the confederate armies. Antrim nominated his kinsman Alasdair MacColla, a veteran soldier with experience of warfare in both Ireland and Scotland, as his major-general (discussed in Chapter 2).

Professional soldiers also fought alongside these baronial commanders. In August 1642 Owen Roe O'Neill, 'a soldier since a boy, in the only martial academy of Christendom—Flanders', arrived in Ireland and took command of the Army of Ulster.[17] However, the fact that he never received overall command of the con-federate armies, combined with the haphazard way in which his forces were sup-plied and armed, left him feeling embittered. To make matters worse, O'Neill's great rival Thomas Preston, who landed at Wexford in August 1642, assumed command of the Army of Leinster. Like O'Neill he had served as a staff officer in Flanders and as a result enjoyed formidable administrative skills which he put to good use at the various sieges, especially at Duncannon in 1645 or at Roscommon in 1646, which he oversaw. Even though Preston enjoyed greater political clout within the supreme council, O'Neill—as his victory at Benburb (1646) high-lights—proved the better soldier; while Preston's performance on the battlefield —as the débâcle at Dungan's Hill (August 1647) demonstrates—smacked of incompetence. Many of the officers who served the confederates were also career soldiers well versed in the ways of continental warfare: Hugh Dubh O'Neill, whose defence of Clonmel in May 1650 won the grudging admiration of Oliver Cromwell himself, fought in the Army of Ulster; while Garret Barry, author of the only contemporary military manual written by an Irishman, served in the Army of Munster and introduced the men to Swedish battle formation; Garret Wall, Con and Brian O'Neill, and many others also had considerable experience of active service, especially siegecraft, in the French and Spanish armies.

RECRUITMENT

Officers apart, who made up the rank and file and how were they recruited? From the outset it seems that 'of men fit for war there are certainly a sufficient number' in Ireland, though these human resources were not always tapped to maximum effect.[18] Initially Irish grandees summoned their followers, tenants, and kinsmen to arms in a time-honoured fashion. Antrim proposed to exploit his position as a Gaelic lord in both Ulster and the Western Isles to levy the 5,000 foot and 200 horse needed for the First Bishops' War; and again in 1644 he summoned the men of his own lordship and of neighbouring sublordships to volunteer for service in Scotland. The rank and file raised by Antrim and the confederates for service in Scotland in 1644 were almost exclusively native Irishmen 'of Ulster, [and] some of the Old Irish in other parts of the kingdom'.[19] A mixture of impressment and voluntary enlistment were also used to recruit troops. The confederates required each county to produce quotas of men (aged between 18 and 60) for service and charged local power-brokers with drilling and maintaining 'trained bands' to be drawn upon in times of emergency. English and Scottish soldiers were also drafted for service in Ireland: by 1643 10,000 Scots had been dispatched to Ulster and by 1649 the English Parliament had sent a total of 20,000 men. Once levied these troops were occasionally left to fend for themselves, much to the horror of the local population, or crammed into already overcrowded garrisons. Up to seven infantry regiments were billeted in houses in and around Dublin during the 1640s and as many as 1,500 soldiers were crammed into Kilkenny. By 1650 the unfortunate town of Clonmel was burdened with two regiments (1,300 men) plus their camp-followers: hardly surprisingly 'many of the poor inhabitants have deserted the town'.[20]

TRAINING AND DISCIPLINE

A large number of 'natives', in Strafford's New Army, had already received some military training in 1640. However, well-drilled and disciplined troops were the exception; much more common were those under Ormond's command during the early 1640s, who were 'only a rabble of disarmed freshwater soldiers, without arms, ammunition or soldier commander';[21] or those Catholic recruits, of whom Owen Roe O'Neill complained in 1642 that there was 'no obedience among the

soldiers, if one call men soldiers who behave nothing better than the animals . . .
I am killing myself bringing them to some order and discipline'.[22]

Yet within a relatively short period of time the continental veterans had
'reduced many of the natives to a more civil deportment, and to a pretty good
understanding of military discipline'.[23] They also introduced modern tactics,
pioneered by Maurice of Nassau at the turn of the seventeenth century and perfected during the Thirty Years War, whereby small tactical units fought in a linear
formation 'in which the firepower of musketeers was co-ordinated with the shock
strength of pikemen'.[24] The Irish victory at Benburb demonstrated the effectiveness of linear formation fighting and how—on occasion—the Irish soldier
appears to have been blessed with remarkable stamina, courage, and endurance.
Certainly the confederate general James Touchet, earl of Castlehaven believed
that though he only led 5,000 foot and 800 horse 'their contentment and courage
. . . does make them in my esteem more than double that number'.[25] By 1646 two
leading royalists maintained that the confederates 'have their men in a better
order of war and better commanded by captains of experience and practice of war
then ever they were since the conquest'.[26]

As in England and Scotland, all sides attempted to maintain discipline among
the soldiers. They issued lengthy lists of regulations which forbade adultery,
blasphemy, treachery, disobedience, pillage, theft, arson, murder, drunkenness,
liaisons with the enemy, boys, or women, and the sale of arms, while promoting
prayer, loyalty, and self-discipline. However, lack of pay and other basic necessities meant that indiscriminate plunder and pillage were commonplace, as
indeed was the case with any army on the move in mid-seventeenth-century
Europe. An added threat came from renegade soldiers who terrorized the local
populace, especially in remote regions, by becoming highwaymen, robbers, and
murderers. One leading confederate complained to Ormond of 'the rapines,
depredations, and disorder of the soldiers (which, . . . eat into the bowels of the
country)'.[27] As the war progressed lawlessness became endemic. In 1647 the confederate General Assembly lamented that the 'frequent committal of murders,
thefts, robberies, forcible entries, extortions . . . do daily multiply and increase
through the want of gaols in several counties, the defect in gaolers . . . and other
officers, to execute and perform their respective duties'.[28] Despite every effort to
control the 'vice and disorder of theft, burglary and robbery' associated with the
army, soldiers continued to exploit and to intimidate the civilian population.[29]
Only regular pay and an efficient system of supply would have improved the discipline, morale, and combat effectiveness of the soldiers fighting in Ireland.[30]

DISEASE

Inadequate shelter, a poor diet, a damp climate, and the rigours associated with
campaigning or with cramped living in unhygienic garrisons resulted in pneu-
monia, flu, and consumption ('the looseness and the malignant fever', 'violent

coughs', 'stopping of the breath') in winter, and in enteric fevers, bacillary dysentery, hepatitis, and typhus (fluxes and agues) in summer. In a single year 300 men, or nearly a third, of Colonel Edward Conway's regiment died for want of quarter and provisions 'whereby the soldiers fell into a disease taken by cold'.[31] Many of the royalist forces stationed in Dublin during the early 1640s were sick—'so many of them being sick as much weakens all the companies'.[32] During the siege of Drogheda over the winter of 1641/2 one combatant noted how 'famine and fluxes with other diseases returned again to their former dominion over us; death began to look more terrible within the walls then without'.[33] In the spring of 1642 an outbreak of fevers and fluxes (probably bacillary dysentery) reduced the royalist forces in Munster by two-thirds; while later that year in one Dublin regiment alone there were 300 foot and thirty officers sick.

To make matters worse, medical services were at best rudimentary. The absence of a doctor during the siege of Duncannon fort in 1645 meant that 'divers men perished of curable wounds'.[34] Medication was also in very short supply. The lords justices complained in April 1642 that 'the want of medicaments here for sick and wounded soldiers is so lamentable as many die daily here under the hands of physicians and surgeons by occasion of that want'.[35] When medical supplies finally arrived they were of poor quality and insufficient quantity. Extant musters indicate that the confederates were somewhat healthier than their royalist or parliamentarian counterparts: less than three per cent of the Army of Leinster was listed as sick in 1649; less than six per cent of the Army of Ulster in 1650. According to one account, the fact that the Irish troops were not confined to garrisons, were apparently better clothed, and enjoyed superior food and quarter helps to account for their hardiness and better immunity to disease.

TACTICS AND STRATEGY[36]

With the exception of seven battles—Kilrush (15 April 1642), Liscarroll (25 August 1642), Benburb (5 June 1646), Dungan's Hill (8 August 1647), Knockanauss (13 November 1647), Rathmines (2 August 1649), and Scarrifhollis (21 June 1650)—few set-piece encounters were fought in Ireland (see map on pp. 34–5). As it was, the confederates only won one of these battles, Benburb, while at Dungan's Hill and Scarrifhollis they lost entire field armies and at Knockanauss a company of veteran Redshanks. One military historian has recently attributed confederate failure on the battlefield to a number of factors. First, the confederates never fully mastered the intricacies of the countermarch which involved the front row (there were usually six) of musketeers discharging their guns and then marching to the rear. The next five rows then stepped forward and the second row (now at the front) fired their weapons. By the time the original first row had progressed back to the front their muskets should have been reloaded. To execute this under fire required soldiers to be exceptionally well drilled, something which the confederates never really were. Second, the confederate pike-heads were smaller and the

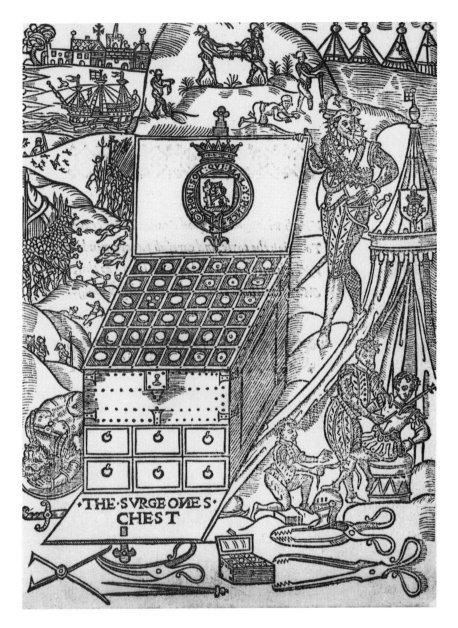

Surgeon's chest

Throughout the three kingdoms disease, especially typhus, dysentery, and bubonic plague, claimed more lives than battlewounds. Field hospitals tried to cater for both but often lacked medical personnel and an adequate supply of medicines. In theory every regiment employed at least one surgeon, shown here on the right treating a wounded soldier. His surgical implements (shown on the bottom) included a variety of scissors, clamps, forceps, knives, and saws. In addition to dressing wounds and setting broken limbs, a military physician would have been expected to perform amputations and other surgical procedures. Anaesthetics remained unknown to the early modern surgeon and many of his unfortunate patients died, often from sepsis and gangrene.

poles less sturdy than those of their opponents and could easily be lopped off in close encounters which, given the vital role played by the pikeman in battle, proved disastrous. Finally, largely due to a shortage of mounts and money, the confederates never maintained the desired 1 : 2 ratio of horse to foot. Moreover commanders, especially O'Neill and Preston, accustomed to fighting in a theatre of war dominated by infantry never employed the small number of cavalry which the confederates did have to the greatest effect.[37]

Instead the confederates favoured siege warfare (discussed in Chapter 6) and adopting tactics which aimed to destroy the enemy's economic base. These 'wars of attrition' dominated the seventeenth-century Irish military landscape. All sides aimed 'to burn all the corn, and kill all the cattle, and to bring famine' to their enemy.[38] Thus in 1646 the Supreme Council ordered its men to burn all grain stored 'on the Liffey downwards to Dublin, and from Dublin to Drogheda' in order to prevent it falling to the enemy.[39] The same year it was reported that the Scottish commander Munro intended to 'burn, kill and prey the counties of Monaghan, the few inhabitants of this county [Kilkenny], Cavan, Westmeath, Longford, and from thence as far as they can in the kingdom . . . They will adventure to hinder the ploughing and sowing of this year'.[40]

By and large, though, any advantage gained by slash-and-burn tactics or the capture of a fortified position was soon largely lost because neither the confederates, the royalists, nor the parliamentarians (prior to 1649) appeared to have a 'grand strategy' for winning the war. On the contrary there was little co-operation between the various commanders. Thus the confederate armies often acted as independent units, advancing, retreating, and occasionally offering battle as the opinion of the commanders and local circumstances dictated. This stemmed largely from the confederate failure to create a central command which would have overseen and co-ordinated the various activities of the regional armies, and from their inability to supply simultaneously four provincial armies (the confederates consistently favoured the Army of Leinster over the other three). To make matters worse the leading Irish generals constantly feuded and bickered with one another over trivial, personal matters. The consequences were often profound: the feud in 1644 between Antrim and Castlehaven over who should be given supreme command of all of the confederate armies ensured that the summer offensive against Ulster ended in a shambles; while the quarrel between O'Neill and Preston, which lost the confederates the opportunity to control Dublin in 1646, was equally devastating to the Catholic cause. The same held true of the armies raised to quell the Irish rebellion. No joint action against the confederate foe was ever arranged between the various forces hostile to the Catholic cause; while the uneasy coalition of those forces loyal to the king and to the English Parliament was then totally shattered by the 1643 cease-fire and from this point on the Scottish and parliamentary forces not only regarded their royalist co-religionists as the enemy but were also intensely suspicious of and uncooperative towards each other. The result, hardly surprisingly, was a military stalemate for much of the decade.

Civil War and Politics, 1643–1649

CESSATION OF ARMS (SEPTEMBER 1643)

The September 1643 cease-fire—known as the cessation of arms—heralded a new departure in Anglo-Irish relations. After much haggling it was agreed that in return for £20,000, troops, and supplies for the English war-effort, the king would consider repealing the penal laws and granting the confederates considerable political independence, freedom of worship, and security of land tenure. It immediately shattered the already strained anti-Catholic alliance; it intensified the war first in Ulster, by driving the Scots into the parliamentary camp, and then in Munster, where many troops now favoured siding with Parliament. It was, however, July before Inchiquin, frustrated by the king's failure to make him lord president of Munster, finally abandoned the royalist cause in Munster. He later claimed that the king was 'deluded' by the Catholics and that it was 'no longer my duty to execute those commands, knowing them to proceed from the advice of those, who expose Religion and the Commonwealth to shipwreck'.[41] His defection opened another active front in the south-west and deprived the royalists of vital towns in Munster, especially Cork, Duncannon, and Youghal. The cessation also embarrassed English royalists, anxious to avoid being tarred as pro-papist, but considering the poor state of the king's affairs they either had to accept it reluctantly or shift their allegiance to Parliament (as some indeed did). As far as the English Parliament was concerned, a 'united' Ireland—however tenuous the union—constituted a major strategic and military threat since the king now had access to previously unexploited assets in terms of men and money.

TROOPS FOR SCOTLAND

Almost at once Charles made use of these resources for his own war-effort. Ormond shipped considerable numbers of largely Protestant troops to Wales. In addition Antrim asked the Supreme Council to provide Charles with a further 10,000 men for England 'to resist the Scotch invasion' and at least 2,000 armed men who who were to join with the Scottish royalists under the marquis of Montrose, as well as with arms for Prince Rupert's forces in England. The council finally agreed to raise troops for Scotland and to provide them with 2,000 muskets, 2,400 hundredweight of powder with match, and 200 barrels of oatmeal. From the confederate perspective, the decision to finance this expedition to Scotland formed an important dimension of the wider struggle to draw the Scots out of Ulster. While the confederates promised to provide the arms and munitions requested for Prince Rupert (see picture on p. 122), they remained reluctant to ship ten Catholic regiments to England at a time when troops were desperately needed at home and refused to commit themselves until they had heard how negotiations between their commissioners and the king (over the redress of their religious, tenurial, and political grievances) were progressing at Oxford. The negotiators sent by the General Assembly to discuss their grievances with the king arrived in the royalist capital in March 1644 (a Protestant delegation sought an audience with Charles the following month). Charles refused to make any significant concessions to any of their demands, especially those concerning religion and the constitutional position of the Irish parliament, and the delegation returned to Kilkenny. Hardly surprisingly, further confederate aid for the royalist war-effort did not materialize.

SUMMER OFFENSIVE IN ULSTER

In June 1644 some 1,600 fully armed soldiers under the command of Alasdair MacColla finally left Ireland. These veterans joined forces with Montrose (see picture on p. 52) and between the summer of 1644 and September 1645 had a dramatic impact on the course of the Scottish Civil War (discussed in Chapter 2). In Ireland, however, the success of the expeditionary force brought the Catholic party little immediate military reward. Although 1,400 Scottish soldiers retreated back across the North Channel to protect their homes, a sizeable force remained in Ulster. Any attempt to use military might to oust the remaining covenanters foundered as Antrim and Castlehaven bickered over who should act as supreme commander of all the confederate forces. As a result, instead of a well-organized two-pronged attack against the Scots, the confederate Ulster offensive over the summer of 1644 was uncoordinated and ineffective, leaving Munro free to campaign unmolested in Counties Down, Cavan, and Monaghan throughout June and July. When the two sides finally met outside Armagh late in July the confederates declined battle and retreated to winter quarters in October. Moreover the need to put into the field simultaneously the expeditionary force and four provincial armies put enormous strain on confederate Ireland's resources. Finally, although the upheavals in Scotland prevented the Scots, who from this point periodically experienced logistical problems, from taking the offensive, this limited feat was only achieved through Antrim's enormously costly expedition, which the confederates had to fund single-handed.

THE GLAMORGAN TREATY

Military defeat in England, first at Marston Moor (July 1644) and then at Naseby (June 1645), strengthened Charles I's resolve to secure immediate and substantial support from Ireland. 'It hath pleased God by many successless misfortunes to reduce my affairs of late from a very prosperous condition to so low an ebb as to be a perfect trial of all men's integrities to me', the king informed Ormond shortly after Naseby, 'and I do principly rely upon you for utmost assistance in my present hazards.'[42] As it was, he had already instructed the earl of Glamorgan, a prominent Welsh Catholic noble, to secure Irish troops for royalist service in return for religious concessions. Glamorgan enjoyed considerable success and in August the confederates, in return for guarantees of complete tolerance for Catholics and other significant religious concessions, agreed to supply Charles I with 10,000 troops. Ultimately the publication in London of the secret terms of the treaty forced both the king and Ormond to repudiate it and in an attempt to salvage the situation Ormond had Glamorgan arrested on 26 December.

In any event the nuncio, Rinuccini, who reached Kilkenny on 12 November, swiftly rejected the 'Glamorgan Treaty' on the grounds that he was unsatisfied with the provisions made for the Catholic religion and because he feared—quite reasonably—that Glamorgan had insufficient powers to implement them. However, he was also aware of Sir Kenelm Digby's mission to Rome on behalf of Queen Henrietta Maria, which resulted on 20 November 1645 in a treaty, known as the 'Roman Treaty', between the pope and Digby. This proved far more favourable to Catholicism than the Glamorgan Treaty since it allowed freedom of worship for the Catholic Church, the abolition of the penal laws, the establishment of an independent parliament, and freedom for Catholics to hold high-ranking civil and military positions. Hardly surprisingly, Rinuccini wanted the Roman Treaty to be accepted in Ireland and so negotiations with the royalists began afresh. A further agreement was finally concluded between Rinuccini and Glamorgan on 20 December.

FACTIONALISM

However, Glamorgan's arrest the following week and Ormond's immediate repudiation of his negotiations with the nuncio threw Kilkenny politics into disarray and further divided the confederates who, instead of concentrating on winning the war, became increasingly factionalized. Since the conclusion of the cease-fire in September 1643, the vast majority of confederates faced the dilemma of how to reconcile their loyalty to the king with their devotion to the Church and how to formulate a moderate settlement which would, in the words of the earl of Clanricard, not cut 'too deep an incision . . . into old sores'.[43] However, it proved impossible to 'staunch and heal the bleeding wounds of this unhappy kingdom'[44] largely because religious differences formed the main stumbling-block to the conclusion of any permanent peace between the confederates and the royalists which, in turn, undermined any real chance of defeating their common enemy, the English Parliament. As the war progressed, some confederates (often Ormond's kinsmen or clients), proved increasingly eager to conclude a settlement with the king, even if it jeopardized the future safety of the Catholic religion. This group—the 'peace party'—held sway over the Supreme Council and clashed constantly with those who favoured complete freedom for the Catholic religion as the inevitable price of any compromise with the royalists. These confederates—the 'clerical party'—included the bishops, returned exiles, and dispossessed landowners usually of 'Old Irish' or Gaelic descent and after 1645 this group turned to the papal nuncio and, to a lesser extent, to Owen Roe O'Neill, for guidance. From the end of 1644 a further interest group, which included individuals who were both pro-peace and pro-clergy, emerged which sought to preserve confederate unity and to seek a compromise between the clerical and peace factions. These moderates, led by the distinguished lawyer Nicholas Plunkett, came to the fore late in 1646 and held the initiative until early 1648 when defeat on the battlefield and the outbreak of civil war within the confederate movement frustrated their attempts to secure a settlement which protected their religious and political position within the context of the Stuart monarchies.[45]

BENBURB

Despite these internal divisions, the confederate armies enjoyed considerable successes throughout 1646. An intensification of the war in England enabled them to capture a number of the parliamentary strongholds, especially Bunratty Castle in County Limerick. Their greatest victory, however, was the battle of Benburb where on 5 June Owen Roe O'Neill and his army of 5,000 at last routed the Scottish army under Munro (discussed in Chapter 2). This was the military highlight of the Confederate Wars and it ensured that Munro's forces (now reduced to c.3,500) no longer represented a threat. Ultimately, Benburb merely served to prolong the war in Ireland, for instead of capitalizing on his victory and ridding Ulster of the Scottish and the rest of Ireland of the parliamentary garrisons, O'Neill marched south to Kilkenny to suborn those who favoured a peace with the king.

THE FIRST ORMOND PEACE

Against the wishes of Rinuccini, the peace faction finally came to terms with the Irish royalists in the summer of 1646. The declaration of the 'Ormond Peace', however, further divided an already fragmented Irish political nation into 'a woeful spectacle, cantonized into several sundry factions, drawing all divers ways, and driving on several interests'.[46] The ranks of the Irish confederates became irremediably split between the peace party, who would have been satisfied with tacit toleration and the freedom to worship quietly while remaining loyal subjects to the crown, and the clerical party, who were loath to settle with a perfidious king without first securing formal freedom of worship for the Catholic religion.

The crisis reached a climax early in August when Rinuccini and the clerical faction convened a legatine synod at Waterford which proclaimed that confederate Catholics adhering to the peace had broken the Oath of Association and declared the Ormond Peace unacceptable. On 1 September the Waterford synod went further and excommunicated all who favoured the Ormond Peace, and two weeks later Rinuccini arrived at Kilkenny to dictate the terms for an acceptable agreement and ordered the arrest of those who favoured a peace. On 26 September the clerical faction appointed a new supreme council—free from Ormond's influence—and ordered the confederate armies to march on Dublin. Possession of the capital would have placed the confederates in a superior position to the parliamentarians, who were their only real opponents by the winter of 1646. Although their armies reached Lucan, possession of Dublin—defended by a force of 3,000–4,000 troops—eluded them largely because O'Neill and Preston failed to act decisively, ending in the latter entering into secret negotiations with Ormond. As a result the confederates abandoned the siege and lost a great opportunity to take the city and thereby prevent Ormond from handing it over to a parliamentary army.

DUNGAN'S HILL AND KNOCKANAUSS

The factional divisions among the confederates were perpetuated and exacerbated by defeat on the battlefield. In June 1647, after long preparation, Ormond handed over Dublin and all the remaining royalist strongholds to a parliamentary army of 1,400 foot and 600 horse under the command of Colonel Michael Jones and the following month, after securing favourable financial terms for himself, withdrew first to England and later to France. For their part, the confederates launched a campaign against the parliamentarians, and Preston, after taking Carlow in May and Naas and Maynooth in July, decided to invest Trim and thereby put pressure on Dublin. Reinforced by Protestant troops from Drogheda and Ulster, Jones first relieved Trim and then moved against Preston (see map on p. 99). The two armies met at Dungan's Hill on 8 August, where Preston's force of 6,000 men was virtually annihilated despite being strengthened by a significant number of veteran Highlanders under Angus MacDonald of Glengarry. Jones then marched into south-west Ulster before returning to Dublin on 17 August, having cleared eastern Leinster of confederates. In October he took the offensive again, proceeding against O'Neill's forces in northern Leinster and placing his own men in important strongholds along the River Boyne. These brief but carefully planned campaigns had effectively destroyed the Army of Leinster, the country's 'national' force, and shifted the military balance in Parliament's favour.

The military fortunes of the confederates fared no better elsewhere. Reinforced with English supplies and soldiers, Inchiquin led 4,500 troops against Dungarvan (which fell in May) and in September he sacked Cashel and wreaked havoc throughout County Tipperary, destroying £20,000 worth of corn around Cahir alone and reducing the inhabitants of Upper Ormond 'to eat their garrans and plough-horses'.[47] When Inchiquin heard that Theobald Taaffe, together with 1,200 horse and 7,000 foot (including a contingent of veteran Redshanks),

Michael Jones (d. 1649)

The son of a Welsh bishop who had settled in Ireland during the early seventeenth century, Jones defected from the service of the king to that of Parliament after the declaration of the 1643 cease-fire with the confederates. He distinguished himself as a cavalry commander in England. After June 1647 he took over command of Dublin from Ormond and immediately launched an offensive against the confederates, winning a major victory at Dungan's Hill (1 August 1647). More important still was his decimation of Ormond's army at Rathmines (2 August 1649) which enabled Oliver Cromwell and his troops to land unmolested near Dublin two weeks later. One of the most talented military commanders to serve in Ireland during the 1640s, Jones fell ill shortly after the abortive siege of Waterford. He died early in December 1649, much to Cromwell's distress.

had taken the field near Mallow, he immediately prepared for combat. On 13 November, at the battle of Knockanauss (County Cork), Inchiquin's army routed the Army of Munster after two hours of heated combat. As far as the confederates were concerned, incompetence and lack of decisive leadership were the hallmarks of the battle. After Alasdair MacColla had launched his classic Highland charge against the parliamentarians, his men dispersed to loot the baggage train. By the time they had regrouped the Munster cavalry and Taaffe had fled, leaving MacColla and his men to be put to the sword by Inchiquin. The parliamentarians now controlled all of the major towns in the province except Limerick, Waterford, and Clonmel. Only the outbreak of the Second English Civil War in May 1648 prevented Jones and Inchiquin from continuing their onslaught against the confederates and a shortage of supplies instead forced them to resort to slash-and-burn tactics.

FOREIGN AID

Confederate defeat on the battlefield had immediate political repercussions. According to the papal nuncio, the eighth confederate General Assembly, which convened on 12 November 1647 at Kilkenny, was faced by 'a country not only divided but full of suspicion of treachery, [and] without a chief ruler capable of cutting the knot of difficulty'.[48] The confederates had three options open to them. First, they could continue the war, alone, against the English Parliament. Second, they could invite one of the European Catholic powers—Spain, France, or the papacy—to become the 'protector' of Ireland in return for military and financial support. Finally, they could persuade Charles I or his son to continue, with confederate support, the royalist war-effort from Ireland in return for certain concessions over religion, either in person or through a Catholic deputy who would rule Ireland on their behalf. The military disasters of the late summer and autumn of 1647 forced the confederates to give serious consideration to all three possibilities.

To begin with, the assembly debated whether to secure the support of the queen and prince of Wales, or to invite either Pope Innocent X, Louis XIV of France, or Philip IV of Spain to become Ireland's saviour. Certainly France and Spain welcomed these overtures. After 1643 both nations had recruited large numbers of troops in Ireland for their own continental war-efforts and, as the 1640s progressed, the desire to become Ireland's protector and to interfere directly in Irish politics became a marked objective of French and Spanish diplomacy for, as one foreign agent noted, 'whoever protects Ireland will control it'.[49] Ideally, France wanted Charles I to rule Ireland; but failing that, Cardinal Mazarin wished Ireland to become a French satellite state (like Catalonia or Savoy), and his agents suggested to the General Assembly that Louis XIV should 'not only become arbiter but absolute master of all the affairs of the confederates'.[50] In contrast, Philip IV, while not opposed to Charles I, was a staunch supporter of the clerical faction and wanted Ireland to return to the Catholic fold. Predictably this destabilized domestic politics and further divided the Irish political nation into the 'Francophiles' (largely Old English and pro-Ormond), who wanted to aid Charles I in return for the best political, religious, and tenurial concessions they could extort, and those (largely Gaelic Irish) who favoured Spain and advocated abandoning the king altogether and making Catholic Ireland, with the aid of foreign powers, impregnable to invasion from England.

A ROYALIST REVIVAL

In the end the assembly opted to invite the prince of Wales either to come in person to Ireland as their protector or to nominate a Catholic lord deputy. On 24 December 1647, after appointing agents to discuss this further with the royal court in exile, the assembly broke up. In the spring of 1648 these confederate agents met with the queen and leading royalists (including Ormond) near Paris and set in motion an ambitious plan, which was supported by the French, to use Ireland 'as the great and principal instrument to reduce Scotland and England'.[51] According to one well-informed observer this involved Ormond's return to Ireland in order to unite the Irish confederate factions and to join forces with the 'Baron [Inchiquin] and the Presbyterians in England, Scotland and Ireland', who 'all form against the present parliament and the Independents'.[52] Once the forces of Clanricard, Inchiquin, Taaffe, Preston, and O'Neill had been amalgamated, their army was to take Dublin and then send an expeditionary force under the prince of Wales's command to invade England and Scotland.

Back in Ireland this royalist revival crystallized with Inchiquin's declaration for the king on 3 April and with the conclusion of a truce with the confederates on 20 May. At this point the Scottish 'Engagers' also made a tentative alliance with the Irish royalists and with those confederates who favoured a peace with Ormond and the Stuarts. This coincided with the revival of the king's cause in England: towards the end of April English royalists seized Berwick and Carlisle while the following month a rebellion broke out in Kent and the navy, stationed in the Downs, declared for Charles. The Second English Civil War had begun.

CIVIL WAR WITHIN CONFEDERATE RANKS

These developments alarmed Rinuccini and other members of the clerical party who tried to sabotage the royalist design to unite Ireland under Ormond's authority by excommunicating the supporters of the 'Inchiquin Truce'. On this occasion the Supreme Council was not intimidated by the nuncio and in retaliation appealed to Rome against the excommunication. So by the summer of 1648 there were two *ad hoc* alliances among the Catholics: on the one hand stood a coalition of royalists, led by Inchiquin, and of more moderate confederates who enjoyed the support of what remained of the Army of Leinster; while on the other were the nuncio and the clerical party, who depended for military assistance exclusively on Owen Roe O'Neill and the Army of Ulster. Just as conflicting loyalties to the king and the Kirk divided—and ultimately destroyed—the covenanting movement, so too the desire to remain loyal to Charles I, without compromising their Catholicism, tore the confederates apart.

The battle-lines between the 'moderate', pro-Ormond party and the 'violent', pro-nuncio faction were formalized on 11 June when Owen Roe O'Neill and the Army of Ulster declared war on the Supreme Council and marched on the confederate capital. Having failed to take Kilkenny by force O'Neill and his troops wreaked havoc throughout the county for much of August until the combined forces of Preston and Inchiquin forced them to retreat. Thus, instead of concentrating on getting rid of their parliamentary opponents, the confederates devoted precious resources to defending Leinster and Connacht from the Army of Ulster. This is turn enabled Jones to campaign into Catholic-held territory, destroying where possible the harvest, and allowed George Monck to seize Carrickfergus, Belfast, and Coleraine in September from their small Scottish garrisons.

A *rapprochement* also occurred between the clerical party, represented by Father Edmund O'Reilly, vicar-general of Dublin and later Catholic archbishop of Armagh, and the parliamentarians, represented by Henry Jones, Protestant bishop of Clogher (Michael Jones's brother). By mid-November the two sides were 'in daily treaty'.[53] Jones's willingness to parley can be explained by his shortage of supplies and his determination to prevent the Army of Ulster from joining with those forces under Ormond and the Irish confederates in a combined assault on the capital. Members of the clerical party also initiated talks with the English Parliament. In London Patrick Crelly, Cistercian abbot of Newry and a supporter of Antrim's, dealt directly with a committee of Independents.

THE SECOND ORMOND PEACE

The defeat of the king's forces in Lancashire (August 1648) and the subsequent overthrow of the royalists in England, combined with their demise in Scotland, greatly increased the importance of Ormond's mission in Ireland, since any hope of continuing the royalist war-effort in the other two kingdoms now depended exclusively on the ability of the lord lieutenant to unite the divided factions in Ireland under the authority of the king (now a prisoner of his English opponents). Ormond finally landed at Cork on 30 September with arms (paid for by the French) for 4,000 foot and 1,000 horse, and immediately joined forces with Inchiquin. Almost at once he secured the full backing of the ninth, and final, General Assembly, which had met on 4 September in order to negotiate a new peace with Ormond. The nuncio's followers refused to take their seats or even to recognize the assembly, which they claimed had been unlawfully convened; in retaliation the assembly condemned the nuncio's followers and declared Owen Roe O'Neill a traitor. Interestingly the output from the confederate press in Kilkenny increased very significantly during these months as the peace party tried to whip up popular support and to undermine O'Neill. One broadsheet of 13 August threatened to punish severely any person 'who shall join with, or adhere unto, supply, relieve, or assist the said Owen O'Neyll'.[54]

On 17 January 1649 the Second Ormond Peace was signed. In return for supplying the king with 18,000 troops, the lord lieutenant verbally agreed to 'give unto the Roman Catholics full assurance that they shall not be molested in the possession of the churches and church livings, or of the exercise of their respective jurisdictions as they now exercise the same' until the king heard their case in a free parliament.[55] All attainders against Catholics issued since 7 August 1641 were to be declared null and void, and there was to be some provision for the security of Catholic property. By the treaty, the confederate government was formally dissolved and twelve 'commissioners of trust' were appointed to mediate between Ormond and the confederates. News of the Second Ormond Peace increased parliamentary fears in London that Ireland would now become the hub of royalist activity. The arrival of Prince Rupert in Kinsale in February 1649 fuelled these worries and put additional pressure on Jones who was becoming increasingly isolated as the confederates regained many of the strongholds he had captured in his 1647 offensive. By June 1649 only Dublin, Drogheda, and Derry remained outside royalist control. In July Drogheda fell and Ormond prepared to besiege Dublin.

Only Charles I's alliance with the Scots had prevented an army being sent to reduce the rebellious Irish in 1648; now in the spring of 1649, with Scotland temporarily subdued and royalist resistance in England totally crushed, Parliament was at last ready to deal with the 'Irish problem' and commissioned its most successful general, Oliver Cromwell, to lead an expeditionary force across the Irish Sea.

War at Sea

As the Catholic war-effort disintegrated on land, their naval strength posed, especially in the wake of the naval revolt of May 1648, a very real threat to Parliament. While no major sea battles were fought between the Irish and their parliamentary enemies during the Wars of the Three Kingdoms, the war at sea nevertheless formed an important dimension of the conflict and naval encounters between confederate-sponsored privateers and enemy Irish, Scottish, and English shipping were both frequent and bitter (also see Chapter 5).

PRIVATEERS

By the mid-1640s cosmopolitan privateering communities had established themselves in Wexford and Waterford which were made up of Flemish, Irish, and even English and French privateers. Their ranks were swollen by the exodus of privateers from Dunkirk after October 1646, when the port fell to the French. A contemporary estimated that in Wexford alone that there were 'twenty-one ships or (as popularly called) frigates'. This figure had roughly doubled by the end of the decade and there were still 'about forty good vessels in the harbour' at Wexford when it was stormed by Cromwell in October 1649; while other frigates were stationed at Waterford.[56] A more reliable figure for the size of the fleet would therefore be between fifty and sixty warships.

The privateering flotilla consisted of relatively small ships which were heavily armed and manned. The *Harp*, owned by Captain Stafford, was a frigate of fifty tons and had five pieces of ordnance together with forty seamen; Vanderkipp's *St Francis* was a frigate of 200 tons and was equipped with eighteen guns, four of which were brass. This made them effective instruments of offence and enabled them both to capture and hold the prize itself, along with its cargo. Their effectiveness was further enhanced by the frigates' habit of hunting in 'wolf packs'. For instance, a parliamentarian commander complained early in 1648 that 'eleven sail of Irish together', sighted between Tor Bay and the Isle of Wight, had 'divided into three squadrons, two consisting of three ships in sum, the other of five', intending to pick off any isolated parliamentary vessels patrolling the Channel.[57]

The privateers maintained an active presence in the St George's Channel, cruising the south-east coast of Ireland between Wexford and Dublin in order to intercept merchant shipping from Whitehaven, Egremont, Liverpool, Chester, Aberystwyth, Milford Haven, and Bristol. By November 1646 it was feared that so many frigates from Wexford and Waterford had 'overspread the seas between Dublin and Chester, that thereby all intercourse between Dublin and Chester and Liverpool and other sea ports of England would be interrupted'.[58] Others attacked the Dutch and Scottish fishing fleets off the Western Isles of Scotland and interrupted communications between Scotland and the north of Ireland. They also patrolled the North Sea and picked off merchantmen trading with Aberdeen, Leith, Berwick, Newcastle, Hull, Great Yarmouth, and Ipswich. Further south the privateers lurked off the coast of Cornwall, particularly between Lands End and the Scilly Isles and took ships bound to and from Bristol, Plymouth, Torbay, Lyme Regis, and Weymouth. The most lucrative prizes in English waters, however, were to be found in the English Channel and, more particularly, in the stretch of sea between Dover and the mouth of the Thames which simply teemed with rich trading vessels sailing to, and from, London or the international entrepôt of Dover. In 1644 one privateer took, near the mouth of the Thames, an English ship of 400 tons, armed with twenty-four guns, *en route* from Amsterdam with £3,000 worth of silver, 400 barrels of powder, and 'great store' of muskets, carbines, and arms on board.

When parliamentary warships stepped up their protection of these profitable waters, the privateers merely sailed further afield in search of booty. By the autumn of 1649 it was even rumoured that Irish men-of-war had ventured into the Mediterranean 'and that more are to follow to take there what English merchants they can'.[59] No wonder Prince Rupert, who now commanded the royal navy, sought refuge in Kinsale in the spring of 1649 and hoped to join forces with the most successful privateering fleet in the king's service; fortunately for Parliament Admiral Blake (see picture on p. 188), prevented them from jeopardizing supply lines to Ireland on the eve of the Cromwellian conquest.

Cromwellian Conquest

Prior to leaving for Ireland Cromwell secured from Parliament an army of 12,000 veterans, a war-chest of £100,000, a considerable arsenal—fifty-six great guns (including four whole cannon and five demi-cannon) and 600 barrels of powder —together with 900 carriage and draft horses and the supplies needed to feed and clothe his army. Throughout the spring of 1649 the parliamentarians had also worked hard to frustrate any reconciliation between the two warring confederate factions and for this reason their commander in Ulster, George Monck (see picture on p. 327), concluded a truce with O'Neill in May 1649. In addition, according to Clarendon, Cromwell also 'entertained agents and spies, as well friars as others, amongst the Irish' who provided him with intelligence on developments within Ireland.[60]

RATHMINES, DROGHEDA, AND WEXFORD

Cromwell's greatest stroke of good fortune came before he had even set foot in Ireland when on 2 August 1649 Michael Jones routed Ormond's army at the battle of Rathmines. In mid-June, after capturing Drogheda and Dundalk, Ormond, with 4,000 foot and 700 horse, had laid siege to Dublin. Despite having half of this number to defend the city Jones attacked Ormond's camp at Rathmines, capturing Ormond's artillery and baggage train and shattering his army. This 'astonishing mercy', as Cromwell dubbed the victory, enabled his army to land unmolested near Dublin on 15 August. Almost at once they moved against the strategically sited town of Drogheda, which was defended by a garrison of 3,000 (later described as 'the flower of all their army') under the command of the English Catholic veteran Sir Arthur Aston. On 10 September Cromwell bombarded the medieval fortifications with eleven siege-guns and quickly breached the walls. As dusk fell on the 11th his infantry stormed the town and in the blood bath which ensued roughly 3,500 soldiers, civilians, and clergy lost their lives, including Aston who was beaten to death with his own wooden leg by soldiers who believed that it was filled with gold. Parliamentary losses numbered 150. Cromwell immediately interpreted the victory as 'a righteous judgment of God upon these barbarous wretches, who have imbrued their hands in so much innocent blood'.[61] Having dispatched Colonels Robert Venables and Theophilus Jones with 5,000 men north (they went on to capture Carlingford, Newry, Lisburn, and Belfast), Cromwell turned his attention to the south and especially to the destruction of the Irish flotilla of privateers stationed in Wexford. He

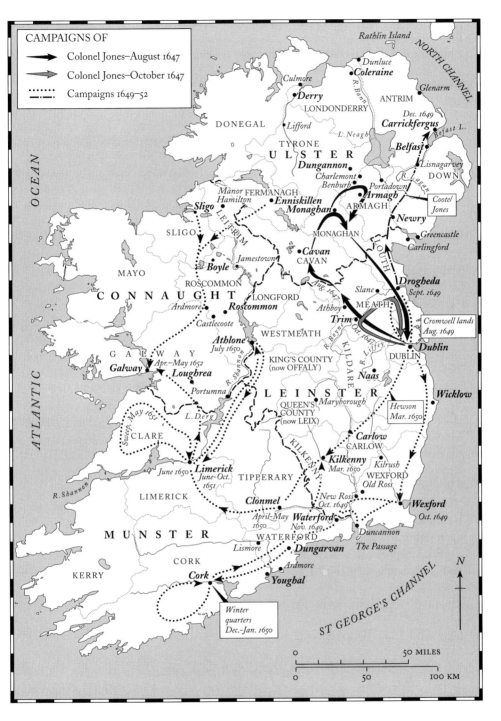

Parliamentary campaigns in Ireland

appeared before the town on 2 October with an effective force of roughly 6,000 men. On the 11th, using eight heavy guns and two mortars, his forces blasted down the walls of the castle, which had not been reinforced with earthworks, at the southern end of the town (defended by 4,800 men). Then, as a surrender was being negotiated, Cromwell's soldiers launched a bloody assault which left 1,500–2,000 dead. The following day Cromwell justified the sack of the town as a punishment for 'the cruelties which they [the privateers] had exercised upon the lives of divers poor Protestants'.[62]

The blood-letting at Drogheda and Wexford spread terror throughout Ireland and the following week New Ross surrendered without a fight giving Cromwell access to the Munster ports. Only poor weather, which frustrated attempts to move his heavy artillery by land; disease, which claimed an increasing number of his soldiers (including Michael Jones); combined with a determined defence by the royalists frustrated Cromwell's attempts to take Duncannon and Waterford in November and December. In March 1650 Cromwell moved against Kilkenny which, after the walls had been breached, surrendered on the 27th. He then turned against Clonmel, which under the command of Hugh Dubh O'Neill put up a fierce defence, massacring 1,500 parliamentarians in the process, but ultimately a shortage of ammunition forced him to abandon the town on 18 May. With the outbreak of the Third Civil War in England the following month Cromwell left the completion of the conquest of Ireland in the hands of his son-in-law Henry Ireton.

By the spring of 1650 the parliamentarians had penetrated deeply into Ormond's territory. The fact that his army had become mutinous and was plague-ridden exacerbated his already dire position. The defeat of his remaining field army, the 6,000-strong Army of Ulster, under the command of the politically astute but militarily inexperienced Ever MacMahon, bishop of Clogher, at Scarrifhollis in County Donegal (21 June) and the subsequent collapse of the remaining garrisons in Leinster and Munster, effectively discredited him. After appointing the marquis of Clanricard as his deputy on 6 December he left for France. Despite this and continued internal bickering over how their war-effort should be conducted, the Irish fought on. Even though the last formal capitulation occurred at Cloughoughter, County Cavan on 27 April 1653, the capture of Limerick on 27 October 1651 and finally of Galway on 12 April 1652 effectively completed the Cromwellian conquest of Ireland.[63]

Conclusion

In just under three years the parliamentary army succeeded in uniting Ireland under one ruler, something the royalist, Scottish, and confederate armies had failed to achieve over the previous nine years. The Catholic insurgents had proved unable to take advantage of a unique set of favourable circumstances in

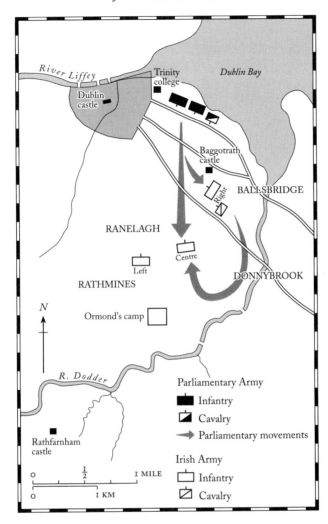

Battle plan of Rathmines

order to win freedom of religious worship and lasting political autonomy within a tripartite Stuart monarchy. Their failure stemmed in part from inept military leadership which had prevented the exploitation of opportunities for strategic success against forces loyal to Parliament in 1643–4 and 1646–7, and eventually gave first Michael Jones and then Cromwell the opportunity to win major battles in 1647 and 1649, paving the way for the English occupation of Ireland. Ultimately, however, military weakness merely reflected the deep-seated political divisions within the Catholic polity, something which mystified foreign observers. The French ambassador in London reported back to Paris late in 1648 that

What really surprises the majority of those who contemplate the affairs of Ireland is to see that people of the same nation and of the same religion—who are well aware that the resolution to exterminate them totally has already been taken—should differ so strongly in their private hostilities; that their zeal for religion, the preservation of their country and their own self interest are not sufficient to make them lay down—at least, for a short time—the passions which divide them one from the other.[64]

Just as in Scotland and in England, these passions centred on their relationship with Charles I. The Irish confederates, like the Scottish covenanters, had failed to reach a satisfactory settlement with their treacherous monarch and, as a result, lost their wars just as he had lost his.

4

THE CIVIL WARS IN ENGLAND

IAN GENTLES

Recruitment[1]

In a country where most of the population deplored civil war, and wished to fight for neither side, how did king and Parliament recruit the armies they needed to wage their struggle—not only recruit about 140,000 men between them, but arm, supply, and pay them as well? At first each side resorted to quasi-legal instruments: the Commission of Array for the king, and the Militia Ordinance for Parliament. Despatched to each county and city, the Commission of Array was a medieval Latin document inscribed on a parchment roll, and impressed with the Great Seal. It empowered the leading men to take charge of their county or city and arm it for the king. The Militia Ordinance was a statute lacking one vital element: the signature and seal of the king. It created committees in each county and major city, charged with raising forces for Parliament.

At first neither instrument was notably successful. When the king declared war against Parliament and raised his standard at Nottingham in August 1642 fewer than a thousand cavalry turned up. What really brought soldiers to the king were commissions to individual men to mobilize regular troops for service under him. While there must have been an element of coercion in all military recruitment, initially the royalist armies did not resort to conscription or 'impressment'. Parliament, which controlled the levers of central power, employed conscription almost from the beginning, while the king did not impress men on a large scale until the spring of 1644.[2] When constables went out to press men their preferred targets were bachelors, idle men, alehouse haunters, vagabonds, and criminals. While parish officers were keen to shovel the dregs of society into the army, county committees insisted that recruits be able-bodied. Boys, the sick, and the aged were not acceptable. It was servants, apprentices, and labourers—landless men still too young to be householders—who were most frequently impressed.

Important as they were, the county trained bands were but one source of manpower for the king. A number of volunteer regiments were mobilized by leading royalists, often out of their own estates. By mid-October 1642 when Charles called his forces together at Bridgnorth they consisted of 6,000 foot, 2,000 horse, and 1,500 dragoons. At the battle of Edgehill, less than two weeks later, the royalist army was probably around 15,000 men (2,800 horse, 11,000 foot, 1,000 dragoons, and perhaps 100 in the train of artillery). The strength of the parliamentary army was similar: 2,150 horse, 12,000 foot, and 720 dragoons.

ARMY SIZE

The armies of both sides were like mushrooms, shooting up almost overnight, and then disappearing even more quickly. During the winter of 1642–3, for example, the earl of Essex's army, with little pay and nothing to do, shrank to a third of its size. Yet by April 1643, when he advanced on Reading, it had swollen to 16,000 foot and 3,000 horse. With that garrison's capitulation one-third of Essex's men promptly departed. By July two-thirds of his army were reported sick, dead, or missing. While the horse had remained fairly steady at 2,500, the foot had collapsed to only 3,000 able-bodied men.[3] In the royalist armies it was normal for the infantry to go home at the end of each campaigning season.[4] However, the big recruitment campaign of the spring of 1645 resulted in the Oxford army being restored to a strength of about 9,500. In addition, George Goring was at Taunton with 5,000 foot and 5,000 horse, while in Wales Charles Gerard had recruited a field force of rather less than 20,000 foot and 700 horse.

In the parliamentary armies it became an increasingly familiar pattern for large numbers to depart after a major victory. Not only did this happen to Essex after Reading, it was also the experience of Ferdinando Lord Fairfax's northern army after Marston Moor in 1644, and the New Model Army after Naseby. The New Model had been given a targeted strength of 22,000 besides officers in the spring of 1645. The goal was quickly reached, but after Naseby where 17,000 had been engaged, about 4,000 of the foot went home to dispose of their rich booty. Victories were fewer on the royalist side, but Prince Rupert, for example, underwent the chastening experience of large-scale desertions after his capture of Bristol in 1643.[5]

Desertion, far more than death on the battlefield, was the reason for the haemorrhaging of numbers on each side. Men frequently 'straggled' before they even saw their first military action. Once in the army lack of pay, clothing, or arms could cause them to steal away or refuse to march. Defeat in battle could trigger large-scale desertions, with many infantry immediately taking up service with the enemy. At Lostwithiel in September 1644, for example, several thousand of Essex's infantry enlisted with the king after the signing of the articles of surrender. After Naseby many of the king's infantry changed sides. Not surprisingly, impressed men were likelier to desert than volunteers. Another headache for the commanders of both sides was the reluctance of men to march outside their county or region. The king failed to persuade any of the Yorkshire gentry to follow him to Nottingham in the summer of 1642. Both Essex and Sir William Waller were plagued with the cry 'home, home!' from the London trained bands who became increasingly nervous the further they found themselves from the capital—at Gloucester (September 1643) under Essex, for example, or Basing (November 1644), and Cropredy Bridge (29 June 1644) under Waller.

RECRUITING GROUNDS

Where were recruits obtained? It was commonly said that Wales and the Marches were 'the nursery of the king's infantry'. Prince Rupert got large numbers from this region and the west Midlands. Sir Ralph Hopton recruited a small army of about 3,000 in the west (Cornwall, Devon, Dorset, and Somerset). The Catholic earl of Derby sent significant numbers from Lancashire to the king's main army in Oxford, while the earl of Newcastle recruited his Whitecoats mainly in Northumberland, Durham, and Yorkshire. By the time he defeated Ferdinando Lord Fairfax at Adwalton Moor (30 June 1643) Newcastle had an army of well over 10,000, of which 3,000 were cavalry. London's population of nearly 400,000 furnished a major recruiting ground for Parliament, as did the agriculturally rich counties of Kent, East Anglia, and the east Midlands. In Yorkshire Ferdinando Lord Fairfax managed to mobilize an army that grew slowly from 900 in 1642 to 8,000 by early 1645. In East Anglia the earl of Manchester was authorized to raise at first 14,000 and later 21,000 men. In reality his infantry, nearly all conscripted, never rose above 6,600, his dragoons 263, and his cavalry 3,500.

FOREIGN AID

Both sides received significant accessions of strength from outside the kingdom. The king suffered a grave propaganda setback from his employment of French mercenaries, perhaps four regiments in all between 1643 and 1645.[6] The cease-fire or 'cessation of arms' (September 1643) in Ireland enabled the marquis of Ormond (see picture on p. 76) to ship men from the king's Irish army. The bulk of these troops were Protestants, while the Catholics who served tended to be of Old English stock; none of the officers was a confederate. Moreover, many of the Irish troops were stationed in Welsh garrisons, and took little part in active fighting.[7] By the spring of 1645 at any rate, there were only 1,200 Irish veterans left in England to bolster the royalist army. The opprobrium that the king suffered from his importation of Irish troops cost him more than any benefit he gained from their presence.

What is often downplayed in accounts of the First English Civil War is the absolutely crucial role played by the Scottish army on the parliamentary side (discussed in Chapter 2). They were at least as cordially hated in the north of England where they were quartered, as were the Irish in Wales, Cheshire, and the west Midlands.[8] Thanks to the treaty negotiated between Parliament and the Scottish Estates at the end of 1643, 21,500 Scots troops entered England under the earl of Leven (see picture on p. 47) in January of the next year. But for their presence at Marston Moor on 2 July 1644 the royalist victories of 1643 might easily not have been reversed. Yet because the Scots were Protestant, and had never been hated to the same degree as the Irish, Parliament paid no discernible propaganda price for its importation of foreign troops.

PAY SCALES

Pay scales were similar in all armies throughout the civil war period: eight pence a day for the private foot-soldier; a shilling and sixpence for the dragoon; and two shillings or two and sixpence for the horse trooper. These sums were not enough to cover the cost of food and lodging for men and horses. Officers were much more generously remunerated. A captain of foot got eight shillings a day; a colonel £1. At the top of the scale, the commander-in-chief in most armies could expect £10 per day. Each higher officer, it should be remembered, was expected to maintain several horses and a small personal staff out of his pay.

WOMEN AND CHILDREN

By convention troop figures did not include officers, who normally comprised ten to twenty per cent, or (in the royalist armies) even more, of the rank and file. Nor is it often remembered that trailing behind the main body of combatants in every army was a substantial 'tail' of non-combatants, mostly women and children, who attended to the physical needs of the soldiers. Women were 'a normal part of European armies, at least from the fourteenth until well into the nineteenth century'.[9] Many of the non-combatants were the soldiers' families; others were whores; still others were nurses, cooks, laundresses, and sutlers trading in meat, drink, and luxuries not part of the regular supply system. What Sir James Turner wrote a quarter of a century later, was probably true of the civil wars:

women are great helpers to armies, to their husbands, especially those of the lower condition, neither should they be rashly banished out of armies; sent away they may be sometimes for weighty considerations. They provide, buy and dress their husbands' meat, when their husbands are on duty or newly come from it; they bring in fuel for fire; and wash their linens, and in such manner of employments a soldier's wife may be helpful to others, and gain money to her husband and herself. Especially they are useful in camps and leaguers, being permitted (which should not be refused them) to go some miles from the camp to buy victuals and other necessaries.[10]

Or, as General Robert Venables commented about his expedition to the West Indies in 1655, 'had more women gone, I suppose that many had not perished as they did for want of care and attendance'.[11]

Mortality

Charles Carlton (see Chapter 8) estimates that over 34,000 parliamentary and 50,000 royalist soldiers were killed in England during the civil wars and

Interregnum (1642–60), with almost all the deaths occurring before 1649. These figures may be on the high side, but his estimate for deaths from disease—roughly 100,000—may be too low. Military historians believe that in the seventeenth century only ten to twenty-five per cent of military deaths were due to battle.[12] Men who had been crowded together in a strange place, ill-clad, poorly housed, and indifferently fed, were extremely vulnerable to those epidemic diseases for which early-modern medicine knew no cure: the 'bloody flux' (dysentery and typhus), 'spotted [or 'camp-'] fever' (typhus or gaol fever), and the bubonic plague. Disease was most devastating in winter and during sieges, when supplies of fresh food and water dwindled to almost nothing, and men found themselves dining off rancid horse- and dog-meat.

If disease relentlessly thinned the ranks, it was officers who suffered the highest mortality in battle. Recent research indicates that forty per cent of the colonels and over twenty per cent of the lieutenant-colonels in the earl of Newcastle's northern army died during the English Civil Wars and Interregnum. The explanation for the high death rate was simple: regimental field officers customarily fought at the head of their regiments. Superficial sword and dagger thrusts to the upper or lower body could often be healed, but an abdominal wound was almost always fatal since peritonitis would afflict the intestines. Penetration by musket-balls and pikes was similarly lethal, producing as it did sepsis and gangrene. While it was standard for each army to have a physician-general and an apothecary-general, these men seem to have attended only to the higher officers. Most regiments, however, could boast a surgeon with a well-equipped medical chest, and two mates. Able to dress cuts and scaldings, seventeenth-century surgeons had also developed considerable skill in setting broken bones and performing amputations. Many lives were also saved by simple nursing in combination with clean dry bedding and an adequate diet.

Social Origins, Age, and Promotion

ROYALIST COMMANDERS

Both king and Parliament aspired to have field armies under aristocratic and gentry leadership. As the wars progressed, however, the social status of officers tended to decline, and the principle of preferment according to merit rather than social status carried the day. During its first two years the royalist army was the military expression of the hierarchical society it was called upon to defend. Of the six regional generals whom the king appointed at the beginning of the fighting season in 1643, five were the greatest royalist magnates of their regions: the earl of Newcastle (the six northern counties); the earl of Derby (Lancashire); the marquis of Hertford (Wiltshire, Hampshire, and the west of England); Lord Herbert, son of the marquis of Worcester (south-east Wales and its march comprising Monmouthshire, Breconshire, Glamorganshire, and Radnorshire); and the earl of Carbery (south-west Wales comprising Carmarthenshire, Cardiganshire, and Pembrokeshire). The sixth, Lord Capel (north Wales and Cheshire, Shropshire, and Worcestershire), was a powerful noble from the east of England who was appointed to a region that possessed no obvious native leader. In the king's Oxford army all officers from captain upward were of gentry or higher status. The typical colonel of foot was a baronet and product of the universities and Inns of Court. In the northern army under Newcastle all the colonels were initially of gentry or noble status, with a mean age of 35. After the initial dismal record of these regional magnates and their gentry followers, the principle of preferment according to merit soon asserted itself. More and more professionals and soldiers of fortune were taken on. Warlords such as the Princes Rupert and Maurice were entrusted with key commands, as were men such as Sir (later Lord) Ralph Hopton in Cornwall, Colonel George Goring, and Sir Marmaduke Langdale in the north, and Sir (later Lord) Jacob Astley at Oxford. Among Prince Rupert's protégés were John Lord Byron and Sir Gilbert Gerard, both members of distinguished military families who had seen continental service. Rather than preferring local men to lead, the king deliberately chose younger sons or gentry from districts distant from those that were placed under their rule. Nevertheless, at all times the direction of the royalist regiments was, as one military historian has observed, 'very much in the hands of solid and respectable gentry and peers',[13] the landed class in other words. A quarter of them had received higher education, but only thirty per cent were younger sons.

PARLIAMENTARY COMMANDERS

All this was in distinct contrast to the armies of Parliament. To be sure, Parliament in the beginning had conscientiously awarded its highest commands to men whose social status was comparable to that of the royalists: the earls of Essex, Bedford, and Manchester; Lords Willoughby and Brooke. However, their numbers remained pitifully small, and their leadership and administrative abilities were appalling. Essex, the commander-in-chief, was according to one recent scholar, 'a mediocre general even by the amateurish standards of the civil war'.[14] Before long the principle of merit upset the applecart of hierarchy, much as most men, including Oliver Cromwell, would have liked to continue respecting it. Less socially eminent men such as Sir William Waller, Colonel Edward Massey, Colonel Charles Fleetwood, Major-General Philip Skippon, and Oliver himself rose to positions of leadership. Even the Eastern Association had to change its tune. The committee in Cambridge, for example, had sought wherever possible to create an officer corps out of local worthies. Thus the higher posts in the Norfolk foot-regiments of early 1643 were filled by men from the county's traditional ruling gentry élite; their captains were cadets of major families, lesser gentlemen, or from the urban patriciate. However, before long officers came to be

The Portraturs of the Comanders in Cheife of the Parlyments Forces by Sea and Land

Rob.t E.t of Essex late Gen: of the Parlim.ts Army

Sr. Tho: Fairfax Gen: of the Army and Constable of the Tower of London

Leivt: Gen: Cromwell

Ma: Gen: Skipon

Lord Fairfax

E.t of Warwick Admi: rall of the Narrow Seas

Alex: Lesley Gen: of the Scots

Earle of Manche.ter

Printed & sould by P.Stent

Robert Devereux, earl of Essex (1591–1646)
by Daniel Mytens

Essex acquired a high reputation as a soldier in the 1620s, and his popularity and military experience made him a natural choice as Parliament's first lord general (commander-in-chief) of the army in July 1642. He was slow moving, ultra cautious, and uninspired as a general, but his soldiers liked and respected him. The support of the leaders of the Long Parliament was crucial to his success in relieving Gloucester in the summer of 1643, and fighting the First battle of Newbury. However, in 1644 he allowed himself to be drawn deep into hostile territory in Cornwall and his army was forced to surrender. He lost his command with the creation of the New Model Army in the spring of 1645 and died the following year. This image of Essex and the other leading parliamentarian commanders (Cromwell and Fairfax are on the left, Warwick and Leslie on the right) dates from the end of the First English Civil War.

selected from counties other than those where the men were raised. Colonel Thomas Rainborough, for example, was from suburban London, while several of his junior officers were New Englanders. The earl of Manchester was also permitted to recruit a Frenchman and thirteen Scots, all of them very likely professional soldiers. Alone among the aristocratic parliamentary generals Manchester, like Cromwell, sought men 'who know what they fight for and love what they know'.[15]

The northern army of Ferdinando Lord Fairfax made no attempt to imitate the social status of its royalist counterpart under the earl of Newcastle. To be sure, only one of Fairfax's colonels was below gentry status, but twenty-six of his commissioned officers who could be identified were less than gentlemen. For his captains he turned increasingly to yeomen and tradesmen. These low-born men rewarded the confidence shown in them by their commander with impressively long service—well in excess of two years in most instances.[16]

THE NEW MODEL ARMY

It was in the New Model Army that respect for social hierarchy was most decisively overturned. Owing to the Self-Denying Ordinance of April 1645 no peer or Member of Parliament was permitted to hold military office, though an exception was later made for Oliver Cromwell. A number of sons of peers and higher gentry were commissioned in 1645, but within two years most of these high-born officers had dropped out. By late 1647, after the purge of conservative officers, not quite half (forty-nine per cent) of the commissioned officers who have been identified could boast aristocratic or gentry origins. Seventeen per cent were professionals, state servants, merchants, or large producers; eighteen per cent were yeomen or husbandmen; and the remaining sixteen per cent were tradesmen, craftsmen, or labourers. Only a handful (nine per cent) of the officers in 1647 had attended university or the Inns of Court. With a median age of only 30 they were considerably younger than their royalist counterparts, and fully half of them were younger sons. A sixth are known to have risen from private or non-commissioned rank, in clear defiance of the practice in all other British armies from the seventeenth to the early twentieth centuries. Denzil Holles then was right: compared to the royalists the pedigrees of the New Model officers were 'a notable dunghill, if one would rake into it'.[17]

THE RANK AND FILE

About the rank and file we know much less than about the officers. This is not a serious drawback since it was the officers who stamped the armies with their distinctive character. In every army the infantry, who after 1644 were mostly conscripts, came from the lowest ranks of society: apprentices, servants, labourers, the jobless, vagrants, and other criminals. Given the low pay, which did not even match that of the agricultural labourer, it is unlikely that anyone above the rank of labourer would have been found among the foot-regiments. Cavalry troopers, many of whom reported for service already mounted, clothed, and armed, were of distinctly higher social status. However, rather than being freeholders and free-holders' sons, they were apprentices, copyholders, husbandmen, small trades-men, and craftsmen, such as tailors, masons, carpenters, blacksmiths, and perhaps a few Cambridge scholars. They were, in sum, men of the 'middling sort' or slightly below. Mostly literate, and animated by a political and religious con-sciousness not found among the infantry, they would play a leading role in the conflict between army and Parliament from 1647 to 1649.

Discipline

That the armies of Parliament were better disciplined than those of the king is a cliché. It is well known that under Manchester, Fairfax, and Cromwell soldiers were severely punished for swearing, drunkenness, and whoring, as well as the more serious offences against military order: negligence, cowardice, plundering, mutiny, and desertion. During the two years after its founding publicists for the New Model Army did not tire of boasting that its soldiers took not so much as an egg from the countryman without paying for it, and that in preference to cards and dice they spent their leisure time in Bible study and prayer. The royalists, by contrast, imitating the example of many of their officers, uttered foul oaths and blasphemies, drank profusely, plundered and terrorized the civilian population, and were sexual profligates. There is some truth to this caricature. When a round-head boasted to one of Sir Philip Warwick's friends of the religious conduct of his army, the royalist answered, 'Faith, thou sayest true; for in our army we have the sins of men (drinking and wenching), but in yours you have those of devils—spiritual pride and rebellion.'[18]

MARTIAL LAW

Every army on both sides was governed by a system of martial law that was codified under the title 'The Articles of War'. The similarity between the royal-ist and parliamentary codes is striking. In fact both of them were modelled on the *Laws and Ordinances of War* issued during the Bishops' Wars by the earl of Arundel in 1639 and the earl of Northumberland in 1640. Innovative in content and organization, these articles became the basis of the military law of the Inter-regnum, and the lineal ancestor of modern English military law. The first article in every code was a prohibition of blaspheming the Holy Trinity or the articles of the Christian faith, 'upon pain to have his tongue bored with a red-hot iron'. Cursing and neglect of divine worship were subject to lesser punishments. Both sides threatened the death penalty for rape, but only the parliamentary codes included 'unnatural abuses' (presumably bestiality and sodomy) as capital sexual offences. In Essex's army over forty offences were punishable by death. The purpose of these harsh punishments was as much exemplary as punitive. In this spirit the royalists would march their army past the bodies of hanged plunderers *pour encourager les autres*. In Essex's army adultery, fornication, 'and other dissolute lasciviousness' were punishable at discretion, usually with a whipping, but the royalist articles were silent on these matters. Both sides punished drunkenness, more severely in officers than in the men, and both sides were silent about gambling. An article unique to the royalist codes stipulated that 'No common soldier shall think himself too good, or refuse to work upon any piece of fortification.' Apparently it was unnecessary to spell out this duty in the codes of Essex and Fairfax. Every royalist soldier was also required to swear an oath 'to be true and faithful to my sovereign Lord King Charles'.[19]

PRISONERS OF WAR

Perhaps the greatest challenge to discipline was in the handling of prisoners and the defeated. A soldier who surrendered on the battlefield had the right to quarter, but in the heat of battle this rule was frequently violated. Defeated troops who had been guaranteed safe conduct often found themselves set upon, stripped, wounded, and plundered. Essex in person drew his sword and attacked his own soldiers when they pillaged the defeated royalists at Reading in 1643. The same thing happened to Skippon's infantry at Lostwithiel the following year: when the king heard of the atrocities being perpetrated he at once sent his officers to beat off and slash his own men. Later, in response to Skippon's protest the king invoked summary justice and hanged seven offenders on the spot. In 1645 victorious New Model soldiers at Naseby massacred 100 women on the pretext that they were whores and Irishwomen 'of cruel countenance'. They apparently went unpunished. The danger of a descent into barbarism was only narrowly averted in the aftermath of Parliament's 1644 ordinance forbidding the granting of quarter to Irish soldiers captured in England. When in February 1645 thirteen royalist Irish prisoners were hanged Prince Rupert protested that the Articles of War had been breached, and retaliated by hanging thirteen Protestant English. Parliament then seems to have thought better of it, and curtailed its policy of treating Irish soldiers as beyond the pale of humanity. However, the judicial executions of defeated royalist commanders—the duke of Hamilton, the earl of Derby, and Lord Capel—at the end of the Second and Third English Civil Wars, illustrate the sober reality that military law provided a safer protection for the rights of the defeated than did parliamentary and civilian law. The picture is therefore ambiguous. While England had atrocities enough during the 1640s, it was spared the full horrors of the Thirty Years War, in part because of the restraining effect of the Articles of War adopted by both sides, which embodied honour, morality, and considerations of reciprocal utility. According to one scholar, 'War crimes did not become policy, atrocities were individual and sporadic, and reprisal was precariously contained.'[20] In fact royalist and parliamentary officers equally regarded their honour as deeply implicated when they granted terms of surrender to a defeated foe. Chivalry more than Puritanism was at stake when Fairfax and his officers repeatedly insisted that Parliament should uphold whatever terms they had agreed to with the vanquished royalists.

ADMINISTRATION OF DISCIPLINE

How was discipline administered? Routine matters such as seeing that quarters were kept clean and that armour was not slovenly, and preventing or breaking up quarrels, were handled in a summary fashion by the officers, as was disobedience on the battlefield. Any soldier who resisted or disobeyed, or drew his sword against an officer was to be punished with death. Police authority in the army was exercised by the regimental provost-marshal, under instructions from the provost-marshal-general. Provosts were not only responsible for the main-tenance of discipline under the Laws and Ordinances of War, but for guarding enemy prisoners. Every commander-in-chief was authorized to establish a court martial that would have the power to inflict capital and lesser punishments for violations of the military code. The court martial consisted of the council of war (the general staff and the regimental colonels) sitting as a court and assisted by a legal official known as the 'advocate of the army' or the 'judge-advocate'. In most large armies there were also regimental courts martial, consisting of the commis-sioned officers. They could try lesser offences, but could not impose the death penalty. Capital punishment usually took the form of hanging, particularly for desertion, but mutineers were commonly shot to death. Lesser punishments tended to be of a corporal nature: whippings, running the gauntlet, having one's sword broken over one's head, or riding the wooden horse. The wooden horse was an especially painful form of humiliation. Consisting of two thin pieces of wood nailed together at a sharp angle and attached to runners, it would be 'ridden' for periods of an hour or two. The pain would be increased by tying mus-kets to the soldier's heels. Unless the victim had taken the precaution of coming with well-padded breeches the punishment could easily leave him with a bloody posterior.

GODLINESS

The superior discipline of the armies of Manchester and Fairfax was not achieved overnight; it was the accomplishment of several years. In both armies heavy stress was laid upon the importance of religion through frequent sermonizing and the encouragement of Bible study. A number of officers transferred from Essex's army, notorious for its 'debauched' behaviour, to Manchester's because of its famed godliness and discipline. Immediately after the founding of the New Model, Fairfax imposed harsh punishments on deserters, plunderers, and muti-neers. He then took aim at lesser sins: swearing, drunkenness, and whoring. There are several documented examples of men in the New Model having

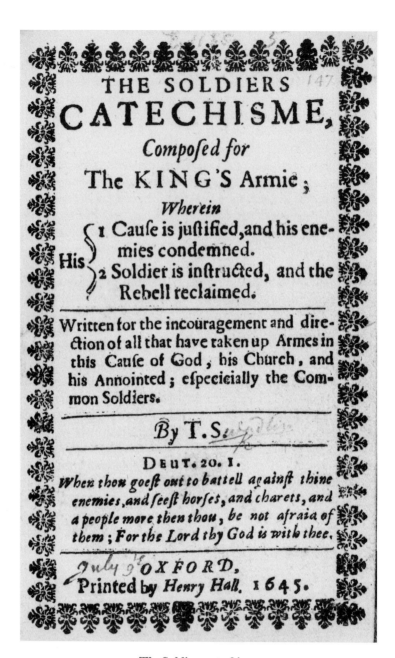

THE SOLDIERS CATECHISME,

Compofed for

The KING'S Armie;

Wherein

His ⎰ 1 Caufe is juftified, and his ene-
       mies condemned.
     ⎱ 2 Soldier is inftructed, and the
       Rebell reclaimed.

Written for the incouragement and direction of all that have taken up Armes in
this Caufe of God, his Church, and
his Annointed; efpecieially the Common Soldiers.

By T.S.

DEUT. 20. I.

*When thou goeft out to battell againft thine
enemies, and feeft horfes, and charets, and
a people more then thou, be not afraid of
them; For the Lord thy God is with thee.*

OXFORD,
Printed by *Henry Hall.* 1645.

The Soldiers catechisme

Robert Ram, Puritan minister and future New Model Army chaplain, wrote *The Soldiers catechisme* in 1644. Reprinted seven times by the end of 1645, it acquired almost official status during the Revolution. It provided a general justification for Christian participation in war and defended the parliamentary soldiers' destruction of crosses, images, and prayer books as legitimate opposition to idolatry and superstition. In strident and confident language it told its readers that the struggle was one between the forces of the Gospel and the agents of Antichrist. Salvation was the promised reward for those who died as martyrs to Christ.

their tongues bored through with a hot iron for blasphemy. While the royalist leadership also fulminated against oaths and swearing, little concrete action seems to have been taken.[21] The parliamentary armies in general were also much less forgiving than the royalists towards those who deserted to fight for the other side. Records from Sir William Waller's army in 1644 show that the crimes most frequently tried by his court martial were plunder or robbery, mutiny, desertion, and neglect of duty. The most common punishment was hanging; next were physical humiliation and cashiering. One in ten of the accused was acquitted.

By contrast, all the evidence from the royalist armies suggests a lax attitude towards lesser crimes, and a failure to call commanders to account for their disobedience. This could have strategic consequences: for example, Prince Maurice's refusal to abandon the siege of Lyme (April to June 1644). Not only did his disobedience throw the main field army on the defensive but the king's failure to discipline his nephew also set in train a dysfunction in the royalist command structure that lasted until the end of the war.

Combat Motivation and Morale

It was Xenophon who pronounced that 'not numbers or strength bring victory in war; but whichever army goes into battle stronger in their soul'. Or, in Napoleon's words, in war 'the moral is to the physical as three is to one'.[22] The great bulk of humanity have little stomach for war. Reluctant to have other men 'sheathe their swords in our bowels', they are mostly unwilling to do the same to others.[23] If forced to don a uniform, many will desert at the first opportunity, or avoid using their weapons, or cross to the other side after their army has been defeated. Yet in spite of this general distaste for bloodshed, men did enlist in large numbers, and several tens of thousands killed one another. Leaving aside those who were coerced into fighting, what persuaded the others to risk their lives in organized violence?

The first argument may be the primordial one of fear. Men who had once openly defied the king feared that if they did not go on to defeat him in war they would be hanged for treason. Men such as John Pym, Denzil Holles, the earls of Essex and Manchester, and the Fairfaxes, were quite conscious of the fate that awaited them should the king wrest a military triumph from them. The marquis of Ormond for his part knew that if the king was defeated he could say goodbye to his property, and probably his life as well. Other men acted out of religious anxiety. Many parliamentarians were convinced that there was a fiendish Jesuitical plot to impose the popish religion on England and exterminate all godly Protestants who refused to convert. This fear seemed to be corroborated when the first atrocity stories from the Irish Catholic rebellion of 1641 reached England. As Richard Baxter commented afterwards, '[t]he terrible massacres of Protestants in Ireland and the threatening of the rebels to invade England were the chief reasons why the nation moved to a state of war.'[24] Those who backed the king remained anxious as well. Committed Anglicans worried that the Puritans in Parliament would abolish the prayer-book, extirpate the Established Church root and branch, and replace it with a Presbyterian worship and doctrine. Most justified in their fears were the small minority who were Catholic. Out of all proportion to their numbers, they flocked to the king's standard in the hope of finding refuge from an intolerant Puritanism.[25]

A sense of honour drove many men on, particularly among the officers. The ideals of medieval chivalry—courtesy, reckless courage, the conviction that a man's word is sacred, loyalty to one's lord, and a hunger for fame—all these still exercised a powerful grip on the imagination of fighting men in the seventeenth century. Prince Rupert thought he could bring the civil war to an early end if he could fight a duel with Essex and have both sides accept the result as binding. It was honour that impelled Sir William Waller to take up arms, even while he assured his royalist foe Sir Ralph Hopton, 'God knows with what a perfect hatred I detest this war without an enemy, but I look upon it as *Opus Domini* [the Lord's work].'[26] It was honour that brought Charles I to sentence to death the governor of Reading, Colonel Fielding for surrendering on too easy terms and agreeing to let Essex hang any parliamentary deserters he found among the royalist garrison. By contrast, when honour was lacking morale could deteriorate alarmingly. Essex's army suffered from the 'European mercenary' attitude of some of his subordinates. Commissary-general Behre, for example, allowed his troops to plunder Buckinghamshire 'more like devils than men'.[27] Others demoralized the rank and file by falsifying musters and accounts.

MILITARY BANNERS

The banners or 'colours' that accompanied each company and troop into battle furnish additional evidence about combat motivation, and illustrate the importance of religion. Belonging to a still-vital tradition of emblematics, these devices served the practical functions of identifying which side the officer and his unit were on, acting as a rallying-point during the terror and confusion of battle, and publicizing the cause the commanding officer considered himself to be advancing. Since officers were permitted to design their own banners, the several hundred drawings of them which survive constitute an exceptionally illuminating source for the combat motivation of both sides.[28]

The bulk of parliamentary colours focused on the constitution and religion. A number of them pictured Magna Carta, sometimes with the Bible beside it, as a bulwark of the rights of the subject against royal tyranny. Other standards dwelt on the familiar theme of a king led astray by evil counsellors. One bore the image of a damaged column representing the commonwealth weakened by the king's wicked advisers, but with the reassuring motto 'still it stands'. Another pictured the king's wicked advisers as bishops, monks, and papists. The most politically

Banner of Captain Sandberd of Devon

Confederate cavalry banner

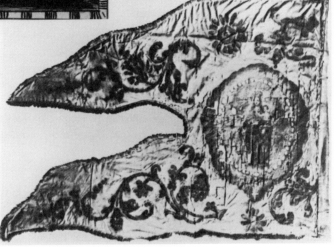

Military banners

(a) Banner of Captain Sandberd of Devon

Every commanding officer of the rank of captain or higher, had the privilege of designing a cornet, ensign, or 'colour' for his unit. Carried into battle, these colours had the practical function of serving as a rallying-point amidst the turmoil and confusion of the battlefield. To desert one's colours was a capital offence; to lose them to the enemy was the deepest disgrace. Drawings of several hundred colours survive. The images and mottoes, mostly in Latin, reveal what the officers on both sides thought the wars were about, and why they were risking their lives. Captain Sandberd's picture of a mocking exchange between a parliamentary swordsman and a terrified cleric ('So you want to be bishop?' 'No, No, I don't!') illustrates both the religious themes and the wit that were common to many colours, both royalist and parliamentarian.

(b) Confederate cavalry banner

This is a confederate guidon, or cavalry flag, measuring 5 feet by 3 feet 7 inches. A figure of the Virgin with the Infant in her arms is painted on to a blue silk background within the surround of a rosary. Religious images adorned other confederate flags together with mottoes like 'Let God arise and let his enemies be scattered' or 'God hath broken our chains'. Other banners displayed an Irish harp on a green background or an Irish cross often with the motto *Vivat Rex Carolus* ('Long Live King Charles'). These flags highlight both the religious nature of the struggle in Ireland and confederate sense of loyalty to the Stuarts.

radical bore the image of a severed head and an axe dripping with blood above the Latin motto 'The safety of the people is the supreme law'.

But the greatest number of parliamentary standards were religious in content. Typical mottos were 'Let God arise and his enemies be scattered' (Psalms 68: 1), 'If God is with us, who can be against us?', and 'For Reformation'. The most frequent images were an arm bearing a sword reaching out of a cloud, and an anchor (peace) hanging from a cloud (heaven). Philip Skippon, major-general of the New Model infantry, designed a colour showing a sword of heaven and a Bible, with the Latin tag 'Pray and fight; Jehovah helps, and he will continue to help.' A cavalry officer proclaimed his faith in the God of battles with the phrase 'I live in this hope' (the sword of heaven). Lieutenant-general Thomas Hammond gave voice to the quintessentially Puritan view that virtue, far from being a passive quality, is restless and dynamic: 'Virtue does not know how to stay standing in one place.' Many colours were openly anti-Catholic. One portrayed a skull and bishop's mitre above the motto 'I would rather die than be a papist'. The exaggerated and inflammatory stories about the atrocities committed by the Catholic Irish rebels inspired a number of bloodthirsty standards. One depicted Ireland as a house on fire, being consumed by the flames of popish rebellion. Another portrayed an Irish rebel slaying a naked (Protestant) woman. 'Heaven avenges cruelty', it warned. What these religious banners bore witness to was a kind of Puritan self-righteousness, stemming from the utter certainty that God was on their side.

The themes on the royalist banners were more varied. The commonest image was a royal crown. A significant proportion were overtly flippant or humorous. Dice were a common motif. The most notorious royalist colour was a transparent reference to Essex's marital embarrassment: 'Cuckold we come', it proclaimed. Others advertised their contempt for the roundheads as traitors or social inferiors, and strove to stir up panic about the threat to landed property and the social order posed by these upstarts. Frequent allusion was made to the king's hapless attempt in January 1642 to arrest the five revolutionary Members of Parliament. One of the most extreme images depicted the Parliament house at Westminster with the heads of two traitors stuck on spikes at either end of the roof above the motto 'as they are outside, so they are inside'.

There were also many royalist colours of a strongly religious cast, but the themes were less triumphalist. Like the parliamentarians the royalists were convinced that they were the instruments of Providence. They were fortified by the certainty that God would not let rebellion prosper indefinitely. More subdued than the Puritans, the royalists focused strongly on the person of the king and the theological obligation of loyalty to him. Typical of many was the banner captured at the 1st battle of Newbury. Beneath a Bible, a sword, and a crown, it proclaimed, 'I live by these things, and I shall die for them.' Constancy in the face of defeat is the explicit message of the one which quoted the Psalmist: 'In the darkness a light has arisen for the upright in heart'. Another favourite motto was also a quotation from the Psalms: 'Touch not mine anointed'. The commonest royalist motto of all came from the mouth of Christ as recorded in Matthew's Gospel: 'Render unto Caesar the things which are Caesar's, and unto God the things which are God's.' In short, for the royalists religion validated the charismatic nature of kingship; it provided consolation and resignation, but it does not seem to have been a galvanizing force. The most extreme instance of this stoical religiosity verging on defeatism was the attitude of the king himself. Charles was morally certain that the civil war was God's punishment of him for having broken his word by permitting the execution of his servant Strafford. At the beginning of December 1642 he expressed to the duke of Hamilton his conviction that if he won the war it would show that God had forgiven him; if he lost, it would prove that his punishment would not be finished until he had left this world. Whatever the outcome he would never yield, 'for I will either be a glorious King or a patient martyr'.[29]

ESPRIT DE CORPS AND MORALE

So much for ideological motivation. What was it that kept men going during the rigours of a long campaign? Normal preconditions for high morale are that the troops should be in good health, with adequate medical care, sufficient food and water, regular pay, and adequate rest and sleep. These are questions not only of available resources, but of a commanding officer's ability to organize and administer them. They were questions upon which an effective commander such as Oliver Cromwell bestowed infinite care. Thus on the way to the battle of Preston in 1648 he stopped for several days until his men had been shod with the boots and stockings fetched from Northampton. His foe the duke of Hamilton was already in the north with 10,000 marauding Scots at his back, but Cromwell refused to be rushed. He halted for another three days until the artillery train from Hull caught up with him at Doncaster. Similarly, the following year Cromwell refused to take his army to Ireland until Parliament had furnished him with a war chest of £100,000. The career of Cromwell illustrates the truth that a military leader makes a crucial contribution to the morale of his troops if he can bring them to feel that they are safe in his hands, that he will not be careless of their lives and welfare. The Scottish general David Leslie, by contrast, failed conspicuously to persuade his troops that they were safe with him. This helps to explain why he lost the battle of Dunbar in 1650 (see picture on p. 68) in spite of being on his home ground and enjoying a numerical superiority of two to one. Distracted by a quarrelsome general staff and an interfering Kirk, Leslie permitted his army to shiver for several days on a windswept hillside where they became steadily more drenched, hungry, and short of sleep. On the eve of the battle, which Cromwell launched at 6 a.m., Leslie had permitted his officers to desert their men for warmer, drier quarters behind the lines (for details see Chapter 2).

Modern evidence suggests that other factors which promote high morale on the field of battle are, in order of importance: prayer, solidarity with the group, hatred for the enemy, and belief in the cause for which the soldiers are fighting. One of the trademarks of the New Model Army was its encouragement of extemporaneous praying aloud. This habit won for it the reputation of the 'praying army'. In the late 1640s several parliamentary companies, troops, regiments, and garrisons, as well as the headquarters staff at Whitehall went further, forming themselves into gathered churches for the purpose of prayer and Scripture study. The palpable result of this religious bonding was articulated by a soldier in Colonel Hewson's regiment who wrote in 1647 about 'the manifest presence of God' among them, exclaiming, 'the sweet union we had with God doth endear us together in love'.[30] This welding of men together through the power of religion had been fostered in the parliamentary armies by continual preaching, the staging of fast days or days of humiliation, and the singing of psalms before going into battle. Song, as most military commanders are well aware, is a primary vehicle of human sociability. So is dance, of which marching is merely a mechanical variety. In the seventeenth century the remarkable discovery was made that long hours of arms- and foot-drill make men more obedient and effective in battle. When a group of men move their arm and leg muscles in unison for prolonged periods a primitive and powerful social bond wells up among them. This bond reinforces primary or small-group loyalty.[31]

Hatred of the enemy was solidly implanted on both sides. The cavaliers were, initially at least, contemptuous of Parliament's roundhead rabble of militarily incompetent rebels against God and king. The roundheads for their part, remained convinced that the cavalier armies were riddled with papists, Irishmen, Welshmen, and (if English), foul-mouthed debauchees. Cordial enmity strengthened the resolve of both. Morale, then, was a complex question, influenced more by religion, honour, politics, and the quality of leadership than by money, weapons, and provisions.

Leadership

CHARLES I

At the beginning of the civil war neither the royalist nor the parliamentarian armies were distinguished by brilliant leadership. The captain-general of the royalist forces was Charles I himself, who like England's medieval kings commanded his army in person. Aged 42 at the outbreak of the war, he had never been in battle, although he had learned something of military organization and administration from the two Bishops' Wars (discussed in Chapter 1). He had considerable personal courage and perseverance, and by 1644 had developed real strategic skill, as evidenced by the successes of his main army against Waller at

Cropredy Bridge (29 June 1644) and Essex at Lostwithiel (August to September 1644). His main shortcoming was poor judgement of human character. His sheltered, ceremonious court life had robbed him of the normal contacts with people necessary for insight into the human heart. He compensated for his lack of self-confidence by an icy restraint which scarcely endeared him to the common soldier. With his advisers he was by turns vacillating and rigid, and was never able to overcome his habit of listening to the advice of the last counsellor he spoke to, nor to subdue intrigue among his entourage.

PRINCE RUPERT

Fortunately the king was able to attract several experienced generals to serve under him. Most outstanding was his nephew Prince Rupert of the Rhine (1619–82). Only 22 at the battle of Edgehill, he was already an officer of experience who had studied his profession deeply. At the tender age of 16 he had seen service at Brabant where he had displayed daring valour. Taken prisoner in 1638, he had spent the next three years improving his knowledge of the military art. Upon his release he devoted all his blazing energy to his uncle's cause. In England he quickly proved himself a master of the rapid movement of troops. Time and again he succeeded in concentrating a superior force at places that his opponents thought he could not reach with such speed. His formidable reputation, combined with his apparent physical immunity on the battlefield, captured people's attention. He appears to have possessed the intangible quality known as charisma. Uninhibited by moral qualms or compassion towards non-military people, he was utterly ruthless in protecting the interests of his cavalry. He also encouraged and developed the leadership potential of his subordinates. John Lord Byron and Sir Gilbert Gerard, both members of distinguished military families, and who had served in the Netherlands, flourished under Rupert's patronage. When it came to handling people who were not under his command, however, his extreme youth became a drawback. Men of dignity and high social rank like Hertford and Newcastle resented his authority. Finding it difficult to cope with disagreement, he quickly conceived a dislike for several of the politicians in the royalist Council of War: Digby, Culpepper, and Hyde; and he was soon on bad terms with independent military leaders like Percy, Wilmot, and Goring. Poor relationships with his peers had deleterious military consequences: for example, Newcastle's sluggishness in bringing his infantry to the battlefield at Marston Moor (2 July 1644), and Goring's refusal to march to Naseby (June 1645). As time wore on Rupert also found himself denied vital finances and supplies, and eventually lost the confidence of the king himself.

THE EARL OF NEWCASTLE AND GEORGE GORING

Of the aristocratic English commanders whom Charles appointed at the beginning of the war only the earl (later marquis) of Newcastle achieved any personal

Prince Rupert, Count Palatine (1619–82)
by William Dobson

Rupert was only 22 when he came to aid his uncle, Charles I, in 1642. Already experienced, he brought to England continental practices of warfare and many foreign military experts. Charles immediately made him commander of the cavalry and he enjoyed a semi-independent role. Rupert showed that he was not only a brave, energetic, and quick-thinking cavalry general but also a good organizer, and he made the mounted arm of the king's army its most formidable weapon. After almost unbroken success in the field in the first two years of the war, when his name alone struck terror into his opponents, he met his match in Cromwell's Ironsides at Marston Moor (2 July 1644). Promoted commander-in-chief of the royalist army in November 1644, he accepted battle at Naseby (14 June 1645), and, although his cavalry wing was successful, the day was lost. He surrendered Bristol shortly afterwards, and was angrily dismissed by his uncle. After 1648 he commanded the royalists at sea.

military distinction—at Adwalton Moor in 1643, after which he subjected all of Yorkshire to the king's authority. However, hampered by the same dilettante attitude as the other royalist peers, and perhaps jealous of Prince Rupert, Newcastle neglected to follow up his victory. On the positive side he displayed shrewdness in his choice of commanders, and attracted intense loyalty from his famed Whitecoats, who fought with impressive bravery at Marston Moor. Yet in spite of his advantages, which included virtually unfettered command in the north and vast numerical superiority over his parliamentary adversaries, he was deficient in strategic consciousness. He missed his opportunity to dispose quickly of Ferdinando Lord Fairfax's army in 1643, when he enjoyed a huge superiority in numbers. Nor was he able to persuade his Yorkshire troops, who comprised the bulk of his army, to march south and help the king. In the supreme crisis of July 1644 he was dilatory about marshalling his infantry to assist Rupert at Marston Moor. Charles's other grandees—men such as the marquis of Hertford, the earl of Derby, the earl of Glamorgan, and Lord Capel—soon showed such ineptitude that before the end of 1643 the king had begun replacing them with professional, experienced soldiers.

Such a one was George Goring. A Spanish veteran, he was held back by a reputation for debauchery, but he fought with distinction as Newcastle's lieutenant-general of horse, demonstrating bravery, administrative efficiency, and gifted leadership. However, when he was rewarded with an army of his own in the West Country, his performance began to falter; he was frequently drunk and his troops, though loyal, were undisciplined. At Langport (July 1645) he proved no match for the New Model cavalry under Sir Thomas Fairfax.

THE EARL OF ESSEX

Like the king, Parliament too was plagued with mediocre leadership at the beginning of the war. In spite of his extensive continental experience, Essex was a lacklustre general whose instincts were defensive and cautious. At Turnham Green (13 November 1642) he could have crushed the king's army, which he outnumbered two to one, but he got cold feet and allowed Charles to withdraw without an engagement. His greatest exploit was the relief of Gloucester (8 September 1643), but his prickliness about his noble status, and his jealousy of more successful men like Sir William Waller made him quarrelsome and ineffective. Thus, his failure to send troops to rescue Waller at Roundway Down (July 1643) earned harsh comment in the London press, and impeded his ability to recruit troops. Devoid of charisma, he found himself shackled when Parliament began diverting resources, first to Waller's and later to Fairfax's army. He exhibited strategic ineptitude by three times undertaking major engagements (Gloucester [8 September 1643], 1st Newbury [19 September 1643], and Lostwithiel [August to September 1644]) where the enemy was positioned between his army and his base. At the last of these the result was disaster as his army was hemmed in with its back to the sea, and Essex himself had to slip away by boat, while Skippon was left the humiliating job of surrendering the infantry.

SIR WILLIAM WALLER AND THE EARL OF MANCHESTER

Essex's junior commander Waller (see picture on p. 314) had a natural aptitude for military command. A few stunning successes early in the war gave him the popular nickname 'William the Conqueror'. His capture of Southsea Castle and Portsmouth showed his ability to conceive a bold plan, the use of surprise, caution in the approach, and an eye for the tactical lie of the land. He also possessed the cardinal military virtue, courage. The other leading pre-New Model Army commander in the south was the earl of Manchester. By able administration, firm discipline, and the adroit use of religion, he welded together the most effective of the regional units, the army of the Eastern Association. Not only did it protect the agriculturally rich territory of East Anglia and Lincolnshire for Parliament, it followed Manchester outside that domain to Yorkshire, where it played a crucial role at Marston Moor (2 July 1644). After that signal triumph, however, the earl seems to have become dismayed at the prospect of total victory over the king. He was lethargic in his response to the orders of the Committee of Both Kingdoms to unite his forces with those of Essex in order to deliver a knockout blow to the king's main army. His reluctance to engage his forces when the king relieved Donnington Castle (November 1644) led to parliamentary hearings into his conduct, and was a material factor behind the Self-Denying Ordinance and the creation of the New Model Army.

LORD FERDINANDO AND SIR THOMAS FAIRFAX

Ferdinando Lord Fairfax, the commander of the Northern Army, was made of sterner stuff than Essex or Manchester. Despite an almost complete lack of support from Westminster he inspired his small force of between 900 and 8,000 men to keep at bay an army twice its size for most of the period between 1642 and 1645. Though chronically short of pay, the Northern Army never mutinied under Fairfax; yet when Colonel Sedenham Poynts took it over between 1645 and 1647 there were several mutinies, despite the army's being more regularly paid than it had been under Lord Fairfax.

His son Sir Thomas emerged as one of the finest military leaders of the entire civil war period. As a young man he had gained military experience in the Low Countries. His excellent record in Yorkshire, together with his friendship with the earl of Northumberland and his relative freedom from political entanglements were enough to secure him the generalship of the New Model Army in 1645. While he cannot be called a great strategist, he showed courage and leadership on the battlefield. Normally a self-effacing, pious, quiet, and even sickly man, his personality was transformed by the challenge of combat. His furious energy and his ability to keep his head 'did so animate the soldiers', in the words

Sir Thomas Fairfax

Of a well-known Yorkshire family, Fairfax fought the Dutch and German wars. His father commanded the Yorkshire forces raised for Parliament in 1642, and Sir Thomas won his spurs defending the county against the much larger forces of the earl of Newcastle. At Marston Moor (2 July 1644) he contributed to the defeat of Rupert and Newcastle. As a successful, experienced, and senior officer, but neither a peer nor a Member of Parliament, he was selected, under the terms of the Self-Denying Ordinance, to command the New Model Army created by Parliament. With Cromwell as his general of horse he won the critical victory of Naseby (14 June 1645) which effectively ended the First English Civil War. He sympathized with his soldiers' postwar grievances, but took no part in the trial and execution of the king.

of one eyewitness, 'as is hardly to be expressed'. At Naseby he responded to the crisis on the parliamentary left wing by arranging the 'timely coming on' of the reserves, and synchronizing the advance of horse and foot in the second great charge which won the day.[32] He was a strict disciplinarian who more than anyone established the high code of personal conduct for which the New Model became famous. At Maidstone in 1648, by his careful planning and personal valour, he effectively crippled the royalist uprising in the south.

OLIVER CROMWELL

It is often forgotten that his lieutenant-general of the cavalry, Oliver Cromwell (see picture on p. 317), did not really come into his own until after the First English Civil War was over. Thirteen years Fairfax's senior, he had no military experience before 1642 when he returned to his native county to raise a troop of horse for Parliament. From the beginning he looked for godly men to be his officers, and managed to infect many of his troops with his own colossal religiosity. Systematic in his training of his regiment, which soon gained the nickname 'Ironsides', he disciplined them to halt and regroup after a charge instead of plunging headlong into pursuit of plunder or the fleeing enemy. He found that he enjoyed the excitement of war, but this did not make him careless of his men's lives. Prior to major campaigns he always took care to see that his armies were well equipped, provisioned, and financed. Another quality was his willingness to give subordinates wide latitude of action, and even on occasion to be guided by them. Thus when Colonel John Lambert perceived the vulnerability of the Scots army at Dunbar (September 1650), Cromwell encouraged him to present his plan for an attack on the Scots army to the Council of War, and gracefully acceded to the request from a member of the council that Lambert should lead the army the next day. Cromwell, like Prince Rupert, possessed charisma. He inspired in his troops a confidence that they were safe in his hands, that he would not be careless of their lives, and that he would extricate them from all difficulties.

Tactics

Seventeenth-century England was much more wooded than today. While enclosure had made steady progress in the farming regions since the late fifteenth century, most arable regions still lay open. What hedges there were could be easily cleared by experienced riders. Apart from London no city or town boasted more than 25,000 people. Internal communications remained poor. Even the main roads were full of ruts and potholes, and liable to turn into quagmires during wet weather. For this reason, in addition to the cold, fighting was normally abandoned during the winter. Poor roads severely limited military movement, especially that of artillery and supplies. Heavy equipment was therefore sent by river or sea whenever possible.

CONTINENTAL TACTICS

Battlefield tactics were strongly influenced by continental developments of the Thirty Years War. Many English commanders had fought on the continent, and while they lacked the innovating genius of a Count Maurice of Nassau or King Gustavus Adolphus of Sweden, they learnt about and imitated their novel formations and techniques. Ever since the invention of the longbow and its widespread adoption in the fourteenth century, the balance of power had been shifting steadily away from the cavalry towards the infantry. Archers were used in the English Civil Wars, but mainly to shoot messages into the enemy camp, or to set fire to the thatched roofs in enemy garrisons or towns. The petition to Charles I from bowyers and fletchers to fight the war with bows and arrows was not as ridiculous as it sounds. Besides being lighter and more portable than the musket, the longbow had a much greater range, and was more reliable in wet weather. Its main drawback was that it required strength and skill to handle, which implied a long period of training for aspiring archers. Muskets and pistols were easier to master, and could inflict more terrible wounds. Squadrons of musketeers were often an effective deterrent to the cavalry charge.

Also effective in stopping cavalry were tightly massed formations of pikemen. In the fifteenth century the Swiss had shown that 'hedgehogs' of pikemen standing shoulder to shoulder could face down an advancing force of cavalry. It has to be remembered that a horse, no matter how well trained, will not run blindly into an obstacle. When units of pikemen came to be interlaced with musketeers life became even more unpleasant for the cavalry trooper. The cavalry's response was to advance in deep formation against the opposing infantry at a trot. The front rank discharged its pistols at a distance of perhaps twenty or thirty feet and trotted to the rear, allowing successive ranks to repeat the process. The intention was to break the infantry with firepower, and then move in for the kill by charging them with drawn swords. The only problem was that a musketeer standing on the ground normally commanded more effective firepower than a man with a pistol or carbine on the swaying back of a horse.

The third factor in the decline of the cavalry was the use of light wheel-drawn field artillery. In the civil wars, however, artillery was confined for the most part to sieges. The use of field guns at major battles such as Naseby was largely perfunctory, and had the principal effect of covering the battlefield in smoke.

The wisdom of the day called for an army to be composed of one-third cavalry and two-thirds infantry, with perhaps a regiment of up to 1,200 dragoons. The artillery train would not normally exceed 200 men. Until the 1640s the infantry had been divided about equally between musketeers and pikemen. Increasingly, however, the view was that the proportion should be two-thirds musketeers and one-third pikemen. Supply warrants from 1645 show this to have been the ratio observed in the New Model Army.

BATTLEFLELD TACTICS

How were troops distributed on the battlefield? Until the innovations of Maurice and Gustavus it had been normal to place the bulk of the infantry in the centre, flanked by cavalry on the right and left wings. Behind the infantry would often be a reserve of veteran infantry and cavalry, and the commander-in-chief's life-guard. The main body of infantry was thus protected from attack on its flank and rear. It should also be noticed, although it is not often mentioned, that one of the principal virtues of this formation was to prevent reluctant, fearful foot-soldiers, who were often the 'offscouring' of the land, from running away. Not only was this possibility very real, officers sometimes had to threaten or cudgel their men to persuade them to advance on the enemy.

A powerful and practical preventive against cowardice on the battlefield was drill. Maurice of Nassau was the first commander of modern times fully to appreciate its importance, not only for weapon training, but also for improving tactical flexibility in battle, and as an essential constituent of morale. In response to the increasingly lethal impact of cannon and musketry he dispersed his armies and thinned them out to two or three lines. His tactical unit was the battalion of 550 men. With smaller, shallower formations it was easier to reinforce threatened portions of his line by transferring units from one sector of the battlefield to the other. The sixteen-foot pike remained essential: a rampart within which or behind which the musketeers could take cover if attacked by enemy cavalry. Because the pike was longer than the medieval cavalry lance (now used only by the Scots), the shock impact of a cavalry charge had been effectively blunted. Gustavus Adolphus carried the process begun by Maurice even further. Firing, which had been conducted by the process of countermarch—each rank firing then marching to the rear to reload—was replaced with the salvo, in which the musketeers, only three deep, all fired at once. The pikemen then clinched the decision by pressing forward into the disordered enemy ranks. The logical next step was what came to be known as the Swedish brigade. Three or four battalions were combined, often into a wedge-shaped formation, with one battalion in reserve. Added firepower was provided by the light 'regimental piece' (three-pound shot or less), which had a devastating anti-personnel effect at close range.

For cavalry the Dutch style consisted of a regiment advancing in six or eight ranks (rather than the traditional ten) towards the enemy and each successive rank halting to fire their pistols or carbines, then retiring for the next rank to do the same, until the enemy was sufficiently broken for a final charge with the sword to be effective. The Swedish development was to charge home with the sword in about three ranks, reserving fire for the pursuit. This was the style used increasingly during the English Civil Wars, and in Scotland. The Swedish king had added firepower to his cavalry by attaching to them bodies of 'commanded musketeers'. Distinguished from the traditional formation of infantry in the

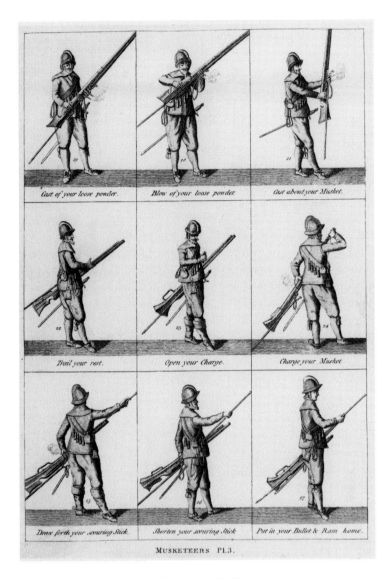

Cast of your loose powder. | Blow of your loose powder. | Cast about your Musket.

Trail your rest. | Open your Charge. | Charge your Musket.

Draw forth your scouring Stick. | Shorten your scouring Stick. | Put in your Bullet & Ram home.

MUSKETEERS Pl.3.

Musketeers' drill

After its introduction in the sixteenth century, the musket, despite being an inaccurate and dangerous instrument, steadily replaced the longbow and the pike as the weapon of choice for the infantry. By the late 1630s musketeers typically comprised two-thirds of the infantry, and pikemen the other third. While the 16- or 18-foot pike remained an effective defence against cavalry, musketeers were more mobile and could, at close range, inflict more devastating wounds. In order to reduce the danger that musketeers all too often posed to their own side, and also to increase their firepower, commanders began around 1600 to subject them to rigorous drill in the handling of their weapons. Contemporary manuals, such as Francis Grose's *Military Antiquities*, detailed as many as forty-three individual movements that the musketeer was supposed to practise in order to master his weapon. Drill made it possible for ranks of musketeers to fire simultaneous volleys at the enemy. This development was to have a far-reaching impact on the character and organization of modern armies.

centre and cavalry on the wings, the Swedish plan presented a chequerboard appearance. There were still units of cavalry on each flank, but they also stretched across the battlefield, interlaced with bodies of musketeers. Perhaps because their infantry were not well-enough drilled, most English commanders did not attempt to implement this more sophisticated formation on a regular basis.

Edgehill

The first major battle of the English Civil Wars illustrates both the extent to which Prince Rupert and Essex had assimilated continental military thinking and the continuing backwardness of English tactical warfare.[33]

In mid-September 1642 the king had marched west from Nottingham, where he had raised disappointingly few troops, to Shrewsbury, hoping to recruit greater numbers from the friendlier territory of Wales and the marches. In mid-October he began his advance on London. Though still inferior in numbers to the parliamentary army, he benefited from superior morale. Shortage of pay combined with absence of training had already rendered Essex's regiments sullen and uncooperative. More significant still, the royalists had just drawn the first blood of the civil wars at Powick Bridge outside Worcester. There on 23 September Prince Rupert, with a detachment of 1,000 horse and dragoons, had routed a similar number of parliamentarians under Colonel John Brown. This action at once made the Prince's name 'terrible indeed' to his foes.

PREPARING FOR BATTLE

Neither side knew precisely when to expect a major encounter. Plagued by atrocious autumn weather, they lumbered slowly across the sodden English countryside, constantly delayed by their even-slower-moving trains of artillery. Neither side had yet recognized the importance of intelligence: Essex would not appoint a scoutmaster-general until the following year, and both cavalries performed inadequately the function of reconnaissance. The result? Each side literally did not know where the other was. When detachments from the royalist and parliamentarian armies bumped into each other by accident at Wormleighton, near Edgehill on the night of 22 October, their units were widely dispersed in villages between Cropredy and Edgecote. By the following morning they had concentrated their forces, the king's at the bottom of the steep, 300-foot incline called Edge Hill, and Essex's in the field halfway between Edge Hill and the village of Kineton. On the parliamentary side the main body of the infantry occupied the centre, two lines deep, and hemmed in by cavalry on both wings. There was also a small cavalry reserve of two regiments stationed behind the infantry. Beyond the cavalry on either wing were detachments of dragoons. On the left Sir James Ramsay had stationed about 300 of them in an advanced position at right angles to the line. This was so that they could subject any attacker to enfilading fire,

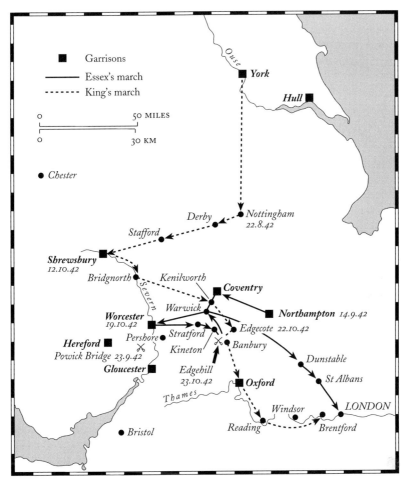

Garrisons

Essex's march

King's march

0   50 MILES

0   30 KM

Ouse

York

Hull

● *Chester*

Derby   ● *Nottingham*
                22.8.42

Stafford

Shrewsbury
12.10.42

Bridgnorth ●   *Kenilworth*

Severn

Warwick   **Coventry**

Worcester
19.10.42

Pershore ●   *Stratford*

Kineton

Hereford
Powick Bridge 23.9.42

Gloucester

Northampton *14.9.42*

Edgecote 22.10.42

Banbury

Dunstable

St Albans

Edgehill
23.10.42

Thames

Oxford

Windsor   **LONDON**

Reading   *Brentford*

● *Bristol*

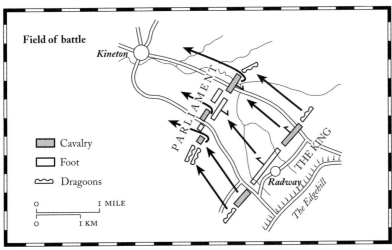

Field of battle

Kineton

PARLIAMENT

THE KING

Radway

The Edgehill

Cavalry

Foot

Dragoons

0   1 MILE

0   1 KM

Edgehill campaign of 1642

meaning shooting at its flank. The guns of the parliamentarian artillery were placed in pairs between the bodies of infantry in the front line. Ramsay had interlaced his squadrons of horse with groups of musketeers, in imitation of the practice pioneered by Gustavus Adolphus. Of the three infantry brigades two were in the front line and one behind as a reserve. We know that Charles Essex's brigade was deployed in a single line, each regiment eight ranks deep, in imitation of the Dutch service, whose tactics Essex was following. Although he had superior numbers and was comforted by the knowledge that Warwick Castle lay behind him as a refuge, the earl did not feel confident enough to take the offensive. For one thing, he had still not concentrated all his forces; in another day he would have three more regiments of foot, eleven troops of horse, and more heavy guns. The king stood between him and London, but the greatest deterrent to a parliamentary offensive was the earl's reluctance to run the risk of killing the king himself during the unpredictable action of a battle.

It took the royalists over six hours to draw up their army in battle formation. The earl of Lindsey, as lord general, favoured the Dutch plan for the army. Rupert, whose commission exempted him from taking orders from anyone save the king, argued for the more complex Swedish brigade. When Charles eventually backed his nephew, Lindsey, piqued by this undermining of his authority, resigned the office of commander-in-chief, and went off to lead his own regiment of foot. The infantry were distributed in five brigades at the bottom of the Edge Hill escarpment, three in front and two behind. On each wing were five regiments of cavalry, Rupert commanding the right and Henry Wilmot the left. The thousand or so dragoons were probably stationed behind the hedges that flanked both wings. The royalist train of artillery boasted only half as many cannon (twenty) as the parliamentarian train, but it was under the able direction of Sir John Heydon. He placed the lighter guns in front of and between the bodies of foot in the first line, and the heavy guns further back on the lower slopes of Edge Hill.

THE BATTLE OF EDGEHILL

The battle began with an ineffective artillery duel and a number of musket skirmishes. Rupert then ordered his cavalry on the right wing to advance. As they rode forward with increasing speed, finally reaching a gallop, Ramsey's horse remained stationary, hoping to absorb their impact. However, they made the grave error of firing their carbines before the royalists were in range, then lost their nerve and fled. Rupert's men pursued them into Kineton, cutting many down. Sir John Byron's two regiments, which comprised the second line of Rupert's wing, now joined the charge, when they ought to have stayed back and attacked the exposed flank of the parliamentary infantry. It was the same story on the royalist left. Wilmot swept away Lord Feilding's regiment, and Lord Digby, commanding the second line, joined in the pursuit. Only a few hundred royalist cavalry remained to participate in the main battle. A bitter struggle now raged as the two infantries came to push of pike. Except for the flight of Charles Essex's parliamentary brigade, both sides stood their ground, and kept up the fight until nightfall.

Essex had wisely kept two horse regiments—Balfour's and Stapleton's—in reserve. These he now committed to the fray. In conjunction with four foot-regiments they attacked Sir Nicholas Byron's brigade, broke into it, and drove it back. The earl of Lindsey and Sir Edmund Verney fell in the fighting, while Sir Nicholas himself was wounded.

Meanwhile Sir Charles Lucas launched the remaining 200 royalist horse against the rear of Essex's army, but accomplished little. Even though the main body of royalist horse was now drifting back to the battlefield, both the riders and their mounts were worn out. The royalist foot therefore made an orderly withdrawal to the bottom of the Edge Hill escarpment where they spent the night.

A STALEMATE

Both armies had been fought to a standstill, and the battle had ended in the stalemate of mutual exhaustion. It is often implied or alleged that the king might have savoured the fruits of victory if Rupert had not allowed his cavalry to leave the battlefield in reckless pursuit of their fleeing adversaries. But the greater blunder was Sir John Byron's, and also Lord Digby's, both of whom should have prevented the second line of cavalry under their respective commands from joining the pursuit. Had Byron and Digby employed their four regiments to attack Essex's infantry in both its flanks they could reasonably have expected to carry the day.

During the night Essex was reinforced by the late arrival of John Hampden's brigade of two regiments of foot and one of horse, but having lost the four infantry regiments of Colonel Charles Essex's brigade, the earl did not share their enthusiasm to renew the fight. The royalists were no better off: many of the horse and about a third of the foot were missing. So both sides withdrew, the king to his previous quarters, and the earl to Warwick.

Edgehill is usually reckoned to be a draw. The losses on both sides were roughly equal, totalling perhaps 1,500. The king lost more officers, but he had cleared the road to London and captured seven guns to bolster his feeble artillery train. While both sides had demonstrated sophistication in their deployment of troops along the Swedish pattern, they had thrown away whatever advantages it might have brought them in the first few minutes of battle.

The First English Civil War

The first shock of war at Edgehill led to a cry for peace, especially in London, where unemployment remained rife and the royalists' seizure of Newcastle had cut off its essential coal supplies. So in December the Lords retreated from the Nineteen Propositions and put forward more modest proposals: that Charles agree in advance to any scheme of Church reform decided on by the Westminster Assembly of divines due to meet in 1643, and that he accept the Militia Ordinance and all other ordinances passed since by Parliament. The Commons added a proviso for the immediate abolition of bishops and archbishops. They were sent on to Oxford, but a month later Charles insisted on the complete restoration of his control over the armed forces and a bill to safeguard the Book of Common Prayer, with a vague allowance for 'tender consciences'. Negotiations collapsed and the war was resumed.

THE PROBLEM OF THE CHURCH

The future of the Church proved the great sticking point, and Parliament's failure to tackle it before war broke out was greatly to its disadvantage, given the issue's crucial importance to so many of its supporters. That said, Charles's undertaking to return the Church to its condition under Queen Elizabeth, which he was still repeating as late as January 1646, meant little because no one could agree on what that condition had been, and he always behaved as if Laud had never given offence to anyone. From February 1641, when the issue was first raised in Parliament, it proved impossible to resolve; on almost any other question the Commons could present the king with a united front, but not on this. There was general agreement that the present bench of bishops must be drastically pruned and their powers curbed, but that was all. Only a minority of Members of Parliament favoured their outright abolition at this stage, but none could agree on the nature of the 'new' episcopacy; still less could they agree on forms of worship and ceremonial. Proposals to abolish the prayer-book provoked an alarming backlash; in fact they soon split the opposition, and by the autumn of 1641 drove some of its leaders into the king's camp. Charles promptly made the protection of the Established Church his rallying cry.

Meanwhile the Lords doggedly refused to ban bishops from their House, and were at odds with the Commons on what forms of worship they were to permit. With Laud in the Tower and his bishops naturally keeping a low profile ecclesiastical discipline virtually collapsed. Into the gap surged the Independents, Baptists, and other sectaries, driven underground since Elizabeth's time but never eliminated. In the metropolitan region they set up new largely working class congregations, which acknowledged no central church at all and were headed by uneducated and unordained 'ministers', usually preaching exclusivist and apocalyptic doctrines at odds with orthodox theology and carrying sinister political and social undertones.

The king and his supporters naturally made hay with these 'mechanics', whose excesses they plausibly blamed on Parliament's irresponsible meddling, but the governing classes of all political persuasions were aghast at this development.

There was general agreement that strict ecclesiastical discipline must be reimposed, but how? The only alternative to episcopacy was Presbyterianism, which was naturally pushed hard by the Scots commissioners in London in 1641, but the ardent support of the Scots was the last thing to convert the English to a system they already distrusted. Presbyterianism certainly imposed a stern discipline, but as practised in Scotland it was aggressively invasive of private life, and gave too much power, it was thought, to the minister and a select junta of elders in each parish. The warning of an Elizabethan Member of Parliament, that 'New Presbyter is but Old Priest writ large', was still heeded, and it is a strange commentary on Laud's Herculean efforts that one of the abiding attractions of Anglicanism was the comparative laxity of its social discipline.

The Irish crisis sidelined the whole question so that by the time it went to war all Parliament could show for its efforts was an Act of March 1642, reluctantly signed by Charles, barring bishops from the House of Lords and from all temporal employments. In September 1642, seeking aid from the Scots, Parliament resolved to abolish bishops altogether, and subsequently seemed to think it had done so, though it did not pass the necessary legislation until October 1646. Archbishop Laud's belated trial in 1644, and his execution early in 1645, was an act of spite which led nowhere. In the meanwhile an assembly was summoned to Westminster in 1643 to tackle the problem, but, shackled to a Parliament divided within itself, it made slow progress. The king declined the invitation to send delegates.

REGIONAL WARFARE

Meanwhile the fortunes of the war had swung this way and that. The king had winning chances at the end of 1642 when his nerve cracked after the skirmish at Turnham Green in early November, and in 1643 at the end of a summer of victories. In 1644, however, his armies did poorly in all sectors, and blunders at the end of the year by all Parliament's senior commanders simply dented a year of progress: they did not write them off.

1643 was pre-eminently a year of largely separate regional wars. The earl of Essex in command of Parliament's main 'marching army' had a miserable time of it. Faced by shrill but contradictory and ill-informed instructions from Westminster he stuck by his own priority of clearing the Thames Valley between London and Oxford of royalist garrisons and that meant that he spent most of the time oscillating between Reading and Windsor, his army ravaged by typhoid and other fevers, increasingly gloomy and demoralized. As Henry Marten put it, 'it is summer in Devonshire, it is summer in Yorkshire, and only winter in Windsor'. In the first eight months of 1643 Essex led his men into three counties and captured three garrisons. Rupert invaded thirteen counties and captured eight major parliamentarian centres.

The greatest success stories from the royalist point of view came in the north and the south-west. In the north the earl, now marquis, of Newcastle began the year seizing castles that gave him control of the Great North Road, including the crucial town of Newark, and mopped up much of the east and North Riding and North Lincolnshire. On 29 June he won one of the biggest victories of the year (about 15,000 combatants) at Adwalton Moor near Bradford—one of the few battles where well-trained artillerymen turned the course of a battle with their deadly fire. His advance south below Newark was blocked by determined and energetic marching and opportunistic counter-punching from Oliver Cromwell and the men of East Anglia, but he had done the king sterling service. In the south-west, Sir Ralph, by the end of the year Lord, Hopton had done even better in turning Devon and Cornwall into a major royalist recruiting ground and clearing much of Wiltshire and Dorset and areas nearer to London (by early 1644 he would trying to break through into Sussex via Hampshire). He had been engaged in a series of running engagements with Sir William Waller, the emerging darling of the war party at Westminster. Their first major clash had been Landsdown, overlooking Bath, on 4 July. The extraordinary courage and grit of the Cornish infantry under Sir Bevill Grenville had seen the royalists storm up a steep incline to occupy the crest of Landsdown Hill. However, a shortage of match and the explosion of a powder keg in which a prisoner of war had imprudently tapped out his pipe, killing several senior royalist officers and temporarily blinding Hopton, made that a pyrrhic victory. Ten days later, with reinforcements from Oxford, Hopton tried again, on Roundway Down on the outskirts of Devizes. This time royalist resolve gained its reward. The parliamentarian horse was put to flight and—in one of John Kenyon's most memorable passages they 'plunged headlong over a concealed escarpment, ending up in a shattered tangle of flesh and bone, equine and human, at the bottom of what is still known as "Bloody Ditch" '.[34] The foot surrendered and the king had control of the west of England.

Elsewhere, things had not gone quite so well for the king. In the north-west Midlands, strong-arm Members of Parliament like Sir William Brereton in Cheshire and Sir John Gell in Derbyshire had at least maintained the area under the control of forces loyal to the Parliament and several royalist attempts to awaken its latent support in East Anglia had failed. However, the real hinge of the war had been in the south Midlands and along the Severn Valley where royalist successes early on at Cirencester and Bristol were offset by losses at Lichfield and Stafford. Rupert had done good—at times very brutal—work to harry that area. It would be fairest to say that the war was shifting too slowly in the king's direction, but the nub of the autumn campaign turned out to be the siege of Gloucester. If the king secured it, he would control the whole of the Severn Valley allowing him to mop up parliamentarian areas in the Marches and Wales and giving him control of the Severn tolls, on the cloth trade, a badly needed financial resource. (The importance of such things should never be underestimated. In 1643 Charles thought it better to allow the Tyne and Tees towns to offer to provide London with massively taxed coal than to deny them the coal and him-self the revenue.) The capture of Gloucester would have capped a good year, and might have caused ragged parliamentary nerves to snap. But at the last moment Essex was persuaded to become proactive. Taking his best troops and the cream of the London trained bands with him—and thus leaving the capital dangerously exposed—Essex trundled across country. As he arrived in Gloucestershire, Charles slipped south and east, placing himself between the earl and London. A knockout blow could now have ended the war. It was the king's best chance but his army was weak and under-supplied and he vacillated. There followed a game of ducks and drakes, as Essex feinted this way and that to get past a back-pedalling royal army. The inevitable confrontation—involving 30,000 men, second only to Marston Moor—took place on the outskirts of Newbury on 19 September. It was a bitter and unflinching fight. The parliamentarians needed to break through and failed to do so. But what turned it from a losing draw to a win-ning draw was that the royalists lacked enough powder to sustain another full day of fighting. Discretion being the better part of a silent musket, they withdrew in good order and allowed Essex to limp back to London. It had not only been Charles's best chance, it was to prove his last real chance.

ROYALIST LOSSES, 1644

For as 1643 had seen steady advances for the royalists, so 1644 saw relentless parliamentarian progress, only mitigated by internal squabbles and indetermin-acy from competing parliamentarian generals.

It is now possible to see that the tide turned in the first months of 1644. An army of 21,500 Scots entered England and quickly secured the north-eastern counties and set to work clearing Yorkshire of royalists. Their presence denied the king men and money, and they represented a distraction to the marquis of Newcastle and his army. The king gained no comparable benefit from the cessa-tion in Ireland. Historians remain uncertain as to the precise number, but several thousand Irish troops streamed across the Irish Sea in small contingents. The only significant body of them was destroyed and dispersed by Sir Thomas Fair-fax on 25 January at the battle of Nantwich after a flash-flood had carried away the bridges which half of the royalist army had crossed and the other half were waiting to cross. These setbacks in the north were then compounded by Waller's comprehensive defeat of the royalist armies of the west at Cheriton not far from Winchester in late March.

From then on the royalists seem to have been constantly trying to recover from their losses and to shore up crumbling positions. Rupert spent the spring and early summer rushing round the east Midlands and then the north-west, reliev-ing sieges and strengthening garrisons. The king and Hopton did the same in the south Midlands—the king winning the one major pitched battle to go the royal-ist way during the year when Waller tried opportunistically to exploit the fact that the king's army was straggling on both sides of Cropredy Bridge near Banbury. It was in fact a messy year, with all the major armies on both sides being broken up so as to pursue several different tasks simultaneously and with sections of several armies being brought together at crucial junctures to fight battles in which the antagonisms of rival generals within their councils of war was almost as great as the antagonisms across the firing-lines. Thus at the greatest battle of the First English Civil War (Marston Moor, 2 July 1644), the royalists were an amalgam of Rupert's army and Newcastle's army, and the parliamentarians a mix of Scots and large parts of the armies of both the Northern and Eastern Associations; while at the 2nd battle of Newbury (27 October 1644), elements of the Southern and Eastern Associations and regiments of the London trained bands and Essex's army took on an equally mongrel royalist force. Victorious units usually broke up and went their separate ways with the result that the fruits of victory often withered on the vine. Only Marston Moor really changed things.

MARSTON MOOR (2 JULY)

What brought well over 40,000 men to that bleak moor north of York in early July was the Scottish encirclement of the capital of the north (discussed in Chapter 2). The earl of Manchester and Oliver Cromwell were there to tighten the stranglehold, Rupert to release it. None of the senior commanders on either side wanted a showdown battle; junior officers and happenstance dictated there should be one. It was a textbook battle: two armies with time to plant themselves in strong defensive positions with massed infantry in the centre and cavalry on either wing; a timeless lull through a torrid July afternoon as both sides stood facing one another a half-mile apart and then, in the early evening at 6 o'clock, a parliamentary and Scottish decision to move forward and engage. Three hours later 6,000 men lay dead, a high proportion of them officers. The accounts of the battle make clear that there were many heroes and few cowards on that field and historians are still unable to decide who takes the credit for the victory. Cromwell claimed it: despite a nasty head wound, he had rallied his men and brought them back into the thick of the action at a crucial juncture when their instinct would have been to harry and plunder the broken regiments they had already defeated. The Scots also maintained that their fearless behaviour across the field and especially in the centre won the day. Recriminations about Oliver's assertion that next to God he deserved the greatest credit, rumbled on for months.

THE SELF-DENYING ORDINANCE

The fruit of Marston Moor was, however, harvested. York surrendered and the marquis of Newcastle, muttering that he 'would not endure the laughter of the Court', withdrew into continental exile. Much of royalist Lancashire and Yorkshire capitulated. The north was lost to the king. In the south, however, all was frustration. Essex had committed himself to the liberation of the south-west,

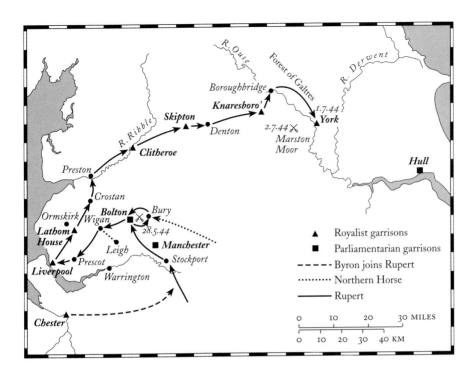

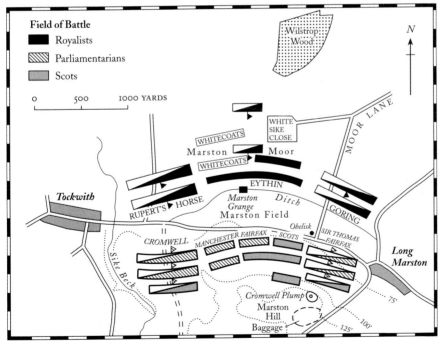

Marston Moor campaign of 1644

but he found himself cut off in Cornwall and forced into a humiliating surrender of his infantry at Lostwithiel (August 1644). A 2nd battle at Newbury was again drawn and the recriminations of the unsuccessful generals—Essex, Waller, Manchester, and Cromwell—was worse than the recrimination amongst the successful generals before York. 1644 ended as a year in which the parliamentarians moved from controlling forty to seventy per cent of England; but it did not feel like it. And the year came to a close with everyone blaming everyone else for the lack of progress. Fortunately, they decided that God was displeased with them and that He was withholding victory because of the worldly pride that governed their actions; and their worldly response to this religious perception was the Self-Denying Ordinance, which made a clean sweep of the high command (all Members of Parliament had to choose between military and parliamentary duties and all chose the latter which left not a single English peer with a military command). The armies of Essex, Waller, and the Eastern Association were fused into a single new strike force—the New Model Army—under the command of Sir Thomas Fairfax, the non-political Yorkshireman. Meanwhile Charles asked for a treaty and desultory negotiations took place at Uxbridge. However, with the king still adamant that he was bound by oath and honour to uphold episcopacy and the Book of Common Prayer, and the parliamentarians and their Scottish minders as adamantly committed to the substitutions of a Presbyterian order and to the new Westminster Directory of Worship, nothing came of them.

PRESBYTERIANISM

Not that all was well in the Parliament Houses. Quite apart from the bitter disputes engendered by the Self-Denying and the New Model Ordinances, there was less agreement on the long-term settlement of Church and State than the firm negotiating stance at Uxbridge suggested. Even if Scottish pressure is discounted, a majority of Members of Parliament were now convinced, with varying degrees of reluctance, that Presbyterianism was the only way forward, the only way to secure religious peace and the suppression of the sects. Nevertheless, a powerful Independent minority in the House of Commons and the Westminster Assembly continued to block further action, giving the impression that the government did not know its own mind. Thus a new Presbyterian prayer-book, the Directory of Worship, was endorsed by Parliament in January 1645, but it did not make its use compulsory, and it did not proscribe the old prayer-book until the following August, when it also set up an elaborate nationwide system of Presbyterian Church government, while offering no means of enforcing it.

END OF THE WAR

On 2 April 1645 the first units of the New Model Army took the field. By June Fairfax had under his immediate command 15,000 to 17,000 men, but all together the field armies under the control of the Committee of Both Kingdoms (including the Scottish Army in England) must have numbered over 50,000 men, with nearly as many again in garrisons all over the country. The king had under half as many troops regimented and in garrisons. Parliament now had control of most of the major ports—the exceptions being Exeter, Bristol, and Chester—and thirty-seven of the fifty largest towns. It also still had the navy to facilitate the coastal supply of its armies and to frustrate royalist seaborne transport, and the area under its control gave it a massively large tax base and—in the City of London—a source of loans for which Charles had no equivalent. The king had no prospect of winning an *English* civil war. He had to strive to keep the war going, avoiding pitched battles except on his own terms, to maintain his hold of the ten county towns and twenty or so medieval castles still in his hands, in order to buy time to bring the resources of his other kingdoms, and just possibly international support, into play. For much of the year Montrose's brilliant victories in Scotland gave him grounds for optimism. Likewise he continued to hope that his supporters in Ireland, especially amongst the Protestant and Catholic Old English, might be brought to see that their long-term security required their participation in the English theatre of operations. This scenario lay within the realm of possibility; but it was not to be (see Chapters 2 and 3).

In its final stages the war turned more vicious. There had been some savage sackings of towns in the first half of the conflict such as Rupert's storming of Bolton in the days before Marston Moor but there was nothing to match the ferocity of his sack of Leicester on 31 May 1645 or Cromwell's brutal slaughter of the surrendered garrison at Basing House (see picture on p. 229) a few weeks later. The royalist armies, increasingly unpaid and with their civilian infrastructure crumbling, became more and more a marauding band living off the land. In the end, the war in England became, as the Irish theatre had always been, too much like the continental wars of the period.

THE BATTLE OF NASEBY (14 JUNE 1645)

In the event, the New Model won the war almost single-handed, without significant help from the Scots who wasted time failing to capture Hereford and Newark (see pictures on pp. 213–14), and in spite of ill-informed and confusing instructions from the armchair generals on the Committee of Both Kingdoms. It fought its way through the Midlands and then on through the west. The king failed to devise a clear strategy and linked up neither with Goring in the west nor with his more scattered forces in the north-west, and he brought his main army of under 10,000 to the field at Naseby against a force at least half as large again. It was the shortest and fiercest of the major battles—all over in barely two hours. It was a battle not unlike Marston Moor in that Cromwell on the parliamentarian right wing routed the cavalry facing him, as Rupert routed Ireton on the royalist

Battle of Naseby (14 June 1645)

If Streeter's engraving (from Joshua Sprigge's *Anglia Rediviva* [1647]) can be believed the parliamentary and royalist battle formations were quite unsophisticated. The infantry took up position in the middle of the front line, flanked by cavalry on the right and left wings. Within the infantry regiments musketeers flanked squares of pikemen, while small field artillery pieces were interspersed between the regiments. In the middle of the picture is the centre and right wing of the New Model Army; facing them are the centre and left wing of the king's army. Not shown is a small advance guard or 'forlorn hope' ahead of the New Model's front line. To the right of Naseby village and its windmill is the parliamentary baggage train which Rupert wasted valuable time attacking after he had driven the left wing of New Model cavalry under commissary-general Henry Ireton off the field. Rupert's failure to regroup his forces allowed Fairfax and Cromwell to carry the day.

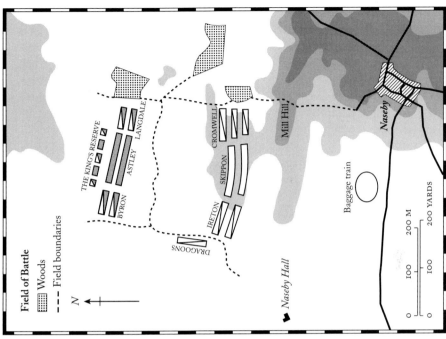

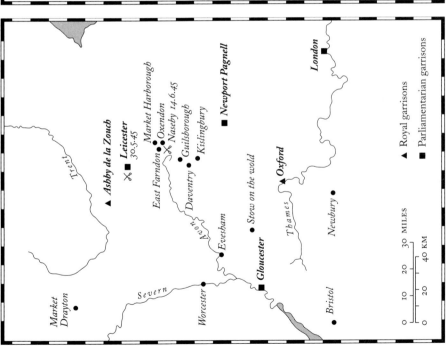

Naseby campaign of 1645

right; and as at Marston Moor, an outnumbered royalist foot showed prodigious courage and might have prevailed but for the towering personal bravery of Sir Thomas Fairfax in their midst and the timely arrival of Cromwell's horse on the flank while Rupert was busy pillaging behind the parliamentary lines. The death rate at Naseby was lower than at Marston Moor, less than ten per cent, but a large proportion of the foot were captured as was the king's top-secret correspondence revealing deeply compromising attempts to secure international aid from the Catholic superpowers and from the Catholic Confederacy in Ireland. Its publication caused a further haemorrhaging of support.

After Naseby, the New Model set off for the west. It was held up initially by the surprising strength of Clubmen (anti-war populist groups) in Dorset and Wiltshire, but within a month Fairfax had lured Goring into a pitched battle at Langport (10 July) between Taunton and Bridgwater. Goring did everything right, occupying a formidably strong ridge and declining to be drawn down from it. However, he was faced by a ferocious artillery bombardment to which he had no reply and by troops buoyed up by recent victories and a conviction of God's presence in their midst. As the cavalry stormed through Goring's position Major Thomas Harrison, watching from the opposite hill, started speaking in tongues and Cromwell burst out: 'to see this, is it not to see the face of God?' Within four weeks, the New Model had routed both of the significant royalist armies. Many months of marches, skirmishes, and sieges lay ahead, both for Fairfax's men and the other regional armies: Hereford was not taken until December 1645, Chester until January, Newark and Exeter until May, Oxford until June, and Worcester until July 1646; and some strongholds and castles were to hold out for longer still. However, the war was effectively over. The question from the high summer of 1645 onwards was not whether Parliament would win the war, but whether it had any hope of winning the peace.

Charles showed his determination to make that as hard as possible for them by surrendering himself to the Scots near Newark on 5 May 1646, after a frantic ride from Oxford. It strengthened their hand and gave him a chink of light as he set out on a prolonged policy of divide and rule amongst the victorious allies. In July 1646 a body of Anglo-Scottish commissioners arrived at Newcastle, where he was housed, with the so-called Newcastle Propositions which resembled those previously offered to him at Uxbridge, and which were still presented to him as non-negotiable.

THE NEWCASTLE PROPOSITIONS

On the armed forces there was some movement; they were to remain under tight control not in perpetuity but for twenty years. This concession was quite overshadowed, however, by a merciless pogrom now launched against the royalists. Here Parliament was in fact bound by the stance it had adopted in 1642. Ostensibly it had no quarrel with the king, only with his wicked advisers. Successive ordinances raising armies to fight the king gave as one of their main aims 'the safety of the king's person', a formula only dropped in 1645, and then after some debate. Up to then the battle-cry of those armies had been 'King and Parliament!', and even the Solemn League and Covenant had been ostensibly designed among other things 'to preserve and defend the King's Majesty's person and authority'.[35] If this were carried to its logical conclusion, then the king must be ruthlessly stripped of his previous advisers, and any of his supporters of like mind who might replace them, so that he would emerge in his proper person, with an unclouded mind. To this end seventy-three persons, beginning with the king's Palatine nephews Rupert and Maurice and comprising most of Charles's ministers and field officers, plus a few bishops, were to be excepted from pardon altogether. A further fifty were barred from public office for life. Furthermore, all men who had fought for the king, or assisted him in any way, were barred from taking office in local government or sitting in Parliament, notwithstanding the fact that most of them had now 'compounded' for their delinquency by the payment of heavy fines. These were terms which even a man much less scrupulous of his honour than Charles I would have found it impossible even to discuss, as he in effect said. Worse still, Parliament would have divided the nation into the sheep and the goats, the haves and the have-nots for at least a generation, and created a resentful and embittered faction which might have perpetuated itself for centuries.

If Parliament was drunk with victory, it soon awoke to a crashing hangover. Even in defeat the king could effectively veto any constitutional or religious settlement he did not like. For virtually everyone, including the Levellers, those violently innovatory radicals who were now emerging as a political force to be reckoned with, assumed in most of their schemes the survival of the monarchy in one form or another together with the House of Lords. Given Charles's character and temperament, deadlock was inevitable, but Parliament, shackled to the unrealistic Newcastle Propositions, lost ground all the time. In August 1646, and again in December and the following May, Charles asked that he be allowed to come to London 'with honour, freedom and safety' to negotiate with Parliament directly, but this was altogether too dangerous. Now that his capacity to do harm was gone he rose in public esteem; while at the same time the unprecedented weight of Parliament's taxation, the all-encompassing tyranny of its county committees, and the impact of its huge armies on the civil population right across the country, rendered it increasingly unpopular, especially since its mandate from the electors, given in October 1640, had lapsed. Nevertheless the parliamentarians bought off the Scots in January 1647 and secured control of the king's person, but they were no nearer controlling his mind and will, and while they futilely tinkered with the Newcastle Propositions the army acted.

England's preservation

This engraving, dating from the end of the First English Civil War, shows the English ark or ship of state, composed of House of Lords, House of Commons, and the Westminster Assembly of Divines, being tossed by a tempest of turbulent royalism. The ark survives, thanks to its own strength, God's favour, and the courageous military leadership of its defenders. Across the top, from left to right, are the earl of Essex, parliament's mediocre lord general from 1642 to 1645; the earl of Warwick, the gifted Puritan admiral of the navy from 1642 to 1645; the earl of Manchester, commander of the Army of the Eastern Association; and David Leslie, commander of the Scottish forces in England between 1644 and 1646. Across the bottom are Sir Thomas Fairfax, the brilliant lord general from 1645 to 1649 when he resigned in protest against the planned invasion of Scotland, and Oliver Cromwell, Fairfax's successor as commander-in-chief. The royalist leaders and counsellors being engulfed by the waves are not identified. On the extreme left, however, one can see Queen Henrietta Maria holding a Catholic missal and rosary, with perhaps the earl of Newcastle behind her. On the right, wielding a sword, is Prince Rupert, with Archbishop William Laud clutching his bishop's mitre. Conspicuously absent from the picture is the king, because it was not against him, but supposedly his 'evil counsellors' that the war had been waged.

The Army and Politics

MUTINIES

By 1647 Parliament, though victorious, faced a staggering political and economic problem: what to do about the £2.8 million that it owed to the New Model, the Northern Army, Massey's brigade, several dozen garrisons and county regiments, and the pre-New Model armies of Essex, Manchester, and Waller. With the undisguised purpose of forcing the disbandment of the New Model and other troops, the House of Lords had been blocking renewal of the monthly assessment since September 1646, while collection of the excise had virtually ceased. The result was a wave of mutinies in at least thirty-four English counties, and throughout most of Wales. Onerous as taxation had been, it was probably less burdensome than compulsory billeting and free quarter. The crisis over pay was a national issue rather than a straightforward conflict between the New Model and Parliament. Organized plunder was the most elementary form of unrest. More direct were the concerted efforts of bodies of men to exact their arrears. Distinct from these mutinies were threats by whole regiments, such as Colonel Duckenfield's in Cheshire, to disband themselves. However, once the king had been vanquished, and troops were no longer needed, such measures, as means of extracting arrears, were self-defeating. As a result, soldiers turned to another expedient: they seized their officers, and in some instances county committee members, sequestrators, and excise men, and held them to ransom. Most sensational was the action of the 500 men of Nantwich Garrison, who in July 1646 captured the Nantwich sequestration committee and threw them in prison among common criminals, 'cavaliers and horse stealers' for two days, where they slept on bare boards, and were denied food, drink, 'or any necessaries'.[36] The most frequent form of mutiny in the years 1646–7 was a refusal to move quarters, or a deliberate march to fresh quarters against orders. Almost all the mutinies were fomented and organized from within the ranks rather than by disgruntled or politically motivated officers. In the spring of 1647, for example, the Northern Army mutinied for the third time against Colonel Sedenham Poynts. Infected by Leveller propaganda, their main demand was to associate themselves with the New Model Army in its demand for arrears and indemnity. Arrest and imprisonment at Pontefract was the reward Poynts earned for refusing to countenance these demands.

DISBANDMENT AND RADICALISM

All the turmoil of 1646–9 was aggravated by a food crisis and massive rise in prices, and leavened by extremist propaganda from the Levellers and other sectarian groups. Alone of all the armies, the New Model's discontent had far-reaching political consequences. That army had been characterized by an advanced political consciousness from the beginning, thanks to the controversies surrounding the Self-Denying Ordinance. As early as autumn 1646 the pro-New Model faction in Parliament had to fend off an effort to transform the Western Brigade of Edward Massey into a self-sufficient army that would challenge the hegemony of the New Model. They turned the tables on the anti-New Model faction by disbanding Massey's brigade and several other provincial forces while preserving the New Model intact. But once the Scots army had been paid off, and quit English soil in February 1647, the last compelling reason for keeping the New Model in existence disappeared. Having gained the upper hand, the Holles-Stapleton group in the Commons cut through the financial Gordian knot by ordering disbandment of most of the New Model *before* its arrears were settled. When the soldiers began petitioning for their back pay, an end to impressment, and an Act indemnifying them for all acts carried out under military orders, they were condemned in a parliamentary resolution as 'enemies of the state'. This, and the refusal to grant more than six weeks' arrears, galvanized the soldiers. In the first English experiment in army democracy, they elected representatives known as agitators, and browbeat most of their officers into joining them to resist disbandment.

The result was a huge explosion which engulfed the general officers and carried them along with it. The New Model, mustered by its regimental officers, rendezvoused near Newmarket, and forced Fairfax to agree to an executive general council which included two officers and two enlisted men elected from each regiment. Then, in circumstances still cloudy and controversial, a troop of horse was despatched to seize the king at Holmby House, Northamptonshire, and bring him back to headquarters. Parliament's furious reaction to these moves caused the army to advance to St Albans, within reach of London, and thence on 14 June it issued a thunderous declaration, claiming that it was a better representative of the people than a decayed Parliament, and demanding that the latter first present its accounts, then dissolve itself. Meanwhile Cromwell's son-in-law, Henry Ireton, consulted with radical peers to draft the army's own blueprint of a future government, the Heads of the Proposals. They were endorsed by the General Council and submitted to the king on 1 August.

At first Parliament resorted to bluster; it passed a resolution declaring its 'high dislike' of the army's proceedings; it tried to turn its other armies in the north and Midlands against it; and it endeavoured to replace its commanders with two Presbyterian veterans, Waller and Edward Massey. This failing, it had second thoughts; it now promised eight weeks' arrears of pay, passed a liberal Indemnity Ordinance, and lovingly declared the New Model to be *its* army, deserving of support. This cut no ice with the army, but it provoked a violent backlash in London, and a wave of rioting which the disaffected trained bands made no effort to control. When a group of Independent Members of Parliament and peers, with their speakers, fled to the camp at St Albans, seeking protection, Fairfax marched

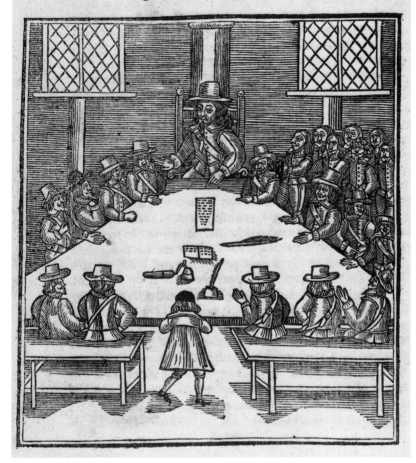

The manner of His Excellency Sir *Thomas Fairfax*, and the Officers of His Armie sitting in C O V N C E L L.

The Army Council

A rare experiment in military democracy, the General Council of the [New Model] Army existed for less than a year. It was created in June 1647 in response to rank and file agitation of the previous year. Though dominated by the officers, it also included two representatives from each regiment of the private soldiers. The Council met intermittently to discuss political issues such as the army's grievances against Parliament, the proposed invasion of London, negotiations with the king, the impeachment of the eleven Presbyterian Members of Parliament, and the Leveller 'Agreement of the People'. It had no jurisdiction over military discipline, strategy, or appointments, which remained the province of Sir Thomas Fairfax and his Council of War. When at Putney in November 1647 the radicals won the majority to their side, the 'grandees' adjourned the council and sent the representatives back to their regiments. The scribe shown here is probably William Clarke, whose extensive notes provide extraordinary insight into the army debates at Reading (July) and Putney (October–November).

his army into London to restore order. Eleven leading Presbyterian Members of Parliament were expelled, and the City government purged.

The New Model was now in the driving seat, but it had nowhere to go. Despite the absence of their leaders, the Presbyterians still had the ascendancy in Parliament, and the army did not cut off their contacts with the king. The Heads of the Proposals were in many ways Charles's best option so far, and if he had accepted them as a basis for negotiation Fairfax might well have taken him with him to London to negotiate with Parliament face to face, as he had been requesting for the past twelve months. The proposals posited a system of biennial parliaments, which were to control the armed forces and government appointments for only ten years (exercising a looser supervision thereafter). They only excepted four (unnamed) persons from pardon (as against the Newcastle Propositions' seventy-three), and all other royalists were to be readmitted to public life after five years. Even the bishops were to be retained, though with token powers, against a vague background of general religious toleration (except for Roman Catholics).

THE PUTNEY DEBATES AND THE AGREEMENT OF THE PEOPLE

However, Charles affected to doubt the New Model's constitutional authority to negotiate, and he had every right to query its stability. A groundswell of distrust in some regiments at the drift of their commanders' negotiations with the king, fanned by the Levellers, forced Fairfax to agree to a celebrated series of debates between the general officers and newly elected agitators from the regiments, together with a few Leveller spokesmen, which commenced at Putney in the last week of October. Here the Levellers presented the draft of a radical republican constitution, the Agreement of the People (28 October), which dispensed with the king and House of Lords, and provided for nearly universal manhood suffrage, religious liberty, and an end to conscription. This led to a far-ranging discussion of natural rights and how far they embraced political rights, that was far ahead of its time. One agitator after another, many of them officers, reminded their commanders, the 'grandees', that they had risked their lives, and many of their comrades had lost theirs, for the good of the commonwealth, and they expected to share in the postwar settlement, which must be an altogether new settlement. Chagrined at the radicalism of these demands, the grandees, led by Cromwell and Ireton, cut off the debate and sent the agitators back to their regiments. While the short-lived experiment in army democracy was over, the grandees still kept up pressure on Parliament, not only to settle its debts to the army, but also to honour its commitment to pay pensions to maimed soldiers and the widows and orphans of the slain. To show goodwill, between January and March 1648 they trimmed 20,000 men from their rolls, or approximately half the army. For a time the army was paid more regularly than ever before.

THE ENGAGEMENT

After an abortive attempt to flee the country in November 1647, Charles ended up at Carisbrooke Castle, on the Isle of Wight, whence he could not escape, but where he enjoyed much greater freedom. The New Model leaders washed their hands of him, and Parliament peremptorily sent him the Four Bills (14 December), demanding his immediate signature without further discussion. The Four Bills were virtually the Newcastle Propositions rearranged, though they did handsomely concede that only seven of those excepted from pardon would be prosecuted on capital charges. However, Charles was now free to accept other delegations, among them one from the Scots, who deeply resented their exclusion from talks with the king, and were alarmed at the prominence of the army in English politics, given its manifest anti-Presbyterianism. If the Long Parliament could not deal with its obstreperous legions, they would. On 24 December Charles rejected the Four Bills and signed an Engagement with the Scots which offered, on the surface at least, his best terms yet, to be enforced by an invading Scots army. He was to acknowledge the Covenant, but only as a voluntary undertaking, and he was to accept State Presbyterianism, but only for a trial period of three years, after which the question was to be reopened. All other issues were to be thrashed out in London later, with Charles's direct participation. In the spring of 1648, while the Scots were raising another army in a last attempt to dominate English politics, sporadic revolts broke out across the south and west, ostensibly in support of the king, but mainly, and especially in Kent and Essex, as a protest against the rule of the Long Parliament.

The English Revolution

THE SECOND ENGLISH CIVIL WAR

In a sense there were four British Civil Wars: the first from 1639–40; the second from 1641–6; the third in 1648; and the fourth from 1649–54. If it is misleading to call any of them an *English* civil war, it is especially misleading so to describe the events of 1648. For that war began with the Engagement between Charles and that section of the Scottish nobility who had secured control of the Northern Kingdom, and its centrepiece was the Scottish 'invasion' of July to August 1648, their defeat in Lancashire, and the subsequent English 'invasion' of Scotland (see Chapter 2). But there *was* an English and Welsh aspect of this British war. In Kent, in south Wales, in Yorkshire, and throughout East Anglia there were uprisings of former royalists and more especially of disillusioned and disaffected former parliamentarians protesting against high taxation, military oppressions (especially the burden of free quarter), centralization, and religious change. In London there were angry demonstrations by apprentices demanding the return of the king and of the good old days. The numbers in all these risings and protests were not large, but for every rebel who declared himself there were ten who wavered and waited upon events. Local militias proved inadequate to contain the protests—and in some cases joined them—so the New Model had to be split up to deal with risings as and when they happened. The most dangerous was a rebellion in Kent which originated in a riot in Canterbury on 25 December 1647 over the county committee's determination to prevent the celebration of Christmas, which Parliament had declared a pagan festival to be suppressed. The trial of those arrested in May 1648 led to spontaneous protests throughout the county. Prompt action by experienced officers of the former royalist army turned this into an organized revolt and within days 11,000 men were regimented. However, as quickly as the brushfire spread, it was doused by Fairfax. Marching against the largest concentration at Maidstone, he encountered stiff resistance but stood his ground and killed and arrested the greater part of the royalists there and occupied the town. The regiments elsewhere melted away, except for 3,000 men who crossed Rochester Bridge into Essex, where they settled down in Colchester, with fresh recruits joining them from all over East Anglia. With royalist numbers growing, Cromwell away with half the New Model dealing with trouble in south Wales, London in turmoil, a major naval revolt breaking out simultaneously in the fleet, and the Scots only weeks away from mounting their campaign in England, this was a genuine crisis. Colchester was too strongly defended for an assault to be certain of success, and a defeat for the New Model detachments would leave London wide open to the insurgents, so Fairfax had to undertake an eleven-week siege almost as debilitating for those camped around the town in unsanitary conditions as for those starving within the walls. There Fairfax was stuck as the Scots crossed the Border in early July. Cromwell's victory at Preston (17 August) was neither guaranteed nor unnecessary. The future of the three kingdoms hung more in the balance than at any time since Marston Moor and perhaps since the 1st battle of Newbury.

A few garrisons in the First Civil War had been denied quarter; and some men had been killed in hot blood after surrendering. But there had been no judicial executions of the losers by the victors. In 1648 all that changed. After the sieges of Pembroke (May–July) and Colchester (June–August) and after the battle of Preston, the leading royalists were put on trial and sentenced to death. Exemplary executions took place. In the view of Fairfax and Cromwell, those who instigated this war were much guiltier than those who fought against them in the first war: that had been a trial by battle and God had declared his mind—the parliamentarian cause was the just cause. To restart the war was to seek to overturn not only the first defeat but the judgement of God. It was to commit sacrilege. So, in the eyes of the army leaders, if those who led the provincial revolts and the Scottish invasion were guilty of sacrilege, how much more guilty was the chief author of the war, that 'Man of Blood' as Charles Stuart was labelled by an army prayer-meeting in Windsor in April. From that moment onwards, the evidence suggests that the army leaders were determined to put Charles I on trial for his war crimes. That meant that for the more pragmatic and secular voices in Parliament, the end of the war replaced anxiety about the external enemy with trepidation about those in their own midst. A majority of both Houses determined to reopen direct negotiations with him and sent commissioners to meet him at Newport on the Isle of Wight on 18 September. However, they could only offer another rehash of the Newcastle Propositions, and Charles insisted on the terms offered by the Scots; he also demanded a complete package, spurning a partial agreement which might have held off the New Model, if only for a while. There is evidence that he was already contemplating his own martyrdom as a decisive ploy which would at once provoke a national uprising in favour of his son. Negotiations were broken off on 27 October.

TRIAL AND EXECUTION OF CHARLES I

When the main body of the army returned to St Albans there were still some who wanted nothing more than the payment of the army's wages and the knitting together of the hearts of the king and the people 'in a threefold cord of love'.[37] Nevertheless, Fairfax came under pressure from his more militant officers, led by Henry Ireton, to reoccupy London and stop the Newport negotiations. Cromwell, though he was preoccupied in Yorkshire, supported these revolutionary moves. Fairfax tried in vain to bring Charles around with a modified version of the Heads of the Proposals. On 15 November he had to agree to submit to Parliament a bullish Remonstrance of the Army, drafted by Ireton, which called for the trial of the king, the abolition of monarchy, and the adoption of the Leveller programme. Further procrastination by Parliament left him at the mercy of the Army Council, and on 2 December he marched back into London and ordered the king to be transferred from Carisbrooke to Hurst Castle, in Hampshire. Attempts to form a provisional government around the Independent Members of Parliament failed, and on 6 December Ireton sent Colonel Pride down to Westminster with a company of soldiers to exclude those members who had voted for the Newport Treaty. This and a wave of voluntary absenteeism in protest or cowardice left a House of about 154. On 1 January 1649 this 'Rump' passed an ordinance setting up a High Court of Justice to try the king. When the Lords refused to comply it simply repassed it as an 'Act', declaring that its authority, as the elected representative of the nation, was sufficient—a ridiculous pretence. On 21 January the king went on trial; such proceedings were unprecedented, but his refusal to accept any constitutional proposals put to him left men with little choice. They might have deposed him, or declared that he had abdicated by inference, as was done with James II in 1689, but with his three sons safely on the continent, ready to take up the succession, this would have been pointless. If Charles had acknowledged the court's jurisdiction, and entered a plea of not guilty, he could have prolonged the trial for weeks, perhaps months, to the embarrassment and danger of an unstable government; but he refused this last accommodation, as he had refused so many before. He was sentenced to death as 'a tyrant, traitor and murderer'[38] on 26 January and beheaded in front of the Whitehall Banqueting House four days later. Although military officers numbered less than one-third of the signatories of the death-warrant (eighteen out of fifty-nine), the army had played a pre-eminent role in bringing the king to the scaffold.

It now seemed that the civil wars were over at last. A republic was rather limply instituted and the monarchy and the House of Lords were abolished without overt protest; isolated mutinies in April and May 1649 served as an excuse for a final purge of the New Model Army which left it for the time being politically inert. However, the Irish Civil War still sputtered on, and the Scots' reaction to the high-handed execution of *their* king without their consent was yet to come.

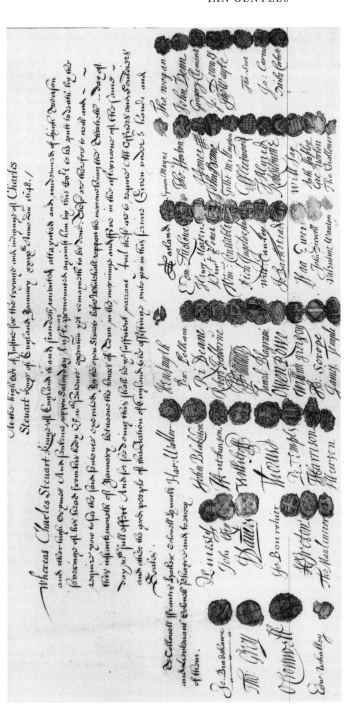

Death-warrant of Charles I

In the wake of the Second English Civil War, the New Model Army united in its determination to treat the king as a criminal and to make him account 'for the blood he had shed and mischief he had done... against the Lord's cause and people in these poor nations'. The Rump Parliament accordingly tried the king on charges of treason against the English people. Charles refused to plead to the charge and denied the legitimacy of the court. In the statements he made at the trial, no trace of his habitual stutter could be detected: he spoke with the utter conviction of a man who knew that he was king and knew what kingship was about. In so doing, he began the image of himself as the martyr king, victimized by traitors, and thereby set the psychological stage for the restoration that occurred eleven years later. Charles I was executed at Whitehall Palace on 30 January 1649 and by March of that year both the monarchy and the House of Lords had been abolished. The signatures on his death-warrant include those of Oliver Cromwell (first column) and Henry Ireton (second column).

5
NAVAL OPERATIONS

BERNARD CAPP

In July 1642 Charles I's splendid navy defected to Parliament without firing a shot. Throughout the First English Civil War the king thus faced the humiliation of fighting his own 'royal' navy. Far more was at stake, of course, than injured pride. As Clarendon observed, the loss of the fleet was 'of unspeakable ill consequence to the King's affairs', and dealt a devastating blow to his chances of winning the war.[1] While command of the navy could never guarantee victory, without it Parliament would have faced almost certain and rapid defeat.

The Royal Navy

Charles had shown an energetic interest in the navy ever since his accession, and indeed before. He oversaw the major shipbuilding programme of the 1630s which added a succession of powerful new vessels to the fleet, including the massive *Sovereign of the Seas* (1637), which in size and design anticipated the warships of Nelson's age. This new armada was designed, as the *Sovereign*'s name suggests, to assert the king's domination over the loosely defined waters surrounding the Stuart kingdoms. After 1635 annual levies of ship-money enabled Charles to set out impressive flotillas each summer in the Channel. While the ostensible purpose was to suppress piracy and privateers, their primary aim was to affirm Charles's honour and sovereignty. Their function was diplomatic rather than military; Charles had neither the will nor the means to be drawn into wars with the Dutch or French, and was relieved that their warships chose to avoid confrontations. The ship-money fleets helped to maintain a naval balance of power in the Channel, and to keep open the Spanish sea route to Flanders. But hopes that Spain would repay him with financial support or diplomatic help to further his aims in the Palatinate failed to materialize. Nor did Charles make much progress in enforcing his claims to maritime sovereignty over the Dutch fishing-fleets in the North Sea, for large warships proved ill-suited to the task of chasing fishing-boats. Nor, ultimately, did he succeed in asserting his authority in the

Channel. In September 1639, while most of the English forces were in the North Sea, Dutch and Spanish fleets met in the Channel. The Spaniards took shelter in the Downs, blockaded by the Dutch under Tromp. Ignoring a warning not to attack in British waters, the Dutch destroyed the Spanish fleet on 11 October, under the very eyes of the English commander Sir John Pennington, whose squadron was too weak to intervene. It was a humiliating blow to national as well as royal honour.

We may see in Charles's aspirations the seeds of later naval developments, but it is hard to judge his policies a success in the short term. Certainly, his own subjects were unimpressed. In the absence of any real threat from the continent, Charles sounded unconvincing when he appealed to patriotic sentiment, and even some of his admirals found the manœuvres of the summer fleets both futile and tedious. It also proved hard to recruit mariners, for the wages paid by the navy fell far below those available on merchant voyages, and with the nation at peace there were no compensating opportunities for plunder, adventure, or glory. While the seamen would probably have been willing to fight any foreign power, if called on to do so, the king's policy of benevolent neutrality weighted towards Catholic Spain held little appeal for them. Perhaps the most telling aspect of the battle of the Downs in 1639 was that the English seamen, looking on as spectators, cheered the Dutch attackers. Charles wholly misread the mood of his seamen, as he had misjudged public feeling over the Scottish crisis (discussed in Chapter 1).

Outbreak of War, 1640–1642

CONTROL OF THE NAVY

Winning control of the navy in 1642 represented a financial as well as military coup for Parliament. It ensured that in the struggle ahead the commercial life of the capital retained some degree of normality, and that customs revenues flowed into parliamentary not royal coffers. Had Charles retained control of the fleet and a major port, the course of events would have been very different. He would then have been able to bring in munitions and supplies from the continent without obstruction. More important, a blockade of the Thames, cutting off London's food and fuel supplies and strangling its economic life, would have triggered mass demonstrations by the hungry and unemployed, and intense pressure from the merchant community. In all probability, Parliament would have been forced to sue for peace on almost any terms the king cared to offer.

How, then, did the king allow his navy to be so easily wrested from his grasp? The issue of allegiance came to a head only in the summer of 1642, but it is clear that Charles had lost a lot of ground well before then. From 1640 Parliament had a say in the appointment of senior naval commanders, and several of the most dependable senior figures of the 1630s were passed over for the summer guard of

1641. Parliament went much further the following spring, by which time war looked increasingly probable. The ineffective lord high admiral, the earl of Northumberland, pleaded he was too unwell to go to sea in person, and in March 1642 he was persuaded by the House of Lords to nominate the earl of Warwick as his deputy. Charles had not been consulted and was outraged, for Warwick had well-known Puritan and parliamentarian sympathies. The king responded by demanding that Sir John Pennington, who had commanded the fleet each year since 1639, should do so again. But Parliament outmanoeuvred him, launching a disingenuous investigation into Pennington's conduct while directing Northumberland on 4 April to confirm Warwick's appointment. Charles at York was presented with a *fait accompli*. To sweeten the pill, Parliament was willing for Sir George Carteret, trusted by the king, to serve again as vice-admiral, but Charles ordered him not to accept, either in pique or because he was unwilling to antagonize Northumberland. Instead William Batten, Northumberland's protégé, became vice-admiral with Sir John Mennes as rear-admiral. Whatever the king's reasoning, the effect was to undermine his position still further. He appears to have decided that Warwick's appointment was the price he had to pay to secure parliamentary funding for a fleet that summer, consoling himself with the belief that at the appropriate moment he could reassert royal authority by turning to Northumberland or exploiting Pennington's hold over the seamen.

WARWICK TAKES COMMAND

This strategy carried a heavy price, as soon became clear. When Charles attempted to seize Hull in April to secure its important magazine and provide a safe landing-place for arms and troops from the continent, the governor, Sir John Hotham, denied him entrance. Warwick, acting on Parliament's orders, had already sent warships to lie in the Humber, and in May the arms and ammunition from the magazine were transferred by sea to London under naval escort. On reaching London the escort commanders, who had flouted direct orders from the king, were called into the House of Lords to be thanked for their 'fidelity'. The navy's aggressive stance, it was rumoured, had also persuaded the Danish king to abandon plans to send a force to Hull to assist the king. There was soon a further reminder of what Charles had lost by conceding Warwick's appointment. Captain Strachan of the *Providence* had taken Queen Henrietta Maria to Holland in February and remained there to wait on her orders, ignoring Warwick's instructions to return to the Downs. At the end of June the queen ordered him to carry over a consignment of arms and ammunition for the king, but Warwick's ships intercepted the vessel and chased her into the Humber. Though Strachan managed to slip into a shallow creek, run his ship ashore, and unload her cargo safely, she was soon taken by parliamentary forces, and the episode made it clear that the king would find it hard to secure much assistance from the continent as long as the fleet remained in hostile hands.

Robert Rich, earl of Warwick, 1587–1658

Prior to the outbreak of war, Warwick had been involved in privateering and colonizing ventures, especially in New England, and was well known for his Puritan sympathies. Throughout the 1630s he became increasingly estranged from court life and after 1640 championed the parliamentary cause, eagerly accepting the command of the navy bestowed upon him—against the king's wishes—in March 1642. Had Charles retained control of his fleet the course of events might have been very different. Under Warwick's able command, the navy intercepted vessels carrying supplies to the royalist armies or the Irish confederates, waged war against numerous Irish privateers, and supported parliamentary initiatives on land, in particular the defence of Hull and Plymouth, the capture of Portsmouth and the relief of Lyme. In April 1645, under the Self-Denying Ordinance, Warwick resigned his commission only to be reinstated in May 1648 in the wake of the naval mutiny in the Downs. In February 1649, following the king's execution, the command of the fleet was transferred to the Generals at Sea and Warwick largely retired from public life.

Stung by these humiliations, and with the country sliding towards war, Charles now attempted to reassert his authority over the navy. As Clarendon later remarked, many wondered why he had waited so long. In late June the king sent a letter dismissing Northumberland, and notified Warwick that his assumed authority as Northumberland's deputy was now void. Charles appointed Pennington to command the fleet, and sent letters to all the captains apprising them of the new situation. Enforcing these orders proved far less easy. Pennington, who was over 70, chose not to go on board to confront Warwick, fearing he might be arrested and sent up to Parliament; instead he asked Sir Henry Palmer, a veteran naval officer living in the Downs, to deliver the king's message. But Palmer showed no sense of urgency, and it was left to the royal messenger, Edward Villiers, to deliver the letters. Villiers arrived on 2 July to find Batten in temporary command, Warwick and Mennes having gone ashore. Batten sent urgent word to Warwick, who hastened back to his flagship and summoned his officers. By the time the eleven commanders and six masters had assembled for the council of war, Warwick had received an ordinance of Parliament, rushed through the previous day, confirming his position as admiral in defiance of the king's letter. Warwick acquainted the council with the king's letter and Parliament's ordinance, and of his resolution to remain at his post. The officers unanimously accepted his authority. Five other captains, however, including the rear-admiral, Mennes, had refused to attend, pleading they dared not disobey the king's express command. Warwick sent a stiff reply, and demanded that the parliamentary ordinance be read out to the assembled company of Mennes's ship. Mennes ignored both this and further summonses, and the five dissenting captains met during the evening to plan their tactics. One, Burley, quickly lost his nerve and submitted to Warwick. Next morning Warwick moved his ships to encircle the remaining four, and sent a new summons. This proved sufficient to bring the submission of Mennes and one of the other captains, Fogge. The remaining two, Slingsby and Wake, held out despite a warning shot. In the event Warwick's ultimatum proved redundant, for unarmed boat parties from his ships scrambled aboard the *Garland* and *Expedition*, seized them without resistance, and arrested the two captains.

SEAMEN

Clarendon later recalled that the loss of the fleet took Charles entirely by surprise and made a greater impression on him than any of his subsequent misfortunes.[2] The king had had total confidence in the loyalty of the commanders and seamen, believing they would oust Warwick and Batten whenever he gave the word. At one level the outcome might be blamed on Pennington's irresolution. Had he gone straight aboard, it is at least possible that most of the captains, with Warwick ashore, would have obeyed the king's orders. It is hard to imagine a less appropriate emissary than Villiers, who had no standing in the navy and was a kinsman of the former royal favourite, the duke of Buckingham, hated by the seamen. However, Pennington's reluctance suggests that he was aware of parliamentary feeling in the navy, and nervous of the outcome. The officers commanding the summer guard in 1642 were very different from those of the mid-1630s. The strength of the older gentleman-commanders, such as Mennes, was already much reduced. The newer men, favoured by Parliament, were former merchant shipmasters, brought into naval service by Northumberland from the late 1630s or after 1640. Batten was typical of them: 'a man of a rough nature, and no breeding but that of a common mariner,' as Clarendon described him with an almost audible sneer.[3] Such men had few court connections; their ties were with the commercial interests better represented in Parliament. They also appear to have had closer relations with their men. Merchant commanders relied on volunteers to man their ships, and it is likely that many of these new captains brought some of their former officers and seamen with them. There was thus a significant division within the officer corps. The older career officers sided with the king, but they were outnumbered by the new men and outmanoeuvred by Warwick. Nor should the ordinary seamen be overlooked. Many of those in the Downs gave strong support to Warwick and Batten, and those who felt differently proved unwilling to risk a trial of strength. Charles's concern for the navy had always focused on his ships, not on feeding, clothing, or paying the men who sailed them, and resentments ran deep. Moreover the political stalemate since 1640 had paralysed royal finances, leaving no money for sailors' pay. In the climate of 1642, disgruntled seamen were more likely to pin blame on 'popish' ministers than on Parliament. On 9 January 1642, a few days after the king's attempt to seize the Five Members, 2,000 seamen from naval and merchant ships had marched to the Guildhall shouting Warwick's name and offering to protect the parliamentary leaders. They remembered the national humiliation of 1639 and the inglorious naval operations against the Scots in 1639 and 1640, and they clearly shared popular sentiment in the capital.

Warwick's first objective was to secure the rest of the summer guard. On 8 July the powerful *Lion*, which had been waiting on the queen in Holland, unexpectedly sailed into the Downs, her captain, Fox, totally ignorant of recent developments. As Fox appeared uncertain how to respond, Warwick arrested him, and the rest of the ship's company accepted Parliament's authority without demur. The Irish guard posed a more serious problem. On receiving secret orders from the king the two admirals, Kettleby and Stradling, deserted their station off southern Ireland in September and took their ships (the *Bonaventure* and *Swallow*) to Newcastle, intending to take in supplies and cross to Holland to join the queen. Their plan was aborted, however, for on reaching Newcastle most of the sailors deserted. The mayor found new crews, of a sort, by pressing men out of colliers, but both ships yielded without firing a shot when Batten arrived with a strong force to challenge them early in October. Stradling fled ignominiously in his longboat, while Kettleby was taken prisoner. The summer guard was re-united under Warwick's command.

Naval Activity 1642–1646

The war at sea might thus appear settled almost before the fighting on land had begun. In the event, the navy was to play an active, varied, and important role in the years ahead. One major task was to help military forces ashore secure strategic positions—usually ports—under threat from the enemy. Another was to turn its overall superiority at sea into effective and tight control, which entailed a long and deeply frustrating campaign against privateers, and constant vigilance to deter foreign intervention.

FLEET SIZE

The war at sea brought no major fleet engagements but years of hectic and con-tinuous activity patrolling, escorting convoys, intercepting privateers, and mounting amphibious operations both defensive and offensive. Each year Parlia-ment set out a substantial summer guard and a smaller winter guard, comprising both purpose-built warships and armed merchantmen. The main force was stationed in the Downs, with smaller squadrons assigned to the Western Approaches, Irish Sea, North Sea, and other stations around the Stuart king-doms. The summer guard for 1644, for example, comprised thirty warships and thirty-eight hired vessels; twenty-one of this combined force were assigned to the Irish Sea. Hiring ships was inevitably fraught with problems, for many own-ers and commanders proved to be mainly concerned with profit and preserving their private property. By 1646 the balance had shifted to forty-four warships and twenty-one merchant vessels, with a further thirty-three hired vessels fitted out but kept in reserve. Over half the warships deployed in the summer of 1646 were small fifth and sixth rates, carrying between six and twenty guns and carrying out the same duties as the merchantmen, in convoys, patrols, and blockades. There was no need to mount operations outside the British seas, for the privateers and royalists operated almost wholly in home waters. Neither did Parliament need to build powerful new warships. What the war increasingly revealed, however, was a shortage of faster, lighter vessels able to match the Flemish privateers. Some of the gaps could be plugged by ships captured or bought, including several Dunkirkers, and towards the end of the war Parliament took more systematic ac-tion. The *Constant Warwick*, built in 1645 for a private syndicate and promptly hired by the state, paved the way for seven new fast warships described as frigates, and classed as fourth rates, which came into service in 1646–7.

OPERATIONS IN 1642–1643

Amphibious operations figured prominently from the start. In the summer of 1642, for example, the navy played a key role in foiling the royalist siege of Hull,

1 11 Oct 1639, battle of the Downs
2 27 May 1648, naval revolt in the Downs
3 29 Aug–1 Sept 1648, confrontation
   between parliamentary and royalist fleets
4 Sept–Nov 1648, confrontation between
   parliamentary and royalist fleets
5 19 May 1652, Blake and Tromp clash in the Downs
6 4 Sept 1652, Blake scatters French fleet,
   ensuring the surrender of Dunkirk
7 1 May 1647, clash with Swedish navy

War at sea, map A

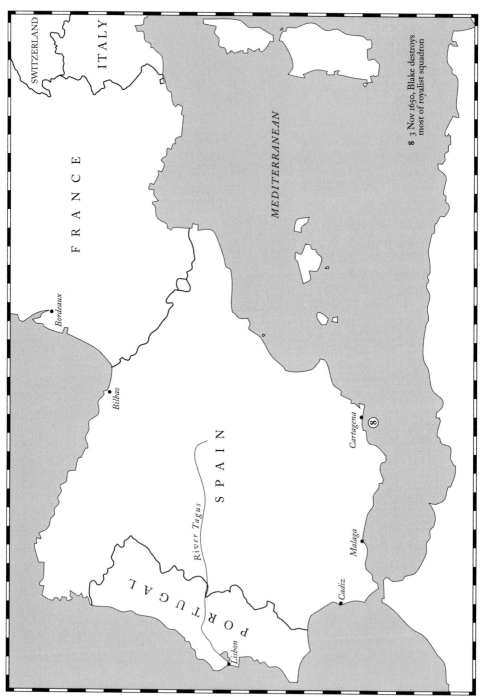

War at sea, map B

8 3 Nov 1650, Blake destroys most of royalist squadron

thus preserving a vital parliamentary stronghold. Captain Trenchfield led a naval force which landed 1,500 men to strengthen the defences, and employed his ships' guns to batter the forts newly erected by the cavaliers. A few weeks later a similar alarm occurred over Portsmouth when its governor, George Goring, declared for the king. Warwick sent the *Charles* with seven armed merchantmen to blockade the port until parliamentary land forces could arrive. In addition one officer, Browne Bushell, led a daring boat-raid by night which boarded the *Henrietta Maria*, lying under the city walls, and brought her away after overpowering her crew and the forty soldiers on board; while Richard Swanley, commanding the *Charles*, launched an equally bold operation on his own initiative, seizing all the forts on the Isle of Wight to secure the rear.

IRISH PRIVATEERS

The threat from privateers, gun-runners, and foreign intervention proved more difficult to deal with. In the winter of 1642 to 1643 the Irish Catholic authorities, the Confederation of Kilkenny, instructed Dunkirk privateers which had shifted their operations to the Irish Sea to capture 'enemy' shipping. Warwick, compelled to keep most of his forces in the Downs to cover potential threats from the continent, found it very difficult to curb these swift raiders, heavily armed and well manned, which from their bases in Wexford and Waterford infested the western approaches and the Irish Sea (also see Chapter 3). Though he stationed warships and armed merchantmen in the key shipping lanes, most of his ships were too slow to intercept the privateers. Warwick enjoyed far more success in staunching the flow of arms from the continent both to Falmouth, which supplied Hopton's army, and to Newcastle, which equipped the earl of Newcastle's northern force. Whether continental powers would have sent substantial military aid to the king had he controlled the sea lanes remains unclear; in the event they were not given the option.

NAVAL SUPPORT FOR THE WAR ON LAND

In the grim military situation that faced Parliament in 1643, the navy's command at sea proved one of its few remaining assets. The earl of Newcastle, dominant in the north after routing the Fairfaxes at Adwalton Moor (29 June), threatened to push south. Hopton's crushing victory at Roundway Down in July secured most of the south-west for the king and hastened the fall of Bristol, England's second city. In September Charles negotiated a cease-fire with the Irish Catholics, clearing the way to bring troops back to England and Wales. Many parliamentarians could feel defeat staring them in the face and, in these circumstances, much of the navy's efforts in 1643 had to be dedicated to mitigating the disasters ashore. With the royalists triumphant in the north, it became all the more important to retain Hull, for Newcastle proved reluctant to move his army south as long as the town held out. A plot by the governor, Sir John Hotham, to betray Hull to the king in

June 1643 was foiled by Captain Moyer of the *Hercules*, who landed mariners to secure the town and magazines until the Fairfaxes could arrive to stiffen the townsfolk's resistance. This story was repeated, with variations, in October, when Newcastle made a direct assault on Hull. Thomas Rainborough of the *Lion* arrived at a critical juncture with a merchantman and 650 soldiers, and on 11 October he helped lead a bold charge by townsmen, sailors, and soldiers to raise the siege, capturing a considerable part of the royalist ordinance. This setback, and the royalist defeat at Winceby on the other side of the Humber on the same day, persuaded Newcastle to lift the siege. There is little doubt that without support from the sea Hull would have fallen at some point in 1643, a major setback to Parliament's military position in the north.

Warwick also attempted to use the navy for damage-limitation in the south-west, though here with less success. In July 1643 he endeavoured to relieve Exeter by sea, only to be driven back by a heavy barrage from the royalist ordinance ashore. The narrow channel limited his room for manœuvre, and his forces withdrew in some disarray, with three ships on fire and three others captured. Exeter surrendered to Prince Rupert on 4 September, and Dartmouth followed a month later. At Plymouth, however, naval support helped the town to hold out against Hopton's army, and the arrival of further ships in late August bringing fresh troops from Portsmouth brought at least temporary security.

FORMATION OF A ROYALIST NAVY

Charles's victories in 1643 in the south-west transformed the war at sea as well as on land. The king could now set about forming a new navy of his own, operating from English ports. 'Royalist' operations at sea in the early months of the war had consisted of privateering raids from bases in Flanders and Ireland, mounted by Irish men and Flemings only notionally under the king's authority. In July 1643 Charles signalled the start of a new phase with a proclamation ordering naval officers and seamen to return to their allegiance by bringing their ships into Falmouth; in return he offered them employment, arrears of pay, and an indemnity. These ships would form the core of a new royal navy, to be commanded by Pennington. On the capture of Bristol late in July, the focus of royalist interest shifted to the River Severn. The owners and masters of eight merchant ships lying at Bristol promptly agreed to serve the king, and the *Tenth Whelp*, an eighteen-gun warship in Warwick's fleet, defected to the new force. Early in August a newsletter reported that Pennington 'was ready to go to sea with 18 tall stout ships'.[4] The Venetian ambassador, writing home in October, even claimed that Pennington's force enjoyed greater strength than the parliamentary fleet, and predicted that the imminent fall of Plymouth would tilt the scales still further. In December Charles tried to establish a further squadron at Dartmouth, under the earl of Marlborough, consisting of ships loaned by local merchants who were to be repaid within six months from prize-money.

It is clear that parliamentary supremacy at sea in late 1643 was much less secure than a year earlier. The king now had ports and shipping in the west. The navy, by contrast, found itself starved of money and supplies as political leaders channelled their limited resources to the war-effort ashore. Warwick and Batten warned that their unpaid, underfed sailors were growing mutinous and might even desert to the enemy. Royalist privateering offered sailors better pay, shorter voyages, and rich opportunities for plunder. Warwick had never had enough ships to meet every demand for convoys, and Parliament's failure to set out a winter guard on time left merchant shipping even more vulnerable. Even worse, the hiatus enabled the royalists to ferry over thousands of troops and supplies of ammunition from Ireland to Wales between October and December 1643, following the cease-fire. Their arrival significantly altered the military balance. As Warwick pointed out to Speaker Lenthall in November, if the winter guard had been set out promptly he could have prevented this operation or intercepted the ships at sea. His deep frustration is evident throughout the second half of the year. From the beginning of August he badgered Lenthall and the navy commissioners to provide additional ships, hasten out the winter guard, and send pay and supplies for his men. At the end of the month he sent Batten to London to press Parliament on all three issues, to no avail. In late November Warwick wrote in despair to Northumberland, the former lord admiral, rehearsing his problems and begging for help: the position in the Irish Sea had become desperate, with Bristol lost, Liverpool threatened, and the royalists building up a substantial counterforce in the south-west. Not until December was the winter guard finally settled, months behind schedule. By then Warwick was already pressing anxiously for the 1644 summer guard to be finalized as a matter of urgency.

The dangers facing the parliamentary navy in 1643 were real and pressing. In the event it weathered the storm. Warwick maintained the allegiance of his men, helped by the fact that Parliament had raised the seamen's pay in January from fifteen shillings to nineteen shillings a month, a positive gesture even if pay was often slow to arrive. The fleet in turn maintained its overall superiority at sea, despite the heavy losses that privateers and the new royalist squadron inflicted on merchant shipping, especially in the Irish Sea. The privateers, driven essentially by the quest for plunder, had no incentive to challenge powerful naval forces. The royalists' own squadron lacked the strength and perhaps courage to risk a major action, and 'Admiral' Pennington remained safely ashore. The royalists' finances too were precarious, moreover, and the loyalty of their own seamen far from certain. When William Smith overpowered the *Fellowship* in August and her commander tried to negotiate a conditional surrender, Smith offered her company employment and arrears of pay if they would yield up their ship, and they promptly complied. Parliamentary commanders achieved several other notable successes, despite their problems. Richard Haddock, patrolling off Newcastle, captured the important fort on Holy Isle as well as several prizes, while Smith overpowered royalist shipping based in Bristol. Far more important, the navy's fundamental loyalty to Parliament remained unbroken. Batten made the point in dramatic style when the queen arrived off Bridlington from the continent in February under the protection of the Dutch Admiral Tromp, bringing money and arms. Unwilling to risk war with the Dutch, Batten chose instead to bombard the house in Bridlington where the queen had taken lodging, forcing her to flee for shelter to a snowy ditch. 'Before we could reach it,' she told the king later, 'the balls were singing round us in fine style.'[5] Batten's cannonade, if not the most heroic action in British naval history, sent an unmistakable message. Not every officer shared his resolution. A few wavered, feeling—like many ashore—that the quarrel with the king was being pushed too far: Browne Bushell, the hero of Portsmouth, defected to the royalists; George Bowden, commanding a hired merchantman, sailed into Dartmouth and accepted a privateering commission from Prince Maurice; while Brooke of the *Providence* wrote to Pennington offering to carry his ship to the royalists at Bristol, though in this case his men intercepted the letter and promptly arrested him. Compared with defections ashore among leading military commanders, however, these were mere pinpricks. There is no evidence of large-scale disaffection or doubts among the officer corps, and at least some of the commanders were driven by strong ideological commitment. Haddock, for instance, dismissed the cavaliers as a 'Romish rout, and anti-Christian crew',[6] while Smith rallied his men with a stirring defence of 'God's cause' as well as the prospect of prize-money. Warwick kept his fleet loyal and largely intact in 1643, and used it effectively to bolster Parliament's shaky position ashore. At the close of the year Parliament belatedly recognized his achievements by appointing him lord high admiral.

OPERATIONS IN 1644

The year 1644 saw dramatic shifts in the fortunes of war on land. The Scots crossed into England, joined up with parliamentary forces in the north, and routed the royalists in July at the battle of Marston Moor. The royalist cause in the north collapsed. In the west and south-west, by contrast, it was the parliamentary cause that foundered.

These events ashore largely drove naval operations in 1644. The North Sea diminished as a theatre of operations with the defeat of the royalists in the north. The navy had mounted a sustained blockade of Newcastle, so tight that only one ship had been able to clear the port in the last six months of the siege (compared to about 1,500 in normal times). Once Newcastle surrendered to the Scots in mid-October Warwick redeployed his ships for service elsewhere. Though the summer guard of 1644 looked formidable with thirty warships and twenty-two hired merchantmen, it had to contend with privateers operating from ports in the West Country, Ireland, France, and Flanders, forcing Warwick to assign many of his ships to routine convoy or patrol work. He also needed to stem the flow of troops and arms from Ireland, which had significantly altered the balance of the war in the west in 1643. In addition he needed vessels to relieve the few small ports in the south-west still left in parliamentary hands, whose only hope now lay in naval support. Much of the naval war-effort in 1644 consisted of amphibious operations designed to help these beleaguered communities, spurred on by the fact that every port that fell to the royalists boosted their strength in seamen, ships, and facilities.

The war against the royalist squadrons and the privateers enjoyed mixed fortunes. Paradoxically it could never be wholly won at sea, for total success required the elimination of their bases, which could only be achieved through victory on land. In February Warwick reported gloomily that the royalists now had the capacity to set out 260 ships of 50 to 300 tons, and painted a bleak scenario of trade devastated or switching to foreign carriers, and of English mariners turning to the royalist privateers for employment. The royalists themselves grew more ambitious. The earl of Marlborough, after ferrying arms and ammunition from France, sailed west in February planning to seize English shipping in the Canary Islands or Azores and then range along the American seaboard, hoping to sweep up enough shipping and sailors to fit out a fleet able to challenge Parliament's navy in the Channel. But such an armada never materialized, and though Warwick failed to defeat the privateers the navy did succeed in containing the problem. The blockade of royalist ports meant that privateers often faced a long wait before they could find an opportunity to slip out, and any prizes they took might be recaptured before they could be brought back to a safe harbour. At Warwick's suggestion, Parliament also licensed twenty-five privateers of its own in 1644, victualled by the state, which were free to take an offensive role.

NAVAL SUPPORT FOR THE LAND FORCES

For much of the year Warwick's energies focused on supporting parliamentary forces on shore, mainly in the south-west. If the navy needed military aid to achieve total victory at sea, Parliament depended on naval support to stave off total ruin. The most dramatic of these episodes was the heroic defence of Lyme, cut off and besieged by strong royalist forces under Prince Maurice. The siege of Lyme took on a symbolic importance that far outweighed its strategic significance (also see Chapter 6). The garrison and townsfolk put up a stubborn and courageous defence, but it became plain that without relief by sea it must eventually fall. Warwick's arrival late in May with arms and provisions put new heart into the defenders, and his men were so moved by their plight that they voted to give up some of their own meagre rations and spare clothing. At the request of the military commanders (among them Robert Blake, the future General at Sea), Warwick sent 300 seamen ashore to strengthen the garrison, and though he had to dispatch most of his ships to other stations he and Batten remained at Lyme, encouraging the defenders and sending urgent pleas to

Parliament to send a relief force by land. On 15 June he reported that Maurice had at last lifted the siege on hearing of Essex's advance. The successful defence of Lyme was widely regarded as one of the greatest feats of endurance of the war. Warwick's ships alone could never have broken the siege, as he was well aware, but without them it is unlikely that Lyme could have survived.

Warwick and Essex now joined in perhaps the most ambitious combined operation of the war. Essex marched into the south-west, a royalist stronghold, shadowed by Warwick's ships in the Channel. The intention was to confront Maurice's army and loosen the royalist grip in the region; in the process Essex would be able to raise the siege of Plymouth and regain Dartmouth and the other ports which had fallen to the royalists, dealing a serious blow to the privateers. It might even be possible to recover Bristol, which would be a major setback to the king's position both by land and sea. The outcome proved very different. After defeating Waller at Cropredy Bridge (29 June), the king pursued Essex as he marched into ever more hostile territory, and at Lostwithiel the parliamentary army found itself surrounded and outnumbered; Essex escaped by sea, leaving his helpless army to surrender on 2 September. Warwick had fully supported Essex's grand plan, but he was furious as well as dismayed at its outcome. For on his march west Essex had stripped Plymouth of most of its garrison, and Warwick protested—well before Lostwithiel—that it had been left desperately vulnerable. Plymouth served as Parliament's only safe harbour in the south-west, and its fall would gravely weaken the naval position in the Channel and the Irish Sea. Warwick himself was forced to sail for London once his supplies were exhausted, but he left Batten and three other ships to give the garrison whatever help they could. It was soon needed, for the king arrived on 17 September, with Maurice and Hopton, and resumed the siege. Lord Robartes, trying to rally the defenders, complained that the townsfolk were apathetic, the soldiers demoralized, and supplies desperately low. Batten sent 300 seamen ashore to bolster the garrison, and the timely arrival of supplies and reinforcements by sea also helped to revive morale. The king eventually moved away, and though the siege continued Plymouth held out for the present.

THE IRISH SEA AND BRISTOL CHANNEL

The other main naval theatre of war in 1644 was the Irish Sea and Bristol Channel. Here, despite many setbacks, events moved slowly in Parliament's favour. By the start of the year the navy had already stemmed the flow of arms and soldiers across the Irish Sea. A squadron based at Liverpool blockaded Dublin and the north Wales coast, while the Irish guard kept up pressure on southern Ireland, south Wales, and the Bristol Channel. These measures proved effective. When the royalist captain Baldwin Wake attempted to break the blockade of Dublin in March, his men mutinied and made him carry the ship back to the safety of Bristol. The earl of Ormond (see picture on p. 76) wrote plaintively that he had both men and materials to send, but no means of transporting them safely to the English theatre of war. Parliament's grip remained precarious, however, with no safe port in Ireland, only Plymouth in the south-west, and Pembroke and the Haven at Milford in Wales. Then, early in 1644, the royalist earl of Carbery overran most of Pembrokeshire, cutting off Pembroke and Milford by land, and then moved swiftly to cut off access by sea by building a new fort at Pill, opposite Pembroke, which would deny safe anchorage for parliamentary shipping. With Swanley, admiral of the Irish guard, away at Plymouth the royalist admiral, Pennington, seized his chance to send arms and supplies to the new fort by sea. Swanley's return on 19 January transformed the situation. He and his seamen roused the demoralized forces at Pembroke, and launched a series of successful attacks on royalist outposts in the area. He and Colonel Laugharne then mounted a combined land and sea attack on the Pill, which surrendered on 24 February along with the two royalist warships lying beneath it. In the wake of this success the royalists fled from Haverfordwest, and another amphibious assault recaptured Tenby on 9 March, with naval officers and seamen first to enter the town. Pembrokeshire was saved for Parliament. More important, the operations blocked a potentially dangerous supply-route for Irish troop reinforcements, and Swanley was summoned to London to receive a medal from a grateful Parliament for his services.

Not everything in south Wales went Parliament's way. Its sweeping gains in Pembrokeshire were soon threatened when Colonel Charles Gerard, one of Rupert's most dynamic and ruthless officers, was sent to restore the royalist position. Gerard swept across the south as far as Pembrokeshire, and the parliamentary commander Laugharne hastily pulled back to Pembroke and Tenby. By July Milford Haven itself was once more at risk, and Warwick warned that if it fell the navy would be unable to maintain any effective Irish guard. In the event the danger passed. In the wake of the royalist disaster at Marston Moor (2 July) Gerard and his best troops returned to Oxford. Laugharne now joined with Robert Moulton, Swanley's successor commanding the naval forces in the area, and launched a series of counter-attacks against the garrisons Gerard had left behind. This secured Pembroke and the Haven and enabled Moulton to crown his fortune by capturing nine rich East Indiamen sailing from Bristol laden with wine and tobacco. Other good news followed. The fall of Liverpool to the royalists early in June proved short-lived; after Marston Moor Parliament soon recovered it. Even more important news came from Ireland. In July the powerful earl of Inchiquin switched allegiance to Parliament, transforming the political and military situation in Ireland. His move proved equally significant for the navy, for by seizing control of Cork, Kinsale, and Youghal he gave the parliamentary navy safe harbours in Ireland itself for the first time in the war and for the first time Parliament could seriously consider taking the war to the privateers. Even though the disaster at Lostwithiel threw a dark shadow over these successes, the parliamentary navy could be satisfied with what it had achieved during the year.

OPERATIONS IN 1645

In 1645 progress proved even greater. This was despite the removal of Warwick, who was forced to lay down his commission in April under the Self-Denying Ordinance. The decision to apply the ordinance to the navy may have reflected a sense that Warwick bore some blame for the débâcle at Lostwithiel, but it was a crass mistake. He had proved himself tough, committed, and energetic. Moreover there was no capable alternative waiting in the wings, no naval Fairfax. After weeks of discussion, Parliament admitted it had failed to find anyone of appropriate 'honour, quality and estate', and notified Batten that he was to command on an interim basis with his old rank of vice-admiral. This was hardly an ideal solution. Batten was a tried and effective commander, but he lacked Warwick's political standing and connections, and almost certainly felt snubbed by the terms of his appointment. Warwick himself, taking his removal in good part, became the driving figure among the new admiralty commissioners directing naval affairs ashore.

There was a further upheaval in June when Swanley, admiral of the Irish guard, was summoned to London to face unspecified charges. These may have concerned his clashes with the Pembrokeshire committee, or perhaps suspicions over his contacts with Ormond, which were intended to persuade him to follow Inchiquin into the parliamentary camp. Whatever the charges, the Irish Sea was now the crucial theatre of naval operations and Swanley's removal was a significant blow, for the struggle for naval mastery had begun in earnest. To fill the vacancy, Parliament appointed Moulton admiral, bringing in William Penn from another station as his deputy. Meanwhile the confederates pressed hard to recover ground lost to Inchiquin. In March the parliamentary stronghold at Duncannon surrendered to the besieging Irish forces and only the arrival of military supplies, brought in under fire by Penn's naval forces, spared Youghal from a similar fate. At sea, the Irish privateers continued to take a heavy toll, capturing increasing numbers of English merchantmen.

SOUTH-WEST INGLAND AND SOUTH WALES

The other main focus of naval activity in 1645 remained the south-west and south Wales. In the wake of Essex's crushing defeat the royalists strengthened their grip on the south-west, and amphibious operations by the navy represented Parliament's only hope of containing the damage. At Plymouth, where the royalists had intensified the siege, naval officers and seamen played a key part in operations ashore, offensive as well as defensive. After one bold sally in February the military governor, Lord Robartes, recorded gratefully that 'All the sea captains behaved themselves stoutly'.[7] Seamen played a still more prominent role later that month further along the coast, securing beleaguered Melcombe and recapturing Weymouth after fierce fighting. The navy also maintained its tight blockade of the ports still in royalist hands. Captain Edward Hall reported that the townsfolk of Dartmouth, finding their trade paralysed, had become mutinous. His ships alone could not seize the place, he observed in August, but if Parliament were able to send any land forces the town would surrender within two days.

In south Wales the situation proved more volatile. The royalist commander Gerard reappeared in Pembrokeshire in late spring, adopting a scorched-earth policy which terrorized the civilian population and penned the parliamentary forces into Pembroke and Tenby. When Batten arrived at Milford on 29 July, Laugharne at once begged him to send sailors ashore to strengthen his own small forces. Batten obliged, and the 200 seamen he landed played a key role in tipping the scales. The combined force launched a successful surprise attack on the royalists at Colby Moor on 1 August and went on to storm the main royalist stronghold at Haverford Castle. Batten managed to send 450 prisoners to Ireland to help Inchiquin hold Youghal. Pembrokeshire was at last safe, and Milford Haven was not to be threatened again. Batten's pride in his sailors was justified, though their dramatic successes were possible only because the king's crushing defeat at Naseby had forced him to recall Gerard from south Wales. The navy played a key part too in foiling Charles's plan to ferry most of his remaining forces across the Bristol Channel to join his best intact army in the south-west. In late July the naval squadron patrolling the Severn captured the sixteen transport vessels intended to carry the troops, forcing the plan to be abandoned. The navy also took part in the final parliamentary triumph of 1645, the capture of Bristol. Marching west after Naseby, Fairfax laid siege to the city in August, and Moulton brought his squadron from Milford Haven to impose a tight blockade by sea. The two commanders met to draw up plans for a combined assault. In the event Rupert, finding himself pressed by land and sea with no hope of relief, surrendered Bristol after a fierce but brief fight on 10 September. With its fall ended the king's dreams of bringing Irish Catholic troops into England, and of building an effective royalist navy.

ENGLISH AND IRISH PRIVATEERS

Paradoxically the parliamentary navy had greater success on land than at sea in 1645, for the privateers remained an intractable problem. The position did improve in the North Sea; with the fall of Scarborough in February 1645, and the capture of 120 ships in its harbour, the royalists lost their last remaining port in the north-east. But in the west Sir Nicholas Crisp, a merchant and shipowner, set out a force of fifteen privateers in the king's name, and Devon and Cornwall provided ideal bases from which to scour the western approaches, the Irish Sea, and the Bristol Channel. Ironically the effective naval blockade of the western ports, which strangled ordinary commerce, had the effect of driving local shipowners and sailors into privateering ventures as their only practicable means of subsistence. In June 1645 ten privateering captains, most of them English, wrote from Ostend warning the bailiffs of Yarmouth not to punish any privateers who fell into their hands: hang any of our men, they declared haughtily, and 'we can, if you compel us, make a hundred suffer for one'.[8] The Fleming Haesdonck also commanded a sizeable force in the king's name; one undated paper listed eleven ships sailing under his commission, for the most part with Flemish captains. Though reliable figures are elusive, there is no doubt that privateers inflicted heavy damage on English merchant shipping. Moreover every parliamentary loss at sea represented an equivalent gain by the enemy. Privateers could sell captured cargoes to buy arms or better ships, while some captured vessels could be turned into privateers themselves. Thus George Bowden, sailing under Crisp's commission, bought a twenty-two-gun frigate at Ostend with the proceeds of a prize he had taken. His lieutenant, Coleman, took over Bowden's original ship, and was soon able to purchase a new frigate for himself with the proceeds of one of his own prizes. Under favourable conditions, privateers could multiply like flies.

In practice, however, conditions proved less than perfect. While they disrupted commerce badly, especially in the Irish Sea, they never looked likely to strangle it, let alone starve Parliament into surrender. The privateers, almost by definition, lacked the will and organization as well as the strength for any concerted action against the parliamentary forces. A naval squadron, based in the Downs, operated a regular convoy system across the Channel, and warships patrolled the main shipping lanes and lay off the privateering bases in the south-west, Ireland, and Flanders. If privateers slipped through the net they faced another gauntlet when they tried to return to port, and their prizes—normally slower sailing—stood a much poorer chance of evading the patrols. Sir Nicholas Crisp, for example, listed nine of his ships which had been captured, sunk, or wrecked; while an Irish royalist lamented in March that Captain Thomas Plunket alone, 'that noted scourge of Irish at sea', had recently taken seventeen of their ships.[9]

OPERATIONS IN 1646

The year 1646 saw Parliament's final victory ashore. The king's last bastions in the south-west succumbed to a twin assault under Fairfax and Batten, who achieved what Essex and Warwick had attempted two years earlier. Fairfax raised the siege of Plymouth in January, and called on Batten for naval support to reduce Dartmouth. Early in April Batten forced the stronghold at Portland to surrender, and then moved to blockade Pendennis Castle, guarding Falmouth; already cut off both by land and sea, it surrendered in August. With the loss of Falmouth the royalists held no harbours in the south-west, a major blow to their privateering operations. Parliament now extended its grip. The prince of Wales had managed to slip out of Falmouth in March and cross safely to Scilly, but on 12 April Batten arrived with a fleet of twenty ships and encircled the island. The prince was 'invited' to return to England and hand himself over to Parliament, though in the event a storm scattered Batten's fleet and the prince was able to flee to the relative safety of Jersey. Scilly eventually surrendered in September, without a fight, to a naval force under Sir George Ayscue. The islanders, Ayscue reported, had held out because of reports that Parliament intended to drive them out and resettle the place, an 'ethnic cleansing' he firmly disavowed.

PRIVATEERING SUCCESS IN IRELAND

The end of the war in England did not spell the end for the privateers, though the capture of their bases in south-west England marked an important shift in their fortunes. The Irish bases, especially Wexford, now assumed still greater importance. The surrender of Dunkirk to the French on 1 October 1646, which meant the loss of another major privateering base, prompted many of the Flemish commanders also to shift their operations to Ireland. It has been estimated that the privateers operating there numbered fifty or sixty ships, a formidable force.[10] It is impossible to measure the damage they inflicted. One Irish contemporary claimed that 1,900 prizes had been captured in six years, almost certainly a massive exaggeration even if small fishing-boats are included. At least 250 prizes were taken by Irish privateers in the period 1642 to 1650, though significantly only about thirty per cent of them were English (and a further sixteen per cent Scottish); privateering captains were never a fastidious breed.[11] Intensive naval patrols and a convoy system provided some relief, and enterprising naval commanders enjoyed some striking successes, but the privateering war was a frustrating business. William Penn, who spent several years serving in the Irish Sea, admitted in 1646 that he had become 'heartily weary of this dull and fruitless employment', and of being 'chained to this coast'.[12] The only permanent solution was to eliminate the bases themselves. Once again, therefore, the navy found itself drawn into amphibious operations supporting military commanders ashore. Early in 1646 Inchiquin and Lord Broghill persuaded Robert Moulton, commander of the Irish guard, to mount an ambitious operation in the south-west: in March he sailed into Dingle Bay where the soldiers sacked and burned the town of Dingle Couch, and then moved into the Shannon to try to forge a military alliance with the earl of Thomond, a wavering parliamentarian. Though the operation eventually failed, the instructions sent to Swanley, who succeeded Moulton in the autumn, directed him to support Inchiquin and Broghill ashore as well as hunting privateers at sea. He was also to provide convoys, as and when needed, for parliamentary troops being shipped to reduce Ireland. The reconquest of Ireland had been pushed close to the top of the parliamentary agenda.

THE NAVY'S CONTRIBUTION TO VICTORY

The First English Civil War was clearly won by the New Model Army, and it is not easy to assess the navy's overall contribution. Certainly the navy enjoyed numerous specific successes against royalist privateers and, arguably more important, in holding on to beleaguered major outposts such as Hull. It would be wrong to underrate these achievements. Had Hull fallen in 1643, for example, Newcastle would have marched his army south and his presence in the Midlands might have altered the military situation decisively when the parliamentary position was at its weakest. But in most cases the navy's triumphs at sea were marginal to the war-effort, and it might be argued that Parliament paid very dearly for them. Putting a fleet to sea proved an expensive operation. Warwick estimated the cost of the navy in 1644 as £392,000 (over half the sum of £641,000 allocated to the New Model Army annually from 1645). Inevitably naval operations diverted enormous sums that could have been poured into the war-effort on land. But such calculations miss the point, for without naval protection maritime trade would have been helpless against the massed privateers, and it is not hard to discern a doomsday scenario. Without a stable maritime trade to generate customs revenues, Parliament would have lost a significant part of its income. Even more important, the crippling of London's commerce would have brought tens of thousands of hungry and angry citizens on to the streets. In those circumstances, parliamentary leaders would have had little choice but to settle for whatever terms Charles might offer. Much the same applies to the military situation. In the absence of a parliamentary fleet, continental powers would certainly have poured far more arms and ammunition into the royalist war-effort. It is quite likely too that Parliament would have lost all control in Ireland, and certain that after the cessation in 1643 many thousand more troops would have crossed the Irish Sea to join the king. They would have placed Charles in a very much stronger military position in 1643-4, and it is conceivable that they might have proved decisive before the Scots' intervention in 1644 restored the balance. The navy's greatest contribution, then, lay in defining the terms of the land war in Parliament's favour. It sustained Parliament's economic position and revenues while cutting off the king's main lines of supply. As in the two World Wars of the twentieth century, naval preponderance was essential to avoid defeat, and a precondition for the victory that only land forces could deliver. Modern civil war historians have tended to marginalize the navy's contribution. Perhaps one should reflect on the fact that the parliamentary leaders, however desperate for cash, were never attracted by the option of keeping the navy in harbour to save money. They recognized that it would be a false and perhaps fatal economy.

King or Parliament? 1646–1649

By the end of 1646 the fighting in England was over. If there was no such peace at sea, the situation had changed there too. During the civil war naval commanders had carefully avoided clashing with foreign warships, but a dramatic incident in the spring of 1647 suggested that a more assertive spirit was now emerging. On

1 May Richard Owen, commanding the western guard, encountered a force of six Swedish warships and about ten merchantmen off the Isle of Wight, and ordered them to strike their topsails in recognition of English sovereignty of the seas. The Swedes refused, citing express instructions from their queen, Christina. Owen had only one other ship with him, but he opened fire on the Swedish vice-admiral and shadowed the convoy as it ran for shelter, sending word meanwhile to Batten in the Downs. Batten found the Swedes lying off Boulogne, summoned their commanders on board, and held them prisoner. A council of war decided to take the Swedish vice-admiral and his ship to the Downs, and the others chose to follow rather than return home to face the queen's wrath. In the event Parliament quickly released the Swedes, but the episode did not go unnoticed. It was no coincidence that only two weeks later the French Cardinal Mazarin finally bowed to parliamentary pressure by banning all royalist privateers from French ports, and forced the prince of Wales to revoke the letters of marque he had issued. Though the prince reversed his decision in August, France was no longer available to refit ships or sell prizes and there was yet another exodus of privateers to Ireland.

The crucial role of the Irish ports was clearly reflected in the fleet stations allocated to the summer guard of 1647. Eleven warships (later increased) and five hired merchantmen patrolled the Irish Sea, and a further eleven warships formed the western guard. Twelve ships under Batten were stationed in the Downs, with only three to secure the north. Swanley, Crowther, and Penn, commanding the Irish guard, stepped up the pressure on the privateers and their main ports, Wexford and Waterford. Penn reported in June 1647 that many had shifted to safer bases further west, at Galway and Limerick, and that he was planning to pursue them thither. But hopes of reconquering Ireland and eliminating the bases had by then already faded. The mutiny of the New Model Army in the spring of 1647 and the political upheavals that followed ruled out any invasion for the foreseeable future. The privateers had gained a reprieve.

POLITICS AND THE NAVY

The disastrous splits in the army and Parliament in 1647 posed urgent questions too about the unity and allegiance of the navy. Could the fleet be held together when the parliamentary cause ashore was splintering? Parliament initially worried that the agitation in the army would spread to the fleet. The Levellers appealed to the seamen, and the admiralty commissioners urged Batten to watch out for Leveller-inspired mutinies. Pay had been a major issue in sparking the army revolt in March, and they reminded him that Parliament had paid its mariners far better wages than Charles I. In the event, it was at the top, not the bottom, that naval loyalties wavered, and over ideology rather than pay. Batten and most of the senior commanders were moderates, eager for a settlement with the king on reasonable terms. Batten had become disgruntled at his treatment by

Parliament, and his unease with political developments ashore reached back at least to the winter of 1646 to 1647, when events had brought him into close proximity to the king and the Scots. After surrendering to the Scots, Charles was held as a quasi-guest at Newcastle. Suspicions were aroused when a Dutch warship and a Dunkirker arrived at Tynemouth in November 1646, with no obvious purpose, and rumours spread that some design was afoot to spirit Charles out of England. These suspicions were well founded, for Charles had indeed asked the prince of Orange to send a ship to help him escape. At the end of December Parliament sent Batten north to foil any such design, with orders to stay the two ships, search every ship leaving the harbour, and detain the king if he was discovered on board. During his stay in the area Batten had many contacts with the Scots, and his chaplain Samuel Kem preached before the king. Kem's sermon urging a negotiated peace, 'An Olive Branch found after a Storm in the North Sea', probably reflected Batten's own views, and was well received.

When the Scots handed Charles over to Parliament late in January 1647 Batten returned to the Downs, but his doubts about the direction of events continued to grow. The army mutiny in the spring, the seizure of the king, and the army's entry into London in August were all alarming signals. Batten himself became accidentally caught up in these events. Six of the eleven Members of Parliament impeached by the army, including Denzil Holles and Sir William Waller, hired a ketch at Gravesend from one Greene to carry them to safety abroad. Greene promptly double-crossed them by raising the alarm, and the warship *Nicedemus* overhauled the ketch and brought it into the Downs, on the evening of 16 August. Batten examined the Members of Parliament and their papers, and found they had passes from Lenthall and an order from both Houses. A council of war next morning agreed that there were accordingly no grounds for detaining them, and he permitted them to resume their journey. What seemed reasonable to Batten and his captains, however, appeared otherwise to the army and Independents. Rumours quickly spread about his motives in allowing them to escape, and he felt obliged to publish an account to clear his name, in which his sympathy for their views is evident. By the time it appeared, 26 August, Batten was already scheming to turn the navy against the army and its Independent allies. He had sent word to the Scottish earl of Lauderdale that he would be willing to declare for the Scots and the English Presbyterians and bring over twenty-two ships—the larger part of the summer guard—if arrangements could be made to victual them. That would be beyond the means of the Scots, but he thought France might be willing to help. Lauderdale contacted the French ambassador in Scotland, who sent word to Cardinal Mazarin. Events quickly overtook these manœuvres. By early September 1647 rumours were circulating in Deal that Batten had been overheard saying he feared the army would eventually execute the king. He was promptly summoned to London to be questioned by the admiralty commissioners, among them the radicals Sir Henry Vane, Henry Marten, and Colonel Rainborough.

Without waiting to hear what they would object against him, Batten delivered up his commission, while insisting that he had served Parliament faithfully and would be willing to continue. Probably he thought they knew or suspected his dealings with the Scots; whatever the case, they promptly accepted his resignation. Batten's conduct was treasonable by any normal standards, though in the confusion of mid-1647 he might well have felt that it was an open question where legitimate political authority now lay. He did not regard himself as betraying the parliamentary cause. As he later insisted, he had always fought to bring the king to Parliament, not to overthrow him. It was the army leaders who had betrayed that cause.

THE RIFT BETWEEN ARMY AND NAVY WIDENS

Batten's removal served only to widen the rift between the army and their Independent allies and the navy. Batten proved a popular figure, and his views were widely shared; his abrupt removal seemed a gratuitous insult to the navy as a whole, fomenting the inter-service rivalry that had been in the background throughout the war years. On 27 September the Commons nominated Colonel Rainborough to replace him in command of the fleet, and the House of Lords eventually concurred (against Warwick's advice). Rainborough came from a maritime background and was a courageous man with naval experience, but his nomination proved a major error of judgement: as an army officer, he symbolized the triumph of the land forces over the navy; as a well-known radical, he confirmed fears about the prospects ahead; and his prominence among the army radicals in the autumn and involvement in the near-mutiny at Ware was to leave the navy without a head at all. When Fairfax informed the House of Lords of his conduct, they forbade him to take up his new post until the matter had been fully examined. Rainborough made a humble recantation, and by the end of December Fairfax's main concern was the effect on the navy of leaving it without a commander for three months, at a time of extreme political tension. He urged Parliament to send Rainborough to the fleet without delay. The House of Lords still refused, but on 1 January 1648 the Commons dispatched the new vice-admiral to the Isle of Wight, with orders to prevent the king escaping to the continent. His arrival in the fleet, after months of delay and with such a questionable authority, boded ill. While Rainborough's commitment to his task was not in doubt, the mood of the fleet remained to be seen.

OPERATIONS IN 1648

The year 1648 saw the parliamentary navy tested almost to destruction, as political turmoil ashore triggered confusion in the fleet. This drama was played out against the background of continuing operational pressures, with the Irish privateers now reinforced by Flemings from Dunkirk. In February Rainborough reported that privateers infested the Channel as well as the Irish Sea, hunting in 'wolf-pack' squadrons strong enough to repel any parliamentary frigate they met. The problems appeared likely to grow, with the earl of Ormond plotting to return to Ireland to head the royalist cause, and determined to impose more concerted tactics on the privateers (discussed in Chapter 3). In response Parliament assigned almost half the 1648 summer guard to the Irish Sea. But events ashore, initially in south Wales and Ireland, conspired to distract naval forces from the war at sea. In March 1648 Colonel Poyer defied an order to hand over Pembroke Castle to a new commander, an act which ignited the Second English Civil War. Meanwhile, across the Irish Sea, Inchiquin changed sides again and in April made peace with the Catholics, transforming the military and political situation in Ireland and closing its ports to parliamentary shipping. The crisis in south Wales, at least, ended in May when Cromwell crushed the rebels at St Fagan's; but by then a far more pressing danger was looming in Kent.

THE SECOND ENGLISH CIVIL WAR

On 19 May 1648 a young man stepped ashore near Sandwich claiming to be the prince of Wales. Despite his shabby appearance his assertion was widely accepted, and his arrival triggered a general rising in Kent demanding free negotiations between the king and the two Houses of Parliament, and the disbanding of the New Model Army. With the whole of Kent in turmoil it was impossible for the fleet in the Downs to remain unaffected. The three small forts in the Downs (Sandwich, Deal, and Walmer) were manned by seamen, many of them local men, and as Rainborough admitted on 24 May, 'these parts are wholly for the king'.[13] Moreover royalist agents had for some time been negotiating with Batten, the former vice-admiral, to bring the fleet over to the king. Batten had retained close contacts with the seamen, partly through his former chaplain Samuel Kem, now minister of Deal. The conspiracy was carried on mainly by warrant officers in the fleet, who served on a more permanent basis than captains and lieutenants and often held great sway over the men; they assured Batten that their captains would not dare to resist, a claim that was soon to be put to the test. The Kent revolt took Batten by surprise, for his plans were not yet mature, but the plotters in the fleet decided to strike without delay. When Rainborough went ashore on 27 May to visit the forts in the Downs, his lieutenant Lisle and a boatswain's mate named Lendall, soon to be acclaimed the mutineers' 'Admiral', persuaded the seamen to seize control of the flagship, the *Constant Reformation*. Rainborough returned to find himself barred from his own ship. An angry altercation followed, with some of the mutineers demanding to take him captive, until he was eventually allowed to leave ignominiously in a small pinnace. The mutineers then summoned the captains to a council of war, where most of them agreed to sign the Kent Petition. Captain Penrose of the *Satisfaction*, who had come only under duress, suggested they should choose an honourable person to take command of the fleet, at which someone shouted for Warwick and the rest

The Constant Reformation

Built in 1619, this vessel of 742 tons carried a crew of 250 men and 46 guns. Described by Warwick in 1644 as one of the 'best sailers' in the parliamentary fleet, she played a key role in the struggle at sea and was serving as flagship when her crew declared for the king during the naval revolt of May 1648. She then became the most important warship in the royalist fleet, serving as flagship for the Prince of Wales and later Prince Rupert before sinking en route to the West Indies in September 1651 with the loss of over 300 lives.

took up the cry. It was settled that Penrose should go to London to report these developments to Parliament, with authority to pledge the mutineers' allegiance to Warwick if he would agree to resume command. These hasty decisions probably upset the conspirators, who had been looking to Batten, not Warwick, as their saviour. But they had ousted Rainborough, and for the moment the fleet remained firmly in their hands.

THE FLEET REVOLTS

Once he was safe Rainborough sent an agitated message to Lenthall, Speaker of the House of Commons, reporting the disaster and urging prompt action to secure the rest of the fleet. The mutiny, he warned, was likely to spread. Parliament responded swiftly and decisively by reappointing Warwick lord high admiral on 29 May, brushing aside a petition from the mayor and aldermen of London calling for Batten. Warwick boarded the small *Nicodemus* without delay, and set sail for the Downs to reassert control, coming up to the fleet by 10 a.m. on the 30th. The leading officers of the revolted ships came aboard, along with Kem, two gentlemen representing the Kent commissioners, and some of the original mutineers from the flagship. The seamen had apparently been intending to accept Warwick, but the Kent gentlemen had persuaded them to demand first that he take the engagement for a personal treaty and the disbandment of the New Model. His refusal created a tense situation, with some of the mutineers now pressing to turn him out of his ship, as they had Rainborough. In the event Warwick was allowed to sail away in his own ship, with a few shreds of dignity to cover his failure. On his way back he received word of Fairfax's crushing victory over the Kentish rebels at Maidstone on 1 June, and promptly sent a summons to the rebel 'Admiral' Lendall in the Downs, offering an indemnity and threatening destruction if he refused. Lendall ignored it.

For the moment Parliament could do nothing about the rebels in the Downs. The six ships initially seized by the mutineers were quickly joined by the *Convertine*, and by the *Greyhound* and *Warwick* from the North Sea squadron. Many other ships' companies were known to be wavering. To stop the rot spreading further Warwick and Batten hastened to Portsmouth to secure the ships there—a decision which indicates that Batten's dealings with the royalists remained as yet unknown. Warwick arrived in Portsmouth on 4 June, and after lengthy talks with the seamen reported that they had pledged their loyalty to Parliament; at the same time he warned that discontent remained widespread, and that it would be prudent to try to recover the revolted ships by conciliation rather than force. The situation elsewhere remained confused, with the companies of the *Tiger* and *Providence*, at Harwich, described as mutinous. But the mutineers too faced problems. Their hopes of winning over the Portsmouth squadron had been checked, at least for the present. They also quickly lost two of the ships in the Downs, for Captain Coppin managed to escape with the *Greyhound*, and the

Warwick also slipped away. Coppin reported that divisions wracked the rebels. The collapse of the revolt in Kent had left them now exposed in the Downs, with only two realistic options: to surrender on terms or join the genuine prince of Wales in the Netherlands. The seamen alone might well have sought an indemnity, but fired by Kem and the Kentish gentlemen still on board they chose the alternative and sailed for Holland on 10 June. The prince soon joined them, naming himself admiral and Lord Willoughby of Parham as vice-admiral. Batten promptly followed suit. In the first week of June Parliament had begun to learn something of his earlier intrigues, and was alarmed to find he had gone to Portsmouth after Warwick had left and tried to subvert the seamen. Instead of accounting for his actions, Batten boarded the *Constant Warwick*, a privateer he part-owned, persuaded her company to follow him, and sailed for Holland. The prince knighted him and appointed him rear-admiral.

THE PRINCE OF WALES TAKES COMMAND

The crisis now entered a new phase. While the prince of Wales was deciding how best to use his new weapon, Parliament stamped out disaffection in its remaining ships and assembled a reliable counter-force to challenge the rebels. Warwick's task proved far from easy. He reported that many of his ships, especially those at Portsmouth, were too unreliable to be allowed to put to sea, while the crews of the powerful *Garland* and *John* refused either to fight the rebels or to leave their ships until they were paid. In despair Warwick ordered the sails and rigging to be taken ashore, which rendered the vessels safe but also useless. Even the ships of the Irish guard posed problems. Though they were desperately short of supplies, it was judged too risky to let them come into Portsmouth lest their men be 'contaminated'. As a result the Irish coast remained almost wholly unprotected. His mission to assemble an armada to challenge the prince proved equally fraught. Three of the four greatest ships of the Channel fleet were in royalist hands, and the fourth, the *Garland*, immobilized at Portsmouth, so Warwick ordered two of the most powerful ships lying in reserve, the *George* and *Unicorn*, to be manned and prepared for sea. Refitting took so long that he strongly suspected subversion, while the problem of manning them was complicated by the fact that most mariners and shipmasters apparently sympathized with the revolters. Warwick found some disaffected men even in his own flagship, and the Derby House Committee had to take urgent steps in July to stop able seamen trying to join the rebel ships.

In July the prince took his new force back to sea. Before sailing, the officers and companies of ten of his ships issued a declaration explaining their actions and inviting the rest of the fleet to join them. They voiced anger that extremists now dominated Parliament and the army and condemned Rainborough's appointment as part of a conspiracy to bring soldiers into every ship 'to master and overawe the seamen'.[14] A few weeks later Batten issued his own, more personal declaration. He was no turncoat, he declared; 'we fought all this time to fetch the king to his Parliament, and yet now it is made treason to offer to bring him thither'.[15] A personal treaty, he urged, remained the only way to guarantee both free parliaments and the royal prerogative.

CONFRONTATION IN THE DOWNS

The rebel fleet arrived off the Downs in mid-July, while Warwick was still preparing his ships in the river, which gave the prince a clear advantage. He then threw it away, however, by failing to pursue any coherent strategy. There were several options: he might intercept and seize merchant shipping, to increase his own strength and put pressure on London; or he could sail into the river to find Warwick's ships, and either persuade the men to bring them over or fight them before they were fully ready and before the Portsmouth squadron could join them. The mariners were eager to sail into the Thames and challenge Warwick, convinced it would then be easy to overpower the Portsmouth squadron. However, the prince and his advisers prevaricated. They stopped numerous merchantmen in the Downs, but then allowed them to proceed, probably because Charles proved loath to antagonize the London merchant community which he knew strongly supported his cause. This pattern continued after Batten arrived to join them. The seamen were outraged, and suspected Batten of taking bribes to release the merchantmen; some charged him to his face with treason and corruption. Though Charles's dilemma was real enough, it was pointless to remain in the Downs with no clear objective and victuals running down. Eventually, in late August, the prince decided to return to Holland, leaving most of the force in the Downs under Lord Willoughby, a man with little experience or standing. The decision provoked a near-mutiny. The seamen demanded to 'try their fortunes' in the Thames before giving up, and when the prince's ship set course for Holland his escorts turned away for the river. Charles had to drop anchor and call a council of war, where he agreed to go into the Thames with them—if they would pledge not to deliver him up to his enemies. This extraordinary proviso laid bare the deep divisions and suspicions within the fleet. With the Second Civil War virtually over on land, and the seamen cut off from their homes and families, the royalist leaders clearly feared the mariners might be ready to buy their indemnity. The whole fleet of about twenty ships (eleven warships and some armed merchantmen) now sailed into the Thames on the morning of 29 August, and found Warwick's fleet, ready at last, anchored off Shoeburyness and waiting to come out on the ebb tide.

During the afternoon Warwick's fleet plied as far as the Oaze where it dropped anchor for the night. The prince anchored about three miles off, and summoned Warwick to submit. Warwick called a council the same evening to decide his strategy. It resolved against risking battle in the shallows and narrow channels of the estuary, aware that in any such action many of the major ships—on both sides—would almost certainly run aground and be lost. Instead it decided to try to defer battle until the Portsmouth fleet, now expected hourly, could join them. Though Warwick insisted on the determination of his officers and men, some of his ships remained undermanned and there must have been some doubts about their steadfastness. For several hours on 30 August the two fleets manœuvred warily; several times they were so close that battle appeared imminent, only for sudden squalls to separate them again. As the wind strengthened to gale force, both fleets dropped anchor. During the night the royalists pondered the risks of losing their entire fleet on the sands, and resolved to draw off to sea in the hope of luring Warwick after them. Similar fears dominated Warwick's own council of war, meeting early on Thursday morning and it decided to continue avoiding battle, but to follow the royalists should they put to sea. At about 10 a.m. on the 31st the royalists withdrew, with Warwick shadowing them closely enough for his forward frigates to be within firing range. He anchored that evening near the Gunfleet, expecting the royalists to anchor too. Instead the prince sailed on, and soon after dark his ships spied another fleet advancing towards them, which dropped anchor before they met. Some of his sailors identified it correctly as the Portsmouth squadron. On the advice of Batten and his friends the prince decided not to engage it, to the astonishment and dismay of the mariners. A night action carried obvious risks, and the royalists may have thought Warwick was still close enough to hear gunfire and come up to the scene. But the prince's cause required decisive action, and his sailors believed that the Portsmouth ships, outnumbered, at anchor, undermanned, and of doubtful resolution, were theirs for the taking. 'Had the prince gone to them we had had them without a blow,' wrote one royalist on board, 'and by consequence entrapped Warwick the next day.'[16] Though it might not have proved quite so simple, it was the best opportunity the royalists were ever likely to have. If they had won over the Portsmouth squadron, Warwick's fleet would have been significantly outnumbered and its morale shattered. Sinking or disabling the Portsmouth ships would have dealt a similar psychological blow, and left the two main fleets roughly equal in strength. In the event the royalists sailed away to Holland, full of bitter recriminations. 'I see no hope to reconcile our differences nor to preserve this fleet,' one lamented.[17] The shadow-boxing in the mouth of the Thames had been an extraordinary episode, perhaps the only major naval confrontation in history where the commanders on both sides harboured well-grounded fears that their men might be ready to desert or betray them.

CONFRONTATION OFF HELVOETSLUYS

The curtain now rose on a new scene, with the previous roles reversed. While the royalists worked to resupply their ships and restore morale, Warwick and his fleet arrived off Helvoetsluys on 18 September, moved into the river, and anchored about four miles from the enemy. His summons to the prince to surrender his fleet was predictably rejected. The fact that the drama was now being played out in foreign territorial waters added a complicating twist. On 22 September a deputation from the Dutch States General arrived to declare Dutch neutrality in the quarrel, and to demand that Warwick should pledge not to initiate violence while in Dutch waters. Warwick agreed. The Derby House Committee, and many in the fleet, thought he should have settled the issue by force when he first arrived, a move the Dutch might privately have welcomed to free them from a difficult situation. That option was now lost, for Tromp arrived with fourteen or fifteen warships and took up position between the two English fleets to maintain the peace. There followed a stalemate deeply frustrating to all the parties. The royalists found their fleet a wasting asset and morale sank low. The prince and many of the sailors had left, and most of the ships' guns and tackle had been carried ashore; but Warwick too found himself trapped in a defensive posture, with the Dutch making it abundantly clear that their sympathies lay with the royalists. After several weeks the prince broke the stalemate, by appointing Prince Rupert (see picture on p. 122) commander-in-chief with orders to find some way to get the ships out to sea. As ever, Rupert proved divisive as well as dynamic. There was soon friction among the royalists, and dismay among the former parliamentarians, who saw him as the epitome of uncompromising cavalierism. It quickly emerged that Batten would not sail with him, and many other sailors followed suit. These divisions appeared to vindicate, at last, Warwick's much-criticized strategy of waiting on events. For after secret negotiations the *Constant Warwick* came in and submitted just before midnight on 5 November. Batten himself made his way back to England, armed with an indemnity. Many of the Dutch warships had by now withdrawn, and Warwick decided to step up the pressure. On 8 November his fleet moved forward and anchored close to the rebels. The *Hind* submitted that night. On the 9th the parliamentary ships moved closer still, while the royalists withdrew to the Sluice leading to the protected inner harbour. The *Constant Reformation*, the royalist flagship, and five others were hauled through to safety, but the *Convertine, Satisfaction,* and *Love* were left outside and forced to submit. The race for the Sluice was a curious action. 'We weighed, they weighed, and the Dutch weighed,' a parliamentarian reported, 'all plying up the river. Our frigates were round their admiral; endeavouring to provoke him to fire (as Prince Rupert vapoured he would), but they then would not take notice of affronts.'[18] Unless Rupert opened fire, Warwick remained bound by his pledge to the Dutch States General not to fire first. Royalist sailors hurled stones and clumps of earth at their opponents, 'but durst not fire so much as a pistol'.[19]

THE ROYALIST FLEET ESCAPES TO KINSALE

The outcome of this bizarre engagement proved unsatisfactory for both sides. The royalists had lost some of their ships, while the Derby House Committee felt that by a more decisive response Warwick could have recovered the entire royalist force. Any further action now looked impossible, so the Committee advised him to send some of his ships home. Instead, to its surprise, Warwick sailed for the Downs on 21 November with his entire fleet. He explained later that he feared his ships would be trapped by the winter ice, with insufficient supplies or victuals, and probably thought there was no chance of the royalists being ready for sea before the spring. This proved a serious miscalculation, for Rupert leapt at the unexpected opportunity. He sent several of his smaller frigates to sea on 5 January, where they promptly snapped up some prizes. On 21 January Rupert himself set sail with a force of eight ships (all he could man), joined later by two others already at sea.

It is easy to appreciate the diplomatic and operational constraints that persuaded Warwick to act with extreme caution throughout the expedition. At the same time it is hard not to share the widespread sense that a bolder strategy might have solved the problem rather than merely containing it. Events in England reinforced the feeling that a change of leadership in the fleet was urgently needed. Only a few days after Rupert's escape Charles I died on the scaffold, and Warwick's brother, the earl of Holland, faced trial and execution for his part in the Second Civil War. Two short Acts of Parliament on 23 and 24 February 1649 revoked Warwick's commission, and appointed three colonels, Popham, Blake, and Deane, as joint admirals and generals at sea. It was the start of a 'New Modelled Navy'.

The New Model Navy, 1649–1652

Warwick's removal initiated sweeping changes in the personnel of naval administration ashore and in the composition of the officer corps at sea. Very many of his closest associates were dropped or refused to serve the new regime. Only one-third of the commanders who had served in the summer guard of 1647 were recommissioned in 1649, or at any later stage during the Interregnum. The new officer corps was moulded from the small radical group among the old captains, such as Robert Moulton, and from radicals among the merchant shipmasters, such as John Lawson and Nehemiah Bourne, energetically recruited by Sir Henry Vane and his admiralty colleagues.

The most pressing task facing the new, republican navy remained of course Prince Rupert's squadron, which had established its base at Kinsale. Rupert and the Irish privateers constituted a formidable force, exacerbating a situation which had already deteriorated sharply with the naval paralysis of 1648. The wholesale reorganization of the fleet, moreover, inevitably delayed the 1649 summer guard. It was not until 21 May that the three new generals at sea arrived off Kinsale with a force of about ten ships and, to their delight, found Rupert's fleet there. Though the harbour fortifications ruled out an attack from the sea, the generals imposed a tight blockade and ended royalist depredations. As Rupert lacked the strength

Robert Blake, 1599–1657

Of humble origins, Blake initially made his career on land and played a key role in the defence of Lyme and subsequent parliamentary assault on Taunton. Despite little naval experience he replaced Warwick in February 1649, as one of three Admirals and Generals at Sea. After pursuing the royalist fleet, led by Prince Rupert, from Kinsale in Ireland to Lisbon in Portugal he finally destroyed most of the king's warships off Carthagena in November 1650. The following year Blake led bloody operations to recapture Scilly and the Channel Islands.

Cherub from the Swan

Relics discovered during recent archaeological excavations from the wreck of a small Cromwellian warship, probably the *Swan*, lying on the seabed off Duart Castle, seat of the MacLeans, in Mull. The wooden cherub is from the ship's decorative carving; in front of it lie the remains of a small keg and a human ulna. The ship was lost during an abortive operation in September 1653 when a task force was dispatched to the Western Isles to suppress Glencairn's Rising.

to break out, another stalemate ensued. It dragged on to the autumn, to be ended at last by the arrival of Cromwell's army of invasion; as his troops marched south, Cork and Kinsale became vulnerable from the land, and on 20 October Rupert took advantage of a storm which had driven Blake off station to put to sea hastily with seven ships. They were all he could fit and man; the rest had to be abandoned. Rupert had contacted King John IV of Portugal over a possible refuge in the Tagus, below Lisbon, and it was there he now made his way.

DESTRUCTION OF THE ROYALIST FLEET

While Lisbon was far safer than Kinsale, the Portuguese made it clear they were offering only a temporary refuge, not a permanent base. They had no wish to be drawn into conflict with England, and by January 1650 they were pressing Rupert to leave. He was still there, however, when Blake arrived in March. Determined not to repeat Warwick's mistake, Blake sailed into the Tagus intending to attack with or without permission, but the wind suddenly dropped and he was forced to anchor and turn to diplomacy. As usual, this proved frustrating, for John refused either to expel Rupert or to allow Blake to attack him. The Council of State sent out reinforcements under Popham, indicating that it was willing to risk war with Portugal as the price for destroying Rupert. Attitudes hardened on both sides, with the Portuguese responding to Blake's increased pressure by fitting out thirteen warships to support Rupert. In the event little actual fighting occurred. Rupert and the Portuguese made three attempts to break out, but each time withdrew after some desultory firing. The stalemate ended in September when Blake shattered a homeward-bound Portuguese Brazil fleet; facing war and commercial ruin, the king sent Rupert packing on 12 October. Rupert and Maurice put to sea with six of their ships, 'poverty and despair being companions and revenge a guide', as one royalist put it.[20]

While Blake took on supplies at Cadiz, Rupert made his way through the Straits into the Mediterranean. He deeply resented Spain's assistance to Blake, and instead of looking for English ships on the high seas entered the ports of Malaga, Velez Malaga, and Motril, and destroyed several English merchantmen in contempt of the Spanish authorities. On 3 November, however, Blake caught up with the royalist squadron near Carthagena; one ship surrendered and all the rest were driven ashore and wrecked. Rupert and Maurice escaped this catastrophe, having left their companions a little earlier to pursue a prize. The French offered them shelter in Toulon, for the moment, but it became clear that the Mediterranean was no longer safe. After refitting, Rupert slipped out early in April 1651 and passed back through the Straits. Blake had returned to England in February, welcomed home as a national hero.

The final stages of the royalist campaign at sea, though packed with adventure, amounted to very little in strategic terms. Rupert had two powerful ships left, the

Constant Reformation and *Swallow*, and picked up several prizes. But his force proved too weak to remain in European waters, and he eventually persuaded his men to try their luck in the West Indies. Disaster struck before they arrived. Rupert's flagship, the *Constant Reformation*, sprang a leak in a storm and sank on 30 September 1651, and though Rupert himself escaped in a small boat over 300 companions drowned. The remaining ships returned to the Azores, and then scoured the African coast, where the pickings proved meagre. In May 1652 he sailed for Barbados a second time. However, on 13 September a hurricane scattered the rest of the small force and caused the *Defiance* to sink (with Maurice aboard). Rupert headed back to Europe once more, and learning that Portugal had made peace with the republic, took the *Swallow* into the mouth of the Loire on 4 March 1653. He may have hoped to fit her to sea again, but it was not to be. Probably too worm-eaten for any further service, she was apparently left to fall to pieces where she lay. It was an inglorious but symbolic end to the royalist adventure.

CROMWELLIAN NAVAL SUPREMACY

Much had changed since Rupert had sailed from Holland in January 1649. The Cromwellians had captured the leading Irish privateering bases of Wexford (October 1649), Waterford (August 1650), and Galway (April 1652). Blake had led bloody but successful operations in 1651 to recapture Scilly, Jersey, and Guernsey. In the New World Barbados submitted to Ayscue in January 1652, soon followed by the other West Indian islands and Virginia. The repercussions of the civil wars were over at last, and a new agenda began to unfold. If the royalists no longer represented a threat, the new republic found itself hated throughout Europe and dependent on naval protection for its security and perhaps even survival. Instead of cutting back, the regime therefore embarked on a massive programme of naval expansion. By the end of 1651 twenty new warships had been built, and a further twenty-five added by purchase or capture. There was no shortage of work for them. Though Spain soon courted the new regime, the close ties of blood between the Bourbons and Stuarts triggered a state of undeclared war at sea between England and France, in which English shipowners suffered heavily in the Mediterranean and Atlantic as well as the Channel. By the end of 1650 the republic had established a system of regular convoys to the Mediterranean. In the late summer of 1652 it sent Mazarin a much blunter message by forcing Dunkirk to surrender to the Spaniards. Closely besieged by the Spaniards, Dunkirk's last hope had lain in a fleet despatched by Mazarin for its relief by sea. On 4 September Blake attacked and scattered this fleet, and Dunkirk's surrender, now inevitable, quickly followed. The republic explained blandly that Blake's action had been a mere act of reprisal. It was enough to convince Mazarin that he had no choice but to recognize the new regime.

That left only the Dutch. They had recognized the Republic in 1650 and had no wish for war, but relations remained beset by political and commercial jealousies. The Dutch, as the carriers of Europe, could never concede the right of English warships to stop and search their merchant shipping; national honour and commercial pragmatism were equally at stake. They also deeply resented the new restrictions imposed on their trade by the Navigation Act of 1651. The new republic, for its part, found odious Dutch sympathy and covert support for the Stuart cause, and feared that the Dutch would exploit its diplomatic isolation to squeeze English commerce to near extinction. Neither side wanted war, but both felt their vital interests could not be compromised. In May 1652 Blake and Tromp met off the Downs, and a fierce action ensued.

The Anglo-Dutch War of 1652–4 lies outside the scope of this chapter and is discussed in the postlude. It witnessed a series of massive and bloody fleet actions, on a scale far greater than any of the clashes at sea during the civil wars. The war inaugurated a new era of British naval history, marked by the state's vigorous use of naval power to defend commercial and colonial interests and assert its political will. A decade of almost continuous operations at sea in the 1640s had given England a powerful fleet and an experienced, pugnacious officer corps unmatched in Europe. The new Commonwealth had rapidly embarked on a major naval rearmament in the face of a hostile Europe. By the end of 1651 it had launched twenty new warships, in addition to many other vessels acquired by capture and purchase. The navy's initially defensive posture had quickly changed to one far more assertive, with the early operations off Spain and Portugal leading on to regular Mediterranean convoys in 1650–2. The dramatic victories against the Dutch in 1653 and the ambitious expeditions in the years following to the Mediterranean, Caribbean, and Baltic contrasted sharply with the navy's record in the 1620s and 1630s, and left European neighbours and Englishmen of all persuasions in no doubt that a new age had dawned. The parliamentary navy had played a significant, if secondary, part in the civil wars; the civil wars played a still more significant part in the navy's own history, accelerating its evolution and fitting it for the primary role it was to play in the colonial and imperial ages ahead.

PART TWO

THE BRITISH AND IRISH EXPERIENCES OF WAR

6
SIEGES AND
FORTIFICATIONS

RONALD HUTTON AND WYLIE REEVES

The characteristic military action of the British and Irish Civil Wars was an attack upon a fortified strongpoint. The First English Civil War began with one on Hull (July 1642) and ended with one on Harlech Castle (March 1647); likewise the Second Civil War was concluded with the reduction of Pontefract (March 1649) and the Third with the storming of Worcester (September 1651). Scotland's troubles were framed between the taking of Edinburgh Castle in March 1639 and the fall of the mighty stronghold of Dunottar in May 1652; while the Irish Civil Wars began in October 1641 with the capture of Charlemont Castle and effectively ended eleven years later in April 1652 with the surrender of Galway after a nine-month blockade. In its first year of campaigning, the New Model Army fought two field actions and conducted a dozen sieges and storms. Prince Rupert, one of the few commanders in history who consistently sought battle as a first and not a last resort, took part in six field actions during the First English Civil War but over twice as many which involved assaulting or defending strongpoints. Similarly skirmishes and sieges, which aimed to capture key forts and towns and to destroy the enemy's economic base, dominated the course of the Irish Civil Wars and throughout the 1640s only seven battles were fought. Cromwell's decisive Irish campaign consisted almost entirely of sieges, and even Montrose's Highland war, which reversed the usual rule in its larger proportion of battles, included assaults upon Aberdeen and Dundee and ended with the reduction of a pair of Hebridean castles. For most of the wars in the three kingdoms, more troops remained locked up in garrisons than took part in mobile operations.

Garrisons and Fortresses

THE IMPORTANCE OF GARRISONS

Why did the various protagonists maintain so many garrisons? Towns were, of course, centres of wealth in their own right, and soldiers lodged in them could

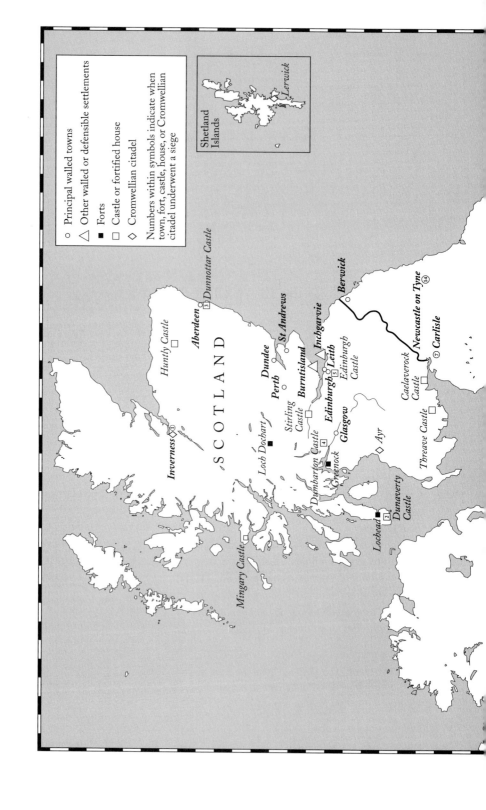

Principal walled towns
Other walled or defensible settlements
Forts
Castle or fortified house
Cromwellian citadel

Numbers within symbols indicate when
town, fort, castle, house, or Cromwellian
citadel underwent a siege

Shetland
Islands

Lerwick

SCOTLAND

Mingary Castle

Inverness ◇ ①

Loch Dochart ■

Huntly Castle

Aberdeen ③ *Dunnottar Castle*

Dundee
Perth
Stirling Castle
St Andrews
Burntisland
Inchgarvie
Leith
Edinburgh ⑤ *Edinburgh Castle*
Dumbarton Castle ④
Glasgow
Greenock

Berwick

Newcastle on Tyne ⑭

Caelaverock Castle
Carlisle ⑦
Threave Castle

Ayr

Locheid ■ ②
Dunaverty Castle

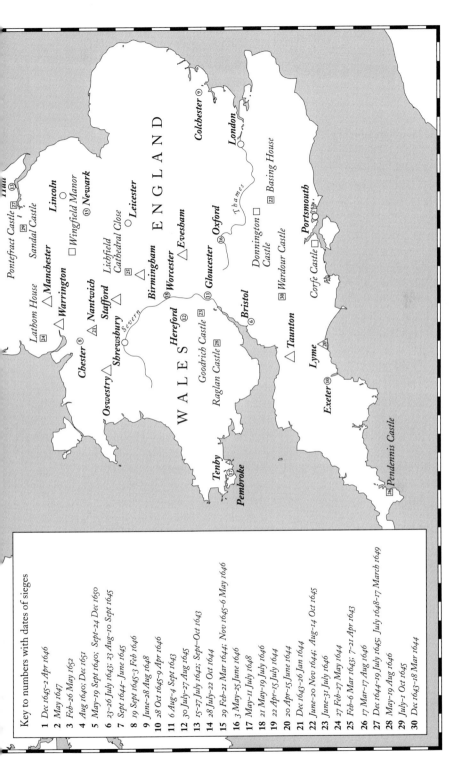

Key to numbers with dates of sieges

1 Dec 1645–2 Apr 1646
2 May 1647
3 Feb–26 May 1652
4 Aug 1640; Dec 1651
5 May–19 Sept 1640; Sept–24 Dec 1650
6 23–26 July 1643; 23 Aug–10 Sept 1645
7 Sept 1644–June 1645
8 19 Sept 1645–3 Feb 1646
9 June–28 Aug 1648
10 28 Oct 1645–9 Apr 1646
11 6 Aug–4 Sept 1643
12 30 July–27 Aug 1645
13 15–27 July 1642; Sept–Oct 1643
14 28 July–22 Oct 1644
15 29 Feb–21 Mar 1644; Nov 1645–6 May 1646
16 3 May–25 June 1646
17 May–11 July 1648
18 21 May–19 July 1646
19 22 Apr–15 July 1644
20 20 Apr–15 June 1644
21 Dec 1643–26 Jan 1644
22 June–20 Nov 1644; Aug–4 Oct 1645
23 June–31 July 1646
24 27 Feb–27 May 1644
25 Feb–6 Mar 1643; 7–21 Apr 1643
26 17 Mar–17 Aug 1646
27 Dec 1644–19 July 1645; July 1648–7 March 1649
28 May–19 Aug 1646
29 July–1 Oct 1645
30 Dec 1643–18 Mar 1644

Sieges and fortifications in the Stuart Kingdoms, map A

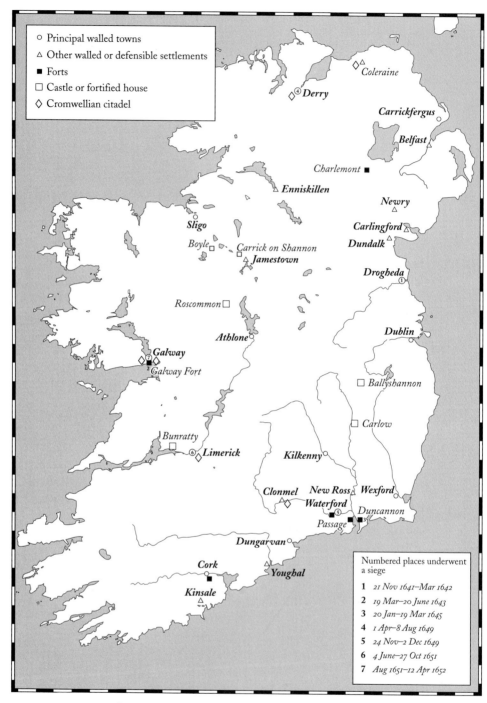

Legend:
- ○ Principal walled towns
- △ Other walled or defensible settlements
- ■ Forts
- □ Castle or fortified house
- ◇ Cromwellian citadel

Coleraine
Derry ④
Carrickfergus
Belfast
Charlemont ■
Enniskillen △
Newry △
Sligo ○
Carlingford
Boyle □   Carrick on Shannon
Dundalk △
Jamestown △
Drogheda ①
Roscommon □
Dublin ○
Athlone ○
Galway ⑦
Ballyshannon □
Galway Fort ② ◇
Carlow □
Bunratty □
Limerick ○ ⑥ ◇
Kilkenny ○
Clonmel ◇
New Ross △   Wexford ○
Waterford ○   Duncannon ■ ③
Passage ■ ⑤
Dungarvan ○
Cork ■
Youghal △
Kinsale △

Numbered places underwent a siege

1 *21 Nov 1641–Mar 1642*
2 *19 Mar–20 June 1643*
3 *20 Jan–19 Mar 1645*
4 *1 Apr–8 Aug 1649*
5 *24 Nov–2 Dec 1649*
6 *4 June–27 Oct 1651*
7 *Aug 1651–12 Apr 1652*

Sieges and fortifications in the Stuart Kingdoms, map B

safeguard them and also control the trading systems which depended upon them; or, if the hinterland was in enemy hands, could block them. In addition, the possession of castles and fortified mansions in rural districts could secure the produce of those areas for the party which held them (see maps on pp. 196–8). All this holds true of any war of the age, but three characteristics of the English and Irish Civil Wars produced an unusual multiplication in the number of garrisons. To begin with, it was a civil conflict, in which—except in Scotland—the dominant party could be confident of the loyalty of all the inhabitants in very few districts. As the demands of the military machines increased and became ever more unpopular, rival commanders needed to keep armed watchmen even in peaceful areas, to overawe the inhabitants and to prevent revolt. Second, by the end of 1643, few areas of England and Ireland, whether controlled by the king or Parliament, were not vulnerable to a sudden thrust from the enemy. To maintain fortresses everywhere therefore secured the combatants against flying columns which might otherwise occupy undefended centres of communication, or simply carry out destructive raids and then retire. This was particularly important for the royalists, as Parliament's control of the navy left virtually no part of the king's quarters in England which was not vulnerable to attack either by land or sea. Third, successful field armies rarely cleared blocs of territory completely; usually they left isolated enemy strongpoints which were intended to be mopped up by local forces, or else planted garrisons themselves and then retired. As a result most parts of England, Wales, and even Ireland sooner or later became chessboard patterns of rival fortresses, the larger of which developed networks of garrisons to hem in local enemies and starve them of supplies. After 1645 Parliament consciously wrecked or demolished most castles or houses which it took from enemy forces, to reduce the number of potential strongholds to a few key fortresses which it could easily control. Extended gradually to the whole British Isles as the parliamentarian armies advanced, it resulted in a considerable simplification of the resources available to garrison warfare. That said, in order to control Ireland effectively during the 1650s the Cromwellians had no choice but to maintain roughly 350 garrisons throughout the country.

There were, then, good practical reasons for the large number of fortresses maintained at certain phases during the Wars of the Three Kingdoms. In addition, particular eventualities could make the reduction of individual strongpoints essential to a party, no matter the risk and the cost. York had to be taken in 1644, Colchester in 1648, Drogheda in 1649, and Worcester in 1651, because all four had complete royalist armies bottled up in them, which could not be allowed to get loose. Oliver Cromwell had to complete the siege of Pembroke in the Second English Civil War, despite the threat from a large Scottish force which was entering England, because the Welsh port represented both a rallying-point for local rebellion and a perfect bridgehead for Irish royalist reinforcements. A failure to secure it would expose Cromwell's forces to the even bigger menace of being caught in a pincer between the Scots and the Welsh and Irish. Fortresses, and siege warfare, became indispensable components of the civil wars.

Were they, however, a regrettable necessity? It is a simple fact of mathematics that the more soldiers a party maintained to hold down its existing territory, the less money, food, and equipment could be spared for field forces which would enable it to win the war; the equation is not altered by the fact that without those stationary troops there would be a grave risk of losing the resources of the area completely. Clearly then garrisons are best regarded as an unavoidable liability. However, whereas field armies tended to thin rapidly from illness, hunger, and desertion, garrison service was popular. Those engaged in it were relatively well paid, fed, and housed. As a result, English royalist armies and the Protestant forces serving in Ireland, in particular, tended to replenish their numbers for summer campaigns from soldiers who had remained in fortresses all winter, often acquiring extra battle experience in local actions. Furthermore, siege warfare and feuding between garrisons loomed large in the popular consciousness, comprising a large part of the subject-matter of newspapers. A daring exploit by the commander of a local outpost could do much to raise the morale of its supporters, giving strongpoints, which had been of particular nuisance to the enemy, a symbolic importance even greater than their strategic one. For this reason in 1645 the New Model Army had twice to make the relief of Taunton an absolute priority, eclipsing any offensive measures.

SIEGES AND PROPAGANDA

Closely linked to this, the rival causes in all three kingdoms made a consistent and illuminating distinction in the use of published narratives of sieges undergone, and survived, by their partisans. To all sides, the fortitude displayed by a garrison demonstrated the fervour with which the cause was supported, and the heroism of the defenders. Likewise, a successful resistance—like a battle won—served as proof of divine favour and of fine moral qualities as well as of practical skills and political commitment. For the parliamentarian press, however, the 'classic' siege story centred on a town defended by its citizens. The anecdotes selected emphasized corporate dedication and mutual support, all ranks and both genders co-operating in the desperate work of digging, repairing, shooting, and running up with supplies. This conveyed the impression of a complete social organism united in a common cause, operating as a microcosm of the nation. The royalist press, on the other hand, took as its favourite narrative the defence of a castle or, even better, a mansion by its aristocratic or genteel owner. The stories selected made a number of different appeals at once. They echoed traditional narratives of chivalry, of the gallant and high-born champion defying and overcoming a multitude of evil opponents. Where the defence was led by a woman, as in the case of the countess of Derby at Lathom House or Lady Banks at Corfe Castle, then the chivalric note could be sounded with even more force. These royalist representations also played upon a social theme, of a monarchy upheld by its 'natural' supporters, the aristocracy, with all the other ranks of the nation, down to the meanest kitchen scullion, united under its command to protect the traditional order. Finally, as the stronghold under attack was also a private home, its resistance could offer a fine symbol of the defence of personal property against a usurping and illegal power. The contrast in motifs was very clearly an artificial one, for there is no evidence that the inhabitants of royalist Chester, York, or Newark laboured with any less corporate determination to hold off attacks, while a parliamentarian chatelaine such as Lady Brilliana Harley at Brampton Bryan Castle could defend her home as nobly as any other. It serves, rather, as a reminder that printed siege narratives became political texts, just as fully as any other kind of propaganda.

CONTROL OF PORTS

In the waging of siege warfare in England, Parliament enjoyed a decided advantage. It rapidly secured control of the three national depots for heavy guns, the Tower of London, Hull, and Portsmouth, and also of the country's main metal-producing area, the Weald, which contained the royal cannon foundry. In addition it held sway over the whole south and east coast from Plymouth to Hull, which included virtually all the fortifications erected or improved since the end of the Middle Ages (see map on pp. 196–7). With possession of the southern and eastern ports went control of the navy, which proved an enormous asset (discussed in Chapter 5). Time and again, parliamentarian strongpoints could be relieved by sea: Hull (1642), Plymouth (1643), Pembroke (1644), and Lyme (1644) all being prominent examples. Conversely, royalist-held ports could be attacked simultaneously from land and water, a combination which proved fatal at Warrington in Cheshire (1643) and Tenby in Pembrokeshire (1644). However, the royalist war-effort responded dynamically to these challenges: it utilized the metalworking regions of the west Midlands to make artillery, and pioneered techniques of both fortification and siegecraft which were, for a time, in advance of those displayed by its enemies.

The Military Revolution

In this respect, as in every other, the civil wars represented a process by which the British and Irish caught up rapidly with military developments which had swept through Europe from the early sixteenth century. The crucial one had occurred in Italy over a hundred years before, with the enclosure of strongpoints within thick, low, earthen walls, studded with polygonal bastions which provided flanking fire along the external ditches. Such artillery fortresses became impervious to all but the most heavy and prolonged bombardment, and turned sieges into protracted affairs requiring considerable technical expertise. This radical development in fortifications has been identified by some historians as the crux of the 'Military Revolution' and by 1600 these artillery fortresses had spread across much of western Europe, the Mediterranean, and the Danube basin, and armies adapted accordingly.[1] Armies increased in size, with much more artillery, and conducted siege warfare by encircling enemy strongholds within a double line of works fortified in the same style. The inner force cut off the besieged from all supplies, while the outer army repelled a relieving force; once within this deadly embrace, a town or fort was almost certainly doomed. However, this proved a very ponderous and expensive way of waging war, while the cost of the new-style fortresses was itself astronomical.

PRE-CIVIL WAR FORTIFICATIONS

Though familiar with these continental developments, the comparatively impecunious and isolated Tudor and Stuart monarchies, lacking both resources and pressing dangers, had generally regarded artillery forts as unnecessary luxuries. As a result the new walls and bastions had appeared in England only at six places, all on the North Sea and Channel coast. They consisted of a chain of small castles with thick, squat, stone walls and rounded bastions, erected by Henry VIII to defend the harbours from Cornwall eastward to Suffolk, together with the border with Scotland. Thus by 1640 the most modern category of fort found widely in England was already a century old. The same held true for Scotland. As recent excavations show, the extensive artillery works at Stirling Castle date from the mid-sixteenth century and are known as the 'French Spur' since they were constructed under the direction of Mary of Guise. The only modern artillery fort had been built by the Campbells at Lochead in Kintyre as a deterrent to any MacDonnell invasion during the Bishops' Wars. While the Privy Council had maintained the defensibility of Edinburgh and Dumbarton Castles, none of the burghs had bastioned artillery defences and plans made in 1627 to fortify Leith (Edinburgh's port), Burntisland (Fife's chief port), Aberdeen, Inchgarvie (an island in the Firth of Forth), and Montrose came to nothing.[2] Defences in Britain, especially inland ones, thus generally comprised medieval castles and town walls constructed before the advent of gunpowder.

By contrast in Ireland, where the threat of foreign invasion and domestic unrest remained very real, the crown had built new artillery fortresses in strategic locations throughout the country. In the 1580s the government constructed modern defences at Duncannon, commanding the approach to Waterford, and by 1590 Limerick enjoyed a star-shaped redoubt outside the city walls, seven new bastions, and a fortified bridgehead. During the early seventeenth century Sir Josias Bodley, assisted by Dutch engineers Levan de Rose and Josias Everard, built Elizabeth fort (near Cork) and St Augustine's fort (near Galway) according to the latest European specifications. Many other fortifications—for example Carrickfergus or Limerick Castles—were remodelled and artillery bastions and earthworks added in order to make the structure more resilient to attack and artillery fire. However any up-to-date fortifications were basically limited to the coastlines of Munster and Connacht, leaving the Leinster coastline relatively unprotected. In particular Dublin's city walls remained old-fashioned and had 'no flankers on them nor places for men to fight on'; while the castle itself was in poor shape 'having on it no modern fortifications'.³

IMPROVEMENTS TO FORTIFICATIONS

However, unsophisticated fortifications could easily be improved. With the advent of war many towns hastily constructed crude earthen works—dug out of a ditch upon the side from which the attack was expected and at a height which protected men's bodies while they shot or thrust over it—which could absorb the impact of shot. Such basic breastworks, quickly scraped out by inexperienced troops at Birmingham in April 1643, repelled an attack by Prince Rupert's crack cavalry regiments; the latter only won the day by outflanking them. To make these defences more formidable still, the size of the bank and ditch could be increased and a parapet built. A flooded moat could replace the ditch, and a stockade of high sharpened posts built on the far side of ditch or moat. 'Storm poles', which were pointed stakes projecting out from the bank, could be added, as could palisadoes or palisades, hedges of posts three or four feet long, with sharp iron tips and circles of nails sticking out from the crowns. Even an old stone wall, itself vulnerable to cannon, could be rendered formidable by packing earth behind it. According to Henry Townshend, under siege in royalist Worcester, a big gun could still breach a wall lined with up to eight feet of soil or dung; but a lining twenty feet thick, to the top, would make the defence invulnerable.⁴ In civil war terms, where there was muck, there was safety.

The whole point about Henry Townshend's comment, however, was that the wall of Worcester did not have twenty feet of dirt packed behind it, but only six. Despite the obvious and urgent nature of their danger, the garrison and citizens had shirked the enormous labour which would have guaranteed their safety and settled for a risky compromise which shored up the wall against a regular bombardment but left it vulnerable to heavy fire at close range. The truth was that security entailed effort and expense, and most occupants of strongpoints, especially though not exclusively the civilians, would avoid both as far as was possible. When a town was exposed to direct attack by an enemy, it is true, inhabitants of all ages and both sexes worked feverishly and without pay to perfect its defences, because of the risk of losing their possessions in the looting which followed a successful storm. Otherwise, however, a military governor or town council paid for labour services or else arranged a regular system of conscription for them. The first involved heavy additional local taxation; the latter a withdrawal of hands from the economy and considerable resentment among those drafted. Digging-tools, timber, and turf, had all likewise to be either purchased or seized. In

December 1642 the king inspected a work-gang deputed to labour upon part of the fortification of his base at Oxford. It was supposed to consist of 122 men; Charles found twelve of them present. When Parliament's main army advanced slowly upon the same city in 1643, every able-bodied man aged between 16 and 60 was ordered to help with the strengthening of the fortifications for one whole day each week, bringing his own spade. The success of this command may be gauged by the frequency, and increasing anger, with which it had to be repeated during the following two months. The programme only began to make real headway during the next winter, when the system of a day's (unpaid) labour out of every seven was maintained with the penalty of a shilling fine for each day missed. The cumulative result was impressive, but only achieved as a result of immense pressure applied over a long period. Towns which considered themselves to be deep within friendly territory rarely bothered to raise covering works at all, sometimes with catastrophic results.

DESTRUCTION OF SUBURBS

Before existing fortifications could be improved, town suburbs, spreading out beyond the medieval walls and offering excellent cover to attackers, had to be razed to the ground. This entailed a huge effort in itself and caused large-scale suffering and resentment on the part of the inhabitants, none of whom received adequate compensation. By 1645 most towns which came under regular siege or which contained garrisons within an area of routine fighting were surrounded by a zone of burnt-out buildings. The alternative was to include the suburbs themselves within new fortifications, incurring proportionately more effort and expense, and stretching the manpower of the defence around a larger perimeter. The inhabitants of Chester attempted this, with disastrous results (see below). Even the repair of existing city or town walls proved a delicate matter because of the number of houses, often the homes of wealthy citizens, which had been built up against them. An effective renovation of the walls would often involve the removal of these, and urban leaders shied away from inciting the anguish and rage of their fellow townsfolk.

CONSTRUCTION OF OUTWORKS

Once constructed, basic defensive lines could be considerably augmented by multiplication, one within another, and by outworks. These included bastions, a projection from the wall normally in the shape of an arrowhead; the half-moon, a semicircular or (more usually) triangular projection; the hornwork, which pushed forward two protuberances like a bull's head; and the battery, which was rectangular. Redoubts were like miniature forts upon the line, with a bastion at each corner, set in the defences or (more usually) lying outside and detached from them. All these earthworks provided flanking fire by musket or artillery, and could be used to strengthen a city wall, cover its gates, or add considerable barriers to earthen lines. A royalist expert on fortifications, Sir Richard Cave, reckoned that twenty men could cast up forty feet of breastworks in twelve hours.[5] Certainly a force of a few hundred determined men, with picks, spades, and axes, could fortify a small town within a week. The 'chains and mudwalls at the town's ends', put up hurriedly at Manchester in September 1642, under the direction of a German engineer, Roseworm, repelled the assaults of a larger royalist force under the earl of Derby.[6] However, Derby's men were every bit as inexperienced as the defenders, and his largest gun fired a six-pound ball; with veterans, and heavier weaponry, he could have breached the walls.

Siege-Guns

In all, ten kinds of siege-gun saw service during the civil wars fought in Britain and Ireland. The smallest three, firing shot of up to four pounds in weight, were essentially field pieces, employed in sieges as anti-personnel weapons. Siege-guns included the saker, which lobbed balls weighing four to seven pounds; the demi-culverin, firing those from seven to twelve pounds; and a culverin, firing those from twelve to twenty pounds. A saker weighed up to 1,800 pounds and was up to ten feet long; a culverin could be 5,000 pounds in weight and thirteen feet long; while up to a dozen horses—or thirty-five men—were needed to drag one demi-culverin and even more to haul a culverin. The saker and demi-culverin could knock in gates and windows and bring down battlements and turrets, while a culverin could crack stonework. None of them, however, could break open a stone wall.[7] The early modern siege weapon *par excellence* was the demi-cannon, which, firing a ball from twenty to forty pounds in weight, could smash down the wall of a typical medieval castle or town. Developed by the Spanish Army of Flanders as the standard component of a siege-train, its supremacy in this field remained unchallenged until the mid-nineteenth century. Thus shortly after the outbreak of the Irish rebellion the insurgents, with the aid of a demi-cannon, 'took all the castles and [strong]holds that were invested by the English' in County Limerick. Very often the English surrendered, realizing that they could not have withstood a battery.[8] However, it weighed between 4,500 and 6,000 pounds and needed an average hundred men, or thirty to forty draught animals, to move it. This at least made it more portable than the biggest guns, the whole cannon which weighed 6,000 to 8,000 pounds and the cannon royal which was larger still. Hurling shot between forty and eighty pounds in weight, these were even more formidable against fortresses, and even harder to shift. They also took at least twice as long to reload and consumed at least twice as much powder.

In addition, early modern besiegers often used a mortar—a fat, squat tub of metal, designed to stand at a forty-five-degree angle and fire grenadoes, or grenades, over the defences of a strongpoint. The latter were primitive shells, ignited by fuses of heavy rope or linen tow soaked in a solution of alcohol or water

Roaring Meg

The mortar cast at Hereford, for the reduction of Goodrich Castle. This squat tub of metal fired twenty-two explosive grenades, each one weighing two hundred pounds, over the walls of the castle into its interior. The damage it did was enormous, turning most of the internal buildings into wrecks. Yet the walls remained intact and the royalist garrison continued to hold out until cannon arrived which would breach the shell of the castle. Only the spectacular remains of the medieval sandstone fortress remain today.

mixed with saltpetre and run into the shell along wooden or iron tubes. The standard textbooks directed that the shell itself should be a globe of copper, filled with gunpowder; in practice they were made of any hard and brittle metal, or of glass, or of clay, or even of canvas.[9] Mortars were of no use in damaging fortifications, but instead served (and still do) as weapons of terror. The exploding grenades could damage the bodies and nerves of defenders, and destroy their living conditions with blasts which could themselves start major fires. They did, however, also have liabilities for the besiegers. It proved hard to calculate the length of a fuse so precisely that it neither exploded the charge in mid-air nor burned long enough after landing to give its intended victims the opportunity to extinguish it. Furthermore, whatever their exact size (which varied greatly) mortars were heavy and clumsy objects, about as hard to move as a demi-cannon.

THE CAPTURE OF A FORTIFIED POSITION

To operate effectively, siege-guns had to be fired less than two hundred paces from their target, at which distance they would also be vulnerable to the firepower of the garrison. To protect them and the gunners, therefore, it was necessary to erect earthworks, supplemented by gabions (wickerwork baskets six feet tall and filled with earth) and turnpikes (wooden spars with sharp stakes projecting in circles from them). Gabions made the provision of defences for batteries much swifter, and turnpikes could stop sallies of horsemen from the garrison, trying to spike the guns; both could be equally useful in fortifications. A good battery combined a number of different sizes of artillery; the cannon or demi-cannon weakened the walls, while smaller pieces loosened cracked masonry still further and drove off people trying to plug the breach. By this means the attackers maintained a continuous rate of fire. Breaching defences was, however, often only a first step, for, as the Cromwellian assaults on Kilkenny and Clonmel highlight (see below), determined defenders could turn what appeared to be a highway to victory into the mouth of hell.

Nor was it necessary to break open fortifications if they could be climbed over. Yet storming a strongpoint required a wholly different set of priorities and alternative equipment. It was usually carried out just before dawn, to give better cover to the attackers and to catch the defence at its lowest ebb, and was dangerous enough to require special incentives. Soldiers were universally promised the plunder of a town or fortress taken by assault, and the New Model sometimes offered cash bonuses to the front-line troops, no matter the outcome of the assault. As this set of instructions for royalists attacking Nantwich in January 1644 highlights, the order of a storm was usually carefully arranged: 'Major Harwar with the regiment under his command, and the firelocks, with the scaling ladders, they and all the dragoneers, armed with firelocks or snaphances, to fall on first...Then to be second with a hundred musketeers; then a strong body of pikes; then a reserve of musketeers; and let the soldiers carry as many faggots as they can; this to be at five a clock in the morning . . . Word. God and a good cause.'[10] The ladders were to scale the ramparts, the faggots of wood (sometimes supplemented by carts) to fill in the ditches, and the password to enable soldiers to recognize friends in the wintry night. Assault troops and defenders of works favoured firelocks and snaphances since they proved more reliable than the usual matchlock muskets, and did not require the glowing cords of the latter which could give away the owner's position in the dark. They also used hand-grenades. However, even such careful preparations never guaranteed success; the order quoted above was taken from the pocket of the captain who wrote it, as the defenders of Nantwich stripped his corpse after beating off the attack.

As well as trying to get over defences, besiegers could attempt to get through them by blowing open the main gate with a petard, a container like a grenade, filled with up to six pounds of powder and hung, fuse burning, in the centre of the gate. This could only be accomplished, however, when defences were still relatively primitive. Beyond that point, the only realistic alternative to bombarding was to mine. According to contemporary manuals a mine needed to be seven feet high, five feet wide, and lined with planks. It was sunk at the end of a trench dug towards a town or fortress wall, and culminated in a chamber excavated under the wall itself. This was filled with barrels of powder, which were supposed to blow out that section of defences when detonated. This proved a difficult enterprise: first, it was long and laborious; second, a mine usually needed professional miners, skilled in making shafts; third, there were few places in Britain (or anywhere else) where the ground was not either too hard, too soft, or too wet to make digging one worth the effort, and, finally, the digging proved a noisy business, and usually audible to attentive defenders who would then tunnel above the workers to drop explosives or pour boiling water on to them. An astute garrison would prepare countermines in advance beneath sections of the wall which seemed particularly vulnerable, and so render itself virtually secure against the threat. Prince Rupert's attempts to reduce Lichfield Cathedral Close in April 1643 reveal the problems as well as the potential of the tactic. His miners, from the coalfield of Cannock Chase, had to work past the springs which abounded around the close. They sank four shafts, of which three were countermined, and when the fourth reached the wall Rupert found that he could not spare enough powder to create the necessary explosion. Eventually more arrived, and a hole was blown in the wall, only for the royalists to be beaten back from it by hand-grenades. The latter, however, consumed so much of the defenders' own store of gunpowder that they asked for terms.

SKILLED PRACTITIONERS

Clearly, taking a fortified stronghold required a knowledge of siege warfare almost entirely lacking, especially during the early years of the wars, among native soldiers. All sides therefore depended on foreign experts who 'spend their whole time in the exercises of military discipline, to whom fights, sieges, batteries, approaches, and underminings were as familiar as were the wearing of their corsletts'.[11] Prince Rupert brought with him to England two professional engineers, Bernard de Gomme and Bartholomew de la Roche, the former of whom became the royal engineer-general. Two Dutchmen, John Dalbier and Peter Manteau van Dalem, fulfilled the equivalent function for the earl of Essex and the New Model Army respectively. A Swede, Beckmann, aided local royalist forces, and the vital role of the German Roseworm at Manchester has already been noted. In 1642 the confederate general, Owen Roe O'Neill, begged for 'some engineers, at least six mining engineers, and some petardeers' to be sent from the Netherlands, together with 'two large pieces of artillery' and 'four or five field pieces' which, he believed, would make short work of the fortifications in Ulster.[12] And indeed a number of foreign technicians skilled in the ways of war did move to Ireland. After serving in the royalist cavalry in England, John Vangyrish, a German engineer, joined the Army of Connacht and appears have designed the confederate fort in Galway using a configuration strikingly similar to defences at Newark master-minded by de Gomme. A Frenchman, Monsieur Laloe, became engineer-general for the confederates and used his 'bombs and fireworks' to great effect at the siege of Duncannon and elsewhere.[13] Thomas Harley served as chief engineer in Munster and was skilled in the destruction of strongholds, as was his counterpart in the Scottish army in Ulster, Henry Jardine.

ARTILLERY TRAINS

If experience was lacking among native troops, then so were the funds necessary to support lengthy sieges or to increase firepower. Back in the late fifteenth century, the Spanish sovereigns Ferdinand and Isabella had deployed 180 pieces of artillery in their conquest of Granada. The Dutch brought eighty against Groenlo in 1625, and used 116 in their siege of 's Hertogenbosch four years later. Gustavus Adolphus had fifty-seven heavy guns on the battlefield of Breitenfeld in 1631, and forced the passage of the River Lech with ninety of them the following year. By contrast, Charles I took twenty-seven on his first campaign in 1642, of which the largest were two demi-cannon, two culverins, and two demi-culverins. By the following summer an extra demi-cannon and culverin had been added to his artillery park, and two of each accompanied the royal army against Bristol and Gloucester. In 1644, when speed was essential, the king's army carried only four demi-culverins and four sakers, while the following summer it deployed a pair of demi-cannon and a culverin with devastating effect against Leicester.[14] The guns initially ordered for the New Model Army included two demi-cannon and three culverins, and it soon added to these the three big pieces from the royal army, captured at Naseby.[15] This gave it a siege-train of unprecedented power, which was further augmented by the arrival of a whole cannon when it was outside Sherborne Castle. Cromwell borrowed this, two demi-cannon, and some culverins when he was sent to take out a set of royalist fortresses in Wiltshire and Hampshire in September 1645 and his total success upon this expedition owed virtually everything to his extraordinary weight of fire. The train brought to Ireland by Cromwell included eleven siege-guns and twelve field pieces, containing more heavy guns than those of all the other armies in Ireland put together!

These big guns often acquired the status of personalities. The two demi-cannon owned by Newcastle's northern royalist army, and almost certainly brought by Henrietta Maria from the Netherlands, were known variously as 'the Queen's Pocket Pistols' or 'Gog and Magog'. The Hull garrison captured one in a sally against royalist siegeworks, and the other was lost when York surrendered to Parliament; both were subsequently used to batter royalist castles in Yorkshire. 'Sweet Lips' was the nickname of the most notorious (or popular) whore in Hull, and applied by its garrison to a demi-cannon. Sir John Meldrum borrowed it to besiege Newark, and surrendered it to Prince Rupert when the latter relieved the town; 'Sweet Lips' remained in the hands of the Newark garrison until hostilities ceased. Parliament favoured keeping siege-pieces at provincial strongholds, notably Portsmouth, Northampton, Hull, Stafford, and Manchester, and loaned them out to local commanders, usually after heated argument. This allowed minor armies to travel very light indeed; the Midland forces of the earl of Denbigh had a permanent train of just two sakers and two drakes.[16] As a rule, garrisons preferred to deploy many small pieces in their own defence, as the weapons primarily needed were those effective against personnel; when Prince Rupert took Bristol in 1643 he found almost a hundred guns in the city, but the largest were two demi-culverins and most had barrels which were hammered together.[17]

Initially the Irish insurgents relied on artillery captured from English strongholds. For instance, at the siege of Limerick in June 1642, they took 'three pieces of ordnance, whereof one of them weighted near 8,000 weight [eight cwt] mounted' and a 'battering piece of such large dimensions, that it took twenty-five oxen to remove it' and fired a thirty-two-pound shot.[18] Presumably this was a whole or a demi-cannon. The Irish also augmented their stock of artillery with cannon recovered from ships and imported from abroad. By the later 1640s some towns had assembled considerable arsenals: Wexford, a major confederate port, together with its fort, contained at the time of its surrender to Cromwell in 1649 'near a hundred cannon'.[19] On the Protestant side, the outbreak of the First English Civil War prevented the dispatch of artillery intended for the English army in Ireland. Yet by February 1643 the Scots in Ulster possessed six 'battering pieces', while Ormond had seven. The combatants fighting in Ireland may have possessed artillery but the rarity of roads and the ubiquity of bogs ensured that heavy guns tended to be used against coastal or riverside strongholds.

Cities and Towns

LONDON

In 1643 Parliament refortified London on a scale and with a sophistication unparalleled elsewhere in the three kingdoms. Its medieval walls were ignored, and a completely new circuit of works constructed around city and suburbs eleven miles in length, of 'turf, sand, wattles and earthen work'. The bank rose eighteen feet from the bottom of the ditch and was studded with storm poles a foot apart. Upon its line were twenty-three forts, redoubts, breastworks, or batteries, mounting a total of almost 200 guns. They included such rarities as a fort with nine angles, one upon two levels, and parapets and bastions covered with tiled roofs for the comfort of defenders. The wealth of the capital and its degree of politicization facilitated this achievement. The livery companies competed with each other to build the defences, their young men marching off to the work 'with roaring drums, flying colours, and girded swords', as girls cheered them.[20] Yet none of this extraordinary sequence of fortifications was ever put to the test.

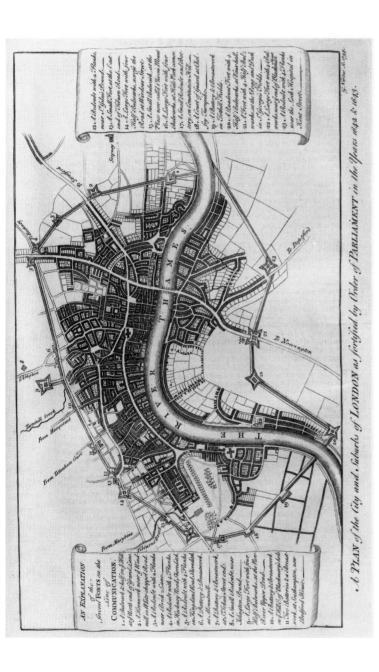

A PLAN of the City and suburbs of LONDON as fortified by Order of PARLIAMENT in the Years 1642 & 1643.

Plan of London's fortifications in 1642–3

This was the circuit of newly dug fortifications, of which the City and Parliament were so justly proud. As well as furnishing comforts for the defenders apparently unique in the English Civil War, such as tiled roofs for parapets and bastions, it provides a textbook illustration of the varieties of defensive structure possible upon a line of earthworks, including angled forts, half-moons, hornworks, and redoubts. The king's failure to capture London in November 1642 (he was turned back at Turnham Green) proved disastrous since it allowed his enemies control of England's political, economic, and administrative infrastructure for the duration of the wars.

EXETER

Far more typical was Exeter, where the survival of exceptionally good document-ary and archaeological evidence illustrates the progressive refortification of the town. It began with the unusual advantage of a complete wall already lined with earth, presumably a legacy of the experience of having got stuck in the teeth of two major Tudor rebellions. Nevertheless, by 1642 the lining had become over-grown and encroached upon by building, so the first task was to restore it. By the end of the year the citizens (now formally adhering to Parliament) had also re-paired the wall, blocked up vaults beneath it, mounted twenty-five guns upon it, and dug outworks. However, a royalist attack revealed the town's continuing vulnerability, and so in the first half of 1643 the gates were given ditches, draw-bridges, turnpikes, and flanking earthworks with guns. The townsfolk dug a trench outside the walls and built outlying forts in a ring around the city. It was all in vain, for when the royalists returned in June they easily overran most of the outworks and penned up the defenders inside the walls. Three months later they stormed the bulwark protecting the south gate before dawn, and the garrison sur-rendered before they blew in the gate itself. Once in charge, the king's men sur-rounded the city with a completely new outer ring of defences, consisting of at least three large bastioned forts and a bank and ditch, the latter seven feet deep and twenty-seven feet wide. These deterred even the New Model Army from making a direct attack when it arrived in October 1645. It preferred to establish a strengthening ring of garrisons of its own, which blockaded Exeter until the be-leaguered city surrendered in April 1646.

NEWARK AND COLCHESTER

The fortifications at Newark were rebuilt in a similar fashion. When the royalists occupied the town at the end of 1642 they found its walls to be decayed beyond the point of repair. They therefore had to construct new defences, and initially produced 'most pitiful works . . . very low and thin, and with a dry ditch which most men might easily leap'.[21] This is exactly what happened during the first parliamentarian attack upon the town, which washed back and forth across the defences as if they hardly existed. Having repelled it, the garrison strengthened the line with storm poles and palisades, and a better bank and ditch, and it held during a siege of several weeks in early 1644. Prince Rupert raised the siege and, in an effort to make this isolated and exposed stronghold impregnable, the royal-ists strengthened the earthworks still further, and built two large outlying forts with an arrowhead bastion at each corner.

When the enemy reappeared before Newark in late 1645, they faced a line of royalist defences which, apart from the huge external forts, possessed 'such deep graffs, bastions, horns, half-moons, counterscarps, redoubts, pitfalls, and an im-pregnable line of sod and turf palisaded and stockaded . . . that this bulky bulwark

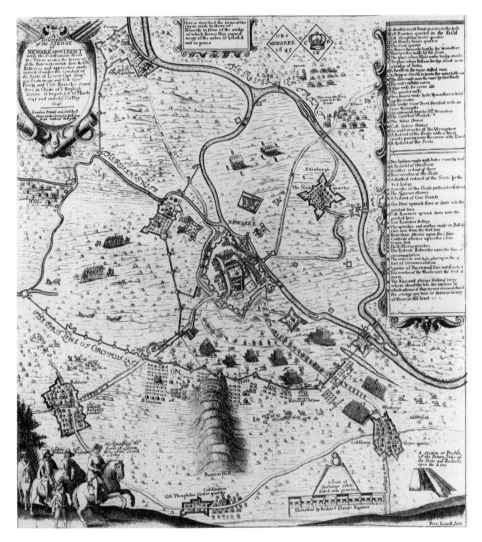

Fortifications at Newark
by Richard Clampe

Newark served as one of the most important royalist bases in the country and as a centre of operations for most of the East Midlands. The garrison resisted repeated attacks and prolonged sieges. The most serious came in November 1645 when a combined Scottish and English force laid siege to the town (the Scottish camp is shown on the right) under the commands of Leven and Poyntz (shown on bottom left). The attackers fortified a ring of towns around Newark—Baledon is shown on the bottom left and Winthorpe on the right—and constructed lines of banks and ditches, interspersed with forts, in an arc to the south. Despite the onslaught the town held out until Charles I ordered it to surrender in May 1646.

Queen's Sconce, Newark

The fortifications at the royalist town at Newark in Nottinghamshire remain the best pre-served of all earthworks dating from the 1640s. Archaeological excavations have revealed that the first bank was made of loose topsoil, while the second was faced with hard red clay that both bonded it and presented a slippery surface. In 1644 the works were all redug with a base of gravel and timber reinforcements, and then almost certainly faced with turf to absorb shot better. The forts surrounding Newark were built in the same way, and one of them, called the Queen's Sconce, seen here from the air, is 300 feet across, with a ditch 70 feet wide and a ram-part still rising 30 feet above it in places. It would also have had storm-poles on the rampart and palisades beyond the ditch. The garrison would have lived in huts or tents inside. Since so many of the other earthworks dating from the 1640s have been destroyed it is impossible to tell whether this was typical of the large bastioned forts built outside many towns during the war, or unusually impressive.

of Newark represented to the besiegers but one entire sconce'.[22] Sconces were forts, graffs were ditches, counterscarps were banks thrown up on the far side of ditches to make it more difficult for an attacker to fire across them, and pitfalls were traps covered in leaves and dug in the ground across which a storming party had to advance to the defences. In response, a combined parliamentarian and Scottish army invested Newark with 9,000 men; the former dug a double line of banks and ditches which cut off the royalists completely to the landward side (the River Trent bounding their other flank). These were weak compared with the defences, but supported by a ring of fortified villages they proved quite effective in preventing sallies. Newark gradually turned into 'a miserable stinking infected town',[23] and would have had to surrender eventually even had the king not ordered it to do so in May 1646. The only other known case in these wars of a complete circumvallation of a town by a besieging force was that of Colchester in 1648. Its medieval walls supplied most of its protection, but within them remained a royalist army of about 4,000 and the New Model Army feared the losses likely to result from taking it by storm. Instead it settled down to starve the defenders out, constructing a continuous rampart and ditch around the town on its side of the River Colne, with five forts, four redoubts, and five hornworks. Five more large forts were built across the river. By the time of their surrender the inhabitants and garrison of Colchester had long been on a ration of seven ounces of bread per person per day, had eaten most of their horses and were working through the local dogs, and were suffering from the bloody faeces which are a symptom of advanced malnutrition.[24]

CARLISLE

Such elaborate siegeworks were a luxury undertaken as much to keep soldiers busy and to reduce the morale of the defenders as for any practical benefit. When the Scots and parliamentarians invested Carlisle in September 1644, they simply built a powerful fort at each of the four cardinal points around it. Small parties of the royalists easily slipped between these and on one occasion even destroyed a fort. It was immediately rebuilt, however, and the garrisons prevented convoys of food from entering the city. By June 1645 hunger reduced the people of Carlisle to eating horses, hempseed, dogs, and rats; little wonder it surrendered. This crude tactic was the usual form of siegecraft adopted in the earlier part of the First English Civil War, more often combined with direct attacks upon the defences. Only towards the end, when they had plenty of time and little fear of being disturbed, did parliamentarian units besieging the remaining enemy cities, such as Chester, Oxford, and Worcester, bother to join up some of their fortified camps with lines. No protagonists attempted the normal continental procedure of a double circumvallation, the outer one intended to deter a relieving army. When one of those did approach, the besiegers always broke up the investments either to retreat or to offer a pitched battle.

LIMITATIONS OF ENGLISH FORTIFICATIONS

If siege warfare remained primitive compared with contemporary European practice, then so was fortification. Many towns were far less well protected than Newark, because they had less fear of attack. In some cases that confidence proved horribly misplaced. Only a short distance from Newark was Leicester, which by mid-1645 had never been approached by an enemy force and reposed securely in Parliament's hands. When the king's army suddenly appeared before it, it was surrounded only by an old stone wall, in which Rupert's two demi-cannon soon blew a gaping hole. This was not quite the end, for the defenders prepared behind it 'a handsome retrenchment' with three pieces of artillery aimed at the breach, from which the royalists were initially thrown back. The drain of men to this work, however, enabled others of the king's forces, storming the wall at four more points soon after midnight, to clear parts of the parapet with hand-grenades. Once over, they opened a gate and the killing and looting in the town lasted until dawn.[25] Hereford and Oswestry, initially deep within royalist territory, seemed even more secure and were just as badly defended and much more weakly garrisoned when Sir William Waller (see picture on p. 314) suddenly appeared before the former in 1643 and the earl of Denbigh before the latter in 1644. In each case the attackers just knocked in a gate with a saker and entered the town.[26] Lincoln fell almost as easily to the earl of Manchester in 1644, for when his soldiers swarmed up its wall on scaling ladders the royalist defenders ran 'crying that they were poor Array men'; that is, conscripts.[27]

OXFORD AND YORK

The onset of war transformed the fortifications of other cities. For instance, Oxford's initial defences were limited to a log barricade across the nearer end of Magdalen Bridge and a pile of rocks, which could be dropped on the heads of attackers, on top of the college tower. Yet by 1646 the city's fortifications had been totally overhauled. The bridge was now guarded by a bastioned fort upon the far side, and similar works blocked the other approaches to the town. The most open flank, to the north, was now covered by a zigzag pattern of high banks and deep ditches, set with storm poles and palisades. There was an arrowhead bastion at the apex of each salient and a half-moon jutting from the centre of each semi-circle between. Two-thirds of the city was, moreover, covered by natural defences, its rivers which had been allowed to flood the usual water-meadows to create enormous moats. Oxford could only be reduced by blockade.

York also enjoyed a strategic advantage. It lay in the flood-plain of two rivers, the larger of which flowed through its centre. Within the city this was easily spanned by bridges, but besiegers had to communicate clumsily over crossings of boats lashed together. Moreover a medieval wall, standing upon an earthen bank and with more earth packed behind it, surrounded it. The only weakness was the sheer size of the circuit to be defended, but that was obviated when it came under threat in 1644 because Newcastle's royalist field army retreated inside. As a result Parliament had to tie down three separate armies in an effort to block it up. One of these succeeded in bringing down a tower with a sprung mine, but the relations between the besieging forces became so strained, and the communications so bad, that the ensuing storm was not co-ordinated and the defenders slaughtered the assailants who came through the breach. After that the besiegers could only hope to starve York out, and were foiled by Prince Rupert's relieving army. Only the rout of Rupert's and Newcastle's armies at Marston Moor on 2 July, leaving too few defenders to man the walls, enabled Parliament to capture York a fortnight later.

LYME AND BRISTOL

Human resolution could make even unpromising situations formidable. Lyme, in Dorset, was a small fishing port which Puritan evangelism had helped to turn into a notable centre of parliamentarianism. When in April 1644 Prince Maurice's army arrived outside the town it faced a strong line and ditch reinforced by no less than seven bastioned forts which commanded the ground above the port. This concentration of defensive works in such a small span, with 1,100 soldiers inside, made Lyme an impossible target. Maurice's men assaulted it repeatedly, always trying to catch the defenders off guard and never succeeding. Parliament's control of the navy meant that food, ammunition, and reinforcements poured in from the sea. Twice the two royalist demi-cannon made a breach in the line, only for its assailants to find that the defenders had retrenched behind it and could pour fire on to them until they retired and the hole was filled. It was a siege virtually doomed from the start. The garrison at Chester acted with similar determination. There the royalist forces, unwilling to incur unpopularity by burning all the suburbs, put its faith in a string of bastioned earthworks designed to protect the suburbs as well. The folly of this was revealed on 20 September 1645, when the local parliamentarians got over the line with ladders at 3 a.m., at a point where a traitor had informed them that there were not yet any palisades. The governor, Lord Byron, returned to find that the unlined medieval walls provided little protection against two demi-cannon. He was, however, determined to fight it out. Twice sections of the wall were blasted away, and each time Byron had lined houses inside and the parapets alongside with musketeers and halberdiers, ready to receive the storming parties. When the latter staggered back, the breaches were filled with earth, and all the while more dirt was piled behind the rest of the wall. The garrison prepared countermines wherever the ground beneath it was soft, and had a tub of water and pile of raw hides placed outside every house within range of a mortar attack. When the latter came, one inhabitant saw 'our houses like so many split vessels crash their supporters and burst themselves in sunder through the violence of these descending fire brands'.[28] The precautions, however, prevented any general conflagration from spreading. After this the parliamentarians had to settle down to blockade the city into surrender, which took until February 1646.

Other urban centres proved exceptionally difficult to defend. For example, even though Bristol (see picture on p. 253) was situated between two converging rivers (like Oxford and York), to the north it was overlooked by hills, close enough to enable artillery to fire down into it, which had therefore to be included in any practicable defence line. Not only did this mean defending a circumference five miles in extent, but the hills were composed of very hard limestone which resisted picks and spades. When Prince Rupert's army arrived outside the city in 1643, it found about 1,500 opponents strung out along the whole circuit. At most points on the north side the new ditch was less than five feet deep and the wall less than five feet high, and although there were three forts and ten lesser works none provided proper flanking fire. The royalists almost threw away these advantages when indiscipline caused them to attack prematurely, without the intended preparation of ladders and faggots. Three out of their four storming parties were foiled. The fourth, however, easily cleared a section of wall with hand-grenades and then pulled it down into the ditch, letting in heavy reinforcements. After that, Bristol's surrender was inevitable.

Once in charge, the royalists increased the garrison to 4,280 men, a sufficient number to hold the perimeter, and decreed a programme of refortification. The cost of both together, however, came to £2,000 per week, which in the depressed economy of wartime and given the extra demands made for specific royal campaigns, could not be raised in the city and its hinterland. Soon soldiers were deserting, and the local royalist leaders settled for a garrison of 2,300 men and for a single huge new fort and three new outworks on the vulnerable north side. When the New Model Army attacked at 2 a.m. on 10 September 1645, they found the same wretchedly shallow ditch and a weak wall along most of the line, and the poverty and demoralization of the king's cause after a string of defeats had reduced the defenders to about 1,000, many of them raw conscripts from the town and from Wales. At two points on the wall the latter turned and ran as soon as the New Model's veterans swarmed up it on their ladders, and in the darkness the forts could do nothing to assist. Once the line was broken, the defence was doomed just as in 1643. Bristol was a death-trap for any cause which made a stand in it; too important to be abandoned without a struggle and yet too expensive to fortify securely. In the words of one royalist engineer, it was simply 'a weak town'.[29]

GLOUCESTER

Very different was the case of Gloucester, to which Prince Rupert's victorious army proceeded from Bristol in 1643 for what was probably the most significant siege of the English Civil Wars, perceived as a turning-point by many at the time and since. This has in itself bedevilled an objective consideration of it, for in the aftermath parliamentarians tended to exaggerate the vulnerability of the city. However, archaeological excavations have revealed the reality of the situation. Gloucester was defended on one side by a wide river, and on two others by newly constructed earthworks with five arrowhead bastions; the ditch in front of these was up to twelve feet deep and thirty feet wide, and permanently flooded; while the ground beyond it was boggy. Thus the royalists could only approach from the south-east, and although this land was higher and drier it was defended by a medieval wall about thirty feet high and completely lined with earth, and with a ditch fifteen deep. Moreover the garrison of the city was the same size as that of Bristol had been, within a much tighter and stronger perimeter.

Faced with this formidable obstacle, the royalists did their best. They had not expected to meet determined resistance and did not want to sustain heavy casualties in a premature attempt to storm when they needed the army intact for a possible march on London. For two weeks, therefore, they tried to batter down the wall and when this failed, began to mine beneath it, while the classical scholar William Chillingworth designed siege engines which could drop bridges across the flooded ditch before the new works. As both enterprises approached fruition the following week, the wall was so dilapidated from bombardment that the desperate citizens dug a trench behind it. A few more days and the king would probably have had Gloucester, but at that moment Essex arrived from London with his relieving army. The real significance of the siege lay not with the bungled royalist attack but with Parliament's efficiency in providing a relief force with a speed and scale of effort which remained unique in the history of the war.

SURPRISE ATTACKS

Occasionally towns fell to surprise attacks, the outstanding examples being Shrewsbury and Hereford. In neither case could this have been accomplished without precise information brought to the attackers by disaffected individuals from the citizenry or garrison. In the former, the vital work was carried out by a party of carpenters, who sawed and chopped through the palisades at 4 a.m. on a freezing February morning, letting in a squad of soldiers with firelocks and pistols who scaled the rampart and opened a gate to their comrades. The demolition of the palisades still took fifteen minutes, and was seen by sentries who gave the alarm. The crucial factor was that the bulk of the royalist garrison was absent on an expedition, leaving a skeleton force of just 200 to hold the town; too few to mobilize fast enough and in sufficient strength to counter the onslaught. The royalists finally lost Hereford in similar conditions, just before dawn on a snowy December morning. Seven parliamentarian soldiers arrived at a gate disguised as a constable bringing in labourers to help improve the defences. As the guards came out to hear the warrant read, they were rushed by 150 others hiding in a ruined building in the burnt-out suburbs nearby. It is possible that traitors had assisted by drawing most of the usual sentries off that gate; at any rate it was seized and nearly 1,800 more parliamentarians came through it. Even a town with good defensive works and ample warning could not hold out if the garrison was heavily outnumbered. In May 1645 Edward Massey's parliamentarians rushed Evesham in five places at once. Their firepower so outmatched that of the defenders that at one point they were able to fill the ditch with faggots, climb the breastwork, tear down the palisades, and pour over into the streets, overwhelming all resistance.

FORTIFICATIONS IN IRELAND

As in England the onset of civil war transformed the defences of Irish cities and towns (see map on p. 198). The largest earthworks were made around Dublin which was difficult to defend 'in regard of the craziness of the walls'.[30] Nevertheless, as the Down Survey shows, earthen ramparts encircled most of the suburbs to the south and north of the city, reinforced by at least eighteen bastions positioned at regular intervals. A description of these fortifications, dating from 1646, speaks of half-moons before the gates, palisades to strengthen the earthworks, and the destruction of houses outside the walls to prevent the enemy from taking shelter. Perhaps fortunately, Dublin never underwent a full siege. At Belfast, a bastioned *enceinte* was built in 1643; nevertheless the town was surprised twice, in 1644 and 1648, indicating the limitations of the improvements. In March 1642, after five months, a lack of heavy artillery forced the confederates to raise their siege of Drogheda, which had been strengthened by breastworks at every gate and by 'platforms in such places where the walls were defective'.[31] Even though they controlled most of Ireland, the confederates overhauled the defences of the major towns—Limerick, New Ross, Wexford, Waterford, Dungarvan, Galway, and Kilkenny, where, as early as 1642, the townspeople allegedly 'had Dutchmen at work . . . in fortifying the town'.[32] Dungarvan's defences initially withstood an assault made by Inchiquin in 1647: 'I played upon it four days successively with four pieces of battery, yet was not the place made any way assaultable thereby.' He later recorded, 'all prejudice we did them being the beating down a flanker upon the town-wall, which was lined with earth, 14 foot high'.[33]

However, Dungarvan eventually fell, as did most towns faced by heavy artillery manned by experienced gunners and skilled military engineers. In the summer of 1645 forces loyal to the English Parliament took Sligo 'after the batteringe of two houses'. In September 1649 Cromwell's superior artillery made short work of Drogheda's medieval walls. Bombarding the town wall at points where buildings behind it made retrenchment difficult, his powerful artillery pumped nearly 300 shot into the old masonry in about eight hours, tearing two breaches through which his soldiers could enter to commence the notorious massacre of the defenders. The following month at Wexford a castle was the key to the fortifications and 100 shot sufficed to puncture that so thoroughly that the town capitulated; and, shortly afterwards, neighbouring New Ross surrendered as soon as a breach was made. After that, however, the going started to get harder. Bad weather in November and December prevented Cromwell from getting his guns near Waterford by land or sea, and he abandoned the attack. In March 1650 the garrison in Kilkenny prepared two palisaded trenches behind the piece of wall being pounded, and beat off the storming party as it came through; but its nerve failed when a second gap was made elsewhere. Worse followed at Clonmel in May, where the continental veteran Hugh Dubh O'Neill ambushed Cromwell's infantry as it stormed a breach in the walls. The troops found themselves between two newly made walls of piled stones and timber, lined with musketeers and converging upon an apex where artillery waited behind a deep ditch. The survivors staggered out, leaving between 1,000 and 2,500 dead behind them; but the defenders had to evacuate that night, having used up all their ammunition. Limerick, again under O'Neill's command, proved the greatest challenge of all. The city's modern fortifications, dating from the 1590s, had received considerable additions during the 1640s, making them, according to one Italian observer, 'almost impregnable, being surrounded with a triple wall, the three walls in turn being protected by water'.[34] Unable to take the town by storm, Cromwell's son-in-law and successor Henry Ireton erected an extensive circumvallation, which included two forts (Fort Cromwell and Fort Ireton), and set up a battery of twenty-eight guns and four mortar pieces. The siege dragged on until October 1651 when a defector told Ireton of a single stretch of the wall which had not been reinforced. He shot this down and so obtained a surrender.[35] After Limerick, the Cromwellians turned their attention to Galway. Unable to storm the extensive, modern, stone-faced defences which the townsfolk had constructed over the course of the 1640s, Sir Charles Coote blockaded the town, forcing it to surrender nine months later in April 1652.

FORTIFICATIONS IN SCOTLAND

The state of fortifications in the major Scottish towns and cities varied enormously (see map on pp. 196–7). The alarming regularity with which Aberdeen fell to a variety of assailants suggests that its defences remained basic. Similarly Dundee's sixteenth-century walls offered little resistance to Montrose, who breached them in 1645, or to George Monck's artillery, which blasted them down in 1651. Other centres enjoyed superior fortifications. The battlements at Inverness withstood a siege by Montrose. Defensive earthworks connected Leith and Edinburgh and despite attempts to take the city over the summer of 1650, the Cromwellians had to wait until after their victory at Dunbar in September before entering Edinburgh. Even then the royalist garrison in the castle, where the fortifications had been revamped, held out for a further two and a half months.

Dunluce Castle

This majestic castle, perched above the rugged County Antrim coastline and overlooking the Western Isles of Scotland, was the seat of the MacDonnells of Antrim and, according to one contemporary, was 'the strongest piece of this realm'. To the left of the castle, shown here from the air, the outline of the village of Dunluce, which was burned by Irish insurgents early in 1642, is clearly visible. Early intelligence of the rising ensured that the castle itself remained in Antrim's hands. However, in May 1642, the Scottish commander in Ulster, Munro, tricked the earl into surrendering the stronghold and then garrisoned troops from Argyll's regiment in it. Though the castle fell into disrepair during the course of the wars, Antrim recovered it at the Restoration.

Edinburgh Castle

James Gordon, minister of Rothiemay, drew this view of Edinburgh castle from the south in the 1640s. The palace block and King David's tower are clearly visible to the left, while the half-moon battery dominates the right. The ancient citadel still featured predominately during the civil wars: the covenanters stormed it in 1639 after Leslie blasted open the main gate with a petard while the following year the royalist garrison succumbed to starvation. The covenanters kept the castle as an artillery magazine and state prison until September 1650. The fall of the castle on 5 September 1648 marked the most significant military success of the Whiggamore Raid. In the aftermath of Dunbar (3 September 1650), the Scots hoped that the castle's elevated position would occupy Cromwell's forces for some time. However, the governor, Walter Dundas of Dundas the younger, surrendered prematurely after a siege lasting less than four months.

Castles and Forts

BOMBARDMENT

Besiegers faced similar problems and possibilities, albeit on a smaller scale, when they tried to capture a castle or fort. For example, in August 1644 Major-General Crawford, a parliamentarian commander, found Sheffield Castle protected by two rivers, an outwork in front of the gate, and the solid rock on which it stood, which could not be mined. He used his sakers to chop down the battlements and to prevent the garrison from sallying out, while the culverin put a crack in one wall. However, without heavy artillery Crawford failed to take the royalist stronghold. Everything changed on the sixth day, when a demi-cannon arrived from York. Trained upon the fissure made by the culverin, this brought the wall crashing down within one morning, and the garrison asked for terms. At Sherborne Castle in Dorset, the New Model Army demonstrated its capacity for undertaking an operation with such strength that the results amounted almost to overkill. It deployed both a whole cannon and some demi-cannon, and simultaneously used Mendip lead-miners to tunnel underneath the walls. Ten days were spent in preparations, and then five more in blasting two huge breaches, bringing down three towers, getting a mine laid, and making 6,000 soldiers ready to storm. Small wonder the royalists surrendered as their enemies came flooding in through the breaches. The confederate general, Thomas Preston, went to similar lengths during his three-month assault on Duncannon Fort (County Wexford) in 1645. He 'made trenches a far off, and by degree both day and night, by triangle and quadrangle work, came a pistol shot near the fort'. According to a contemporary writer it was 'the very best siege that was yet in Ireland . . . the ordinance and bombs going very thick', and an engraving shows that Preston commanded seventeen guns and three mortars.[36]

If cannon proved fatal to some castles, a mortar could be equally effective against others. Lichfield Cathedral Close had been turned into a fortress by a medieval bishop, and the first garrison to occupy it, a set of local royalists, easily repelled a succession of assaults. When a mortar arrived, however, and ten-inch shells began raining down upon them, they gave up at once. A parliamentarian in the force beleaguering Banbury Castle in Warwickshire recorded with grim satisfaction how screams were heard from inside every time another grenade exploded. However, Banbury did not surrender largely because the mortar fire did not intimidate the garrison. Goodrich Castle in Herefordshire, held for the king in 1646 by Sir Henry Lingen, also successfully withstood a mortar attack. To reduce it, the parliamentarian governor of Hereford, John Birch, had cast a mortar capable of throwing a grenade weighing 200 pounds; 'Roaring Meg', as it became known, survives in Hereford Museum. Birch fired twenty-two of these into the castle, almost all with his own hand, removing most roofs and damaging every single room. Lingen and his men simply gritted their teeth, and the castle only fell when siege-guns arrived and opened up the interior by bringing down a whole tower.

SIEGES

Even the heaviest artillery was not effective against all fortresses. At Castle Coote (County Roscommon) in 1643 the engineer Saint Loo, 'an experienced Low-Country soldier', made a 'regular circumvallation about the castle; yet the garrison so nobly attacked each redoubt, as greatly disappointed the besiegers'.[37] Scarborough Castle stood upon a steep headland, which rendered most of it inaccessible even if it were breached. In 1645 the parliamentarian Sir John Meldrum bombarded it with a whole cannon and two demi-cannon, which beat down the gatehouse and half a tower. The royalists had raised new, strong, earthen defences across the front of the castle which were impervious to fire, and this was the only part of it which could be approached. When Meldrum was killed by a stray shot, his men gave up the battering and settled down to blockade the fortress. It surrendered after seven months, because scurvy killed the occupants at the rate of ten per night and left them too weak to grind corn; a beleaguered stronghold did not actually have to run short of food for its inhabitants to suffer fatally from dietary deficiency. At another Yorkshire castle, Pontefract, the royalists had a long period in which to prepare for siege, and used that time to ram up to fifteen feet of earth behind the walls after the manner of people defending a town. As a result, when the northern parliamentarian forces eventually pounded it with a whole cannon and two demi-cannon during the spring of 1645, they could only knock down the tops of the towers. When stonework did flake away from the face of the wall, the defenders just packed on proportionately more much behind. In two weeks about 1,400 shot were fired at the castle, to no effect, and once again the siege turned into a blockade which lasted seven months until the garrison's supplies ran out. There was a repetition of the same process in the Second English Civil War, with a mortar being added to the siege equipment. This merely wrecked some rooms in the castle and so replenished the defenders' stock of firewood. Once again, starvation proved the only solution.

A short distance to the south was Sandal Castle, where the royalists prepared for siege by putting the earth outside the walls, in the shape of a new rampart and bastion covering one side. Unhappily for them, they lacked either the time or the imagination to screen the other in the same way, and a cannon and demi-cannon reduced this, in the words of the excavator, to 'little more than a tumbled mass of masonry among which the defenders had formed gun emplacements and access trenches'. One particularly vivid discovery by the archaeologists was a meal laid ready in one room, which had been abandoned when the wall came crashing down on it. After a few days of this the garrison surrendered.[38] Very different was the situation at Donnington Castle, an isolated royalist fortress in Berkshire, where bastioned earthworks were constructed all around it. In September 1644 siege-guns beat down four of its towers, and in early 1646 a mortar caused the garrison to evacuate the shell of the castle altogether for a time. The works around, however, were so strong that they held out to the end of the war. Equally formidable earthen defences were built around the marquis of Worcester's massive castle at Raglan in Monmouthshire, which became the last English royalist fortress to surrender in the first English Civil War.[39] It only did so when Fairfax concentrated more than 7,000 men around it, equipped with miners and a record six mortars. Faced with a nightmarish experience and absolutely no hope of relief, the marquis gave up.

Some of the artillery forts constructed by Henry VIII performed well during these wars, although admittedly most of them were away from war zones and they were usually small enough to be blocked up and left to run out of supplies without great effort on the part of besiegers. Only one, Southsea Castle by Portsmouth, was ever taken by direct attack, and this fell at the very opening of the First English Civil War before allegiances had hardened and standards of competence risen. The circumstances, in fact, defy parody; when Parliament's troops stormed it in the early hours of 4 September 1642, there were only twelve men inside and the governor was too drunk to get out of bed. He woke up in the morning to find himself a prisoner, and promptly changed sides. Very different was the fate of Pendennis Castle in Cornwall where King Henry's work had been accentuated by the addition of bastioned earthen ramparts under Elizabeth. The royalists eventually concentrated nearly 1,000 men inside, under Sir John ('Jack for the King') Arundell, and they were safe against anything except starvation. This took five months to work its effects, which were eventually so dramatic that upon its surrender almost half the garrison was too weak to walk out.

MINING

Mining occasionally accomplished what gunfire could not, although geological conditions seldom permitted it as most castles, like Sheffield, were perched on rocks. In November 1650 Cromwell, using Scottish colliers, tried to bring down Edinburgh Castle by driving tunnels into the crag below the southern walls; however, the rock was too hard and he abandoned the operations. The case of Lichfield has been mentioned, and two parliamentarian fortresses in Herefordshire, Hopton and Brampton Bryan, surrendered on the mere threat of a mine being sprung, as they stood in well-drained parkland. Another small castle in the same terrain was the Wiltshire one of Wardour, held for Parliament in 1644 by Edmund Ludlow. The royalists used Mendip miners, and when the explosion occurred, Ludlow 'was lifted up with it from the floor, with much dust suddenly about me; which was no sooner laid, but I found both the doors of my chamber blown open, and my window towards the enemy blown down, so that a cart might have entered at the breach'. Nevertheless, the latter was plugged with furniture before the storming party could get through, and the garrison only capitulated because its corn supply had been blown up as well.[40] At the weakly defended castles of Powis, near Welshpool, and Farnham, in Surrey, those miniature mines, petards, blew open the gates and enforced surrender.

BLOCKADE

Most castles in these wars, like many towns, were reduced by blockade. The huge medieval fortresses of Wales, almost all held for the king, were taken in this lengthy but straightforward fashion because they were too remote and isolated to require other treatment. The work of blocking up could be very simple; at Beeston in Cheshire during 1645 the parliamentarians simply constructed an earthen fort in front of the castle gate, and left it there with its own garrison like a cork in a bottle. When the royalists made terms after eighteen weeks, they had nothing left to eat but 'a piece of Turkey pie, two biscuits, a live peacock and a peahen';[41] one admires the aesthetic sense of hungry men who would spare a peacock. In general it was food which gave out first, most castles surrendering with plenty of ammunition left and more arms than there were men to use them. A number of Scottish strongholds fell through starvation during the 1640s: the covenanter garrison in Mingary Castle on the Ardnamurchan peninsula succumbed to MacColla in July 1644; while hunger finally forced the royalists garrisoned in Huntly Castle, near Aberdeen, to yield to the covenanters late in 1645. Similarly the Cromwellians starved the royalist garrison in Dunnotter Castle into submission in May 1652 after a nine-month siege.

TREACHERY

A few forts yielded to treachery or trickery. Late in 1644 Montrose overcame the Campbell stronghold at Loch Dochart in the central Lowlands by deceit: a party of royalists approached the island fortress by boat, claiming to be carrying letters from Argyll, and quickly overpowered the small garrison. At Corfe Castle in Dorset a royalist traitor opened a side-gate. At Portland in the same county a parliamentarian dashed up with a royalist horse troop disguised as their opponents, and called to the guards for admission. The ruse succeeded. In mid-December 1643 nine intrepid royalists carrying firelocks climbed into the upper ward of Beeston Castle soon after the moon had set. When day broke the governor found them lodged in his own citadel, and not knowing their numbers he decided to surrender, inviting their commander genially to lunch. Unsurprisingly, he was subsequently shot by his own side after a court martial; the king's men were left to hold the castle and keep exotic birds.[42]

Unable to withstand battery, many Irish and Scottish castles surrendered upon sight of artillery. For example, in August 1651 Stirling gave in to Monck when its Highland defenders panicked upon being treated to their first experience of mortar shells. Occasionally, even in this phase of the conflict, medieval strongholds still yielded to medieval methods. During 1651 Edward Ludlow, long recovered from his ordeal at Wardour, attacked a castle at Gourtenshore in western Ireland which had a river on one side and an earthwork on the other. His men carried faggots in front of them as shields against fire, and threw these into the ditch of the work on running up to it. Ladders got them over the banks and then over the wall of the castle courtyard beyond. They prised out the iron bars covering one window of the keep and so climbed into the interior and took it.[43]

Mansions and Manor Houses

LATHOM HOUSE

Castles and fortified houses enjoyed many common characteristics; indeed, Gourtenshore might well be classed among the latter. Some like Lathom House, the famous Lancashire residence of the earls of Derby, proved more formidable than many castles. It had been built after the advent of gunpowder, with walls of stone six feet thick bearing nine towers and surrounded by a moat six feet deep and twenty-four feet wide. The royalists inside had plenty of warning to prepare for the attack, which they used to pack six more feet of earth behind the walls and erect palisades on both edges of the moat. Nevertheless, when the Lancashire parliamentarians arrived in February 1644 they brought a perfect local siege-kit, including both a mortar and a demi-cannon. They surrounded the house with three successive banks and ditches, and eight bulwarks, and opened fire. Then their problems began. First, even the demi-cannon could not make much impact on walls that were thick and well lined. Second, the besiegers ran low on ammunition, so could not fire it much anyway, while they had neither the powder nor the containers for grenades. Thus the mortar fired rocks for a few weeks, until a proper supply of shells arrived on 24 April. On discovering this, the royalists realized that they were in serious trouble, and seized the initiative. That night, they sallied forth and captured the mortar itself, dragging it back into the house 'like a dead lion lying quietly among them'.[44] In the final analysis, their greatest asset had been their own high morale, inspired by the presence of the courageous countess of Derby. After that, the parliamentarians settled for trying to starve the house out, which was eventually accomplished, after successive attempts, at the end of 1645.

BASING HOUSE

The war's other epic resistance by an aristocratic mansion was at Basing House in Hampshire, home of the royalist marquis of Winchester. The original fortifications here were much more modest, consisting of an old round tower, but that and the new house beside it were surrounded by earthworks and ditches covering fourteen and a half acres. The banks were faced with brick and enough

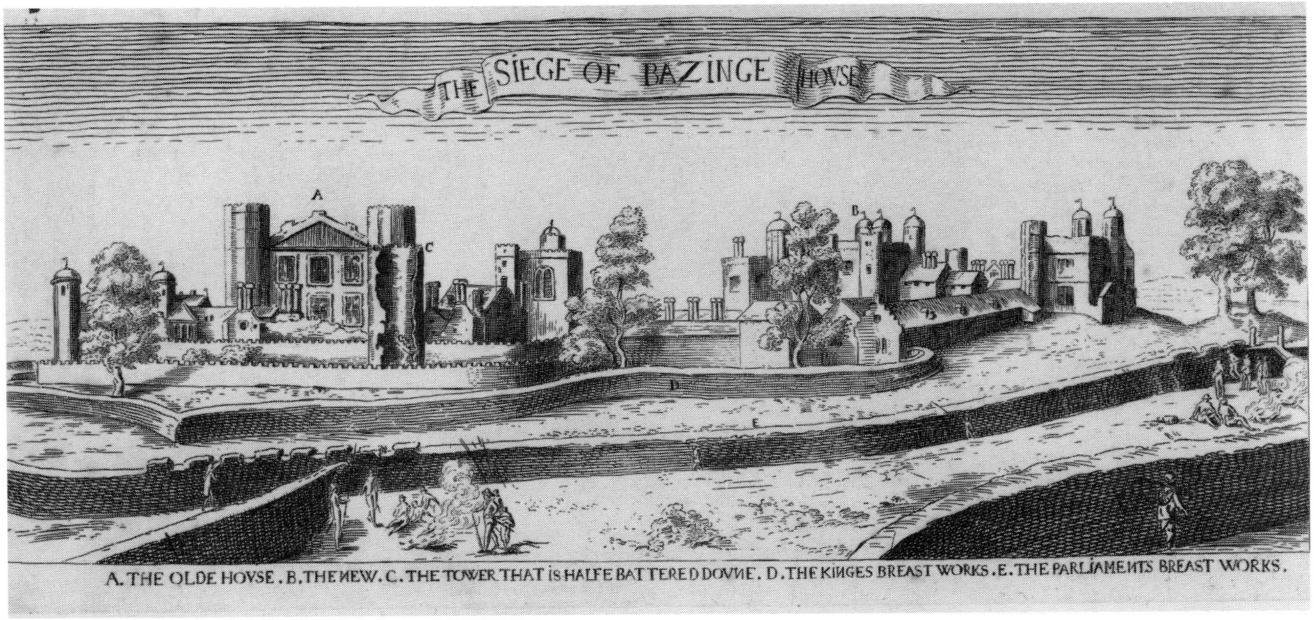
THE SIEGE OF BAZINGE HOVSE
A
B
C
D
E
A. THE OLDE HOVSE . B. THE NEW . C. THE TOWER THAT IS HALFE BATTERED DOVNE . D. THE KINGES BREAST WORKS . E. THE PARLIAMENTS BREAST WORKS .

Siege of Basing House in Hampshire

Few contemporary pictures illustrate so perfectly the importance of low, thick, earthen defences to both besiegers and besieged during the English Civil Wars. The sketch portrays the scene towards the end of the six-month parliamentary siege of late 1644. The main medieval towers inside the defences made a perfect target for a demi-cannon, and have been bombarded into a ruin. The encircling earth-banks, however, proved effective against the same treatment, and therefore the garrison managed to hold out. The besiegers in turn erected works to protect themselves from the shots and sallies of the royalists. Basing House finally fell to Cromwell in October 1645 after a six-day bombardment and assault which left 100 defenders dead and a further 200 (including its owner, the marquis of Winchester) in parliamentary hands. The house was also sacked and, apart from the medieval earthworks, little remains.

earth was piled into them to make them proof against a demi-cannon. Sir William Waller deployed one in November 1643, and made no impression upon them at all. During another siege in 1644, which lasted five months, a whole cannon, a demi-cannon, and a mortar were used separately. Between them these pieces managed to destroy or damage most of the buildings inside the works but, just as at nearby Donnington, the latter held up so well that the royalists could keep on fighting. Basing was only extinguished in October 1645 when Cromwell arrived with, as so often in his career, resources denied to any previous commander. Against a garrison of about 300, he deployed nearly 7,000 soldiers, plus a cannon, and two demi-cannon, with culverins to support them. The besieged were penned in to await his approach, with lines of circumvallation almost one and a half miles around. He took three days to plant his battery, with 100 shot ready for the cannon and 300 for the demi-cannon. When the firestorm broke, it ripped two huge gaps in the defences, and Cromwell's soldiers attacked these and three other points at 6 a.m. on 14 October. The collapse and surrender of the defenders—or those who survived—was inevitable.

PRIMITIVE DEFENCES

Few other great houses were as well protected. Throughout the three kingdoms, landowners had abandoned fortified castles in favour of stately manor houses during the late sixteenth and early seventeenth centuries. As one Kerry gentleman lamented shortly after the outbreak of the Irish rebellion: 'My house I built for peace, having more windows than walls.'[45] Nevertheless many grandees made valiant efforts to defend their homes with earthen works. Wingfield Manor in Derbyshire was sheltered by a steep hill upon three sides and the parliamentarians who fortified it plugged the fourth one with earthworks fifteen feet high and ten feet thick. In August 1644, however, when it was in royalist hands, enemies arrived with a siege-train including a demi-cannon, and although this could not breach the bank, the concussive effect of the bombardment, in such a confined space, proved too much for the defenders. One has sympathy for them, as the din of the guns was so powerful that for some time the garrison could not make themselves heard when beating a drum for a parley to settle terms. While most manor houses and country seats could serve as posts from which soldiers could enforce taxation and monitor (or plunder) trade, they became sitting ducks for armies with artillery. Typical of many was the fate of Rushall Hall in Staffordshire, before which the earl of Denbigh arrived in 1644 with a single big gun borrowed from Stafford. In half a day this had made a breach in the courtyard wall wide enough for eight men to pass abreast, and the royalists gave up. A saker proved sufficient to knock in the roof and windows of Grafton House in Northamptonshire and Compton Wynyates in Warwickshire, and so deprive the king of two more outposts. As with castles, primitive methods sometimes sufficed against simple defences. Blazing gorse branches put paid to Abbotsbury

House, in Dorset, being used first to burn down the gate to its courtyard and then being thrust into the porch and windows while musket-fire pinned down the royalists inside. The whole building was soon ablaze, along with its defenders, but the parliamentarians were repaid for their ruthlessness when the powder magazine inside blew up and took eighty of them with it. Some of the most brutal incidents of the British and Irish Civil Wars took place in these squalid little local struggles.

Conclusion

EUROPEAN CONTEXT

In the context of contemporary continental developments the siegecraft associated with the conflict in Ireland and Britain remains modest. The one to three miles of siegeworks put around Colchester, Newark, Lathom, or Basing hardly compare to the eleven miles of siegeworks, including six huge fortified camps and nine major bastioned forts, with which Prince Frederick Henry had encircled 's Hertogenborsch in 1629. His Spanish enemies had besieged Breda five years before with a ring of ninety-six redoubts, thirty-seven forts, and forty-five batteries. The complete lack of double circumvallation shows how limited the adoption of European siege practices was; and this also holds true in fortification, where virtually none of the new works were revetted with stone and even the eleven-mile circuit around London remained primitive compared with those about the cities of the Netherlands and of Lombardy. Mercifully, the scale of suffering was proportionately minor, for the 3,500 defenders whom Cromwell butchered at Drogheda compare favourably with the 25,000 who allegedly perished at Magdeburg in 1631. Even the level of hunger at Colchester or Carlisle was low compared with that at La Rochelle in 1627–8, when almost a quarter of the population starved to death under siege. In 1677 an ageing Anglo-Irish soldier and politician, Roger Boyle, earl of Orrery, published *A Treatise on the Art of War*. He paid full tribute to the overwhelming contemporary importance of fortification and siegecraft, declaring that 'we make war more like foxes than like lions; and you will have twenty sieges for one battle'.[46] Orrery proceeded to illustrate this assertion lavishly, and entirely from continental examples. Although he had lived through the whole of the British and Irish Civil Wars, and commanded forces in them, he did not think a single episode of them worthy to represent the practice of European siege warfare; and he was surely correct.

INNOVATIONS

The only novelty in those wars, after all, consisted of the introduction to the British Isles of practices already familiar abroad, and in textbooks. The few attempts to produce genuinely original solutions to specific problems almost all ended in failure, and usually in farcical failure at that. Had Chillingworth's siege-towers ever got to the point of lumbering towards the defences of Gloucester then the tale might have been different, but the relieving army arrived too soon, and discovered them abandoned, half-completed, in a marsh. In October 1645 the royalists at Hereford decided to attempt the recapture of an outpost at Canon Frome House by constructing what they termed a 'sow', a wooden tower drawn on wheels by a team of oxen and filled with musketeers firing through loopholes. The idea was that in this fashion the defenders would gain no protection from their earthworks and be forced to quit them under a withering fire from above. Again the device might have worked, but it was too cumbersome to be transported swiftly. Its progress between Hereford and Canon Frome gave the latter garrison ample opportunity to receive warning and summon up a relief force which routed the royalists and captured the machine a few miles short of its objective. A pair of similar structures, likewise termed 'boar and sow', were made for the first siege of Corfe Castle, in 1643. They were composed of boards covered in wool to repel musket-shot, and in this case their function was to enable the parliamentarian attackers to get their own firepower much closer to the walls with impunity. The defect in this case was simply shoddy construction, for although the structures protected the bodies of the men inside, they left their legs exposed and the royalist sharpshooters concentrated upon these with such devastating effect that the occupants of the 'sow' abandoned it, while those of the 'boar' retreated. After this reverse, the besiegers preferred to give up the whole idea, rather than try to improve the design. At Basing House in 1644 a different set of parliamentarian attackers managed to build a better version of it, covering the whole of the men within. The result in this case, however, was mere anticlimax, for the defences of the house were so strong that the experience of musket-fire at a close range did little to deter the defence.

It can be no coincidence that the only totally effective local innovation of the whole series of conflicts was also the simplest, being represented by the New Model Army's assault upon Bridgwater in July 1645. The main strength of the defences lay in the moat in front of them, thirty feet wide and linked to a tidal river. This made them virtually impregnable to any storming tactics, but the New Model did not wish to get tied up in a prolonged siege. Its council of war decided accordingly to make eight portable wooden bridges between thirty and forty feet in length. The work took eleven days, and the bridges were thrust into place at two o'clock in the morning, catching the royalists completely off guard. They had trusted so much to the water barrier that the earthworks on the near side were weak and easily climbed by the parliamentarians swarming over the bridges with ladders. After that the town was doomed. The circumstances at Bridgwater were so unusual that the device remained unique although it has a common parallel in the frequent use of pontoon bridges and bridges of boats to cross rivers, seen to greatest effect at the battle of Worcester or during Cromwell's Irish campaign.

It does nothing to alter the general insignificance of these sieges in the history of war.

DEMILITARIZATION OF BRITAIN AND IRELAND

Nevertheless siege warfare formed a major—often the major—component in what was arguably the most important single set of conflicts which the British Isles have ever endured. The consequences of that warfare were also very significant. In military history they represented a process by which, on a characteristically reduced and parochial scale, the British and Irish finally caught up with continental developments of the previous hundred years. The greatest single result, however, was not a more pronounced degree of militarization but its exact opposite. The 'slighting' of enemy castles (such as the earl of Worcester's seat at Raglan, near Monmouth or the royalist stronghold of Sudeley Castle in Gloucestershire) and demolition of captured aristocratic and gentry seats by the Long Parliament's forces represented an enormous reduction in the number of actual or potential fortresses in all three kingdoms.

The same forces also made a point of levelling the new fortifications, and although the parliamentarian and republican regimes retained garrisons in a few towns, these were progressively reduced in number. They almost vanished altogether after the Restoration when the government of Charles II, as precautions against further unrest, pulled down the medieval walls of Gloucester, Coventry, and Northampton and demolished the artillery forts built by the Cromwellians, such as those at Inverness and Ayr. A dual process had thus been completed: on the one hand, hundreds of medieval strongholds had been rendered indefensible throughout the archipelago; while, on the other, the new 'works' of the wars had been demolished, so thoroughly that the few survivors represent one of the scarcest classes of monument from the past. The story of fortification and siegecraft in these civil wars is best seen not as an episode in the history of warfare but a key one in the transition of the British and Irish from warrior to civilian societies.

7

LOGISTICS AND SUPPLY

PETER EDWARDS

War everywhere tested a society's capacity to provide logistical backing as much as its ability to raise soldiers. This was certainly true of the British and Irish Civil Wars, for the business of supplying weapons, ammunition, provisions, and transport (in the form of horses) to the various armies fighting in England, Scotland, and Ireland proved to be no easy matter. The raising of money—the sinew of any war—to pay, clothe, arm, and care for the troops proved an even greater headache. How then did the combatants acquire their weapons, munitions, rations, uniforms, and mounts? What impact did a decade of incessant warfare have on domestic economic development, especially the arms industry, and on commerce and trade? Finally, to what extent did logistics determine the outcome of the various civil wars?

Arms and Equipment

INFANTRY

Civil war armies comprised three elements—infantry, cavalry, and artillery—each with its appropriate weaponry and equipment. The majority of musketeers carried a matchlock, which fired by igniting gunpowder in the 'pan' or breech with a smouldering match, and despatched a round lead ball. While it proved woefully inaccurate, difficult to handle, and slow to reload, it was quite effective in volleys. Snaphance and flintlock muskets, with a mechanism similar to a modern petrol lighter, were more efficient, but more expensive and difficult to make. By and large, only troops guarding the artillery and ammunition wagons, where a lighted match could spell disaster, used them. Originally, dragoons (mounted musketeers) used a 'dragon', a short-barrelled carbine; later a flintlock musket became more usual. (None of these firearms were accurate enough for snipers, who tended to fire civilian birding and fowling pieces.) In addition, each musketeer needed cartouches for his powder, carried on a bandolier slung across his

Musketeer

The musketeer wears no armour and carries a matchlock musket and a smoking length of match in one hand and a rest in the other. From his bandolier, draped across his shoulder, hang a dozen cartouches, each with a charge of about one half ounce of powder. Bandoliers were cumbersome pieces of equipment to wear; the cartouches swung to and fro and rattled or jangled as the person moved. Apart from the danger that the noise might advertise one's presence, there was always the possibility that a spark might explode the entire belt and blow up the soldier with it.

shoulder, a bullet pouch, and a small flask for his fine priming powder. He also possessed a short sword.

Beside the musketeers stood pikemen. In theory the pike, normally of ash, was sixteen feet long, including a pointed steel head; in practice many soldiers cut a couple of feet off the bottom, making it easier to carry. In battle, too, enemy soldiers lopped off the end of their pikes. For example, after a royalist excursion into Hampshire in July 1643 most of the 112 pikes returned to the king's magazine were unheaded. To prevent this happening steel languets might be added. Pikemen, like musketeers, used a short sword for close-quarter work. Officers carried a partizan, a short spear, apparently as a badge of rank; lieutenants sometimes a poleaxe, and non-commissioned officers a halberd. To boost morale and facilitate communication and identification, each regiment also needed colours and drums.

CAVALRY

Cavalry troops each held a sword, sometimes a poleaxe as well, but their main weapons were firearms. Fully armed they bore a harquebus, a short musket between two feet six inches and three feet three inches long, and a pair of pistols, triggered either by a wheellock or flintlock mechanism. Flintlocks were cheaper, less complicated, and more reliable than wheellocks, which, although technically more advanced, had to be wound up with a spanner and often seized up if not used immediately. Some residual units of lancers survived, especially among the Scots, but they remained few in number. One or two detachments of cuirassiers, clad in full armour, also made an appearance. However, they were handicapped by their lack of mobility and by the difficulty of finding horses strong enough to carry them.

ARTILLERY

In battle the artillery used a variety of cannon. In accordance with the contemporary stress on transportability, the smaller more manœuvrable guns of saker size down to the three-quarter-pounder rabinets proved popular. Even lighter ordnance, the so-called leather gun, consisting of bronze tubing strengthened with iron and bound with rope and leather, saw service, esecially during the Bishops' Wars. The larger field pieces, the demi-culverin and the occasional culverin, tended to be placed in fixed batteries. Culverins were also used in sieges but as they often proved to be ineffectual, the largest ordnance pieces of all, demi-cannon, cannon, and cannon royal, together with mortars of various sizes, were preferred.

Shot for the weaponry had to be made in different sizes of bore, and in huge quantities, but its manufacture proved comparatively simple. The New Model Army carried the necessary pigs of lead, pots to melt them in, ladles, and moulds, so that it could augment its supplies on the march. However, it often proved

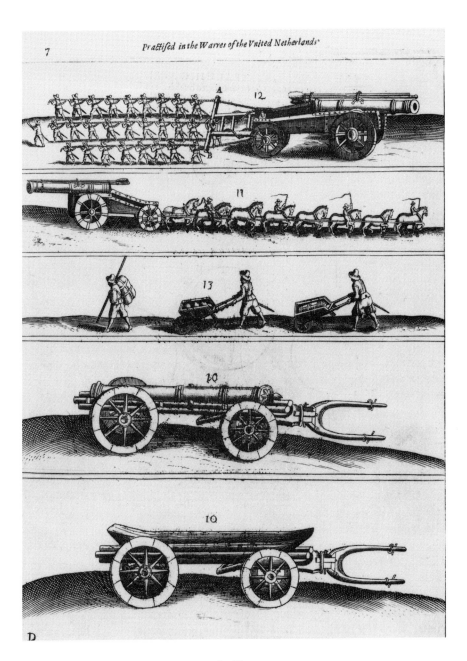

Artillery

All sides used artillery but, unlike the navy, tended not to employ them to the same effect. One of the main problems in taking heavy artillery along with a field army was the difficulty encountered when trying to negotiate the unmetalled roads of mid-seventeenth-century Britain and Ireland. The largest pieces required far larger teams than the one indicated here, perhaps as many as seventy at a time. By the mid-seventeenth century draught horses of a reasonable standard could be obtained, especially in the mixed farming regions of lowland England. In certain parts of the country oxen were used but horses were preferred if at all possible.

difficult to make bullets of the correct size. For example, Lord Broghill, a parliamentary commander in Ireland, complained that his musketeers 'were forced to gnaw off much of the lead [and], others to cut their bullets, in which much time was lost, the bullets flew a less way and more uncertainly; and, which was worse, so many pauses animated the enemy by making him think our courages cooled'.[1] Cannonballs, called round shot, were cast from iron. Artillery pieces also fired case shot, that is, tin canisters full of musket-balls. Mortar shells differed from shot because they contained explosives and required skilled engineers to fire them effectively. Unlike shot, gunpowder proved more difficult to produce since its constituents of charcoal, sulphur, and saltpetre (potassium nitrate) did not combine well when ground together by hand. 'Corning', that is, moistening the powder, then 'incorporating' it by prolonged pounding, produced much better results because the cake so formed could be broken into smaller particles or grains. However, the process called for horse- or water-driven mill machinery and specialized handling.

HORSES AND UNIFORMS

In addition to arms and munitions, armies needed horses. Cavalrymen required 'serviceable' mounts of a certain size and strength; ideally they stood at least fifteen hands but in practice many were an inch or two smaller. Other characteristics were equally, if not more, important. As the cavalry re-emerged as an instrument of 'shock' in the early seventeenth century, sheer bulk counted for less than mobility, and lighter, more nimble animals replaced the traditional 'great' horses. Cheaper mounts sufficed for the dragoons. Cavalry saddles had to be of better quality too, costing on average twice as much as dragoon saddles. Troopers carried their pistols in holsters across their saddles. In the artillery train, mobile field pieces, as well as the carts, had teams of up to five horses but the larger cannon required far greater numbers. Culverins might demand a team of seventeen horses and cannon royal up to seventy. During Cromwell's Irish campaign of 1649 infantry regiments received twelve horses to pull each cart and wagon while a further 900 beasts serviced the artillery train of eleven siege-guns and twelve field pieces. Numbers increased in bad weather. At Lostwithiel (1644) the narrow lanes became 'so extreme foul with excessive rain' that teams of thirty horses could not move three demi-culverins and a brass piece.[2] If no alternative existed, oxen might be used in place of horses, especially in areas where farmers and wagoners kept them.

Each side also needed to clothe its armies. Throughout the three kingdoms the ordinary dress of the footman usually consisted of a cap, doublet, cassock (or coat), breeches, a shirt, and a pair of stockings and shoes. In the covenanting army in Ulster in 1642 the Lowland infantry units were dressed in suits of hodden grey and the Highland ones in belted plaid or—in at least one case, trews—together with long white shirts (some with cravats). For footwear, the infantry had shoes, whereas the cavalry tended to wear thigh boots as this would help to protect their legs in action. Many soldiers wore some sort of armour, though given the amount of ammunition, weapons, and spare clothing an infantryman had to carry, he often discarded it while on the march. Sir Arthur Hesilrige equipped a regiment of cuirassiers, the famous 'Lobsters', with plate armour, but this was unusual; cavalry troopers usually contented themselves with a small helmet (pot) and a corslet (back- and breast-plate). Troopers and pikemen might wear a leather buff coat, a garment which could deflect a sword-cut.

To what extent did these clothes constitute a uniform? While individuals raising troops no doubt strove for uniformity in dress, financial limitations often prevented it from happening. For example, Essex's army at Edgehill (1642) fought in a variety of colours. The absence of a standard uniform caused problems of identification and hampered the fostering of *esprit de corps* and in order to distinguish friend from foe some other means, such as a coloured scarf, sash, ribbon, or plume, had to be employed. It was only with the creation of the New Model Army that a measure of consistency emerged; on 7 May 1645 it was reported that the 'men are Redcoats all, the whole army only are distinguished by several facings of their coats'.3

Procurement of Matériel

ARMS

In the build-up to the war all sides sought to take possession of existing stores of military hardware. On balance, Parliament did better than the royalists. In particular, because of its dominant position in London, it could obtain the arms and munitions kept by the ordnance office in the Tower and those lying at Woolwich and Greenwich. By the end of September 1642 the well-stocked magazines at Hull and at Portsmouth were in its hands. Many of the coastal forts along the south coast similarly came under its command. Moreover, the navy declared for Parliament, bringing along its store of cannon and munitions. In Ireland, the insurgents' failure to capture the extensive arsenal kept in Dublin Castle mirrored the king's unsuccessful attempts to secure such important storage centres as the Tower and Hull. This deprived the confederates of vital war material during the early months of the war. Of course, one can overestimate the amount and quality of the arms that might be found, for many county magazines, for instance, had been allowed to run down in the long years of peace. The Tower itself ran short of supplies and in February 1642 desperately required cannon, match, muskets, and gunpowder (none had been delivered to the Tower for the previous thirteen months).

In addition, each side in England appealed to its supporters for arms, equipment, and money. On 9 June 1642 Parliament issued the 'Propositions', asking people to contribute money and plate or to equip and maintain horsemen. As the horses and arms were brought in, they were to be valued and their owners promised repayment at eight per cent interest. In June, too, a number of royalist peers signed the 'Engagement', pledging to protect the king against his enemies and subscribing horses and equipment. Wealthy individuals, such as the earl of Cork, the earl of Argyll, or the marquis of Worcester, raised whole regiments and companies of soldiers, furnishing and maintaining them at their own expense. Others put their own magazines at the disposal of a particular party. Exhortation was accompanied by a certain amount of pressure and, inevitably, all those who did not actively support a particular side were seen as suspect and treated more harshly. In Shropshire the royalists asked the bailiffs of Ludlow to order recalcitrant gentry to muster with their horses, arms, and equipment at Shrewsbury on 15 December 1642 or face the consequences.

None the less, neither side in England was fully prepared—or indeed expected —to fight a long-drawn-out war. At Edgehill there were insufficient arms to go round. When the king left Shrewsbury on 12 October 1642 an observer commented that some of the infantry were armed with 'but pitchforks and such like tools, and many only with good cudgels' and that 'there was not one pikeman had a corslet, and very few musketeers who had swords'.[4] One explanation was the inadequacy of existing stocks in both private and public hands, the result of the compatively peaceful conditions of the early seventeenth century. Even Ireland was affected. Whereas one Ulster settler in eight owned a musket in 1619, in 1630 the proportion was down to one in thirty-three. In 1631 there were only twenty muskets apiece in Carrickfergus and Derry. Such shortcomings never ceased. Indeed, once the war began, the authorities had to deal with the problem of the turnover in arms and equipment. As the committee of the Scottish Army plaintively told the commissioners in London on 16 May 1644, 'Our arms and ammunition are continually wasting'.[5]

Clearly, existing reserves of weapons could not sustain a war. Therefore the confederates and covenanters, as well as the royalists and parliamentarians, turned to military suppliers on the continent (see below). In addition, all sides sought to increase domestic output of arms and munitions. Parliament, with its control of the capital and south-eastern and eastern England, exploited the arms and armaments industries concentrated in the region. The royalists, on the other hand, created an arms industry, both plant and personnel, virtually from scratch. At the hub stood Oxford, the king's headquarters. Not only did the city house his central ordnance offices and magazines but it also became the centre of arms production, with local craftsmen manufacturing and repairing weapons. Artisans resident in neighbouring villages were also put under contract. For the Scots, the cannon foundry for three-pounders which the general of artillery, Alexander Hamilton, established in Potter Row, Edinburgh, in 1638, produced excellent iron field pieces that constituted the main field gun of the covenanter armies. In

Ireland the confederates manufactured a variety of weapons throughout the country. For instance, one smith from County Meath allegedly produced 'a great piece of ordnance' from 140 pots and pans; not surprisingly the gun burst shortly after being discharged.[6]

THE ORDNANCE OFFICES

Rival ordnance offices controlled the supply of arms and equipment in England. The original office was based at the Tower of London and its officers took responsibility for all matters relating to arms and munitions, ranging from the purchase, storage, and distribution of *matériel* to quality control and the standardization of weapons. The titular head was the master of ordnance but in practice his deputy, the lieutenant-general, carried out the work. Other senior officers included the surveyor-general, the clerk of the ordnance, the storekeeper, the clerk of deliveries, and the treasurer, whose titles indicate the nature of their job. Although Parliament seized the Tower, the king did have the support of Sir John Heydon, the lieutenant-general, and later in 1642 the services of six of the nine principal ordnance and armoury officers. They brought their expertise to the task of developing the new ordnance office set up in New College, Oxford. Heydon provided the essential professionalism and continuity necessary in such a crucial position, especially as from May 1643 to August 1644 the nominal head (entitled general of the artillery in the war) was the arrogant but ineffective Lord Percy. Parliament, by contrast, had difficulty in filling some of the leading posts in their office, still situated in the Tower. Sir Walter Erle, the new lieutenant-general, might have retained the services of minor officials and artificers but the loss of top men hampered effective administration.

During the English Civil Wars both ordnance offices continued to act in the traditional manner, though not all of the *matériel* passed through the hands of the officials. Commanders often dealt directly with manufacturers, artificers, and merchants. For Parliament, authorization for the issue of arms was given (at various dates) by the Committee of Safety, the Committee of Both Kingdoms, and the Army Committee. Until December 1642 a small committee of men, known as ordnance or artillery commissioners, directed royalist operations. They had their own magazine and arms workshops in the Schools' Tower. In December the old ordnance office officials resumed their places, freeing the commissioners to organize supplies for the train.

Much evidence survives to show the ordnance officers at work, receiving goods, putting together consignments (as best they could), organizing transport, and sending off arms and equipment. None the less, neither set of officials had complete central control or possession of all war materials and in consequence the system became rather complex. Indeed, the royalist marquis of Newcastle had a virtual independent command in the north and appointed his own general of the ordnance, Sir William Davenant. Both sides had other magazines, each exercising a certain amount of freedom of action and running separate distribution networks. The king held important ones at Bristol, Reading, Weymouth, and Worcester, while the port of King's Lynn, with its coastal and inland waterway links, served as a supply base for Parliament.

For the ancillary but none the less vital task of equipping and provisioning the soldiers, whether in garrisons, field armies, or county forces, a parallel organization, the commissariat, took charge. Each army had its own set of commissary officers, responsible for such items as victuals, clothing, draught animals, and fodder (and even arms and munitions). They might buy goods privately or on the open market and some of them spent large amounts of money. Lieutenant Russell, for instance, paid out over £6,000 on horses for the Eastern Association army in 1644. They also requisitioned goods and enforced free quarter, actions which made them unpopular with the local residents.

Procurement of Munitions

The English armaments industry on the eve of the First English Civil War was not a monolith and its various branches had distinct forms of organization. A handful of large-scale producers continued to dominate the manufacture of ordnance and munitions much as they had during the 1630s when the ordnance, shot, and gunpowder industries had been made into monopolies. The processes involved in manufacturing these products were the ones naturally suited to a capitalist form of organization. Money had to be spent on processing and manufacturing plants, on power sources and machinery but the investment brought tangible rewards in the form of greatly increased output. Although it was possible to make these wares by hand—gunpowder could be ground with a pestle and a mortar and bullets and round shot cast in portable moulds—it was a laborious and inefficient way of operating.

PARLIAMENT AND THE ARMAMENTS INDUSTRY

For its ordnance, Parliament continued to deal with John Browne, Charles I's gunfounder: in 1635 he had paid £12,000 to acquire the sole right to make ordnance and shot. Though allegedly a royalist, the location of his business, set firmly in the parliamentarian sphere of influence in the south-east, determined that Browne worked for Parliament. In 1645 alone his estimated charge for the cannon, shot, and grenades required for the summer fleet amounted to over £2,500, much of which originated in his furnaces at Horsemonden and Brenchley in Kent. He also had a house in Martin Lane in London from where he dealt with consignments earmarked for Parliament, while his agents, Richard Pearson and Samuel Ferrers, handled goods destined for the open market. Similarly, in the supply of ammunition to Parliament Daniel Judd attained a dominant position. Although on the payroll of the ordnance office as the master plumber, he formed one of a group of large-scale contractors who did a good deal of outside work as well. An entrepreneur rather than a specialist, he dealt in gunpowder, match, clothing, and swords. Together with John Freeman and Thomas Steventon, he regularly delivered consignments of match to the Tower, or occasionally directly to the army.

Gunpowder-making was another pre-war monopoly where the patentee, Samuel Cordwell, had to switch sides to remain in business. He, briefly with George Collins, had obtained the exclusive right to manufacture gunpowder in the country on 1 November 1636. By the terms of his contract he had to make 240 lasts of gunpowder annually for the king (one last equals twenty-four hundred-weights), a total which, owing to shortages of saltpetre, he did not always meet. The monopoly itself ended in 1641, another victim of parliamentary hostility to such practices. During the war others entered the business, perhaps attracted by the money which could be made from the manufacture of such a highly prized commodity. Cordwell's main competitor was John Beresford, a London grocer, who in 1642 leased the Temple mills at Leyton on the River Lea in Essex and converted them to gunpowder production. Beresford had probably begun to manufacture gunpowder before the end of 1642 and certainly had deposited gunpowder in the magazine of the City of London militia at Leadenhall in February 1643. Later in the war other sites along the Lea were developed, notably by Beresford at Sewardstone Mills and by John Samyne at Walthamstow. Elsewhere, Daniel Judd produced gunpowder at the Home Works at Faversham.

Although metropolitan manufacturers and dealers who contracted with Parliament for ordnance and munitions dominated the market, there were local suppliers too. The furnace at Newent in the Forest of Dean, still in parliamentarian hands, supplied Gloucester with bullets, grenades, and petards in the first half of 1643. Other furnaces were located in Carmarthenshire, Denbighshire, Shropshire, and Staffordshire. Several provincial gunpowder mills mushroomed up, helping to overcome local shortages. Hardly surprisingly, powder-makers were highly valued; indeed, in November 1643 one of them became the subject of a tug-of-war amongst parliamentarians in Derbyshire and Staffordshire.

THE ROYALISTS AND THE ARMAMENTS INDUSTRY

The royalists, placed at a disadvantage by their inability to deal with established contractors, had to create alternative sources of supply. At Oxford newly built or converted foundries and mills provided ordnance and munitions. William Baber, a gunpowder-maker, delivered his first recorded batch (four barrels) to the king's magazine on 8 January 1643. In May his output peaked at fifty-five barrels, a level which his successors, the ordnance commissioners, Strode and Wandesford, did not attain until the end of the year. Between January 1643 and June 1644 production averaged between thirty-two and thirty-three barrels per month (each barrel contained 100 pounds net weight of gunpowder). Others supplied the king with locally produced match and musket-shot and for the same eighteen-month period manufactured thirty-nine to forty hundredweight and thirty-six to thirty-seven hundredweight respectively.

The most important figures at Oxford were the ordnance commissioners, Strode and Wandesford, who used their position as a means of involving themselves in production as well as administration. In June 1643 they made their first delivery of gunpowder; in July they began to manufacture match and bullet; and in February 1644 they acquired the sole right to produce saltpetre and gunpowder. The two men also cast ordnance and in August 1643 Heydon delivered to them a large copper furnace for that purpose. They seem to have been motivated by a desire for financial gain, justified by the expenditure they had already incurred in supporting the king's cause. Their actions, however, bred resentment in Oxford, especially when they obtained the gunpowder monopoly, and allegations of profiteering were raised against them.

Other centres supplemented the production of ordnance and munitions at Oxford. The major port and industrial city of Bristol, captured in July 1643, emerged as an armaments' centre and one that became increasingly valuable to the king. Richard March, the pre-war keeper of stores in the Tower, was put in charge there and early in 1644 some of Oxford's productive capacity shifted to the city. Not only could Bristol easily draw on supplies of raw materials from south Wales and the Forest of Dean but it also proved less vulnerable to parliamentarian attack from London.

For iron ordnance and weapons the royalists exploited the raw materials and well-established ironworks in south Wales, the Welsh border, and in the west Midlands. As early as August 1642 the Foley furnaces at Stourbridge and Dudley (Worcestershire) turned out bullets and in December the governor of Worcester, Sir William Russell, paid out money for ordnance and shot. He also obtained ware from Shropshire ironmasters working at Bouldon, Bridgnorth, and Leighton. Francis Walker of Bouldon produced large quantities of shot and many cannon and in September 1643 received almost £1,000 for his work. Ordnance and munitions from the west Midlands were transported to the central magazine at Oxford, via the Severn to Worcester, and thence by cart. Munitions from the Forest of Dean and south Wales tended to be employed locally. In 1643 Lord Herbert's forces obtained cannon, armour, and pike-heads from ironworks in Glamorgan and Breconshire, as well as in the Forest of Dean. Similarly, Sir John Wyntour's works at Lydney supplied *matériel* to the royalists in the West Country. Somewhat ruefully, a parliamentarian supporter in Gloucester commented that his mills and furnaces 'were the main strength of his estate and garrison'.[7]

SHORTAGES OF MUNITIONS

In spite of the scale of production both sides at times experienced serious shortages of munitions. Apart from cannon-balls, munitions could only be fired once and stocks had to be constantly replenished. Moreover, they were used up at an alarming rate. In December 1645 Sir William Brereton asked for more gunpowder, protesting his economy but complaining that 'it is incredible how much is spent'.[8] Much match was unavoidably wasted because musketeers had to keep their matches lit throughout the course of an action or when close to the enemy. The supply of gunpowder and match posed a particular problem because of inadequate home production. Both commodities required sulphur, only obtainable abroad, while domestic stocks of saltpetre barely met peacetime needs, let alone the requirements of war. In the months leading up to the outbreak of the conflict in England, moreover, gunpowder production was at a low ebb, the result of tensions created by the ending of the monopoly. To make matters worse, existing sites were destroyed in the initial stages of the war. At Chilworth, Cordwell's mills were put out of action and did not reopen until the middle of 1643. With the country divided between two warring parties, raw materials were even scarcer to find. Neither side achieved self-sufficiency and only the parliamentarians ever managed on occasion to reach pre-war production levels. The royalists never got close.

Procurement of Small Arms and Equipment

The small arms and equipment industries were organized in a different way, in a manner that conformed more closely to the typical small-scale pattern of economic activity. In England, both sides therefore had to deal with large numbers of craftsmen and artificers of comparatively modest means. None the less, in London where they were organized into companies and guilds, groups like the gunmakers, armourers, and swordsmiths took on large contracts. The Company of Gunmakers was incorporated on 14 March 1638, an important development since it overcame the problems caused by a division of work between blacksmiths and locksmiths. Similarly, individual craftsmen might be organized by wealthy merchants, who, having contracted to deliver substantial consignments of goods, put out the work to others.

CENTRES OF PRODUCTION: LONDON AND OXFORD

For Parliament, London served as the main market-place for domestic weapons and equipment and was patronized by local commanders as well as by the ordnance office and Essex's army. Over time, the importance of the capital increased, a development which seems to be associated with tighter bureaucratic control of the armies and the rationalization of the system of supply. In the Eastern Association the trend towards centralization and the associated rise in the size of the purchases is discernible from the end of 1643. Early in 1644 its officials began to deal regularly with London arms merchants. One agent, Captain West, bought £6,665 worth of arms. Their most important supplier was Edward Barker of the Coldharbour, who delivered several consignments of firearms, valued at about £7,000. Men like Barker did not manufacture arms themselves but sub-contracted the work to others. To fulfil one commitment to the earl of Manchester Barker obtained swords from William Pinkham of St. Helen's parish, London, while, on another occasion, Mr Churchill, a cutler living at Holborn Bridge, furnished him with 'a great quantity of swords'.[9]

For the royalists, production at Oxford developed. Contracts were given to local craftsmen and by the beginning of 1643 *matériel* arrived in the stores. Strode and Wandesford became involved; in December 1642 an order from the council of war ordered them to co-operate with Heydon to produce and repair small arms, especially muskets. As a result, gunmakers were set to work in the commissioners' armoury in the Schools' Tower. In June 1643 production of swords increased, as did the provision of other arms, such as pikes.

LOCAL PRODUCTION

In spite of the increase in output at London and Oxford, the nature of the small arms industry meant that it was possible for commanders and commissary officers to procure small arms locally. Craftsmen capable of producing weapons could be found in many parts of the country. In 1639 Sir Jacob Astley had noted that there were four gunsmiths at Hull, one of whom produced very good fire-locks, while swordmakers in Birmingham reportedly provided 15,000 swords to the earl of Essex and other parliamentarian armies. Everywhere, one could find blacksmiths who could make parts like pike-heads and gun-barrels and assemble the entire weapon. The accounts bristle with small-scale purchases, designed to top up stocks or to repair arms and equipment. For the royalists, the ironworking areas of the west Midlands and south Wales produced pikes, as well as ordnance and munitions. Bristol's gunsmiths helped to provide new firearms and by February 1644 output reached 200 muskets and bandoliers a week.

Unlike munitions, weapons, if kept in good working order, could be reused. Wherever possible, weapons were retrieved from fleeing or dead soldiers: on 1 July 1645 Parliament paid Richard Whitton and five others £1 for looking for arms left on the field after Naseby. Soldiers were expected to look after their guns and perhaps pay for any losses incurred through negligence. Defective arms were routinely returned to the central magazines for repair where individuals like George Fisher, the keeper of the small guns office at the Tower, overhauled them.

SUPPLY OF HORSES AND UNIFORMS

The war also took its toll on horses, especially cavalry mounts. Many were killed or maimed in action, losses running at a higher level than they did for soldiers. Apart from those killed, many more were worn out by the rigours of campaigning. In January 1647 Sir Samuel Luke calculated that losses amounted to 116 out of the 156 horses for which he accounted. As a result of increased demand, prices soared, reaching levels up to fifty per cent higher than they had been before the

Councell of warre att Oxford 19th of Aprill 1644.

His Maty

Present

Lord Treasuror
Marquesse of Hertford
Lord Chamberlayne
Lord Dunsmore
Mr Secretary Nicolas

Duke of Richmond
Lord Great Chamberlaine
Earle of Bristoll
Lord Savill
Mr of the Rolles

Sr Edw: Nicholas

Consideration being then taken of compleating & giving all fitt encouragemt to the Citty Regimt. It was thereon ordered by his Maty by the advice of his Councell of warre, that the said Regimt should bee compleated to the number of 800 men in five Companyes, being about 137 in a Company, of which not above 120 to bee obliged to appeare to doe duty every night, for as they bee not under that number.

That duty shall bee done but by One Company in a night, soe eury man will watch but one night in five.

That the freemen, & auntient Inhabitants of this Citty shall bee of the Citty Regimt and of noe other, to which purpose the Governor to have notice given him hereof.

It was farther ordered that all suche freemen of this Towne or other auntient Inhabitants, or their servts who shall refuse to pay their Assessmts towards the charges of this Regimt (they being indifferently layed) or who shall refuse to list themselves and to doe duty in this Regimt shall bee looked upon as persons that thereby give just cause to bee suspected of their Loyalty and Affection to his Maties service, and if they shall not speedily comply, soe that his Maty may bee confident

Minutes of the King's Council of War in Oxford on 19 April 1644

In this extract the royalist Council of War, which probably met in Christ Church, ordered that the 'Citty Regiment' should be increased to 800 men, with at least 120 men in each company, and that 'each man will watch but one night in six'. According to the order, anyone refusing to serve in the regiment or to pay for its upkeep was to be treated as a traitor. For over three years Oxford served as Charles's capital and administrative centre, as the seat of the court, and as a military stronghold.

conflict. Specialist middlemen dominated the supply of horses. Parliament, for example, conducted a good deal of business with a small group of horse-dealers who lived in and around the Smithfield, London's leading livestock market.

Merchants, rather than manufacturers, took the lead in equipping soldiers with uniforms. For example, Stephen Estwick supplied Essex's army with clothes in August 1642 and later on formed consortia with a number of woollen-drapers. In the provinces men such as Thomas Buckley, a merchant from Cambridge, supplied garments in bulk to the Eastern Association army. Entrepreneurs provisioned the royalist side too. In March 1643 Thomas Bushell, an ex-monopolist, proposed to send to Oxford reasonably priced suits sufficient to clothe the whole army. He must have fulfilled his part of the bargain for eight months later he received £2,000 for his services. Such men subcontracted the work out. For instance, John Davies and his partners, suppliers of arms, equipment, and victuals to the Scottish forces in Ulster, subcontracted the making of garments to woollen-drapers like Richard Downes, Arthur Dew, and Edward Harris, men experienced in supplying large quantities of uniforms to the army. They, in turn, hired the tailors.

Orders for dress and footwear recurred constantly throughout the war. Given the wear and tear of marching and fighting, shoes and clothes did not last long. Clothing ripped, came apart at the seams, and frayed at the edges. It also became encrusted with dirt, sweat, and blood. Poor-quality garments disintegrated even more rapidly. Parish conscripts were particularly badly dressed as constables sought to reduce expenditure. Some contractors acted dishonestly, cutting corners by using inferior materials and employing cheap labour. In the case brought against John Davies in 1645 one of the accusations concerned the production of shoddy clothes. Richard Moss observed that soldiers had worn the suits 'but two or three days' before they 'were all torn and ripped in the seams and also the linings' and that 'the clothes were made so straight that the soldiers that wore them, were fain to rip them to pluck them on'.[10] Shoes wore out quickly too and were even harder to replace. The Irish lords justices were not alone in complaining that 'The soldiers' want of clothes is very great … but their want of shoes exceeds'.[11]

As the war progressed, the advantages that Parliament enjoyed became more apparent. The arms and equipment industries, especially those in London, grew in size and their output rose. In consequence, some prices, especially those of small arms, fell. In the first six months of the war Essex and Lord Brooke paid £1 for matchlock muskets, whereas in 1644 the Eastern Association bought them for fifteen shillings. Two years later the price dropped to ten shillings and by 1649 it had fallen to nine.

PARLIAMENTARY SYSTEM OF SUPPLY

Production peaked with the equipping of the New Model Army between 1645 and 1646. To facilitate the task Parliament reorganized the system of supply. In

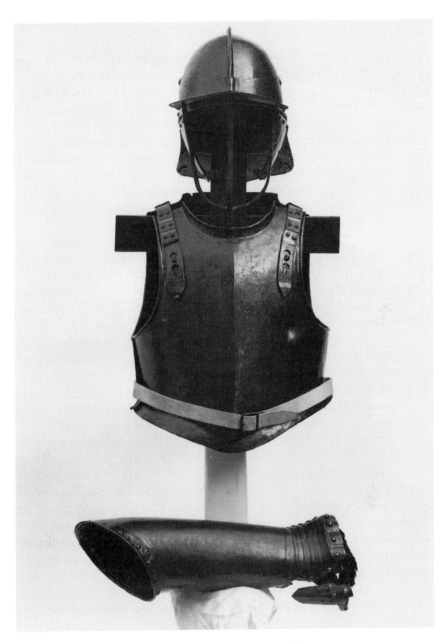

Harquebus armour (c. 1645)

By the 1640s most cavalrymen's body armour comprised merely a pot and a corslet; that is, a breast and back. Of the surviving units clad in full armour Essex's lifeguard and Haselrige's 'Lobsters' are the best known. The development of firepower rendered the use of armour obsolete; although some armour was shot-proof, it was designed to turn a sword-thrust. Moreover, as it was heavy and cumbersome, the wearer found it difficult to move and became overheated in hot weather. Edmund Ludlow, a member of Essex's lifeguard, recalled that at Edgehill he had found it very difficult to remount his horse. Sir Edmund Verney flatly refused to serve in a suit of armour, claiming that it would kill a man to do so.

particular, procurement became more highly centralized, with the establishment of a separate magazine at Reading where arms and equipment for the army could be stockpiled. The ordnance office expanded its activities too. Hitherto, it had mainly been concerned with the dissemination of munitions, especially to the artillery trains of the various armies, but now it involved itself more deeply in all aspects of arms procurement. To take charge of the business of supplying the army two new committees, the committee of the army and the committee for powder, match, and shot were set up. The committee of the army began its work straight away, dealing with suppliers and negotiating contracts. The new procedures soon proved their worth and almost at once consignments of *matériel* arrived in the magazine at Reading.

Virtually all of the persons who obtained contracts worked in or around London and included people already active in the service of Parliament. By spring 1645 it would have been a relatively straightforward job for the committee to choose the suppliers capable of quickly delivering bulk orders to the new army. As before, the system of production varied between commodities, but a significant difference lay in the size of the consignments and the frequency with which deliveries to the new army were made. In the munitions industry large-scale producers like John Beresford, Samuel Cordwell, and Daniel Judd predominated, while craft companies took the lead in the production of personal weapons. For clothing, Parliament relied upon the merchants who had already served them. Similarly, five Smithfield dealers continued to supply horses, selling 6,708 animals to the New Model Army between April 1645 and August 1646.

ROYALIST SYSTEM OF SUPPLY

The speed with which Parliament equipped the New Model Army, occasional shortages notwithstanding, and the relative ease with which it paid for the goods reflects the underlying strength of its economic and financial position. This advantage increased over time and undoubtedly affected the final outcome of the conflict. In contrast, after 1645 the royalist cause began to decline. From the summer of 1644 the area under Charles's control shrank, making it more difficult for the army to maintain its supply of men, money, and *matériel*. Moreover, while the king might still obtain arms and equipment from abroad, the loss of vital ports like Newcastle-upon-Tyne and Bristol affected the flow. Even allowing for the incompleteness of the royalist ordnance papers, and for the lack of accurate figures both for imports and for output elsewhere in royalist territory, it is clear that production and receipts of arms and equipment fell. As a result, available stocks proved insufficient fully to provision the royalist armies. In Ireland too the king's cause suffered, forcing Ormond to conclude after 1643 a series of annual cease-fires with the confederates.

This is not to say that the parliamentarian forces did not continue to experience difficulties in supply. To a certain extent the provisioning of the New Model

Army had been achieved at the expense of the soldiers serving in garrisons, in local forces, and in the other field armies. Sir Thomas Fairfax's units enjoyed priority treatment, both in terms of arms and money, even though the combined number of soldiers in the armies of Massey in the west and Poynts in the north were nearly as large. Deliveries to the Scottish armies in England and Ireland also used up stocks. Another problem was the need to spread the *matériel* more widely around the country. As Parliament made inroads into royalist territory, it acquired garrisons, some of which had to be defended and supplied with arms and munitions.

Imports

None of the protagonists fighting in the three kingdoms could rely upon domestic supplies and had to obtain war material from abroad. At first, imports helped to overcome the shortage caused by the lack of preparedness at home. However, even when the native arms industries geared themselves up to cater for wartime needs, there remained a significant gap between supply and demand which could only be filled from abroad. Without the substantial help they received from the continent, the royalists would not have had the means to wage war for as long as they did, while the parliamentarian cause would have suffered too. In Ireland, the Irish confederates realized from the outset that without substantial foreign aid their cause was almost hopeless: 'Our wants are money, arms and ammunition; these we have no way to provide for, the country being exceedingly exhausted unless we may be assisted by those who wish well unto our cause beyond the seas.'[12]

This reliance upon foreign supplies made the protagonists dependent upon outsiders, whose political and commercial policies could differ from their own. Monarchs might wish to support Charles in his fight against the rebels but they had to think about practical politics. In the United Provinces Frederick Henry, the Stadtholder, sympathized with the plight of his father-in-law but his primary consideration remained the war against Spain. One possible consequence of his blockade of Flanders, designed to hinder his enemy's trade, was the disruption of supplies to England. Governments also found that, as the Parliament's power grew, they had to pay greater attention to it. For their part, foreign merchants tended to follow their own commercial inclinations, regardless of the political stance of their government. However, they were torn between two different considerations. Commercially, they might wish to trade with all sides but politically they tended to favour Parliament. For Dutch merchants this dilemma proved particularly acute. On the one hand, they used their power in the States General to counteract the Stadtholder's pro-Stuart leanings, declaring a policy of strict neutrality on 1 November 1642. On the other, merchants at Amsterdam and Rotterdam, fearing the loss of trading opportunities, wished to reinterpret the declaration to read the right to distribute arms evenly to both sides. As one historian has noted, 'the two largest towns connived at all kinds of export of war material for Charles I as well as for Parliament'.[13]

CONTROL OF THE PORTS

Because Parliament controlled the harbours closest to the continent they more readily received goods from abroad (see maps on pp. 163–4). In contrast, the royalist ports lay further away in the north and the south-west, thereby lengthening their supply lines and putting their ships in greater danger from bad weather and enemy action. Parliamentary control of the navy enabled it to seize ships on the high seas and to blockade royalist ports, though, in practice, many of the ships carrying *matériel* for the royalists did get through. The capture of Bristol in July 1643 greatly improved the logistical position of the royalists. After Bristol other south-western ports fell to the king, with Gloucester and Plymouth being the two most notable and damaging exceptions. Of those held by the royalists, Weymouth served as an important channel for imports, though shipments regularly passed through Dartmouth, Exeter, and Falmouth too (discussed in Chapter 5).

IMPORT OF MILITARY HARDWARE

In England gun-running began before the onset of civil war. In June 1642, for instance, Prince Rupert arrived at Tynemouth with a shipload of muskets, gunpowder, and arms. The following month a consignment of gunpowder and muskets from Flanders was sent to Ireland. The pace quickened during the conflict. In 1643 300 ships allegedly sailed to England from Amsterdam alone, each one making four trips a year. For that year licences issued by the Amsterdam chamber of the admiralty survive from 12 August to the end of December and twenty-six out of the thirty consignments bound for Britain included arms and munitions. The evidence, which relates to a fraction of the trade, is impressive. Munitions amounted to 51 tons of match, 31 tons of gunpowder, 14.75 tons of sulphur, hundreds of cannon-balls and hand-grenades, and 700 powder horns. The small arms comprised nearly 24,000 guns, 1,200 gun-barrels, over 4,000 swords and blades, 2,500 pikes, and thousands of belts, holsters, and bandoliers. Four thousand and twenty suits of armour were sent too. As the conflict escalated so too did the scale of imports. Side-arms predominated among the cargoes: a minimum of 74,580 firearms, 40,454 swords and blades, 13,700 pikes, and 12,332 suits of armour were exported between 1642 and the end of 1646. Although not so well documented, shiploads of arms similarly left the Spanish Netherlands, many of them heading for royalist and Irish ports. Others came from Spain. The Irish confederates, in particular, benefited from the solicitations of fellow Catholics and remarkably seem to have built up reserves of war materials. The Irish royalists under Ormond also acquired stock from abroad, if not to the same extent, and, as a result, even tried to obtain arms from the Confederation.

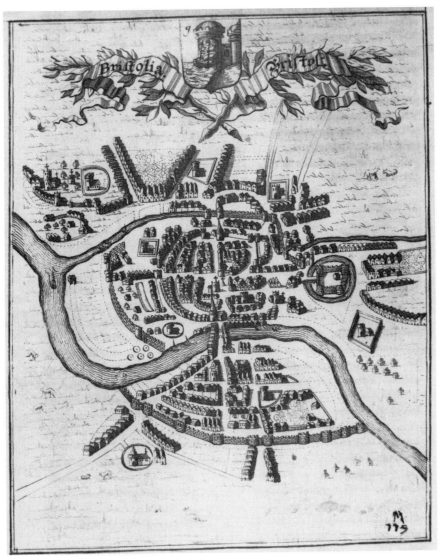

View of Bristol, 1632
by Wenceslaus Hollar

Bristol, the third city in the kingdom in the 1640s, and a thriving port and manufacturing centre, was captured by the royalists in July 1643 and proved to be a priceless asset to them. Because of its easy communication with Ireland and the continent it became an important conduit through which flowed arms, raw materials, and even soldiers from abroad. Moreover its workshops, mills, and foundries turned out ever-growing quantities of arms and munitions for the king. Less vulnerable to attack from the parliamentarian forces, production was being shifted there away from Oxford right up to the time of its recapture by Parliament in September 1645. Ironically, its governor, Prince Rupert, had to surrender the city for the same reason that he had been able to take it in the first place; namely, having too few soldiers to guard the huge 3-mile perimeter defences.

Imported gunpowder and match were particularly welcomed and figure prominently in the consignments coming from abroad, often in large lots. In January 1644, for instance, one shipload of arms landed at Exeter contained 500 barrels of gunpowder. A major problem remained the lack of adequate domestic supplies of saltpetre and brimstone. To make good this deficiency Parliament contracted with a number of merchants, including William Courteen, a pre-war shipper, to import saltpetre. In May 1644 he delivered ten tons to John Beresford and later that year he joined a consortium which agreed to secure £12,000 worth of saltpetre for the navy. Similarly Abraham Pieters Croock, whose company had sold sulphur and gunpowder to the government before the war, continued to supply both items during it; in 1642 forty-five tons of sulphur left Amsterdam and in the last third of 1643 a further thirty-seven tons followed.

Despite customs dues, porterage and transport costs, foreign weapons were not necessarily more expensive. Larger scale production might reduce costs and enable manufacturers to sell their goods at competitive rates. Purchases of match for the New Model Army in mid-1645 illustrate this point. While there were fluctuations in the prices, Dutch and Flemish match was not always more costly than home-produced material.

ENTREPRENEURS AND PROFITEERS

Some of the importers were merchants operating out of home ports. Among the wealthiest royalists were London traders like Sir Nicholas Crisp. An ex-customs farmer, he had been expelled from the House of Commons as a monopolist in 1641 and had put his fortune at Charles I's disposal. He raised troops, equipped ships, and bought arms abroad. Other London merchants, like John Freeman, the supplier of match, served Parliament. Freeman had a number of commercial links with northern Europe and obtained match and weapons on the continent. Provincial merchants also became involved. In East Anglia they operated through ports such as King's Lynn and Boston and supplied the Eastern Association army with a considerable amount of war material. In spring 1644, for instance, Bartholomew Wormall of King's Lynn received £8,000 for arms and munitions brought from the Netherlands. In Ireland, among those native merchants who involved themselves in the trade were John Davis of Carrickfergus, James Maxwell of Strabane, John Stuart and Archibald Moore of Belfast, Francis Dormer of Ross and Patrick Archer of Kilkenny.

To assist them, all sides maintained a network of officials and agents abroad. William Boswell, the king's resident at The Hague, and Lord Goring, the ambassador in France, helped promote the traffic in arms. The Irish confederates sent residents to Holland, Rome, and the leading continental Catholic courts where they acted in the same way. Other activists worked among the mercantile and manufacturing community in ports and industrial centres. One of the king's most energetic agents was William Sandys. While at Dunkirk, he organized numerous shipments to ports in north-eastern and south-western England. Because of their local connections, members of expatriate merchant communities proved particularly useful. Prominent on the royalist side were a number of merchant adventurers, resident at Amsterdam and Rotterdam. John Webster, for instance, did business with foreign arms dealers and sent shiploads of arms and munitions to England. He also supported the royalists with his own money and helped to get them credit abroad. On 6 July 1644 he became one of the five members of the company outlawed by Parliament as 'incendiaries and enemies to the state'.[14] Parliament had its supporters too, merchants like Sir Thomas Cunningham, the conservator at the Scottish staple port of Veere in Zealand. Together with his partners, James Weir and James Eleis, he had dispatched large quantities of arms to Scotland during the Bishops' Wars. In 1640 Cunningham sent a fully armed frigate, twelve 'great brazen canon', and 15,000 muskets. After 1642 he provided all of the arms for the Scottish Army in Ulster and after 1644 he also supplied the Scottish troops serving in England. One consignment, sent over in six ships in 1644, comprised 7,000 pounds of gunpowder and 130,022 pounds of match, together with 12,000 swords and belts, 4,000 pikes, and 500 pairs of pistols in holsters.

Most shippers, however, were foreign merchants. The licensees at Amsterdam were predominantly Dutchmen, including members of the interrelated Trip and de Geer families, who dominated the arms industry of western Europe. Some of the Amsterdam licensees were specialists, perhaps selling their own wares: the Chardinels and Abraham Pieters Croock manufactured gunpowder, while Jan van Os and David Behagel dealt in sword blades. Behagel's blades had come from the noted German sword-making centre of Solingen, suggesting the size of the hinterland served by the port. At Weymouth many of the merchants bringing *matériel* to the royalists there were French, resident at or operating through one of the Channel ports.

The chance of making a profit undoubtedly tempted foreign merchants to get involved in the dangerous business of gun-running. Thus, many were willing to risk travelling to Ireland, which, it was said, was as profitable as going to the East or West Indies.[15] As a result, the country was full of foreign wartime profiteers. The Flemish trader and moneylender Antonio Nicholas Vanderkipp, for example, sold supplies to the highest bidder and hired out transport vessels to anyone who would pay the extortionate rates he charged. The notable Flemish arms dealer, Jan van Haesdonck, operated in a similar way. Although he was intrumental in providing shiploads of arms to the royalists, he did so, according to the Dutch government, purely for commercial reasons.

Merchants were particularly keen to obtain return cargoes. Sandys emphasized this point in a letter to Captain Strachan at Weymouth in January 1644: 'it is the price and good payment and free permission to export all commodities without restraint will make that port thrive and the king well supplied with arms.'[16] Moreover, in May 1644 he suggested to Sir Hugh Cholmondeley, the governor of Scarborough, that in exchange for arms, he might furnish lead, wool, and the finest northern cloths. The wares traded in naturally varied according to region; tin, wool, cloth, and hides from the south-west and coal and cloth from the north. In Ireland, in return for *matériel* for their war-effort, the confederates exported wool, hides, sheep and goat skins, tallow, herring, and salmon to friendly ports in England, France, Holland, Spain, and Germany. However, not all voyages proved lucrative. On occasion royalist officials only accepted consignments when it suited them and paid at their leisure. Significantly, when the queen sent 400 barrels to Exeter in May 1645, she had to pledge her own credit because the merchants were concerned that they would not be paid on arrival. During the early 1640s the troops in Dublin and Cork regularly commandeered the cargoes of merchantmen, hindering further trade.

Food and Drink

Apart from the supply of arms and equipment, consideration had to be given to the soldiers' diet since its quality, good or bad, affected morale and discipline. The standard fare of soldiers on the march was bread or biscuit, cheese, and beer, though this might be augmented from time to time by meat bought or taken from the local population. Infantrymen seem to have carried about a week's supply of food in their knapsacks. On Cromwell's Scottish campaign of 1650 to 1651 the daily ration consisted of a pound to a pound and a half of bread and eight to twelve ounces of cheese. One contemporary later quipped: 'Nothing is more certain than this: that in the late wars, both Scotland and Ireland were conquered by timely provisions of Cheshire cheese and biscuit.'[17] Soldiers in garrisons might do much better, benefiting from a more varied and plentiful diet, though this was by no means certain. Much depended upon the resources of the locality, as well as on the attitude of the inhabitants. At Hereford the earl of Stamford's troops had withdrawn from the city by the end of 1642 partly because of the hostility of the local population and their reluctance to provide them with food and drink. In November 1645 Ormond (see picture on p. 76) petitioned to be allowed to resign rather than be driven out of Dublin through want of bread.

Horses had to be fed too and, given the large numbers involved, the search for fodder presented the armies with one of their most serious problems. War horses could not subsist on grass or hay alone and the need to supplement their diet with oats and pulses added to the cost and increased the difficulty of finding sufficient supplies. It has been calculated that the normal daily requirement for such a horse was fourteen pounds of hay, seven pounds of straw, one peck of oats, and half a peck of peas. This sort of allowance, though somewhat generous in peas, seems to have approximated to the amount of fodder given to horses in the civil wars. In

July 1643 the daily ration of some of the earl of Denbigh's horses was sixpence worth of hay, a peck of oats, and some peas or beans.

It proved a difficult logistical task to obtain sufficient quantities of food and drink for so many soldiers and horses. On average a troop of horse, comprising seventy officers and men on basic rations, would consume in a month about 1.5 tons of bread and 0.75 tons of cheese. Their horses would require over 13.5 tons of hay, 271 bushels of oats, and 5 bushels of pulse. Inevitably shortages occurred. During the Marston Moor campaign, for instance, the Eastern Association army suffered badly. After the battle a captain reported that provisions were 'very scarce amongst us: and our soldiers hungry and tired with a lingering siege'.[18] In Ireland semi-nomadic herders ('creaghts') accompanied the confederate Army of Ulster, providing them with provisions out of their large herds and flocks. The other Catholic armies fared less well and experienced logistical problems intermittently throughout the war. A lack of adequate provision had military consequences because it made the soldiers mutinous. As Sir Lewis Kirke, the governor of Bridgnorth, noted in a letter to Prince Rupert in April 1644, 'Here is a great want of provision for the soldiers ... And that pay which is allowed them not yet paid them, makes them apt to mutter out their discontents and will adapt them to quit the service.'[19]

Considerable emphasis was placed upon obtaining victuals from the countryside through which the soldiers were passing. Many English parishes and Irish counties paid part of their assessment in kind, though the bulk of the victuals and fodder were requisitioned. If accommodation were required, the troops were billeted in the homes of householders. Yet goods and services had to be paid for. In the New Model Army the rate for fodder per night ranged from threepence for grass to seven pence for a peck of barley or malt. The infantry were allowed sixpence a day, dragoons seven pence, and troopers eight pence. Because their wages were often in arrears, soldiers tended to take free quarter, giving the householders a voucher which could be cashed in later. Some people did get their money. Within the home territory of the Eastern Association army most people received repayment within a year, though those living outside did not fare as well. The royalists' record was not as good and grew worse over time. As their cause began to fail, they not only issued more vouchers but were also less likely to honour them. By the end of the war unredeemed royalist vouchers proved worthless! Communities situated along major roadways proved particularly vulnerable. At Dunchurch (Warwickshire), the constable explained the frequent quartering of troops in the village by the aside 'our Town lying on the Road way'.[20] Inevitably, the system bred discontent, especially if the demands became excessive and reoccurred. The spread of the Clubmen movement in a number of western and southern counties of England during the course of 1645 stemmed from the depredations of the armies.

Transport

WATER-BORNE TRANSPORT

All sides gave careful consideration to transport arrangements. After all, goods had to be moved from where they had been manufactured or stored to the places where they were needed. Water transport proved the more efficient and in this respect, Parliament had the edge. Its control of the navy and the command of the seas around Britain gave it an unrivalled logistical advantage (see Chapter 5). Moreover, it possessed the ports closest to the continent, with London the focal point. From the capital, *matériel* made locally or imported from abroad could be sent out via the Thames river system or round the coast. In 1645 a good deal of the arms and munitions destined for Reading, the storage depot for the New Model Army, sailed up the Thames. The Eastern Association army chose King's Lynn as its supply base for the same reasons. As a port, situated at the head of an extensive river system, it could receive goods from London or from abroad and redistribute them efficiently and with greater security. Keelboats from King's Lynn helped stock the magazine at Cambridge, while coasters provisioned the parliamentarian army besieging York.

Cromwell's conquests of Ireland after 1649 and Scotland after 1650 illustrate the importance of water-borne communications. By shipping arms, equipment, and victuals from England in bulk, he secured adequate supplies for his men independent of local resources. At least twenty ships were regularly employed for the Irish campaign and at least 140 were used in Scotland. A considerable number of flatboats carried soldiers and goods up the Forth. Control of the sea and the capture of vital ports eased his task and the ships regularly plied between England and Irish or Scottish harbours. In August 1649 Cromwell had access only to the Irish ports of Dublin and Derry but the seizure of Belfast, Cork, Wexford, and Duncannon opened up the country to him. In Scotland the capture of the ports of Dunbar and Musselburgh in July 1650 gave Cromwell a bridgehead and enabled him to supply his army throughout the summer and the acquisition of Leith provided him with a sheltered port in winter.

Royalists, dependent to a greater extent on imports, had less certainty of delivery. While most ships got through, Parliament took a number of prizes, thereby reducing the resources available to the king. Royalist and Irish privateers did enjoy considerable successes against enemy shipping but their attacks remained more sporadic and less damaging to the supply links. The royalists also transported goods by water wherever they could. In the south-west, where their influence remained strong, they had a relatively free hand, though the survival of Plymouth as a parliamentarian outpost proved an obstacle. They obtained supplies from Ireland too, notably to provision their bases in the Isle of Man, north Wales, and at Chester. Arms and munitions from Oxford flowed along the

Thames to garrisons like Abingdon, Wallingford, and Reading. Naturally, they used the Severn as a means of transport. The strategic importance of the river as a link between the royalist heartland and Bristol and the outside world, however, was seriously affected by the parliamentarian hold on Gloucester.

ROAD TRANSPORT

All sides still had to make provision for road transport. Armies on the march took with them artillery and baggage trains, while consignments to and from stores and from ports and places of manufacture regularly travelled overland, at least for a part of the journey. When Sir William Brereton moved 4,000 arms, earmarked for Ireland, from Hull to Chester in February 1642, the goods sailed along the Trent via Nottingham to the King's Mills at Donington (Leicestershire). From there, the arms travelled by cart through Swarkeston and Uttoxeter to Chester. Goods travelling by road went either by packhorse or cart. The most common road vehicles were the four-wheeled wagons and the two-wheeled carts and wains. Each horse in cart shafts could move nearly three times as much weight as a packhorse but the latter, being smaller and more nimble, proved more economical and especially effective on long hauls. They were faster, could travel over rougher ground, and were more flexible in their use.

From the point of view of road transport, Oxford's position served as a source of strength and weakness to the royalists. Located in the south Midlands, it was close to one of the most keenly contested parts of the country and therefore had short supply lines to its garrisons and forces in the region. Moreover, as arms and men continually passed through the south Midlands, the area resembled a military thoroughfare and one which the royalists could hope to control. Yet Oxford remained vulnerable to attack. Parliamentarian troops, stationed in garrisons relatively near to the city, vied with Oxford for local resources. Its supply routes, both inward and out, depended partially upon road communications and were exposed to enemy attack. The establishment of separate manufacturing and distribution centres helped reduce the problem for outgoing goods but not for those coming in. Indeed, the integration of the various centres made it easier for parliamentarians to intercept convoys of goods passing between them. This problem grew more serious over time. By the end of 1644 royalist setbacks had had a damaging effect on supply lines, especially in the north and south-west. In the spring of 1645 the link with the West Midlands was lost. Meanwhile, as the débâcle at Lostwithiel in 1644 (when forty heavy guns fell to the king) highlights, Parliament experienced its own problems when transporting goods by road, especially to its forces in the north and west. As a result, it, too, established local magazines which might act as distribution points for an area.

Because carrying war materials by road proved slower and more dangerous than river transport, convoys had to be heavily protected. Consequently, large bodies of soldiers might be tied up on escort duty. This increased costs and reduced the number of available troops. On one occasion, in May 1643, Major Craffaud felt it necessary to protect a convoy of ammunition to Marlborough with a whole regiment rather than the 150 cavalry asked for because the enemy was in strength nearby. For Parliament a particularly hazardous undertaking was the transportation of a huge store of supplies, collected in London, to Gloucester in the winter of 1643 to 1644. By the time the convoy left Warwick in mid-March 1644 troop numbers had risen to 3,150 horse and 3,500 foot.

CARRYING SERVICES

Given the fluctuating demand for carrying facilities and the cost of maintaining horses, it made sense merely to maintain a pool of vehicles and animals, augmenting them from outside, if necessary. Horses and carts often formed a part of local assessments, with a certain number being fixed on a parish or a division. More commonly, carriers were hired. The daily rate for each draught horse seems to have been two shillings and sixpence, though in the first few months of the conflict Essex paid three shillings and sixpence, a reflection of the difficulty he experienced in obtaining a sufficient number of animals. For a packhorse the rate varied between a shilling and one shilling and sixpence. Because of the scale of demand, however, compulsion might also be needed, with warrants issued authorizing the impressment of horses and carts. In addition, soldiers seized vehicles and animals of opponents and neutrals.

Contemporary records reveal that though soldiers might pay for the carts and animals they hired or impressed, they tended merely to issue vouchers at the time and allow arrears to build up. Some of those working in Essex's artillery train in 1643 and 1644 were not fully paid until March 1645. Others proved even less fortunate. In September 1642 Robert Bennett, a wagoner on his way from Devon to London with a load of cloth, was impressed into Essex's service and found himself involved in the Edgehill campaign. As a result, he lost his wagon and seven horses, worth at least £82, and with them his whole livelihood. At the end of the war horses formed the single biggest category dealt with by the indemnity committee, set up in 1647 to protect soldiers and others from prosecution for acts committed in the name of Parliament. Of the 1,116 military cases, almost one-third (30.6 per cent) related to disputes concerning horses.

Yet the enormous increase in the demand for carrying services generated by the war had an impact on society and the economy as a whole. For carriers it provided a lucrative source of income; that is, as long as they were paid regularly and they did not have their horses and carts stolen. Farmers might benefit too. Apart from the market in draught and pack animals, there was the opportunity to make some money carrying at slack times of the year. Unfortunately, the soldiers did not normally see beyond their own immediate needs and these might conflict with the interests of others. Not only did individuals lose their livelihood but trade was disrupted as carriers were plundered of their wares, as well as their horses and carts. In agriculture, the effect could be disastrous, especially if large numbers of draught animals and farm vehicles were requisitioned at critical points of the year like seed-time and harvest. Thus, after taking Cirencester in February 1643 the cavaliers seized between 200 and 300 horses from the nearby divisions of the Seven Hundreds, an action which, the royalist commissioners told the king, had prevented the farmers from sowing their land, forcing them to let it lie waste.

Financial Management

In spite of comparable problems and the adoption of similar fiscal measures, there were differences between the parties, both in style and effectiveness. In its financial demands, for instance, Parliament acted more decisively than the king did. Individual ordinances placed the burden of each tax on the whole country, or at least in those areas where the parliamentarian writ ran. The king, more sensible of the wishes of his supporters and seeking to gain local approval for his actions, proceeded in a more cautious fashion, county by county. Administratively too the king proved more conservative, utilizing the traditional machinery of government, including the exchequer. However, through the pressure of events, the position of the exchequer was progressively challenged by the creation of a special treasury at war. Parliament, starting from scratch, created a number of central financial institutions to deal with raising income from particular sources. In its anxiety to prevent an abuse of power the revenue from each was kept distinct and out of the control of money-raising bodies. To assess and collect revenue both sides used people in the county, working in local committees and groups. Commissioners of array acted as the main agents for the royalists, while Parliament worked through the financial subsection of the county committee.

MILITARY COSTS

An army is a beast with a great belly and this makes war a costly business. By the end of the English Civil Wars both sides had been bankrupted, Parliament just as much as the king, by their efforts to feed the insatiable appetites of their military establishments for money, weapons, and supplies. An examination of available evidence indicates that during the first two and a half years of the war the parliamentarian Treasurers at War received £1.1 million from all sources. From 1645 to 1649 Parliament's military charges average £1.7 million yearly, but revenue only approximated £1 million. The result was that Parliament owed over £3 million by the time it executed the king. To get out of this financial box confiscated Church, crown, and royalist lands had to be sold off. Between 1646 and 1653 £3.7 million was realized in this way, with a large chunk of it (£1.4 million) earmarked to pay off soldiers' arrears.

The Charge of Subduing the Irish Rebellion in 1641.

An Account of what the subduing the Rebellion of Ireland, begun the 23d of October, 1641. hath cost, and what Damage the Protestants there have sustained thereby, and what Lands have been forfeited and disposed of to Adventurers, Souldiers, and other English, and what to the Irish, and now in their possession: Abstracted out of the Accounts of Moneys in the Exchequer, during such time as any regular Accounts were made up, and by probable and rational Estimates, for the time in which no Accounts were kept, by reason of the general Rebellion and Confusion, and out of the Surveys, Decrees, and Settlements, made by His Majesty's Commissioners, for executing the Acts of Settlement and Explanation in Ireland.

I. Moneys receiv'd and issued from the 6th of July 1649, to the 1st of November 1656, being 7 Years and 4 Months, according to an Account thereof, remaining as a Record in the Auditor General's Office in *Ireland.*

	l. s. d.
Transmitted out of *England, in specie*	566848 13 4
Assessments in *Ireland*	1309695 14 11½
Rents of forfeited and sequestered Houses, Lands, Fishings, &c. 161598 8 7½	
Tythes sequestered	135524 3 1½ } 3509396 17 0½
Customs and Excise	252474 18 10½
Preys of Cows, Horses, and other Goods, taken from the Rebels, and for other casual Revenue } 083258 18	

l. s. d.
3509396 17 0½

Money issued in *England* towards transporting Armies, raising Recruits, buying and sending over Provisions of all sorts for the Army, and other Moneys issued by Warrant from the then Council, or the Committee of the Army in *England*, which was not accounted for in *Ireland*, the Warrants and Accounts being never transmitted thither, of which there is a Reference in the account of Record, in the *Exchequer* above mentioned, which is estimated to be as much, if not more, than the above sum of 3509396 *l.* 17 *s.* 0½ *d.* In that all Cloths, Linnen and Woollen, Stockings, Shoes, Boots, Horses, Saddles, Arms, Ammunition, Tents, Bread, Cheese, and all other eating Provisions, were sent from *England*, and the Price thereof deducted from the weekly Pay of the Army, and not brought to Account, and so estimated as above

l. s.
3509396 17

The Charges of the Armies in the several Provinces of *Ireland*, from the 23d of *October* 1641, the time the Rebellion broke out, to the 6th of *July* 1649, from whence the Account is stated, as above, being about 7 Years and 9 Months, when no regular Accounts were or could be kept, by reason of the Confusion in which the Kingdom was by the Rebellion, there may be by probable Estimate added, without any Allowance, for Provision of all sorts after the Rate of what was paid the Army after the 6th of *July* 1649, when Provisions were deducted } 3760068

l.
3760068

l. s. d.
22191258 3 0½

The Loss of Rents for 14 Years, from *October* 1641 until the Year 1655, reckoning the Land but at 12 *d.* an Acre yearly, is 7608264 *l.* 6 *s.* and reckoning all the Corporations, Houses and Tythes, but at a Moiety thereof, comes to } 11412396 9

l. s.
11412396 9

Besides the Loss by the Devastation of Houses, Orchards, Gardens, Improvements, Houshold-stuff, Corn, Cattel, and the impairing the value of Land unto that time, not to be estimated, but in reason to be accounted, as much as before, is computed for all other Charges, Losses and Expences, if not much more, the same extending to the whole Kingdom.

II. By the Surveys of *Ireland*, there is in *Ireland*, as forfeited by the Rebellion, and belonging to Protestants not forfeited, of Plantation-Acres, accounting 21 Foot to the Perch, and 160 Perches to the Acre, in the respective Provinces, the quantity of Land hereafter mentioned.

	Acres	
Leinster	1603520 }	
Munster	3255874 {	*Acres*
Ulster	2777875 } 10868949	
Connaght	2231680 }	

The which Lands are divided and distributed, as by the Surveys and Records of the Court of Claims will appear, as followeth:

To the Protestants, and others, that proved their constant good affection, including the Bogs, Loughs and Mountains in *Ireland*,	6110292 }	
To Adventurers	396054	
To the Officers and Souldiers	1442839	
To the Officers that served his Majesty against the Rebels in *Ireland*, before the Year 1649	278041	
To his Royal Highness the Duke of *York*, as Regicides Lands	111015 } 2717549	10868949
To Protestants, on Provisoes by the Acts of Settlement and Explanation	383975	
To the Bishops for their Augmentations, of which some have possession	118041 }	
Reserved to His Majesty as un-disposed, upon the account of *Lewis Dyke* and *Thomas Conyngham*, being set out on fraudulent Adventures } 14006		
Left of course Lands un-disposed, the Title to the greatest part whereof was doubtful	73578 }	
Restored unto the *Irish* upon Decrees of Innocency	965270 }	
Restored to them by special Provisoes in the Acts of Settlement and Explanation	408083 } 2041108	
Set out upon their Transplantations of *Connaght* and *Clare*, over and above what is confirmed to *English* Protestants, who purchased Interests there from the *Irish* } 667755		

So that the *Irish*, notwithstanding the Rebellion, and their great complaints of losing all their Lands, are restored unto, and possessed of, almost one half of all the Lands formerly accounted forfeited by the Rebellion. Besides, that the 2717549 Acres granted to the *English*, hath cost as before (besides the loss of Hundreds of thousands of Men murthered by, and killed in subduing the said Rebels) the sum of 22191258 *l.* 3 *s.* 0½ *d.* And accounting the said 2717549 Acres to be worth 12 *d. per* Acre, one Acre with the other yearly, they will come to 135876 *l.* 9 *s.* which for the Purchase thereof, at 10 Years Purchase, comes to 1358764 *l.* 10 *s.* After which Rate the Lands, granted to the *English* and Protestants are not the 15th part of what the Money expended in subduing the said Rebellion would have bought, accounting the Devastations and loss of many Thousands of Mens Lives for nothing.

ADVERTISEMENT.

☞ *The History of the Execrable* IRISH REBELLION, *Traced from many preceding Acts to the grand Eruption the 23d of October 1641, and thence pursued to the Acts of Settlement 1662. Printed for Robert Clavell at the Peacock, and Charles Brome at the Gun near the West-end of S. Pauls.*

Charge of subduing the Irish rebellion

This account, published after the Restoration, suggests that the outlay in maintaining the army in Ireland throughout the 1640s, together with losses of rents sustained by Protestant landlords, amounted to over £22,000,000. Sir William Petty, the father of political economy, included the destruction of grain and livestock in his calculations and concluded that a decade of strife had cost over £32,000,000. In the absence of accurate data for the 1640s calculating the costs of the Irish rebellion and civil wars will prove impossible. Historians have, however, estimated that the total cost of the Cromwellian conquest of Ireland between 1649 and 1656 amounted to £3.8 million, which would suggest that these figures for the 1640s are grossly exaggerated and merely designed to whip up anti-Catholic sentiment.

Clearly, all parties had to dig deep into their pockets. In the wake of the Second Bishops' War, the English Parliament spent £850 per day to maintain the Scottish army. The covenanters later alleged that the conflict had cost them £515,000. In Ireland, just over £10,000 was needed to keep the 6,000 Irish confederate foot and 800 horse in the field for six months, while the Scottish Army in Ulster required £16,000 per month to maintain its force of 10,000. By 1644, when English administrative records became less chaotic, Essex's army of 10,500 was reckoned to cost £30,000 a month. Essex complained that Manchester's army of the Eastern Association, which was no larger, was allowed £34,000. A year later it was estimated that the pay of the 22,000-strong New Model Army would amount to £45,000 a month. This proved to be a serious underestimate, since the monthly assessment of £53,000 did not prevent arrears from piling up. In March 1649 there was at last a realistic appreciation of the cost not only of the New Model, but of all the parliamentary forces in England and Ireland. The monthly assessment was raised to £90,000, and a year later to £120,000 a month.

The presence in England from January 1644 of the Scots army added to the difficulties, especially in the North. Not only did the 20,000 men cost up to £30,000 a month but because they had to be given priority, the northern army under Ferdinando Lord Fairfax was starved of funds. Revenue from sequestrated property in the region, originally earmarked for Fairfax, was diverted, to the tune of over £220,000, to the Scots. The northern parliamentary army got only £20,000. It was the same with the Yorkshire assessment: collected partly in corn and meat, almost all of it went to the Scots army. In consequence, Lord Fairfax's officers, who had already footed the bill to recruit and equip their forces, found themselves often paying their men out of their own pockets. At the end of the First English Civil War, moreover, Parliament agreed to pay the Scots £400,000.

DONATIONS AND LOANS

Initially the protagonists fighting in all three kingdoms had tried to finance the war through loans and voluntary contributions. Sensible of his inability to tax his subjects without their consent in Parliament, Charles fell back for a while on the goodwill of his friends. The wealthiest ones, the marquises of Worcester and Newcastle, asserted after the wars were over that they had each poured over £900,000 into the royal coffers. In Ireland, Ormond allegedly lost £1,000,000 in the service of the king, while the earl of Clanricard contracted debts amounting to £60,000. These figures evidently included losses from the plundering and sequestration of their estates. For his part, the king also sold titles and honours—sixty-seven baronetcies, for example, within three years. Loyal clergy hastened to help him as well, while Catholics were asked to pay their recusancy fines in advance. Oxford colleges were squeezed to melt down their plate, and send the proceeds to the new mint at Aberystwyth. Many of the king's regiments were financed by the personal contributions of the peers and gentry who raised and commanded them. For example, the earl of Cork largely financed the war-effort in Munster. In addition to maintaining his own company at Lismore (at a weekly cost of £20 plus provisions) and funding the defence of Youghall (£2,100), the army regularly siphoned off any spare cash he managed to accumulate, leaving the family virtually bankrupt by the end of the 1640s.

Foreign support was solicited too. In February 1642 the queen fled to Holland where she raised £180,000 by pawning the crown jewels and in the same year the Stadtholder, Frederick Henry, used his own credit to obtain on her behalf a loan of 300,000 guilders. Parliamentarian sympathizers in the country were similarly active, sending over aid that totalled £31,218 in the five years 1643 to 1648. In this context it should be noted that the consignment of arms which Thomas Cunningham, the conservator at Veere, sent to the Scottish army in 1644 was purchased using the credit of the Lampsins family of Middelburg and Flushing. Catholic countries, naturally enough, provided financial support for their co-religionists in Ireland. The confederates received £56,000 in cash and in bills of exchange from the papacy, nearly £6,400 from France, and £5,000 from Spain, mostly in gold coin.

At the same time, all parties negotiated commercial loans. The London mercantile community advanced large sums of money to the House of Commons against the security of future revenue, including roughly £333,000 for the Irish war-effort. This enabled Parliament more effectively to meet immediate calls on expenditure. The successful provisioning of the New Model Army derived in part to an £80,000 loan obtained from the City. In 1640 the city of Edinburgh loaned the covenanters £100,000 for the upkeep of the army and throughout the 1640s leading merchants, such as Sir William Dick of Braid, continued to provide considerable amounts for the war-effort (Dick went bankrupt as a result). Six leading citizens of Glasgow donated nearly £6,000 Scots (£500 sterling) for the Bishops' Wars, while the city as a whole expended £1,630 sterling for the 1638–40 war-effort. Elsewhere, leading Irish merchants made funds available to royalists and confederates alike: by 1645 Patrick Archer of Kilkenny, for instance, provided the Catholics with cash or goods to the value of £5,000 and at the Restoration claimed that Ormond owed him £10,000.

TAXATION

Controlling the central administration, and enjoying a superior constitutional position with regard to taxation, Parliament quickly abandoned voluntary contributions. The three pillars of its fiscal policy were the assessment, customs, and the excise tax. Parliament first gave authorization for a weekly assessment on 24 February 1643, initially for a three-month period, although this proved merely to be the first of a series of orders. Committees were appointed in each county under parliamentary control to assess and levy the tax. Resistance to this extraordinarily heavy tax prompted Parliament to resort to armed force to extract it. Although only a sixth of the assessment was actually collected in 1643 and 1644, it became the largest single source of parliamentary revenue between 1643 and 1660. Much of it was spent in the county where it arose, and so never reached the Treasurers at War in London. After 1645 the assessment, now levied on a monthly basis, was devoted mainly to the New Model Army under Sir Thomas Fairfax. In part because of the co-operative spirit displayed by the leaders of London's financial and commercial community, four of whom constituted the Treasurers at War, the assessment was brought in much more efficiently from 1645 onward.

Because Parliament gained control of the navy and all the major ports except Bristol and Newcastle-upon-Tyne it could count on the bulk of the income derived from customs receipts. It used the receipts principally to pay the navy. The excise, introduced in 1643, helped fund the armies. Prior to 1645 it was used to pay the armies of Essex and Waller, and the navy. From that year onward most of it went to the New Model Army. A value-added tax, it was targeted at consumable items that were evidently thought not to comprise the necessities of life: tobacco, alcohol, dried fruit, sugar, and so on. Like sales taxes in all ages it proved unpopular and initially difficult to collect. Gradually the range of goods taxed was broadened: alum, copperas, hats, and silk goods in 1644, and meat in 1645. By this point it had to be levied at gunpoint; nevertheless it raised over £1.3 million from 1643 to 1647, most of which went to the army.[21] The remaining sources of parliamentary income were the traditional subsidy (the so-called 'fifteenth' and 'twentieth'), rents from sequestrated property, delinquency fines, and, after 1646, the sales of confiscated property—Church, crown, and royalist.

The king also found that loans and freewill offerings soon ran out, though in Worcestershire, at least, voluntary donations continued to be his largest single source of income until the end of the war's first year. Thus, in royalist areas a system of regular taxes, similar to the one introduced by Parliament, gradually emerged. In early 1643 Charles began appointing commissions 'for the guarding the county' whose principal duty was levying monthly taxes. The fifteen counties under royal control furnished £6,700 per week, of which £6,000 went to the army.[22] In 1644 the royalists similarly adopted the excise. Unlike the parliamentary version it was levied on necessities such as salt, soap, wool, meat, bread, butter, and cheese. While it seems to have brought in very little, relatively large sums were paid in by the farmers of the great farm of the customs, and the court of wards.

In Ireland, the confederates drew an income from the profits of the Church lands, tithes, and Church livings and taxed freeholds at a third and movable goods at a tenth. Apart from earmarking two-thirds of the receipts from the tithes and livings for the army, they ordered that 'each man grants the fourth part of his estate towards the maintenance of the war'.[23] When the system proved ineffective it was replaced with one based on county contributions. As a result of the Cromwellian conquest, the system was progessively tightened up. By 1652 the country was being charged £24,770 in 'cess' and a further £6,495 5s. 6d. in 'forage'. An excise was also introduced in the country, unfortunately for the royalists to no great effect. In 1644 the total yield was a mere £200 per week. The confederates did find that the impost had a value, however. In March 1646, for example, they raised a loan of £3,000 in a week, using as collateral the 'profits of the excise at Waterford, Kilkenny and Limerick and in the towns of Galway, Wexford and Clonmel'.[24]

Taxation also supplanted private donations and loans as a means of funding the Scottish covenanters' cause. After 1640 they had to impose an innovative national levy (known as the 'tenth penny') which aimed to tax all kinds of income. After 1643 they also required each shire to pay a lump sum towards the upkeep of the army (in a fashion similar to England); however, payments were constantly in arrears and by 1649 just over half of a loan voted in July 1643 had actually been accounted for. Inspired by the English example and desperate to repay their vast public debt, the covenanters also introduced, despite widespread hostility, the excise in January 1644.

SEIZURE OF PROPERTY

All sides quickly realized the benefits to be obtained from seizing the property of opponents, a practice which added to one's own resources while denying them to the enemy. Parliament was the first to make it official policy, issuing a sequestration ordinance on 27 March 1643. A further ordinance of 18 August 1643 softened the blow by allowing up to one-fifth of the estate to be used to maintain a delinquent's family and in practice the treatment may have been more lenient. The king took longer to agree formally to sequestration in spite of sanctioning some of the local initiatives which had continued unabated. For instance, in January 1644 he allowed the Gloucestershire committee to seize estates on its own initiative. Incidentally, this measure was less profitable for the king for the simple reason that parliamentarians owned much less property than did the royalists. In a similar fashion, the confederates confiscated the estates and goods of those in arms against them. Between Michaelmas 1646 and July 1647 the confederates received £627 10s. 0d. from 'the enemies' and neuters' rents in County Carlow, alone; while a note of the rents of those liable to sequestration in Wexford, Carlow, and Kildare in 1649 gave a total rental of over £2,700. From the summer of 1644 it became increasingly possible for owners of sequestered estates to buy back their property, the amount determined by the extent of their delinquency. None the less, it was August 1645 before any system of compounding was formally established, first by Parliament.

CIVILIAN REACTION

The demands of the various protagonists drove taxation to unprecedented heights in all three kingdoms. Warwickshire, for instance, was rated at £600 per week, as compared with a total of £4,000 a year in ship-money. Royalist quotas were also high, counties agreeing to pay up to £7,000 a month. The exigencies of war, moreover, led to the imposition of special levies on particular areas from time to time. Cumulatively, the various financial measures put immense strain on the country. The most vulnerable communities lay on the border of rival spheres of influence. In north Warwickshire the inhabitants of Grendon and Wishaw said that they had paid contributions to the royalist garrisons of Ashby (Leicester-shire), Dudley (Worcestershire), and Lichfield (Staffordshire) as well as to the parliamentarians. In addition, Wishaw claimed that 'the daily losses we sustained by continual pillaging and plundering of our goods and cattle is greater than we can well express'.[25]

At the same time the populace was being subjected to free quarter and other depredations, especially when money was scarce. Even when reimbursed, people did not receive the amount it actually cost to feed, much less lodge, the soldiers quartered upon them. Moreover, when horses were grazed the owners of the pas-tures were rarely compensated. Loud complaints against the 'insupportable' and 'intolerable' burden of free quarter were heard from very early in the civil wars, right up until the end. More than any other military practice free quarter pro-voked civilian hatred of soldiers, and a near-universal yearning for peace at what-ever cost. The anger caused by outright plunder was even greater. Prince Rupert's cavalry, for instance, fell into the habit of rounding up large numbers of cattle on their sweeps through the countryside.[26] Whether the animals belonged to the friends or the foes of the king scarcely mattered. The royalists, on balance, were worse culprits, though the Parliamentarians were by no means innocent parties. Raiding enemy territory, however, did constitute the main activity of garrisons in the frontier zone. Conquered towns would be subject to levies as an alternative to being sacked.

Not surprisingly, taxpayers objected to the amounts they had to pay. Early in 1644, shortly after the introduction of the excise, John Spalding, the royalist his-torian from Aberdeen, lamented: 'Thus is this miserable country overburdened with uncouth taxations … which this land was unable to bear.'[27] In spite of special pleading, many experienced genuine hardship, notably at times when commun-ities were subject to free quarter and requisitioning of supplies. To some extent the Mauchline Moor Rising (June 1648) in south-west Scotland came as a reac-tion to a decade of war, or in the words of Robert Baillie, 'the extreme great oppression of the army'.[28] Similarly, in England on 3 November 1645 two of the inhabitants of Andover (Hampshire) wrote to the county committee at South-ampton to say that they could not raise much money in rents from sequestration because 'of free quarter, contribution and other extraordinary impositions a long time laid on us'.[29] People were particularly aggrieved when the demands appeared arbitrary, the method of collection brutal, and the officials tyrannical. The use of soldiers to enforce payment and to intimidate the population caused particular offence. In the winter of 1644 to 1645, for instance, Colonel Bridges threatened the constables of Twyning (Gloucestershire) with a 'troop of horse' if they did not bring in their contributions.[30]

In their attempts to fill up their central treasuries and finance their field armies the royalists and parliamentarians were hamstrung by the strength of local sentiment. Among those contributing to the Propositions were men like Sir William Paston of Norfolk, who stressed that his contribution should be used 'for the defence of the county, not to be sent out'.[31] While it made sense to retain a proportion of the revenue in the area to meet local expenses and to avoid the cost and danger involved in transporting large sums of money around the country, it accentuated the problem of channelling money to places where it was most needed. There was particular opposition to the decision to allow royalists to compound for their estates since the process was administered from London rather than in the county. Within the associations themselves tensions emerged between the individual counties and association officials. The earl of Denbigh, the commander of the West Midlands Association, faced opposition from the county committee of Warwickshire in particular. Only in the Eastern Association did an effective organization develop in which the revenues from the counties were channelled to a central association treasury.

The authorities patently met resistance to their demands but did they manage to secure sufficient funding to wage war effectively? Numerous references indicate that money was not always forthcoming. The Hertfordshire Committee observed on 4 December 1644 that 'Taxes are so frequent in the country for one thing and another, that when warrants are issued, the returns are often complaints and tears and not moneys as are expected.'[32] The royalists rarely had enough money to buy all the arms and equipment they needed and this made manufacturers and merchants reluctant to deal with them. In Bristol lower-than-expected receipts from customs and contributions from Somerset had a damaging effect on the production of weapons in the city. Richard March warned that the artificers, whose pay already stood £1,200 in arrears, could not continue to work unless a regular source of income could be found, perhaps from the excise at Bristol. In spite of its superior financial resources Parliament suffered too. Its local forces, in particular, were dependent upon money given them by the county committees and this was often well in arrears. Sir Samuel Luke, the parliamentarian governor of Newport Pagnell, had to send out numerous letters, asking them to make good their contributions. He painted a terrible picture of soldiers without pay or adequate food and clothing and with insufficient money to buy arms. On 13 January 1645 the soldiers were said to be so desperate that they were pawning their clothes for bread!

In Ireland, while the confederates enjoyed the advantage of controlling most of Ireland's taxable resources, they failed to exploit them to full effect. For instance, contributions raised throughout confederate quarters in the spring and

summer of 1646 were expected to yield nearly £19,000; yet of this it was anticipated that 'a good part ... will be lost by desperate delinquency, wastes, paying of
garrisons, six pence per pound to the commissioners and receivers, and it is conceived probable that £8,000 may be had clear thereof for this harvest service'.[33] In
an attempt to improve their crude and inefficient financial machinery the confederates farmed out the excise, overhauled the collection of tithes, and punished
tax-evaders. To no avail: by August 1648 the confederates were virtually bankrupt
and had few prospects of raising money 'from a country so totally exhausted, and
so lamentably ruined'.[34]

Conclusion

KING AND PARLIAMENT

To what extent then did logistics determine the outcome of the English Civil
Wars? Reputedly, the king's cause failed in England not only because he did not
have the same financial and economic resources as Parliament but also because he
did not exploit what assets he did have as well as he might have done. Certainly,
his organization appeared more ramshackle and less ruthless (yet in practice
more arbitrary) than the system devised by Parliament. None the less this comparison may have been overdrawn and by 1643 the royalist administration had
begun to operate with increasing efficiency. The reduction in the amount of unpaid taxation in Worcestershire, and later Herefordshire and Monmouth as well,
highlights this. While the taxable capacity of the regions under royal control was
much less than the south and east controlled by Parliament, the necessary funds
were raised, at least until the beginning of 1645. It was not lack of money that ex-
plains the royalists' defeat, even if the incessant conflict between the exchequer,
headed by Edward Hyde, and the war treasury, headed by John Ashburnham,
hampered the king's cause. As one leading authority points out, in the mobilization of its strictly military resources the crown kept pace with Parliament, and
'actual shortages, in arms, men or money were largely overcome'.[35]

What really weakened the royalist war-effort was the fact that the conflict had
a greater impact on its territories than on those of Parliament and thus the financial machinery could not be established properly. In particular, the war impinged
closely on some of its most prosperous areas, creating a general sense of insecurity there and affecting the amount of revenue received. This, in turn, necessitated
the introduction of various expedients to obtain money and essential supplies, including special levies, free quarter, and requisitioning. As final defeat stared them
in the face, royalist units engaged in ever more self-destructive activity just to
keep themselves alive. They started a vicious circle by robbing their own shires.
Looting engendered hatred from civilians; it also rendered the countryside
incapable of paying the tax upon which the soldiers' pay depended; this in turn

drove the soldiers to more frantic looting. As long as the royalists had an army it could be used to coerce the population but the catastrophe of Naseby in June 1645 took away even this.

Parliament initially encountered the same obstacles as confronted the king: a largely indifferent population and a distinct reluctance to contribute to the war-effort. This is apparent even in areas such as Kent and East Anglia, located at the heart of its territory. Thus, it, too, had difficulty in paying for supplies. Between September and December 1642, for instance, the City of London militia committee acquired £7,300 worth of arms and equipment but by the end of 1644 only £2,670 seems to have been paid for them. To keep tighter control of finances Parliament set up the committee for taking the accounts of the kingdom in February 1645. Over time, however, the situation improved because the machinery which Parliament put in place established itself in comparative peace. Arrears were never written off and gradually the money came in. As a result, Parliament gained a much higher yield from the main tax, the assessment. The Eastern Association had the best record, with a 95 per cent success rate. Even if the money only came in slowly, this was a remarkable achievement, given the scale of the demand made on the region. The greater certainty of obtaining the tax revenue served as the basis of Parliament's success; in particular it enabled its officials to raise loans on the security of tax revenue in the knowledge that money would be available to repay them. It also allowed Parliament eventually to settle many of its outstanding debts. In December 1645, as part of this process, the committee for taking the accounts dealt with all undischarged warrants and settled many claims.

A quick victory offered Charles the best chance of winning the war. In the autumn of 1642 he had an opportunity to do so but failed for reasons that were not primarily due to deficiencies in supply. There certainly were shortcomings in this area but Parliament had its own problems too. The longer the war went on, the more likely it became that Parliament, with its commercial and economic superiority, would win. The royalists did make good use of the facilities at their disposal and focused their efforts on the production of war *matériel*. They exploited their natural resources, developed existing industries, and founded new ones where necessary. However, their workshops, mills, and furnaces could not produce enough goods to meet the demands of their armies, forcing the king to rely increasingly upon imports.

COVENANTERS AND CONFEDERATES

For most of the 1640s the covenanters drew resources from the wealthiest regions of Scotland and, given the country's lack of natural resources, raised remarkable sums of money. However, in the spring of 1645 they teetered on the verge of bankruptcy: the Scottish royalists, under Montrose (see picture on p. 52), controlled parts of Argyll and the Northeast as well as Moray (and what they did not command, they plundered and destroyed) while an already dire situation was exacerbated by the spread of the plague from the south and the inability of the English Parliament to subsidize the Scottish forces in Ulster and England. Only the defeat of the royalists in England (at the battle of Naseby in June 1645) and in Scotland (at the battle of Philiphaugh in September 1645) solved this financial crisis, enabling the covenanters to collect the monthly maintenance and excise at home and to receive English subsidies. The bulk of their creditors, however, remained unpaid. By 1649, according to Sir Thomas Cunningham, the covenanters still owed him and his partners over £16,000.

In Ireland, the inability of the protagonists—especially the royalists, the Scots, and prior to 1649 the parliamentarians—to care for their soldiers either physically or financially also had serious implications. Thus, even though by the summer of 1642 anti-Catholic coalition had a numerical advantage over the confederates, they failed to use this to full effect due to a lack of money, food, and equipment. The Irish royalists attributed their military ineffectiveness during the early 1640s to logistical difficulties and in 1643 believed that they were 'equally in danger to be devoured through our wants, or to be destroyed by the rebels for want of needful habiliments of war'.[36] Little wonder that they eagerly concluded a cease-fire with the Catholics in 1643. Likewise, in 1647 Ormond claimed that logistical problems were one reason why he handed Dublin over to the parliamentarians. Despite the despatch of over £2 million for the Irish war-effort prior to 1649, parliamentary forces were nevertheless so poorly supplied that they signed informal local truces with the Irish late in 1648 and again in May 1649.

By contrast, the confederate victory at Benburb (June 1646) can be attributed as much to the ability of the Catholic party to pay and supply the Army of Ulster with victuals, arms, and munitions as to Owen Roe O'Neill's abilities as a military commander. The same was true of Cromwell's Irish campaign which was a logistical triumph: Cromwell's troops were well supplied, well equipped, and well paid—but this feat cost the English government £3.8 million (or the equivalent of £37,000 per month) between May 1649 and November 1656. One Irish military historian even suggested that 'Without this increased financial efficiency, it is doubtful whether even Cromwell's military genius could have forced the decisive action he did in so short a time'.[37]

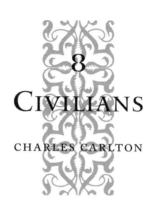

8
CIVILIANS

CHARLES CARLTON

At the height of the First English Civil War, and faced by the intolerable pressure of placating both roundheads and cavaliers without alienating either, a Wiltshire village constable wrote a note to himself: 'Woe is me, poor Bastard'.[1] During the British and Irish Civil Wars millions of men, women, and children must have expressed similar sentiments, for the conflict made a misery of the lives of both civilians and soldiers alike. Hardly a parish remained untouched. As General Robert Venables, a parliamentary commander, afterwards recalled, the wars 'were so general that almost every man was in action or affection engaged in them in one part or another'.[2]

Although perhaps as many as one adult Englishman in four served in the armed forces, the vast majority of the population remained civilians. Unlike noncombatants in a modern war they were rarely the target of military actions, such as bombing. Since the weapons of the seventeenth century lacked modern destructiveness, not many civilians become 'collateral casualties'. Compared to other wars, both ancient and modern, few folk became the victims of atrocities. Yet the lot of the civilian was unpleasant: armies constantly marched through towns and villages, trampling crops, plundering homes, abusing women, the old, and children. And as they did so they spread diseases that killed as many, if not more, people than combat itself.

Women and children were almost by definition civilians. For men, however, the line between civilian and soldier became a blurred one. For instance, the militia units which were mobilized to fight the war, had a strong non-combatant tradition that tended to lessen their military effectiveness. Uniforms, the most obvious visible distinction between soldier and civilian, did not become widespread until the third or even fourth year of the First English Civil War, while in Ireland and Scotland they remained the exception rather than the norm. Troops did not enlist for a set period of time. Desertion and re-enlistment became so widespread that soldiering was more a revolving door than a long-term commitment. In many ways the story of the British and Irish Civil Wars was the story of the growing militarization of society. In England on both sides aristocrats were replaced by those whom Oliver Cromwell described as 'plain Russet coated Captains who knew what they fought for and loved what they knew'. Although Cromwell continued to insist that 'On becoming Soldiers we have not ceased to be citizens', in fact at the end of the war under his rule the latter lost out to the former.[3] However, in the long run—no matter how terrible the experience of war had been—the civilians triumphed.

Civilian Casualties

While casualties for a war—any war—are notoriously difficult to ascertain with accuracy, figures for the conflict in England and Wales derived from a statistical analysis by computer suggests that in some 645 incidents ranging from major battles to minor brawls in England and Wales 84,830 people died in combat, of whom 34,130 were parliamentarians and 50,700 were royalists. Many more lost their lives in Ireland and Scotland. How many of these were civilians remains hard to estimate.[4]

DEATH IN COMBAT

Few civilians lost their lives in the war's fifteen largest pitched battles in which over a thousand people died. Stories of 'she soldiers', women who fought dressed as men, were more figments of imagination than reality. The massacre of the Welsh women (whom the roundheads apparently mistook for Irish Catholics) in the royalist baggage train after Naseby, was so unusual that is caused considerable comment. Anyway, it was matched by several incidents in which civilians killed defenceless soldiers. Nearly half those who died in combat did so in encounters in which the total dead were under 250.

It seems reasonable to assume that the smaller the incident the more likely civilians were to be involved, particularly as such incidents tended to take place very quickly, giving non-combatants little time to get out of the way.

SIEGE WARFARE

Escaping a siege proved far more difficult. Indeed, besieging soldiers often tried to ensure that civilians could not leave. In addition to eating food badly needed by the defending garrison, they pressured its commander to surrender so as to avoid the sack which was the inevitable consequence of a storm. That on Burton-on-Trent in April 1643 was all too common. 'Having taken the town,' declared a parliamentary intelligence report, 'the cavaliers drove at least thirty civilians into the church, had cut all their throats, doing great spoil in the town, ravishing the women, forcing many of them to take to the river, where they drowned.'[5] During the sack of Bolton a year later the royalists killed 1,200 to 1,500 people of whom 700 were civilians, nearly half the town's peacetime population. Thus sieges were not

Burial Register, 1644

This page from an Oxfordshire burial register illustrates the plight of ordinary people caught up in the parliamentarian siege of Banbury Castle (August–October 1644). In August and September a total of forty-eight people died, thirty of them allegedly of plague. Of these latter unfortunates ten, a third, were listed as children. The plague not only devastated communities throughout the three kingdoms, especially in the later 1640s, but also often claimed the lives of entire families. Gabriel Gubbins and his two children died in August while the following month another of his children also succumbed to the plague. Among those who died were a tailor, a glazier, a carpenter, an attorney, a number of soldiers, and an unfortunate civilian, James Hawkins, 'slaine with bullett from the castel'.

only extremely atrocious affairs, accounting for twenty-four per cent of the war's total combat deaths, but were especially hazardous to civilians (see Chapter 6).

ACCIDENTAL DEATH

In addition to falling victim to atrocities, ordinary folk died accidentally. Gunpowder, muskets, and cannon are inherently lethal combinations. While mixing a batch of powder for the royal army Edward Morton blew himself, his four children, and house to smithereens. Soldiers frequently discharged muskets inadvertently. During an argument with a couple of Oxford undergraduates, Captain Stagger's musket discharged—by mistake, or so he claimed—hitting a woman who happened to be shopping at the butcher's stall next door. The parish register for Romsey, Hampshire, noted the burial on 25 May 1645 of 'Frances Nash, daughter of Francis, mortally wounded by a soldier *per infortuniam*'.[6]

DISEASE

By far the largest cause of civilian deaths, however, resulted from the diseases armies spread as they campaigned across the land. Epidemics were, of course, no strangers to early modern Britain and Ireland. It has been estimated that between 1570 and 1670 660,000 people died of the plague. Before the technological advances in medicine and in public health and the development of weapons of mass destruction of the First World War, many more soldiers died of war-related disease than from combat itself. The reasons were simple. From the crowded royalist base of Oxford, Lady Anne Fanshawe wrote that 'the sad spectacles of war', plague, and sickness came 'by reason of so many people being packed together'. John Taylor, the poet, who was appointed water bailiff for the besieged city, vividly recalled the bestial condition of the River Thames:[7]

> Dead hogs, dogs, cats and well flayed carrion horse
> Their noisome corpses soiled the water courses;
> Both swines' and stable dung, beasts' guts and garbage,
> Street dirt, with gardeners' weeds and rotten herbage.
> And from this water's filthy *putrefaction*,
> Our meat and drink were made, which bred infection.

Essex's troops brought camp-fever with them into Devon during the 1644 campaign. In December seventy-nine people fell victim to it in Ottery St Mary, the parliamentary headquarters for the siege of Exeter. Pestilence lingered long after the troops left. In 1646 a contemporary estimated that of Barnstaple's population of between 4,000 and 5,000, 1,500 fell victims—276 victims were interred in the suburban parish of Pilton alone. Camp-fever was most likely a variant of typhoid. Its symptoms were small spots. With a seventy-five per cent fatality rate, it was a truly terrible experience. 'As soon as I felt my disease, I rode the six or seven miles back into the country, and the next morning (with much ado) to

Bath,' recalled one survivor, who gratefully recorded that after a fortnight 'the fever ended in a crisis of sweat and urine'.[8]

BUBONIC PLAGUE

Even more devastating than camp-fever was that perennial seventeenth-century scourge, the bubonic plague. During the strain of war plague was especially catastrophic. In Banbury between 1643 and 1645 there was an average of 255 burials per annum, compared to seventy-three a year before the war. Between 22 June 1647 and 20 April 1648 2,099 people died of the plague in war-torn Chester. War-related plague so devastated Stafford that it took a generation for its population to recover. During the 1646 siege plague became so serious in Newark that the authorities ordered every infected house shut up, with a sentry posted outside. Between July and September 1645 there was not a single christening in Manchester's parish church: they were too busy burying 748 corpses, a fortyfold increase over the norm. Indeed so virulent was the plague there that many folk vowed that 'they would rather be hanged at their own door than enter such an infected town'.[9]

Between 1645 and 1649 bubonic plague allegedly claimed 30,000 lives in Scotland. For instance, Perth may have lost nearly forty per cent of its inhabitants to the disease during the later 1640s; while between April and December 1647 roughly 1,700 people, or between fifteen and twenty per cent of the city's pre-war population, died in Aberdeen. Similarly in Ireland thousands of urban dwellers died of bubonic plague. Sir William Petty asserted that in 1649–50 it killed 1,300 people per week in Dublin alone; certainly the numbers of burials in one city parish, where the records have survived, soared during the summers of 1649 and 1650. One-third of the population of Kilkenny allegedly died of plague in 1650; while one contemporary estimated that roughly 20,000 townsfolk died in Galway during the epidemic of 1649–50. Thomas Dekker was not exaggerating when in his play *Dialogue Between Ware, Famine and Pestilence* (1604), Pestilence boasts:[10]

> War, I surpass the fury of thy stroke
> Say that an army forty thousand strong
> Enter the crimson lists, and of that number
> Purchance the fourth part falls, marked with Red Death?
> Why I slay forty thousand in one battle.

ENGLISH DEATHS

Estimates of the ratio between the number of people who died from disease and those who died from the effects of war vary. It has been calculated that of the 11,817 people who died in Devon between 1643 and 1645, 4,193 did so as a result of the war. To put that another way, directly or indirectly the war increased the county's dead by fifty-five per cent. If this total of 4,193 is compared to the 1,634 people that the computer data base lists as having been directly killed in combat, then it would appear that during the First English Civil War 2.57 times more people died in Devon from indirect rather than direct causes. The death of 2,845 people from disease during the siege of Plymouth would support this conclusion. A French demographer estimated that during the seventeenth century only ten per cent of military deaths were due to battle; while another scholar put this figure at twenty-five per cent. Certainly during the American Civil War, when figures are more accurate—for every casualty in battle a further two people died from war-related diseases.[11]

Using the computer-generated figure of 84,830 as a basis, and a fairly conservative ratio of 1 battle to 1.5 non-battle deaths it would not be unreasonable to suggest that 127,000 people died of non-combat deaths in England and Wales. If, say, sixty per cent of these were soldiers it would mean that during the civil wars in England and Wales some 40,000 civilians lost their lives.

SCOTTISH DEATHS

Such a total for England is, it goes without saying, a wild, although not reckless, guess. Those for Scotland are even more speculative. A survey of some forty-six incidents north of the border gives a total of 27,865 casualties. Since fighting in Scotland was far more brutal than England many more civilians died as a direct result of combat, while the ratio of indirect deaths such as those from disease would be as high as in England. In particular, the Campbell–MacDonald feud left many dead. One Gaelic poet lauded Alasdair MacColla for 'burning, killing, wreaking destruction' on the followers of Clan Campbell.[12] Over the winter of 1644–5 alone 895 men allegedly lost their lives on Maclean lands without any formal battle occurring. On another occasion, later dubbed 'The Barn of Bones', MacColla's men fired a barn filled with Campbell women and children and then set light to it. Thus it would not be fanciful to suggest that perhaps 15,000 civilians perished in Scotland.

IRISH DEATHS

Figures for Ireland are even more difficult to ascertain because the historical record is slight. Certainly the devastation the civil war inflicted was unbelievable. As early as 1642 Owen Roe O'Neill reported that most of Country Donegal 'not only looks like a desert, but like Hell'.[13] Having travelled extensively throughout Ireland in 1652 and 1653 Colonel Richard Lawrence stated that 'the plague and famine had swept away whole counties that a man might travel twenty or thirty miles and not see a living creature, either man, beast or bird'.[14] A Gaelic bard lamented:[15]

> I hear not the Duck's call nor goose there,
> Nor the eagle by the harbour proud,
> Nor Even the bees for their whorl there,
> To give honey and wax to the crown.
> No melodious songs of birds there . . .

Writing in 1672, after the civil war and the land confiscation and deportations decreed by the draconian Act of Settlement, Sir William Petty, the father of modern demography, estimated that between 23 October 1641 and 23 October 1652 618,000 people lost their lives in Ireland. Although Petty's figures are, according to a leading Irish historian, 'the best we have', they none the less remain extremely tentative.[16] On the one hand, his figures for 37,000 Protestant civilians massacred in the autumn and winter of 1642 is far too high, perhaps by as much as a factor of ten; certainly more recent research suggests that a more realistic figure is roughly 4,000 deaths. On the other hand, Petty does not include those, possibly as many as 40,000, driven into exile or sold into slavery to the West Indies (where most were worked to death). If we say that Petty's exaggerated his figure threefold, that only 200,000 Irish died during the civil wars, and that of these a third were soldiers, this would mean that 137,000 civilians died directly or indirectly as a result of the civil wars. If we add in the estimates from England, 40,000, and for Scotland, another 15,000, we get a total of 192,000, or roughly 2.5 per cent of the civilian population.

When these figures are compared with modern wars, the findings prove instructive. As a result of the First World War perhaps as many as 150,000 civilians died, or 0.36 per cent of the population, most of them during the 1918/19 Spanish flu epidemic; while during the Second World War 50,000 civilians or 0.11 per cent of the population lost their lives largely as a result of enemy bombing. So without doubt as far as civilians were concerned the British and Irish Civil Wars remain the bloodiest man-made event in the history of the three kingdoms.

Families

BY THE SWORD DIVIDED

The war divided families, the basic building blocks of civil society, in three main ways: through the death of a father, son, or brother, because of geographical separation, and as a result of conflicting political loyalties. Of the gentry who participated in hostilities six per cent in both Lancashire and South East Berkshire, seven per cent in Suffolk, and sixteen per cent in Yorkshire were divided, as compared to fifteen per cent of the aristocracy, and twenty per cent of the 159 families listed in the *Dictionary of National Biography*.

At Edgehill, to take but one example, William Feilding, earl of Denbigh, and Henry Carey, earl of Devon, charged against their sons, Basil and John; while Sir Edmund Verney died trying to save the royal standard from the parliamentary army whose cause his eldest son Ralph supported. Sir Edmund's youngest son, also christened Edmund, reproved his elder brother: ''tis most unseemly done, and it grieves my heart'.[17] Three of the cousins of Denzil Holles, who commanded a roundhead regiment, were royalists, as were at least six members of

Atrocities in Ireland

No images prepared civilians and soldiers alike more for the horrors of war than depictions of atrocities in Ireland, which were supported by tales and, grossly exaggerated, by the Protestant refugees who flooded into Britain after the outbreak of the rebellion in October 1641. Thus instead of 154,000 Protestants who were allegedly murdered, c.4,000–6,000 died. Here a violated woman, surrounded by corpses, symbolizes the outrages of war, which civilians, both male and female, dreaded.

Cromwell's family. Sir Thomas Maulever's son fought and was imprisoned for the king his father voted to execute. Divisions permeated all levels of society. Peter and Christina Daniels of Over Tably, Cheshire, had four sons and four daughters. Two of the boys, Peter and Thomas, served the king, being killed at Gloucester and Brentford. Their two brothers John and William sided with Parliament, both surviving to become colonels. Three daughters married royalists, and one a roundhead. 'Sir John, you are my kinsman, and one I have much honoured,' Colonel Boynton told Governor Hotham as he grabbed his cousin's horse as he was deserting Parliament for Charles, 'but I must now wave all that, and arrest you as a traitor to the kingdom.'[18] Soon afterwards Parliament shot Hotham and his son for treason.

Family members not only fought on different sides, but most worrying of all could actually kill each other. 'My dear heart, my dear life, my sweet joy,' wrote Elizabeth Bourchier to her husband (who was fighting for Parliament as her father served the crown), 'I hope God will preserve you from your father's and everybody's hurt.'[19] In only one case did one family member personally kill another. As he lay dying from musket-wounds sustained in an unsuccessful storm of Wardour Castle, Private Hillsdeane, a roundhead, confessed that his royalist brother had fired the fatal shot. He forgave him, saying he had only been doing his duty. The pain of a death in a family was even more intense. Lady Denbigh's son Basil was a roundhead while her husband William was a royalist who lost his life in April 1643 storming Nottingham.

The effect on young children who lost fathers to the war was incalculable, even if their mothers remarried. Less serious was the impact on families if the father was away fighting. Oliver Luke proved fractious when his father left home to serve as parliamentary governor of Newport Pagnell. Samuel Luke wrote to the lad telling him that if he caught the fever that was going around it would be a sign of God's displeasure. The threat worked. A month later Samuel Luke wrote to Oliver saying how glad he was to learn from his mother that he had turned over a new leaf. In preparation for the siege of Scarborough, which lasted for twelve bitter months, Lady Elizabeth Cholmley sent her two children to Holland: 'whom I parted with not without great trouble, for I was fond of them,' explained the royalist governor's wife.[20]

Most women strove desperately to keep their families together with or without husbands, in the face of the perils of war. Elizabeth Moore tried to do so. From the borders of Hertfordshire and Bedfordshire she wrote:[21]

2 June 1644.
Good Sister:
I had written to you before this time, but that I have had an extreme sore eye, and is not very perfect. Little Will hath been much set back with the breeching of his teeth . . . He grows very much in length though not in breadth. We ask for your company here many times. Here are great fears at this time for it is reported that the enemy is at Bedford, and

that they have plundered Hatch in Hertfordshire. The countrys are all in arms. There is no place free from distraction and trouble, I pray God fit us all for what he please to impose on us, for these are bad times. My uncle in Lincolnshire is ill done by the Cavaliers, they have taken all his writing and books . . . He is in Norfolk at my cousins. Thus we see how uncertain the world is. I pray God set an end to all these troubles that we may have a happy putting upon again, for which I pray and ever remain your loving sister, Eliz Moore.

Whatever happened to Elizabeth Moore, whether she found the happiness for which she prayed, or else had her hopes, home, and family destroyed, remains unknown. None the less her letter is worth quoting at length because it conveys the anguish and uncertainty, the courage and determination ordinary women showed as they faced the face of war.

Indeed, most families pulled through to become a source of quite pride and warm solace. Sir John Gibson of Wilburn, Yorkshire, wrote in his *Autobiography*:[22]

> When uncivil war withal
> Did bloodshed bring and strife
> Twelve sons my wife Penelope
> And four daughters had,
> Which was a comfort to me
> And made my heart full glad.

Children

Children rarely fought in combat. William St Lawrence and John Gandy, two schoolboys who ran away from Bury St Edmunds 'to the intolerable grief of their parents' to enlist in Waller's army, were unusual.[23] Sometimes boys served as drummers, or were used for intelligence work, particularly carrying missives. One lad, Richard Clark, carried messages for the parliamentary garrison at Wem, Shropshire, by putting them in a hollowed stick, its ends sealed with dirt. Whenever he came across a party of cavaliers he would play the simpleton, throwing his stick at a bird, to pick up after the enemy had gone.

Had Richard been caught he would have been severely punished. During the sieges of Wardour Castle (1643–4) and Limerick (1651) the defenders tortured boys suspected of smuggling intelligence to traitors within. In the summer of 1644 Colonel John Hutchinson, governor of the besieged parliamentary garrison of Nottingham, used burning cord to coerce a lad into confessing that he had carried messages to Private Griffith, a royalist masquerading as a roundhead.

War could effect children indirectly, almost randomly. Richard Gough never forgot an incident at Myddle, in Shropshire, 'which I saw when I was a schoolboy'. By accident royalist and roundhead patrols bumped into each other at the village smithy, and in the ensuring fire-fight Cornet Collins, an Irishman from King's garrison at Shrawardine Castle, was shot, toppling into the village pond, and two of his troopers were killed. The villagers dragged Collins out of the pond, and carried him bleeding profusely to Allen Chaloner's house, where they dumped him on the floor. He begged for a feather mattress to relieve the pain. There was none, Mrs Chaloner replied: he had thrown it into the pond yesterday for spite, after plundering her house. None the less she retrieved the tattered, and still wet, palliasse and slid it under the officer, before summoning the local minister. 'I went with him,' recalled Richard Gough, 'and saw the Cornet lying on the bed, and much blood running along the floor.'[24]

The effects of the war on Captain Thomas Wathen's son must have been equally traumatic. When the soldiers entered the family house, Mere Court, Hereford, to steal the family's pack horses, one of them saw Wathen's son rocking his baby brother in a cradle. Picking up the infant, playing, and kissing it, the trooper soon won the boy's confidence. Asked where his father was, the lad replied that he had gone to hide the horses in a specially dug pit.

Women

Although they did not alter attitudes to children, the civil wars challenged the basic assumptions about women characteristic of early modern Britain and Ireland. In 1646, looking back on women's achievements, Edward Foord wondered:[25]

> Women they say the Weaker Vessels are,
> If so, it is a paradox to men
> That those were never trained up in war
> So often should obtain the victory.

CROSS-DRESSING

A few women even dressed as men in order to remain with their husbands or lovers or else for the excitement of combat. The story that the 2,000 royalists Fairfax captured at Acton church, Cheshire, in January 1644 included 'a female regiment' of about twenty-one well-armed, bloodthirsty Amazons is incredible: most likely the women were camp-followers.[26] 'Molly' the landlady of the 'Mad Dog' pub at Blackheath supposedly fought dressed as a man. Jane Engleby, the daughter of a Yorkshire yeoman, is said to have charged with the king's cavalry at Marston Moor, and wounded, escaped back to the safety of her father's farm. A newspaper reported the capture of a woman dressed as one of General Lindsay's cavaliers in 1642. Oliver Cromwell surprised a small raiding party under Henry, Lord Percy at Andover in March 1645, which included 'a youth of so fair a countenance', and such a high voice, that Lord Percy, 'in some confusion did acknowledge she was a damsel'.[27] Eight months later Sedenham Poynts's men apprehended a cavalier corporal who turned out to be a woman. A horrified House of Commons was informed that two of the hundred whores Prince

Rupert kept were dressed as boys. Charles thought the cross-dressing of women as soldiers so pernicious and common that in July 1643 he issued a proclamation forbidding the practice (*inter alia*) as 'a thing which nature and Religion forbid, and our Soul abhors'.[28]

Reports of 'she-soldiers' were rife if only because they made excellent copy. In 1655 the popular ballad 'The Gallant She-Soldier' described the career of a heroine who served in the army under the alias of 'Mr. Clarke':[29]

> Her Husband was a soldier, and to the wars did go,
> And she would be his comrade, the truth of all is so,
> She put on man's apparel, and bore him company
> As many in the army for truth can testify.

SIEGE WARFARE

Far more women fought in sieges than served in the army (also see Chapter 6). When a sixty-pound shell fell in the street during the siege of Gloucester, a quick-witted women doused the fuse with a bucket of water. Women knew only too well what could happen if the town was taken by storm. A maid servant who witnessed the brutal massacre of the garrison of Hopton Castle, Herefordshire, suffered the mental trauma for the rest of her life. William Summers, declared that, after she lost her son, and all her possessions following the royalist sack of Leicester in 1645, his 'wife hath been distracted'.[30] Sadder still was the case of Lady Jordan, who was caught in the siege of Cirencester in February 1643. The bombardment, which included a shelling by a large mortar, as well as the subsequent sack, reduced her to behaving like a tiny child, being able to find happiness only by playing with the dolls that were made specially for her.

After the parliamentarians finally captured Basing House in October 1645 they brutally murdered many women. Dr Griffith's daughter had her brains smashed in when she tried to stop a roundhead from beating her father. When eight or nine gentlewomen tried to run away they 'were entertained by the common soldiers somewhat coarsely, yet not uncivilly,' reported the Reverend Hugh Peters; 'they left them with some clothes upon them'.[31] In June of the previous year after the royalists gave up their long and brutal siege the victorious defenders of Lyme Regis allegedly seized an old Irish woman. Some say that the sailors, with their swords drawn, drove her through the town into the sea; others report that a mob tore her to pieces or else rolled her around inside a nail-studded barrel.

One possible explanation for the assaults on women after the captures of Lyme Regis and Basing is that women took an active part in the defence. From the walls at Basing they hurled sticks and stones down on the attacking roundheads. At Lyme some 400 women assiduously supported the parliamentary cause by putting out fires started by incendiary arrows fired over the walls; by standing guard at night; by reloading soldiers' muskets; and even by firing at the attacking royalists. When the enemy temporarily abandoned the siege the enraged women rushed out with picks and shovels, levelling the earthworks in three days. During the siege of Withenshaw House, a royalist base in Cheshire, a serving-girl turned sniper, shot and killed Captain Adams. During the siege of Worcester 400 'ordinary sort of women out of every ward' worked daily, often during bombardments, on the defences. Cannon killed several; others lost their lives while filling in as snipers as the men got some rest.[32] At Bristol Dorothy Hazard (an appropriate name) and her friends rushed in to seal a breach in the wall with sandbags. Then they stood behind the guns to see that the men fired grapeshot at any roundhead who dared poke his head through the gap.

DEFENCE OF LONDON

The most important military operation in which large numbers of women became involved was the defence of London in late 1642. Terrified by the sack of Brentford on 12 November 1642—the details of which grew more horrendous with every telling—some twenty thousand citizens built an earth wall eighteen feet high, eleven miles in circumference, with a ditch in front, and straddled by fourteen forts (see picture on p. 211). Many foreign experts believed the capital's defences impregnable. Certainly they were strong enough to deter Charles I from advancing on the city, and thus losing his only real chance of capturing London, and winning the English Civil War. Many of those responsible were women, about whom Samuel Butler, the royalist poet sneered.[33]

> From Ladies down to oyster wenches
> Laboured the pioneers in the trenches
> Fallen to pickaxes and tools
> And helped the men dig like Moles.

ARISTOCRATIC WOMEN

Better known were the high-born ladies who commanded the defence of the family home during the absence of their husbands. Two months after the outbreak of the Irish rebellion Lady Elizabeth Dowdall raised a company of soldiers in Munster. When the 'rebels' tried to plunder her fortified house, she seized their horses, and hanged the men. When Richard Stephenson arrived with 3,000 men and with drums beating and pipes wailing to demand her surrender, the indomitable Lady Dowdall 'sent him a shot in the head that made him bid the world good-night, and routed the whole army, we shot so hot'.[34]

Elizabeth, the widow of Maurice Cuffe, a merchant, held out her family's Irish castle for six weeks against the Irish insurgents. When they demanded her surrender, she replied that 'by the help of God this castle should to the hazard of life be kept for the Kings Majesty's use'.[35] The countess of Portland vowed personally to fire the first cannon rather than surrender Carisbrooke Castle on the Isle of Wight. Lady Mary Winter's refusal to give up Lydney House did much to thwart Parliament's attempts to control Gloucestershire. In the summer of 1643 Lady Mary Bankes defended Corfe Castle, Dorset, during the absence of her husband, Sir John, the chief justice of common pleas, who was serving the king at Oxford. When the roundheads, some of whom were freed felons, and all of whom were well lubricated with 'hot waters', assaulted the castle, her ladyship, her daughters, and serving-women, plus five soldiers, threw burning embers and stones from the battlements with such effect that the enemy could not scale their ladders.

'My Heart: Our Condition is at this time very desperate,' wrote Lady Helen Neale to her husband on 9 May 1646 from Hawarden Castle, near Chester, which was under siege. Although the parliamentarians had brought up heavy cannon to batter down the great round tower Lady Neale vowed, 'I am purposed to hold out as long as there is meat for man, for none of these eminent dangers shall ever frighten me from my loyalty, but in life and death I will be the king's faithful subject and thy constant loving wife and humble servant.'[36]

While royalists could understand and even approve of such defiance, they could not fathom Lady Brilliana Harley's refusal to surrender Brampton Bryan Castle, Herefordshire. When this 'woman of great spirit' spurned the king's demand of August 1643 to surrender, Charles blamed her defiance on evil counsellors who had taken advantage of a woman's weaker nature. Lady Harley replied with fitting female humility that she could not possibly surrender without her husband's permission.[37]

On the royalist side the countess of Derby dramatically displayed the tension between behaving properly as the weaker vessel and showing courage above one's sex in February 1643 by refusing to surrender Lathom House, her husband's ancestral home in Lancashire, while he was off fighting for the king in the Isle of Man. 'Though a woman, and a stranger, divorced from her friends, and robbed of her estate,' the countess declared 'she was ready to refuse their utmost violence, trusting in God for both protection and deliverance.' Lathom House was a mighty fortress, with walls six feet thick, nine towers, and a moat eighteen yards wide and a fathom deep. The siege proved long and bitter. Cannon-balls crashed through the windows of the countess's chamber: the garrison suffered dreadfully from a mortar that lobbed eighty-pound shells. Confident of victory, Colonel Rigby (who had specially invited his friends and neighbours along to see the fun) demanded Lady Derby's surrender. The countess told the herald that 'a due reward for his pains is to be hanged up at her gates, but thou art a foolish instrument of a traitorous pride'. Summoning the garrison, she vowed to fight to the death rather than surrender. The pep-talk worked. Cheering troops vowed, 'We'll die for his Majesty and your honour—God save the King!' Emboldened by the countess's defiance two days later they rushed out, captured the mortar, and broke the enemy's will.[38]

WAR AND LOVE

There is no doubt that there is something erotic about war, with its handsome uniforms, romantic trappings, macho values, and opportunities for casual coup-lings. Lonely and frightened soldiers have always sought the security—no mat-ter how brief and impersonal—of a woman's embrace.

How effective they were in finding such solace remains difficult to say. Baptis-mal registers do not record a bumper crop of bastards. So the evidence remains impressionistic. 'The young women conversed without any circumspection or modesty,' remembered Sir Edward Hyde, the contemporary historian.[39] Like the GIs based in Britain during the Second World War, many county folk thought the troopers oversexed and overpaid. The soldiers had a swaggering self-confidence that the local lads interpreted as arrogance, and some of the local lasses found irresistible. With looted coins jangling in their pockets, troopers might offer a simple village girl excitement undreamed of in her usual rural round. Such goings-on outraged village worthies—not to mention the fathers of daughters. When a sanctimonious Somerset householder espied a woman dally-ing under a hedge with a soldier he drew his sword and stabbed the man. On an-other occasion, after watching a servant woman traipse into a barn with a trooper, her mistress peeped around the door, and saw 'the soldier lying upon her and her clothing up so that she saw her naked skin'. Outraged, the mistress called a posse of local lads, who threw the offending lass into a mill-stream.[40]

Moral outrage could, however, all too easily become hypocrisy that turned vic-tims into scapegoats. When in late 1645 some of Goring's defeated royalists ar-rived in the village of Doulting, Somerset, 'they were very rude and beat up most of the people'. Demanding a woman to 'dress their meat', the villagers bought them off with Joan Easton, who spent 'all the day and night with them'.[41]

Troops also genuinely fell for local women. Many of the Scottish and English soldiers serving in Ireland took local brides. Major-General Robert Munro married the widow of Lord Montgomery of the Ards and later settled in County Down. A number of his officers did likewise: the veteran Major James Turner, for instance, wed a Catholic woman whom he had met while his regiment had been garrisoned in Newry. In the wake of the Cromwellian conquest, the frequency with which English soldiers fell in love with Catholics led the government to issue orders forbidding intermarriage. Captain Innis, the commander of a Scots company billeted in Hipswell, Yorkshire, was smitten by Alice Townsend, offer-ing £3,000 and then £4,000 for the 17-year-old's hand: it did his wooing no good. The captain 'was so wild a blood looking man,' Alice recalled, 'that I trembled all the time he was in the house'. So she ran away from home. When Innis threatened to have his men smash up her mother's cottage unless she told him where her daughter was hiding, Mrs Townsend complained to General Leslie, who told Innis to stop, allowing Alice to return home. She must have been an attractive woman for soon afterwards Captain Jermyn Smith asked her to marry him. She refused. Luckily one of his troopers, Private Thomas Binke, told her, as she was bandaging his wounded hand, that Jermyn was planning to abduct her during her usual walk to Lowes, 'and force me on horseback away with them, and God knows what end he would make of me'.[42]

A few women liked such a rough wooing. Sir John Gell hated his royalist rival Sir John Stanhope so bitterly that after his death he plundered his house, and broke the nose and fingers from his stone monument in the parish church. He even dug up the flower-beds that were Lady Stanhope's pride and joy. Far from loathing him, the widow allowed Gell to court her, and accepted his marriage proposal. Similarly in 1649 Jean Gordon, widow of Baron Claud Hamilton of Strabane, married Sir Phelim O'Neill despite the fact that late in 1641 he had taken her prisoner and burned her castle at Strabane in County Tyrone.

Even more surprising was the behaviour of Susan Denton, a middle-aged spinster long past making a good match. The roundheads captured her after storming Hillesden House in Buckinghamshire. 'We were not shamefully used in any way by the soldiers,' wrote Pen Verney, a fellow prisoner, 'but they took everything, and I was scarce left the clothes on my back.' As the captives were being marched off to be penned for the night in the local church, Susan caught the eye of Captain Jeremiah Abercrombie, the Scotch-Irish commander of the guard detail. It was a case of love at first sight—the slightly desperate spinster, and the rugged Ulster officer. 'I think few of her friends like it a bit, but if she had not him she would not have any,' an aunt sneeringly concluded. The couple married quickly, since Abercrombie had to march on with his regiment. Sadly he was killed near Bristol a few months later.[43]

Abercrombie at least behaved like a gentleman—which is more at least than can be said for some. In the village of Myddle an army captain courted 'a lonely handsome woman' who had married a local landowner more to please her father than herself. Falling for the captain's blandishments to take her away from all that to Ireland, where no one cared about previous marriage vows, she left her spouse and child. However, her officer was no gentleman. He deserted her at Chester, and she had to return home to her husband, who took her back only on receipt of a second dowry. Sometimes it was the wronged husband who suffered the most. Worried sick by his wife's affair with Lieutenant Thomas Corneby, an officer from the parliamentary garrison, an apothecary from Newport Pagnell slit his throat in three places.

Women were, however, less likely to troubled by romantic strangers than persistent neighbours, particularly when their husbands were away at the war. Convinced that Nat Owen, a parliamentary deserter and horse-thief was sleeping with his wife, Richard Manning led a patrol from the roundhead garrison at Morton Corbet to Myddle, to have him arrested. In fact they ran into a cavalier party, killing its officer. Troopers in Newport Pagnell assured local girls that sleeping with them was not really adultery since there was a war on. A yeoman from Clinton, Somerset, tried to persuade the wife of a labourer who had been away with the army in Ireland for two years, to go to bed with him, by explaining that 'her husband used the company and lay with women in Ireland and had the carnal knowledge of their bodies, and he would wish her to do the like with men here in England'.[44] Civilians were not above such spurious arguments. J. Bostock, clerk to the local council of war, was found guilty of committing adultery with Alice Chetwood. Since they did so in a minister's house, on the sabbath, and—worst still—during the hours of divine worship, the pair were lucky to get off with having to stand in Nantwich market-place with a sign describing their crimes about their necks.

WAR BRIDES

Amidst the dislocation and partings of civil war, most husbands and wives remained faithful, as they desperately missed each other. 'In my absence,' noted Chaplain Ralph Josselin, my wife 'was wondrous sad and discontented'.[45] Lady Anne Fanshawe was a typical war bride. After her father, a royalist Member of Parliament, escaped from parliamentary custody he summoned her and her sister to join him in Oxford. Anne recalled the hardships they had to endure: 'From as good a house as any gentleman in England had, we came to a baker's house in an obscure street, and from rooms well furnished, to lie in a very bad bed in a garret, to one dish of meat and that not the best.'[46]

But wartime Oxford was not without its attractions. Raucous sergeants replaced contemplative dons; handsome officers marched where callow students used to stroll. Cavalry patrols jangled through the streets trying to catch the eye of those pretty women who seemed to flock wherever the court met. Attracted by the sound of their drums, one afternoon Lady Anne Fanshawe strolled over to St John's College garden, and leaning against a tree watched the soldiers drill. The commander, a family friend, 'in compliment gave us a volley of shot'. He did not realize that instead of blanks one of his musketeers had loaded a brace of bullets that pierced the bark a couple of feet above Anne's head.[47]

Anne survived to meet and fall in love with Sir Richard, a cavalier officer. She never forgot the day in March 1645 when her husband left for the wars. 'He was extremely affected, even to tears, though passion was against his nature.' Two days later their infant child died, victim of the fevers that ravaged the garrison town. The following May Anne joined Richard to share the adventures of campaigning. After he was captured at Worcester and marched to London, she loyally followed him to the capital, where every morning at 4 a.m., even in the rain, she stood in the street outside Richard's cell window to talk to him. After his release and heavy with child, Anne Fanshawe escaped with her husband first to the Scilly Islands, and then to the Isles of Jersey, where she arrived 'almost dead'. The war forced her to move constantly. Thus Anne buried children in Lisbon,

Madrid, Paris, Oxford, Yorkshire, Hertfordshire, and Kent, she and her family returning home just in time for Sir Richard to join Charles II's invasion of England. Uncertain if he had survived the battle of Worcester in September 1650, 'for three days it was inexpressible what affliction I was in,' remembered Anne Fanshawe: 'I neither eat, nor slept, but trembled at every motion I heard, expecting the fatal news'.[48] Anne was most relieved that her husband had survived and she would not have to bring up her children without a father. Having them in the seventeenth century was hard enough; giving birth during a civil war made it only worse, sparing neither high nor low.

QUEEN HENRIETTA MARIA

The wars' most famous mother was Henrietta Maria (see frontispiece). Seven months in her term, the queen left her husband (whom she never again saw) in Oxford in April 1644 for the safety of the West Country. Desperately worried, the king begged Sir Thomas Mayerne, the royal family physician, 'for the love of me go to my wife, C.R.'. On 14 June Henrietta had a daughter in Exeter. The painful labour left the baby with one shoulder permanently lower than then other, and the mother exceedingly debilitated. 'Here is the woefullest spectacle my eyes yet ever looked upon,' an attendant wrote home, 'the most and weak pitiful creature in the world, the poor Queen.' Yet Fairfax refused to grant her majesty a safe conduct to travel to take the healing waters at Bath. Thus less than a month after a painful confinement the sick, helpless, and hated queen had to take ship at Falmouth, and after being fired upon by a parliamentary vessel she landed at Brest, so ill that the doctors concurred that 'her days will not be many'.[49]

The queen and her daughter, Henrietta-Anne, were fortunate to survive this ordeal. Frightened by the sudden appearance of a cavalier patrol near Plymouth, Colonel Robert Bennet's wife went into premature labour, and died, losing the child. Simple war-weariness and excessive childbearing killed Lady Dunley. In the absence of her husband on royal service, she had to manage the estate, and put up with 'the horrid rudeness of the soldiers and Scots' billeted upon her. 'The troubles and destruction of those sad times did [so] much affect and grieve' the poor woman, her sister recalled, that as a result she expired giving birth to her sixteenth child.[50] When Thomas Springett, a member of the parliamentary garrison of Arundel Castle, fell dangerously ill in 1644, his pregnant wife Mary had to travel through terrible winter weather to join him. Her coach skidded into a ditch, she had to take a boat through flooded countryside, and walk many miles across wet cold ground to reach her husband, who was delirious by the time she arrived. Having sat up with him for forty-eight hours until he passed away, Mary Springett survived to bear his posthumous child. Lady Anne Saville, trapped in the siege of York, suffered a similar ordeal. Having just lost her husband and been denied a midwife by the parliamentary attackers, she gave birth the day after York fell. After marrying Edward Heath when she was only 13, and enduring much of the war in disease-ridden Oxford, where three of her babies died, Lucy Heath was given permission to return to her home near Oakham to have a child. The baby died aged 6 months, and half a year later its 27-year-old mother passed away, worn out by war, worry, and pregnancies.

WAR WIVES

Wives were petrified of being widowed. 'What can be more doleful, or greater terror,' asked *The Widowes' Lamentation* (1643), than 'our husbands should be taken from us by violent deaths'.[51] 'I am in perpetual fear for you,' Lady Bourchier wrote to her husband, the earl of Rutland, in August 1644; 'I would rather live with you with bread and water than from you with all the plenty in the world.'[52] The wives of ordinary folk shared the same fears and hopes as high-born ladies or gentlewomen. Susan Rodway, the wife of a common soldier in the London trained bands, off fighting at the siege of Basing House (see picture on p. 229), wrote to 'My Dear and loving husband, my king love,' how worried she was not to have heard from him, especially after her neighbours had received letters from their husbands. She was worried about their son: 'My little Willie has been sick this fortnight.' She was frightened to be on her own: 'You do not consider that I am a lone woman, I thought you would never leave me this long together.' But most of all she was desperately scared of being left a widow ending her letter: 'So I rest ever praying for your safe return.'[53]

WIDOWS

Being widowed, wrote Margaret Eure, whose second husband, Colonel William Eure, perished in 1644, was 'the greatest misfortune that could ever happen to me in this world . . . the death of the gallantest man that I ever knew in my Life'.[54] Two days after hearing that her husband Lord Charles Moore had been killed in a skirmish near Meath in September 1643, Lady Alice described herself as 'a wretched woman, desolate and distressed . . . I am not capable of receiving comfort myself in this dreadful extremity.'[55] Typical of the trauma of losing a husband to the war was that experienced by Carey Verney. She was only 16, 'as sweet a creature as any living', when she married Thomas Gardiner, the son of the prominent lawyer and the recorder of London. Three months after their wedding day he joined the army, leaving her pregnant. In July 1645 he died in a skirmish at Ethrop, Buckinghamshire, leaving 'a sad disconsolate widow, great with child', and 'not a penny in the house'. Carey tried to get the £80 her brother-in-law Harry Gardiner owed her, but he too was killed. Her own brother was in France, unable to help. Her in-laws were cruelly indifferent, even after she gave birth to a weak, sickly, almost blind baby. So Carey Verney returned to her family's house in Claydon. Two years later, most folk thought her lucky to remarry John Stewkeley, a widower with several children.[56]

Many women did not learn the fate of husbands who went to the wars never to return. Susan Rodway's husband, Richard, almost certainly perished in the assault of the great barn at Basing House, where most of his unit was wiped out. In desperation some women even turned to the occult to discover the lots of those missing in action. The files of William Lilly, the century's most famous astrologer, are full of enquiries from desperate widows.

All too often the sad fate of widows became grist for propaganda mills, or, sadder still, fodder for callous comedians. At the start of hostilities one pamphlet maintained that 'there was not a widow amongst us, from old crocked bedames of four score and fifteen to the young buxom widow of twenty' who could now hope to find a 'young lusty husband'.[57] The following year *The Virgins' Complaint for the Loss of their Sweethearts* argued that war had deprived them of their rightful role of being 'a helper for man in his necessities'. The death of so many young swains, the virgins complained, forced them to 'betroth ourselves to frosty bearded usurers, that are as cold in their constitutions and performances as they are in their charities'. At times this pamphlet became crassly comic, with its images of ancient 'bumbling fumblers' trying to satisfy young females, as they tottered on their crutches. Underneath the pamphlet's bawdyness was a message serious enough to sell five editions between 1643 and 1646: 'To shed human blood is against all divine and human laws, and barbarous it is for men, handsome young men, with their weapons.' Of course, the reference to men's weapons was a crude pun, yet it touched on an important issue for a society that believed the women's sexual urges were far stronger than men's, and if aroused and then not satisfied within marriage were a threat to social stability:[58]

> No fleety potion
> Not other notion
> Of Physic for our sickness can be found
> Only one thing makes us this consold
> The oil of man can ease us in this hold.

At the end of the First English Civil War, *Hey-Hoe for a Husband, or the Parliament of Maids*—allegedly written by a gaggle of virgins that included a Miss Priscilla Prick-Story—proposed legislation that would forbid old widows from marrying young men, and force every tenth man in each parish to wed every tenth woman, regardless of their looks. Of course, all these pamphlets were written tongue in cheek, yet one suspects that their humour was wasted on the many thousands of women widowed by the civil wars. Certainly it did not amuse 'The many thousand Wives and Matrons' who in February 1643 purportedly petitioned for peace. They explained that 'each of us has a loving and kind husband as ever lay a leg over a woman,' yet now they were 'poor distressed wives this cold weather lying alone in our beds without the warm touches and embraces of any man to comfort us'.[59]

PHYSICAL ABUSE

Women have always been more vulnerable to violence, which is overwhelmingly a male activity. The 1641 depositions which detail events following the outbreak of rebellion in Ireland contain numerous descriptions of women who were both physically and mentally abused: many were stripped, robbed of their possessions, and forced out of their homes during the bitterly cold winter of 1641 to 1642. In 1645 according to a parliamentary spy in Northampton, one of Sir Marmaduke Langdale's cavaliers, angry that a large sum he had taken in loot had been picked from his pocket, seized a young woman, stripped her, and scattered gunpowder over her breasts, setting them alight. Bruno Ryves, one of the king's most zealous propagandists, claimed that as the roundheads were marching through Chipping Norton a women called out 'God bless the Cavaliers'. They tied her to a cart, stripped her to the waist, and scourged her back to the bones with horsewhips. Then they dragged her through the mud still tied to the wagon, the stones cutting her bare feet, and as a result she died a few days later.[60] At Lostwithiel the townsfolk were even more vicious. 'I saw them strip a woman,' wrote an eyewitness of the parliamentary surrender in 1644. 'She had lain in but three days before. They took her by the hair of her head and threw her into the river, and there almost drowned her. The woman died within twelve hours.' So horrible was this crime that Charles ordered the murderers hanged.[61]

None the less incidents such as these against women were remarkably rare—at least in the First English Civil War. In all of these cases the perpetrators were under some degree of provocation, which the helplessness of their victims seemed to exacerbate—a royalist officer described the roundheads taken at Lostwithiel as sheep.[62] Just like the massacre of the Welsh women (who spoke no English) after Naseby, they were crimes of power committed by frightened, angry men, who were relieved at being alive, against those least able to defend themselves.

RAPE

Rape is, of course, just such a crime. Rape is not so much a crime of sexual passion as it is one of hatred and violence. As the Russian Army demonstrated in 1945, or the warring factions in Bosnia have shown more recently, the ultimate act of aggression and humiliation of an enemy is the systematic violation of their women.

There was no shortage of stories about rape during the civil wars. According to Bruno Ryves some roundheads propositioned a couple of chambermaids at the Swan Inn, Wellingborough. When they refused the soldiers shot one woman, and wounded the other. *The Scourge of Civil Warre: the Blessings of Peace* (1645) reported how a mother was forced 'to behold the Ravishment of her own daughters'.[63] William Trumbell, a gentleman from Berkshire, alleged that troops

The Thirty Years War
by Vrancx

Long before hostilities started in the three Stuart kingdoms civilians were only too aware of the horrors of war from events on the continent. Pamphlets described atrocities in graphic terms. Conditions became so bad in Germany that Nehemiah Wallington, the London artisan, was convinced 'they did boil whole pots and kettles of frogs and eat them with their entrails'. Vranx's painting shows soldiers plundering a German village, the body of a raped woman being clearly visible in the foreground.

billeted in his house snatched a servant from her bed and assaulted her.[64] General Fairfax explained the rape of a farmer's wife at Otley, Yorkshire by reporting that the three cavaliers were French mercenaries. Sir Samuel Luke, the parliamentarian scout-master who ran a fairly reliable spy network, reported that during the spring of 1645 in Northamptonshire Sir Marmaduke Langdale's men plundered and ravished without mercy. They tied up the men, before debauching their wives and daughters before them. They raped a pregnant wench, and, worse still, violated a gentlewoman and her daughter.

At the time many believed such tales. For one thing they were perfectly possible. The abuse of women, particularly by soldiers, has always been far too common. Stories of rape frightened the 'The Virgins of Norwich' into raising money to equip a troop of horse, known as 'the maiden's troop' to protect their hymens from cavalier lusts.[65] Nehemiah Wallington, the London artisan, recorded numerous atrocity stories in his commonplace-book. 'Women and Children put before the cannon', 'plundering and firing at Oakingham', 'savage cruelty at Bristol', he noted with credulous horror. He also copied out reports of the massacre of the Welsh women after Naseby with obvious satisfaction.[66]

Few soldiers were punished for rape. On 24 May 1645 Captain Richard Symonds watched every carter in the army's baggage train give a soldier, who was tied to a tree naked from the waist up, a lash for ravishing two women. The two sets of surviving civil war court martial papers contain few cases of rape. None of the thirty-seven soldiers tried by court martial in Sir William Waller's army between April and December 1648 were charged with sexual offences. Six of the fifty-five cases tried by Cromwell's forces in the Dundee area between September 1651 and January 1652 dealt with sexual matters. Yet five of these were for fornication, while one was for attempted rape—for which the soldier was sentenced to sixty lashes and imprisoned during Cromwell's pleasure.

It could be argued that rape has always been an underreported and underpunished crime, particularly by armies which stress masculine violence. Some feminists have argued that rape is 'The mother's milk of militarism': inevitable whenever men go to war. Yet the punishments handed out by the Dundee courts martial were particularly ferocious especially when the crimes involved women —forty to sixty lashes being the norm for fornication—because the army was trying to rebuild relations with the local population. Commanders have traditionally punished rape less for the hurt it inflicts on the victims, than for the damage it does to military discipline and civilian relations. The fact that propagandists did not include stories of rape in their descriptions of atrocities would support the view that it was surprisingly absent during the civil wars. While both sides attributed all too many atrocities to each other during the Irish massacres of 1641, violation of women was conspicuous by its dearth. For instance, the few references to rape in the 1641 depositions usually relate to servant girls whom the Irish insurgents 'took to themselves to keep and to use or rather abuse as a whore'.[67]

Though rape may have occurred rarely in Ireland the experience nevertheless left another young woman feeling physically sick and believing that 'she would never be well nor in her right mind again the act was so foul and grievous unto her'.[68] Similarly in Scotland, despite the extreme brutality of some of the campaigns, cases of rape appear to be rare. However, they did occur: in the wake of the First Bishops' War Argyll's followers raided the island of Colonsay, stripping and raping the women, 'which barbarity was never practised by the Turks'.[69] When Montrose's troops captured Aberdeen they 'spoiled the houses and deflowered the women. Such was the wickedness of the villains,' Robert Douglas sombrely noted in his diary.[70] A 1644 pamphlet described the many outrages committed by recently demobilized troopers. It gave details of gangs operating in Hull, Berwick, Cambridgeshire, Hyde Park, Southwark, Cheapside, Watford, and Islington and even described how at Berwick Trooper John Hawkins and 'his Irish accomplice held up half a dozen young ladies 'and robbed them of all but of what? Their Maidenheads'.[71]

Plunder

If few women were robbed of their maidenheads during the civil wars, many civilians were at one time or another plundered of their possessions. The English language reflected this important change. Although the word 'plunder' was first used in 1632 it became commonplace a decade latter. In November 1642 *A Relation of the King's Army* described how after capturing Brentford 'they plundered it without any respect of persons'. The same month the mayor and corporation of Sandwich complained that 'the cavaliers are extremely outrageous in plundering when they come, putting no difference at all between friends and supposed enemies'.[72] At Weverham, they rounded up all the elders, tied them to a cart, and dragged them through the mud to a dungeon, in which they spent the night without food or light to persuade them to reveal where they had stashed their goods. On the following day—a sabbath, Puritans noted with added horror—the royalists plundered the village without let or hindrance.

Plunder was widespread in both Scotland and Ireland. In August 1640 Argyll's men did 'most cruelly and barbarously burn the principal dwelling house' at Keppoch, while furniture, outhouses, barns, crops, and livestock belonging to other MacDonalds were either pillaged or destroyed.[73] The covenanters repeatedly ransacked the homes and estates of Scottish royalists, especially those living in the north-east; while between 1644 and 1645 Montrose and his forces systematically plundered the lands and goods of their enemies, especially the Campbells of Argyll. Urban centres also suffered, particularly Aberdeen, which was situated at the epicentre of the civil wars in Scotland and between 1639 and 1646 changed hands nineteen times. By 1650 the combination of plague and pillage had reduced the city to the brink of demographic and economic disaster.

The English Irish soldier

For soldiers plunder was a great motivation. It was not only profitable, but gave them a sense of power over those who in normal times were their social superiors. Conversely, plundering terrified civilians not merely because they lost property, but because it violated their self-respect. This 'English-Irish soldier', who 'had rather eate than fight', is from a broadside ballad of 1642.

In Ireland the lack of regular pay and other basic necessities meant that in-discriminate plunder and pillage were commonplace. For example, in July 1647 parliamentary troops garrisoned in Dublin plundered the local markets, shops, and homes before breaking into and robbing the excise house. The citizens were horrified and remonstrated at once to Westminster about 'the enemy abroad and the soldiers at home'.[74] An added threat came from renegade soldiers who ter-rorized the local populace, especially in remote regions, by becoming highway-men, robbers, and murderers. Garrisons like the one in County Roscommon were, according to one source, 'continually active, plundering and preying the country at their pleasure'.[75]

Surprisingly many young men—once law-abiding, sober citizens—felt hardly a scrap of shame after they joined the army and became enthusiastic pillagers. Take Nehemiah Wharton, the London apprentice, whose war began in August 1642 with an orgy of plunder. Near Acton he and his comrades robbed an old man of all his clothes, furniture, and fittings. 'I found him sitting on his only stool, with tears flowing down his hoary beard,' reported a bystander. At Wendover Sergeant Wharton's regiment chopped up the altar rails for firewood. They 'pillaged to the skin' the rector of Southam, Warwickshire—, 'a very malignant town', Wharton explained by way of excuse. They poached so many deer from the parks of great houses that the sergeant boasted to his master back in London that 'venison is almost as common with us as beef is with you'.[76]

There was something casually cruel about the looting by Wharton and his comrades, who cynically maintained that 'all rich men are Roundheads'. They plundered the house of John Penrudock, a Catholic from Ealing, taking all his furniture, leaving him not even a chair or bed, before maliciously vandalizing his garden and ripping up all his fruit trees. At Castlemorton, Worcester, they looted Rowland Bartlett's house.[77] Far from expressing any remorse, Wharton, a religious young man, described this experience in Bunyanesque terms as his 'pilgrimage'. Having presumably been well brought up to respect property, he pillaged with the brutal enthusiasm of a godless veteran of the Thirty Years War. And if the troopers did feel any guilt about stealing the goods of their fellow countrymen they soon assuaged it by listening to 'a famous sermon' or two from the regimental chaplain.

VICTIMS

The victims were not able to overcome the experience so easily. The author of *A Relation of the Rare Exploits of the London Soldiers* (1642), wondered how 'these strange inhumanities' were possible, particularly when 'they are practised amongst Christians against Christians'. The excuse that the prey were papists rang hollow. 'Were they Jews or Atheists it is a stain,' the pamphlet indignantly maintained. Anyway, religion was all too often a rationale for vandalism and greed. During the sack of Winchester in 1645 'our unruly soldiers' looted all the houses, and then 'found a great store of Popish books, pictures and crucifixes,' which they triumphantly carried through the streets to the market-place with an enthusiasm apparently enhanced by the excessive use of liberated alcohol.[78]

The first—and quite literally vital—lesson the victims of plunders then (like those of muggers today) had to learn was not to resist. In October 1642, when the war was but ten weeks old, Mr Rellisone tried to use his bow to stop Sir Francis Wortley's men from pillaging Bakewell House, Warwickshire. They murdered him. The following year a foraging party shot and killed Edward Morgan when he tried to prevent them requisitioning two of his master's oxen from Brampton Park. In 1644, just outside Leicester, a hapless carter met the same fate trying to stop a patrol of Lord Hasting's royalists from seizing his load of plums and spices. That June a cavalier raiding-party shot dead the landlord of the Red Lion Inn, Dunstable, when he protested against the seizure of his horses. The following year Andrew Pottinger, a substantial freeholder and parliamentary partisan, with a wife and six young children, died from being hit on the head as he tried to stop roundheads from the Newbury garrison rustling his sheep.

William Harvey, the physician who discovered the circulation of blood, frequently declared that, of all the losses he sustained at the hands of the roundheads during the civil wars, 'none was so crucifying to him' as the malicious destruction of his papers, including the only manuscript of his book *De Insectis*.[79] Bulstrode Whitelocke described how in November 1642 Rupert's troops plundered his house, Fawley Court. The royalists ate all his food, killed his deer, presented his prize hounds to Prince Rupert, broke open his trunks and chests, slashed up his beds strewing feathers all over the place, and stole his coach and horses.

The experience could leave scars that might last a lifetime. Take, for example, the Reverend Ralph Josselin, minister of Earls Colne. When the royalists entered the Essex village on 12 June 1648 they plundered indiscriminately and started looking for roundheads. Fearing arrest, Josselin, who had served as a parliamentary chaplain, escaped to the neighbouring village of Coggeshall. The next day he returned. The royalists spotted him when his baby daughter cried out for her father. Josselin ran, trying to take refuge in a neighbour's house. But she refused him sanctuary for fear of being further plundered. 'It cut my heart to see my life no more regarded by her, and it was the greatest danger and trouble to my spirit for present that I ever met with,' wrote Josselin.[80] One wonders how over the years, for the minister lived in Earls Colne until his death in 1683, he and his unnamed neighbour felt as they met on the street, raised a glass in the inn, or worshipped together at divine service.

This sense of being ravaged by foe and fair-weather friends alike was not confined to parliamentarians. Having his horse stolen by a roundhead troops so upset Alexander Brome that he wrote a poem trying to sort out his feelings, which ranged from a violent desire to see the thief hanged, to the philosophical resignation 'that all worldly goods are frail'.[81]

Memorial of Dr William Oldys

Fearing for his safety, the Anglican vicar of Adderbury, Oxfordshire, Dr William Oldys, had sought refuge in the royalist stronghold at Banbury. However, as he accompanied his family on a trip to nearby Oxford in September 1645 a party of parliamentarian soldiers intercepted and shot him. The family memorial in Adderbury church remembers him as 'a strenuous upholder of the threatened cause of religion and majesty, struck down by rebel soldiers near this town, 1645, aged 55'.

Some tried to avoid being plundered by moving away. In late September 1643 Mrs Joyce Jeffries shut up her house in Hereford, which she believed was vulnerable to attack, to move to her country home in Kilkinton. It did not work. The following month Captain Hammon 'and his barbarous company spoiled her of her goods, coaches linen and money'.[82] Desperate, the widow paid a neighbour to hide her few remaining valuables. The tactic backfired. When the troopers returned the following March they were so angry to find the cupboard bare that they smashed in all the locks to her house. Most folk soon learned how to conceal their valuables. Lady Sussex put them in the turret room over her bedroom which she walled up. As she ostentatiously dined off pewter, she told enquirers that she had sold all her silver. The owner of Dimsdale Farm near Edgehill hung his plate down the well, while Abel Barker, a gentleman from Hambleton, Rutland, kept no cash on his person lest it be stolen.

The trouble with running away from plunderers was that they also plied their trade upon the way. Eight highway men relieved Lady Lambert of £8 on the road near Alton. Colonel Hasting's troops based in Asby-de-la-Zouch became so notorious that they were known as the 'Rob-carriers' because they plundered so many pack trains. One of their victims was Daniel Gittins, a farm manager from Blackwell Hall, who was travelling on business when they robbed him of his horse, saddle-bag, cane, and buck-skinned coat at the Wheatsheaf Inn, Daventry. When their efforts to use soap and water to pry off his wedding ring failed, the troopers threatened to smash his brains out, and trample him under their horse's hooves. Only the intervention of the serving-girls from the inn saved Gittins's life.

COMPASSION AND CRUELTY

Occasionally plunderers showed compassion. Billeted in the house of a heavily pregnant gentlewoman near Appleby during the 1648 invasion, Sir James Turner discovered a cache of gold coins hidden under the floorboards. In tears the lady explained that her husband was such a spendthrift that, without him knowing, she had to skim the money from her allowance to save it for a rainy day, such as her impending confinement. Turner returned the coins.

Most victims were not so lucky. Perhaps the most heart-rending story concerned Margery Royston, a widow from Warwickshire, who was robbed of the money she had painstakingly saved to reclaim her 9-year-old daughter who had been shipped as an indentured servant to Virginia. As she mourned for the child she would never see again so that a few troopers could enjoy an evening's carousing, Mrs Royston must have pondered the capriciousness of her fate. Innocent and guilty, friend and foe, honest men and crooks seemed to suffer equally from the whims of plunder. When the royalists took Cirencester in 1643 they freed John Plot, whom Parliament had imprisoned for his loyalty to the crown. He walked home from his cell only to find his house full of the king's soldiers who stole £1,200 which he never recovered. Plunder could destroy a lifetime's work. After watching the royalists rustle cattle in Worcester in 1646 a diarist noted, 'and so a poor honest man ruined in a one night what he hath laboured for all his days'.[83] In a similar vein, the earl of Clanricard complained that his estate in Galway yielded virtually no income because it was 'spoiled and pillaged by English and Irish, what one left always destroyed by the other'.[84] A doggerel verse summed up the pain of being plundered by both sides without rhyme, reason, or mercy:[85]

> I had six oxen the other day
> And them the Roundheads got away.
> A mischief on them speed.
> I had six horses in the hole
> And them the Cavaliers stole.
> I think in this they are agreed.

THE WORLD TURNED UPSIDE DOWN

The implicit violence and irrationality of plunder made many lose faith in a reasonable orderly world. After some cavaliers stole his possessions, John Jones, a royalist from Flint, complained that their action was 'against the Laws of this Land, the Covenant of this State, and the Oath of a King'.[86]

Interestingly enough the perpetrators accepted a similar argument. Thomas Chadwick suggested to Hugh Kidd that they should break into Beresford Hall since 'there was no other law now'.[87] And to prove the point that the rule of the gun had replaced that of the law, Chadwick was shot and killed during the robbery. Captain Antonio Vernatti used the same rationale to excuse the protection racket he and his troops set up at Hatfield Close, Yorkshire. Having escaped from a debtor's prison in London, Vernatti broke into Herbert Le Roy's home, stealing £10. He threatened to burn down Charles Weterlow's house if he did not hand over his livestock and plough, and spurned the orders of the earl of Newcastle, the local royalist commander, to stop by, explaining that there was no longer any law in force forbidding his extortions.

Plunder often reduced victims to despair. After losing all his goods worth several hundred pounds Silvester Warner of Marston, Warwickshire, prayed 'God will either take him out of this world or make him more able to undergo these burdens'.[88] In the spring of 1644 Ranulph Crewe told a friend that having being pillaged on several occasions of everything he owned, he had nothing left in life to lose. 'I mourn and groan to think' Ranulph concluded, 'of the coming campaign season, with its devastation and impoverishment.'[89]

RAMPAGING ROYALISTS

If the campaigning season of 1644 was bad for the royalists, that of 1645 proved even worse. Vanquished troops tend to plunder more than victorious ones,

MAD FASHIONs,
OD FASHIONS,
All out of Faſhions,
OR,
The Emblems of theſe Diſtracted times.

By *Iohn Taylor*.

LONDON,
Printed by *Iohn Hammond*, for *Thomas Banks*, 1642.

The World turned upside down

While war might be the natural order for soldiers, in those distracted times everything was out of fashion for civilians. This woodcut shows a mouse chasing a cat, a rabbit hounding a dog, a horse driving a cart, and a human body completely out of order. The same could be said of the body politic.

because they not only need food and money as their supply systems break down but seek an outlet for the anger and frustration of defeat. While no means unique, the experience of the villages of Brent Knoll, Somerset, in March 1645 is perhaps the best recorded example of what such a clash between desperate soldiers and vulnerable civilians was like. Men broke into John Jones's house to steal twenty-five shillings, and took twelve bushels of malt and six yards of cloth from William Weakes' home. Three troopers, Francis Swift, Richard Hutchings, and John Parsons, who were billeted on Henry Simons, stole his 'fat Bullock', which they gave to a servant. When Simons tried to reclaim it they beat him up, and threatened to run his wife through with their swords if she did not fetch a rope to hang her husband. Discretion proved the better part of matrimony. Having placed the noose about Simons's neck, with many foul oaths the soldiers swore to string him up. Only the immediate offer of twenty shillings assuaged their anger and saved his life. Over a period of eleven days (that included an Easter Sunday) the royalists plundered £687 worth of goods from eighty-five inhabitants of Brent Knoll. (In the same time they took £850 from the smaller adjacent hamlet of Berrow, after threatening to burn every house there to the ground.) Losses suffered in Brent Knoll ranged from Thomas Coulbroke's four shillings to John Somerset's £100.

Thus it is no surprise that John Somerset—who had once served the crown as a captain—became the village Hampden. On 4 April he led a spontaneous attack against the soldiers. Armed only with pikes, staves, and muskets they caught the troopers napping. Although no one died, several were wounded, including an officer who was shot in the thigh. When he banged at Thomas Gilling's door demanding sanctuary from the pursuing mob, Gilling told him to 'begone, begone'. Once reinforcements arrived from royal garrison at Bristol the villagers did not have a chance. They were harshly fined. Colonel Ascough had Somerset and Gilling arrested on the general charge of leading an 'insurrection' against his majesty's forces, and specifically for ordering Private Abraham Williams to be beaten up. Ascough could well have trumped up the charge to justify his men's plunder. None the less their lawyer, William Morgan, advised Somerset and Gilling that if they went before a court martial they had not a chance of proving either their innocence or the soldier's crimes. From Bristol gaol the pair petitioned Sir Ralph Hopton and the prince of Wales to be released, and after five weeks they were freed on bail. Never brought to trial, and having forfeited their bail money, they returned home to survive as best they could.

Neutralism: Clubmen

John Somerset and Thomas Gilling—together with the vast majority of the inhabitants of not just Brent Colne but every hamlet, village, and town in the land—would have said a heartfelt 'Amen' to the suggestion from Henry Townsend of Gloucester that a new verse should be added to the Church's litany: 'From the plundering of soldiers, their insolence, cruelty, atheism, blasphemy, and rule over us, Lord Deliver us.'[90] While still trusting the Almighty, some civilians, known as the clubmen, tried to deliver themselves from the insolence, cruelty, and plunder of soldiers. As one of their banners pithily put it:[91]

> If you offer to plunder or take our Cattle,
> Be assured we will bid you battle.

The clubman movement consisted of a series of spontaneous jaqueries— revolts of desperate peasants—which erupted in parts of the country that, as one of their leaders put it, had 'more deeply . . . tasted the Misery of this unnatural in-testine War'.[92] While clubmen occasionally voiced fairly sophisticated ideas, such as those drawn up on 24 June 1645 in 'The Desires and Resolutions of the clubmen of the Counties of Dorset and Wiltshire', the movement remained a disorganized gut reaction against the war and 'the outrages and violence of the soldiers'.[93]

In the first three months of 1645 clubmen revolts took place in the bitterly con-tested border counties of Shropshire, Worcestershire, and Herefordshire. Be-tween May and June they broke out in the western counties of Wiltshire, Dorset and Somerset. On 30 June–1 July 10,000 clubmen assembled at Cefn Oun, and Llantristant, Glamorganshire, to proclaim themselves the 'Peaceable Army'.[94] From September to November there were clubmen risings in Berkshire, Sussex, Hampshire, South Wales, and the Welsh borders. Notwithstanding the taunts of their opponents that they were nothing but a 'vulgar multitude ignorant of man-ners', all but the highest ranks of rural society joined the clubmen.[95] Quantity, admittedly, exceeded the quality. Twenty thousand clubmen were reported in Wiltshire and Devon, and 16,000 in Berkshire. Oliver Cromwell described the 10,000 protesters, whom he dispersed from Hambledon Hill on 2 August 1645, as 'poor silly creatures, whom if you please to let me send home, they promise to be very dutiful'.[96]

Perhaps as many as 600 clubmen were killed in the war, and about 700 briefly detained as prisoners, which would suggest that they were not as significant a force as recent research might imply. Yet the clubman movement, which was the most dramatic expression of a desire for neutrality, enhanced civilian control over the army, and the deep-seated determination that insolent, cruel, plundering, blaspheming soldiers would never again rule over free-born subjects was one of the most profound legacies of the civil wars.

Conclusion

The British and Irish Civil Wars turned the civilian world upside down. The Reverend Hinson, rector of Battle, Sussex, was one of tens, perhaps hundreds, of thousands to discover this terrible truth after the roundheads arrested him in July 1643. Taken to the local lock-up, he was put in a loathsome cell with a tinker, 'and he none of the jolliest', recalled the priest. Claiming seniority of tenure over his social superior, the ragamuffin refused to share the cell's single bench, forcing the Anglican divine to walk up and down all night to keep warm, the stone floor being too cold to sleep on.[97]

Such experiences profoundly affected civilians. 'As for soldiers,' wrote Sir Roger Burgoyne in 1645, 'I could never trust them.'[98] Bulstrode Whitelock, whose house Fawley Court was plundered to the bare walls in 1642, declared over two decades later that what most upset the English people was seeing 'servants riding on horseback and Masters in great want'.[99] William Dugdale agreed, when he declared that:[100]

> Beggars are Lords and Lords are beggars made
> The Holy war hath had a gallant trade,
> Knaves are ennobled, good men undone we see,
> Can a more thorough reformation be?

By 1660 the English people had had more than enough of 'reformation'. They had seen the growth of a powerful standing army under Cromwell and the development or radical military movements such as the Levellers, and had suffered under the rule of major-generals. They wanted a restoration not just of monarchy but of civilian hegemony. Once it returned William Blundell could rejoice:

> The husbandman may now enjoy his own
> And look the armed soldier in the face.[101]

Perhaps the abuses of the Cromwell's major-generals were exaggerated, but the fear of a standing army turned, in England at least, the revolution of 1688 into as bloodless a one as that of the 1640s had been bloody. This almost unconscious memory of the war remained within the Anglo-American tradition long after William Walker, the last surviving civil war soldier, died in Chelsea Hospital in 1736. The ghost of Oliver Cromwell sat with the Founding Fathers as they wrote the American Constitution in 1787; while in England the system of purchasing commissions remained in force until 1871 to make sure that no russet-coated captain could turn against his social and civilian betters. Since then, through two world wars, and the trauma of decolonization, civilian control over the armed forces has remained—a lasting legacy of the experience of the British and Irish Civil Wars.

BETWEEN WAR AND PEACE
1651–1662

JOHN MORRILL

Introduction

Countless historians have spoken of the civil wars ending in 1651; and countless historians have been wrong. The battle of Worcester may have been the last pitched battle of the British and Irish civil wars; but it was far from being the last military engagement of the period. The embers of Catholic royalist resistance in Ireland had yet to be extinguished—the last formal surrender of an organized Irish force took place at Cloghoughter on 27 July 1653—and guerrilla activities there continued throughout the 1650s. There was a major revolt in Scotland in 1653–5. It took 6,000 men eighteen months tramping up and down the glens of the north-west Highlands to put it down. The attempt of Charles II in the spring of 1655 to raise armed revolt in England may have been a series of damp squibs (the choice of Marston Moor and Rowton Heath as two of the rendezvous points for would-be insurrectionaries was unwise), but the second attempt—in the summer of 1659—brought 12,000 men together in a serious pitched battle at Winnington Bridge on the Mersey. Just as significant in different ways, in 1655 and 1656 6,000 British troops failed in an attempt to wrest Hispaniola (Cuba) from the Spaniards but succeeded in taking Jamaica as a consolation prize; and in 1657 a further 6,000 English troops were sent to fight alongside or within the French army in northern France and Flanders, where (at the battle of the Dunes) they came up against a smaller body of British and Irish troops in the Spanish service. This was not a decade devoid of military interest or significance.

The Standing Armies

There was thus no let-up in the sense of military crisis. Between 1651 and 1660 there were never less than 30,000 men in the standing armies of the Commonwealth and Protectorate (the figure stipulated in the Instrument of Government).[1] Indeed at times—as in 1652, in late 1654 and early 1655, and again in 1659—there were well over 50,000 men in arms. This is quite apart from the 'select militias', the highly trained and well-armed reservists who need to be added to any calculation of the forces at the disposal of the state.

Commonwealth and standing army

This engraving is an excellent example of royalist propaganda against the republican Commonwealth, represented here by the fierce Griffon. Ultimately Cromwell's power rested on a bed of pikes and after a royalist rising in March 1655 he resorted to blatant military rule when he divided England and Wales into ten districts and placed them under the command of senior army officers (the 'Major-Generals'). For much of the 1650s the standing army numbered some fifty thousand men and this combined with a navy of nearly 300 vessels gobbled up nine-tenths of the government's revenue. This naval and military might transformed England into a formidable power both at home and abroad. As a result Cromwell, according to one leading royalist historian, mounted 'himself into the throne of the three kingdoms without the name of a king but with greater power and authority than had ever been exercised or claimed by any king'.

IN ENGLAND

Although the total number of men in arms throughout Scotland and Ireland fluctuated wildly from month to month and year to year, the number in England remained fairly static. There was a significant demobilization and reorganization after the battle of Worcester, but from early 1652 to the winter of 1659/60 the number of men in England fluctuated between 10,000 and 13,500. There was a fairly stable presence of around 3,000 men in the City of London, and the remainder were largely distributed between garrisons.

In London, sections of the old royal palaces at Whitehall and St James were rebuilt as military barracks (this is where Cromwell's own regiments of foot and horse were permanently located). Between 1657 and 1650 (as between 1647 and 1649) the nave of St Paul's Cathedral was also used for companies of cavalry. Cromwell's own men apart, most of the other men defending the capital were stationed in the suburbs.[2] Most of the garrisoned towns were situated around the coasts and along the Welsh and Scottish borders, and very few of them contained more than a few hundred troops. Regiments kept their own clear identity, but no regiment in England was kept together in one place. They were usually broken up into companies, one or more company serving its turn either in a series of garrisons or in a tour of duty in Scotland. Over time the number of garrisons was reduced, especially at times of financial shortage. This was not a straightforward matter, for strong fortifications were expensive to build and to maintain; and they could not be left behind by a departing garrison. So a decision to abandon a garrison also involved a decision to sleight defence works often expensively built or strengthened only shortly before. There was considerable debate on this issue. In 1656 the prolix and offensively opinionated William Prynne—who had been sentenced by Star Chamber to lose the tips of his ears in 1633 for libelling the queen and the stumps of his ears in 1637 for libelling the bishops, and who had spent much of the 1640s attacking both clerical power and those who supported religious freedom—turned his attention to the problem of fortifications and the interference of soldiers in civilian life. At inordinate length he denounced the whole strategy of dispersing troops around peripheral garrisons, and he demanded the demolition of *all* forts (see Chapter 6). It was a campaign for which he secured more support than was his wont.[3] In fact, it was already a diminishing problem. Back in 1649 there had been around sixty fortified towns in England and Wales; but by the middle of the Protectorate there were about half of that number, with the result that most of those great medieval castles of England which had not had huge holes blown in their walls at the end of civil-war sieges, were now breached by explosives to render them indefensible for the time to come.

IRELAND AND SCOTLAND

If the number of soldiers in England remained fairly stable over time, the number of men in Scotland and Ireland rose and then fell over the period 1651–60. In Ireland the number peaked at 23,000 in the early part of the Protectorate before falling back to just over 10,000 by early 1659; while in Scotland it rose to almost 19,000 at the height of Glencairn's rebellion in the winter of 1654/5, but was down to 10,000 by the summer of 1657 and 7,700 in the spring of 1659.[4]

The army in Scotland was supposed to be supplied by short tours of duty by detachments from regiments also based in England. There was a notional two-year rota for each regiment (though they were to serve under a permanent general staff there), but this was very slackly observed: only a few men from Cromwell's own regiments served there after 1651, and Lambert's and Whalley's regiments also saw little service, whereas Hacker and Berry's regiments each served in Scotland for four years.[5] None the less there was no distinction between the duty of service in England and Scotland, whereas the army of Ireland not only had its own general staff, but—once the conquest was complete—regiments which were permanently stationed there,[6] all under colonels who had never served in the New Model.

OVERSEAS

The two major overseas expeditions of the 1650s were mongrel armies, made up of men culled from existing British and Irish regiments, from volunteers drawn from soldiers previously demobilized, and from fresh recruits. Few officers with extensive New Model experience were seconded to these expeditions, however. Thus the general commanding the expedition to the West Indies was Robert Venables, whose military career in the First Civil War had been in Sir William Brereton's Cheshire Army, and who had served since 1649 in Ireland, latterly as commander of the forces in Ulster. His regiment was made up of 1,000 men culled from English regiments and 1,500 new recruits (he later bitterly complained that he was not allowed to select men from his Irish regiments). His second-in-command, William Brayne, had served mainly in Scotland, most recently as governor of Inverlochy (the core of his regiment comprised forty-two men drawn from each of the twelve regiments serving at that time in Scotland, and most of his junior officers were raised from the ranks of that army); and the next man in seniority was Anthony Buller who had served in Massey's Western Brigade and then as governor of the Scilly Isles.[7]

The 6,000 men sent to Flanders in April 1657 comprised about 1,500 troops drawn from regiments in England and 4,500 volunteers, many retired veterans. The commander was Sir John Reynolds, the commissary general in Ireland and his number two was Major General Thomas Morgan, currently second in command to Monck in Scotland. Only one of the other four regimental commanders —Roger Alsop—had already held a commission in the regular army; two of the others had experience as mercenaries in the Dutch service; and the fourth was a former Scottish covenanting officer.[8]

The military structure of the 1650s was thus complex. The British army that is, the army of England and Scotland, not the separate army of Ireland—saw very considerable continuity of command—more than ninety per cent of the majors, colonels, and other field officers serving in 1659 had been in the army in 1649. Promotion within the British army throughout the decade was fairly strictly by seniority. Eight senior officers resigned or were cashiered in the period and most of the replacements were 'insiders'; the only outsiders were men sent to bring the Northern Brigade more under Cromwell's control after the fall of John Lambert, the one semi-autonomous regional commander in the Commonwealth and early Protectorate. Almost three-quarters of all promotions to lieutenant-colonel and major went to the senior major or captain already *en poste*. In contrast, there was an enormous turnover of the rank and file. Between 1649 and 1652 crown lands worth £1.5 million had been sold by the Commonwealth. The only way that this land could be acquired was with military debentures—certified statements of arrears owing to each and every soldier. There had been an active debentures market with officers and civilians buying up—at discounts of at least fifty per cent—the certificates of the common soldiers. Be that as it may, it seems that a high proportion of the soldiery took their arrears and left the army.[9] Against the very stable membership of the officer corps, the continuity rate amongst the soldiery may have been as low as twelve to twenty per cent (the figures for the two regiments for which a calculation can be made).[10] There is a similar pattern in Ireland, with a low turnover of officers—except that plague and contagious disease took a grim toll of officers as well as men—and a large replacement rate in the rank and file, especially once the 12,000 men who acquired Irish land in settlement of their arrears had proceeded to settle on it in the mid-1650s.[11] This certainly helps to explain the politics of the army in the 1650s, for while the *officers* at the height of the Protectorate were men who had been serving during the heady days of 1647, 1648, and 1649 when the army debated the future of the king, of the state, of the world, few of the soldiers had been so involved. They had no proud memory of the regimental discussions and petitioning on fundamental human rights, of the great prayer-meetings at which the will of God inspired a select few to exact justice on the men of blood, of seeing king and parliament bend the knee before them. This new army would have to be radicalized all over again and despite arrears mounting inexorably in the late 1650s, it did not happen. The army of the late 1650s may have commanded events, but the officers caballed together; they did not have to hold back a rank and file straining at the leash.[12]

Auxiliary Forces

The Commonwealth and Protectorate were thus highly militarized. By far the greater part of the standing army was stationed outside England and Wales, but that was not because successive regimes were complacent about the security situation. It was because those regimes had consistently to balance the need for a military presence against the need to keep down defence costs: the higher the rates of taxation, the greater the potential unrest and the greater the need for additional troops and thus for extra taxation. To break out of this vicious circle, successive governments tried to transfer much of the business of regional security to local militias paid for by local taxation. To an extent unthinkable in the period down to the 1630s, the standing army and the militias were made to work together as an integrated force. Thus, the 'general militia' of all counties—that is, the regularly trained standby forces supported by a general levy on property holders—was called up to supplement garrisons whenever detachments of the regular army were called away to deal with national crises. This had been successfully pioneered during the Third Civil War: for example, Essex militia troops were made entirely responsible for the defence of Colchester and Mersea Island, and the governors of King's Lynn and Yarmouth were given authority to call in militiamen to supplement their garrisons as they saw need. More dramatically, however, the Rump Parliament gave its Council of State a free hand to deploy the militia as they saw fit: and as a result militia troops from East Anglia and elsewhere were marched across England—without a peep of the protest that deploying militia outside county boundaries had engendered in 1639 and 1642. At the battle of Worcester, more than one-third of Cromwell's army was made up of militiamen.[13] Similar attempts to deploy the general militia not as a fully regimented force, but as a pool of men with basic training for supplementing garrisons and standing regiments, was attempted in 1655 and 1659, although with less impressive effect.

THE MAJOR-GENERALS

There was yet one more piece to the jigsaw. Alongside the general militia, successive regimes encouraged the systematic development of standing volunteers, drawn mainly from demobilized veterans. This policy was most aggressively and damagingly pursued in late 1655 and 1656 when the lord protector divided England and Wales into eleven districts, each of which was sent a senior army commander as 'Major-General' with the express purpose of raising just such stand-by forces maintained by a discriminatory 'decimation' tax on those families ever convicted of royalist leanings. Yet it is often forgotten that there was nothing new about the idea of a select militia, and that the purpose of the 1655 reforms was both to *reduce* the size of the standing army and to halve direct taxation on the bulk of the population in exchange for this less visible and less expensive form of local defence. The principle of licensing well-affected and experienced men to raise, train, and equip volunteer forces dates back to 1648 (and, in a sense, to 1642—what else was Cromwell doing at Huntingdon in the summer of that year?) when Parliament permitted men like Henry Marten, Lord Grey, and John Pyne to do so.[14] In 1651 the Council of State again experimented with volunteer regiments supported by local subscription. The novelty in 1655/6 was not the raising of volunteer regiments of reservists to replace the standing army, but the discriminatory and extra-legal taxation used to maintain them. There are striking similarities between these English schemes and ones attempted by Henry Cromwell in Ireland at the same time, once more focused on demobilized veterans.[15]

The English Navy

At the height of the civil wars, Parliament had forty-four warships, and about fifty armed merchantmen, thirty of the latter in mothballs. Between 1649 and 1660 no less than 216 ships were added to the force, about half of them prize ships mainly captured from the Dutch or from corsairs, but many of the rest purpose-built state-of-the-art warships.[16] The new ships bore the proud names of parliamentarian land victories in the civil wars—the *Naseby*, the *Nantwich*—or of their commanders—the *Fairfax*, the *Warwick*—or of the officers of the Common-wealth—the *Speaker*, the *Lord General*. The greatest increase came for and during the First Anglo-Dutch War (1652–4) but while Cromwell spent much of the later 1650s trying to scale back on the size of his armies, he made no attempt to reduce the navy; and indeed for the first time in its history, the English navy can be said to have ruled the waves.

In the two years after the battle of Worcester, the Rump and its successor spent more money on a naval war against the Dutch than they paid out for the whole of the conquest of Scotland and Ireland—£2.16 million was spent in the calendar year 1653 alone. It allowed them to grind down the Dutch. After a year in which neither gained an advantage, Admiral Blake (see picture on p. 188) won a series of heavily contested exchanges, especially one off Portland Bill in mid-March 1653 which closed the Channel to Dutch merchant shipping and forced it round the north of Scotland. The four-day battle off Harwich in June 1653 in which Blake sank twenty of the 110 ships that Admiral Tromp brought to break the blockade of the Channel and dispersed the rest effectively settled the war and transformed the balance of naval power.[17] For the rest of the decade—for the whole period of the Protectorate—a swollen English fleet took on all comers and challenges: privateers in the Baltic, the Flanders ports, Biscay, the coast of North Africa; offensives against Portugal and Spain; expeditions to the Canaries and the Caribbean; seaborne umpiring in the Baltic. Every year brought its successes and only the Western Design (see below) proved a serious check. By the end of the decade, the navy was engaged in complex and effective amphibious operations to sustain the Anglo-French assault on Spanish Flanders.

Employments of the Army

Between 1642 and 1651 perhaps as many as 80,000 soldiers lost their lives in battle and of war-related physical injury. In the period 1651 to 1660 the number of troops loyal to the Interregnum governments who died as a direct result of fighting was probably in the region of 4,000–5,000 although rather more perished from the scourges of typhoid, cholera, plague, camp-fever, and other contagious diseases especially in the West Indies, Flanders, and Ireland. In addition an unknown number died resisting Commonwealth and Protectorate governments, either as royalists fighting in the British regiments within the Spanish armies, in insurrections within Britain and Ireland, or as guerrillas—tories in Ireland, mosstroopers in Scotland—who were at once freedom-fighters and bandits.[18]

The first task of the soldiery in the 1650s was thus soldiering. Few of the regiments were allowed to go soft. Regiments alternated between turns of garrison duty in England and tours of duty in Scotland, and men from all units were regularly culled—as often as not by lot—to foreign service. A soldier in Whalley's regiment, for example, who served from 1651 to 1660 would have seen active service in six or seven different locations with exposure to differing levels of military risk and action, and that regiment is likely to be typical.[19]

IN ENGLAND

In England, few shots were fired in anger between 1651 and 1655. In the late winter of 1655 the royalists planned a series of co-ordinated risings across the country, but in the event most of those who had pledged themselves got cold feet and dispirited bands of conspirators counted by the dozen not by hundred gathered on blasted heaths near York, Chester, Salisbury, and elsewhere and slunk away. Only the Salisbury band persisted, and that was because while they were furtively gathering, a judge on his way to the assizes rode past and they took him hostage. For several days they moved steadily west, away from London, gathering strength too slowly until finally challenged by a detachment of the New Model. After little more than a scuffle they were disarmed and arrested, subsequently to be executed or transported to Barbados. Elsewhere the army had to assist in the rounding-up and incarceration of suspected insurgents. It was the dampest of damp squibs although when called upon to turn out, the militia had prevaricated almost as much as royalists had done; and it was this which lay behind Cromwell's decision to introduce the Major-Generals and the select militia drawn from the demobbed veterans.[20]

The army was more active in the summer of 1659. Once more a major series of risings was planned but only one of them—that led by Sir George Booth in the greater Manchester area—got off the ground. By now disillusionment with a disintegrating central authority led the local governors to wait upon events. This compelled John Lambert to march from London with 2,000 men and to link up with troops sent over from Ireland and Yorkshire to make a force of 5,000 or so men. Although he had more than a week to take the initiative—to seize Chester, retreat to the Welsh hills or the Lancashire bogs—Booth simply stood still and awaited his fate. Lambert threw his full weight against him at Winnington Bridge near Warrington. Several hundred men were killed and the rest seized or scattered. Although there was skirmishing between detachments of the disintegrating Commonwealth army during the winter of 1659/60, that really was the last battle of the British Civil Wars.[21]

IN IRELAND AND SCOTLAND

The situation in Ireland was consistently more tense: the army was confronted by widespread brigandage and persistent guerrilla-raiding from the bogs of the north Midlands and north-west and the mountain ranges to the south of Dublin. Judges, and other officials such as tax collectors, needed armed escorts and ambushes were commonplace. The brutality of the relations between the communities in Ireland can be seen in the series of proclamations issued by Charles Fleetwood in which he threatened reprisals against the inhabitants within which

Tomb of Sir William Waller (1597?–1668)

In the south transept of Bath Abbey stands a monument to Waller's first wife (d. 1633), with Waller reclining beside her. Waller, a Member of the Long Parliament and veteran of the Thirty Years War, successfully served as a colonel of parliamentary horse during the First English Civil War. The passage of the Self-Denying Ordinance in 1645 ended his military career and he became one of the leaders of the Presbyterian faction in Parliament. His determination to secure a settlement with the king earned him the enmity of the Army and he was excluded from Parliament during Pride's Purge (December 1648). Long stints in prison during the 1650s did not dampen his royalism and he played a prominent role in Booth's Rising (August 1659). The following year he allied with Monck and helped to facilitate the restoration of Charles II. He died in 1668 and lies buried in an unmarked grave in London.

an English soldier was killed: that community would be given a few hours to hand over the culprits or face mass deportation into slavery in the West Indies. Indeed in the course of the 1650s perhaps as many as 12,000 Irish were transported—that is in addition to the 35,000 former confederates driven abroad to seek their fortune as mercenaries.[22]

In Scotland, too, there was constant work to be done. In 1650–2 the armies of the Commonwealth had taken on and routed the armies of the covenant, those who had fought alongside the English Parliament in the 1640s. In 1653 they faced a new challenge from the Highland clans who had remained loyal to Charles I and had never recognized the covenant. These men had loitered in their fastnesses while Charles II dallied with the Presbyterians. Now they made their own bid to restore him at least to his Scottish throne. No less than thirteen Scottish peers pledged themselves to the exiled king, who responded by sending Lieutenant-General Middleton, a veteran of Preston and Worcester from St Germain to be their leader. For the best part of two years they tied down thousands of English troops by refusing to be drawn into an open battle and waging an opportunistic war against successive forces commanded first by Colonel Robert Lilburne and then Lieutenant-General George Monck (see picture on

p. 327). It was a war of attrition with many ambushes and skirmishes, during which thousands of clansmen and hundreds of English were killed; and it involved Monck and his deputy, Robert Morgan, in hundreds of miles of forced marches. There was no question that the English had the superiority of numbers, resources, discipline. The question was whether they had the superiority of will-power and the ability to keep the Lowlands quiet, especially since the costs of the campaign would need to be met in large part from Scotland. The English nerve held, and while taxation was high, so was Monck's willingness to soften the regime's attitude to its previous enemies. A notable easing of the policy of Anglicization and proscription prevented the spread of the revolt; and an iron grip was kept on all the routes from the Highlands to the Lowlands. The unflinching gaze of the English at their Highland foes, together with increasing shortages of supplies made worse by a brutal scorched earth policy, broke the will of the Scottish royalists. Once Monck started transporting to slavery in Barbados all those captured in arms, panic set in and bands of rebels began surrendering themselves. It was not a glamorous campaign, or a militarily interesting one, but it showed a ruthless efficiency and determination lacking elsewhere. Even after the embers of revolt had been stamped out, there was no complete safety. The English did not occupy the Highlands; they sealed it off from the Lowlands and took Danegeld from it, which no more put an end to the Scottish mosstroopers than repression in Ireland put an end to the tories and the woodkerne. As ever in Scottish history, pacifying the Lowlands was not to prove the same thing as pacifying Scotland.[23]

ANGLO-SPANISH WAR

However, if there was plenty to keep the army on red alert throughout the 1650s most of the fighting took place abroad in ambitious (and amphibious) operations on the Spanish Caribbean and in Flanders. In the winter of 1655–6, driven on by apocalyptic hopes and an utter belief that God wanted the English Revolution exported so that the world could be rid of popery and the menace of Antichrist, Cromwell sent an expedition to seize the treasure routes from Spanish America to Europe. The aim was to capture Hispaniola and from there to take over the isthmus of Panama and other key points in the Spanish supply lines. The diversion of gold and silver from Spanish to British coffers would allow the ultimate destruction of the Spanish war machine and of the sword arm of popery. To achieve this an amphibious force with an untried and unfortunate command structure was despatched. Admiral William Penn had executive authority over the fleet and General Robert Venables over the 6,000 horse and foot. Overall control of the expedition was entrusted to a five-man commission comprising the two commanders and three civilians. This turned out to be a recipe for disaster. Penn and Venables disliked one another and despised the civilians. Everyone quickly decided to ignore what everyone else said. Furthermore, the expedition was lavishly but inappropriately provisioned. Venables was used to fighting in

Ireland where food was scarce and water plentiful, quite the reverse of conditions in Hispaniola. A surfeit of knapsacks was no substitute for a dearth of leather water bottles in the parched circumstances of a three-day march across Hispaniola. Diseases induced by heat and insects combined with failures of co-ordination in amphibious operations and better than expected Spanish defence works at San Domingo to make the attempt on Hispaniola a fiasco. Although the effectively undefended Jamaica was claimed for the Protectorate as a consolation prize, a weakened and divided force was in no position to take on the main point of the expedition—the Spanish-American mainland—and no sooner was Jamaica taken than Penn and Venables, deserting their charge, set off in separate vessels in a race to get their version of events to the Council of State before the other one did. It ruined both their careers and broke Cromwell's nerve. He became convinced that the failure was a slap in the face from God, a reproof to the worldliness of his regime, perhaps to his secret musings over the prospects of the crown itself. It was an expensive failure in more senses than one.[24]

The first stage of the Spanish War had thus been a flop and the summer of 1656 saw little alleviation of the frustration. Blake and Montagu failed to deal decisively with the corsairs of either the Flanders ports of Ostend and Dunkirk or of North Africa, picking off a few minor prizes but failing to halt the widespread depredations on English shipping. A long blockade of Cadiz achieved nothing. However, the naval tide turned in September when Captain Stayner intercepted a Spanish treasure fleet and sank or captured all but two of its vessels. News of this reached London on 1 October 1656, the very day on which the second Protectorate Parliament had declared that 'the war against the Spaniard was undertaken on just and necessary grounds and for the good of the people of this Commonwealth'. It seemed highly auspicious. During the winter months that followed, a new dual strategy was planned and set into motion. In November Cromwell and Cardinal Mazarin pencilled an Anglo-French agreement for a joint amphibious assault on Gravelines, Mardyke, and Dunkirk, the first for the ownership of the French, the other two for the permanent ownership of the British (subject to the Protector guaranteeing the religious rights of the Catholic residents of those towns). The French would pay for the entire project and provide 20,000 troops; the English would despatch 6,000 foot and the bulk of the naval support. While preparations for this enterprise went ahead, the council also planned a second and more limited expedition against Spanish America, this time to seek out and destroy the main Spanish fleet and leave the treasure fleets defenceless before a British naval blockade of metropolitan Spain.

This second prong of the war was achieved first: Blake totally destroyed the Spanish fleet in the strongly defended harbour of Santa Cruz in the Canaries. In all, the Spanish fleet consisted of sixteen vessels, including seven great galleons of 1,000 to 1,200 tons, anchored broadside to the sea and protected by massive stone forts covered with batteries. It was a remarkable display of naval discipline and

Tempora mutantur et nos mutamur in illis.

OLIVAR·D·G·RP·ANG·SCO·HIBERNIÆ·PROTECTOR·

RETIRE·TOY·LHONNEVR·APPARTIENT·AV·ROY·MON·MAISTRE·

LOVIS·LE·GRAND·

The difference of Times, between those TIMES and these Times

BRITANNIA'S ISLE, like Fortune's Wheel,
In Politicks does daily reel.
What's up to day, to morrow's down;
And from a Smile ensues a Frown.

She Sits in pompous State you see,
And bears HIS HEAD upon her knee;
Whilst two Ambassadors contend,
Which first shall kiss his nether end.

This MEDDEL was struck in HOLLAND in the time of OLIVER CROMWELL, the reverse of which is, the FR··H, and SP···SH, EMBASADORS contending for the honour of their MASTERS, which should have the favour to kiss his —— so submisive ware those great powers in those days and so much aw'd that they dreaded a FROWN from the PROTECTOR.

Medal

Despite international condemnation, particularly by the Dutch, of the trial and execution of Charles I, the leading continental powers—led by Spain—quickly recognized the Commonwealth. One side of this satirical medal shows the Spanish and French ambassadors squabbling for the privilege of being the first to kiss Cromwell's 'nether end' (ironically war broke out with Spain shortly afterwards in 1656). The other shows Cromwell as Protector of England, Scotland, and Ireland. The medal was struck in Holland, no doubt at the height of the First Anglo-Dutch War (1652–4).

Cromwell dismissing the Rump

The 'Rump' of the Long Parliament was no revolutionary assembly (two-thirds of its members had not supported the regicide). While it made some attempt to create a godly society (it passed the Blue Laws in 1650 which legislated against blasphemy, drunkenness, and adultery), it proved unwilling to overhaul the legal system and refused to hold free elections as the New Model Army demanded. Unable to find a satisfactory compromise between the civilian politicians and his soldiers, Cromwell, as this Dutch engraving shows, expelled the Rump on 20 April 1653.

unflinching artillery action aided—so all reports made plain—by a Protestant wind that blew them into port and then turned round to allow them to effect a speedy withdrawal. Blake was the admiral commanding, but the plan of battle and the extraordinary leadership of the battle lay with Captain Richard Stayner, previously the victor at Cadiz, one of the most unsung heroes of the British navy.

Thereafter the navy was principally engaged in supporting the Anglo-French operations which led to the assault on the Flemish towns. These were far more tenaciously and strongly defended than had been anticipated and it took eighteen and not six months for the aims to be realized: but one by one Mardyke, Dunkirk, and Gravelines fell to them. The part played by the 6,000 soldiers—especially the astonishing assault of Sir William Lockhart's men up a strongly defended sandhill 150 feet high in the 'battle of Dunes' between Turenne's army and a Spanish relieving army during the siege of Dunkirk—should not be underestimated. As one veteran commander wrote: 'it was more steep than any ascent of a breach that I have ever seen'. However, the navy played a part at least as important—intercepting and destroying all manner of relief vessels, supplying the besiegers, and pouring lethal fire into besieged towns. The importance of the military aid afforded by the Protectorate strengthened Mazarin's resolve to honour the treaty and to hand over Mardyke and Dunkirk to English occupancy despite the protests of Louis XIV and the strength of French public opinion. The English honoured their obligations: the rights of Catholics, even of Catholic clergy in Dunkirk, were respected (in stark contrast to Ireland, where all Catholic clergy had been 'knocked on the head' even if they surrendered) and even after the two towns were in English hands, half the English expeditionary force stayed with Turenne and were instrumental in the ensuing capture of Gravelines and many other Flemish towns. Not since the early fifteenth century had the prowess of English arms stood so high in continental Europe as on the eve of the disintegration of the British army at home in 1659.[25]

Civilian Employments

IN ENGLAND

However, there was more to soldiering in the 1650s than fighting. The army in England found itself throughout the 1650s engaged in a wide range of security and civil employments. Small detachments of soldiers were constantly needed to perform guard duties in the movement of vital goods and supplies—such as convoys of timber. More controversially, small bodies of troops escorted collectors of the hated excise and sequestration officials as they moved round to collect rents or to manage the confiscated estates of former royalists—an activity that attracted a blast from John Lilburne in 1651.[26] Even more controversially, they were called in, often in significant numbers, to police civil disturbances.

For example, bodies of troops were used to subdue grain rioters in Wickham and enclosure rioters in Slimbridge, against striking keelmen at Newcastle, and (unavailingly as it turns out) to protect the drainage trenches dug in the Cambridgeshire fen at Bottisham and Swaffham Bulbeck. With an increase in highway robberies, regular patrols were established in the west Midlands, for example, and travellers found themselves required to carry safe conducts from officials of the government to be able to move any great distance from their homes. All these things are usually seen as aspects of the rule of the Major-Generals (1655–7); but as one historian has made clear, they did no more than bring to the fore activities that the army had been less formally handling for some years.[27]

Many parts of the country—especially inland counties—had little military presence and were thus little bothered by such intrusions into local affairs. However, those living in a garrison town would have to put up with such things and more. Newsbooks regularly record stories of soldiers disrupting civilian life, as by breaking up stage-plays, cockfights, morris dancing, and so on; and arresting and interrogating those suspected of threatening the peace—Quakers complain about this quite as much as former royalists. In some places detachments of soldiers would break up Anglican services,[28] in others they would protect sectarian gatherings from local magisterial disapproval and encourage townsmen to join their own free worship. It is no coincidence that some of the strongest centres of Dissent after 1660 had been garrison towns in the 1650s. Garrison commanders were frequently at odds with town officials over the custody of town keys or the costs of maintaining town walls, and many garrison officers intruded themselves on to local committees, including commissions of the peace.[29]

IN SCOTLAND AND IRELAND

None the less the army presence in England made an impact, however patchy and spasmodic. The army was far more active and visible in civil as well as in military affairs in Scotland and Ireland. An essential part of the settlement in Scotland after the conquest and assimilation was an attempted partnership between the English military and Scottish lairds. Thus when sheriffs were established in each of the nineteen Scottish shires in 1655, the initial scheme was to yoke together an English army officer and a prominent local man. Similarly perhaps one in four of all the newly established Justices of the Peace were serving officers in the army of occupation—the proportion of serving officers in England and Wales would never have been higher than three per cent. With time, more responsibility could be returned to 'trusty' Scots—officers ceased to act as joint sheriffs, for example. However, the army remained formally at the heart of law enforcement and 'the number of occasions on which General Monck had to intervene in the work of the justices suggests that the commission of the peace needed constant prodding from Army headquarters to carry out its duties'. The Scottish Council of State played second fiddle to the army when it came to day-to-day supervision of the Scottish regions.[30]

More than 30,000 English soldiers served in Ireland between 1647 and 1653 and each was issued with a debenture or certificate of the amount of arrears owing to them for their service. These certificates were redeemable only against confiscated Irish land. Almost two-thirds of them sold their debentures to their officers or to protestant Old English landowners for as little as forty per cent of their face value, and at least 7,500 but perhaps as many as 12,000 of them settled on the land, creating a new yeoman class. Many of them retained their arms and constituted a volunteer reserve force to supplement the standing army. It was from amongst the officers with their larger holdings made up of their own and the bought-in debentures that the Dublin authorities selected a high proportion of the new sheriffs and Justices of the Peace.[31]

Even with the volunteer reserve, the regime felt the need of a large standing army and the cost of this army over the period 1647–60 was well over £4 million: indeed it was averaging £300,000 in each year of the Protectorate. No more than half of this was raised within Ireland because of the economic recession following the years of destructive war and the systematic exclusion of the Catholic community from participation in trade and all aspects of local government. In a desperate attempt to reduce the charge of Ireland on the English exchequer, there was a marked liberalization in the later 1650s, usually linked to the arrival of Henry Cromwell as lord deputy in succession to his brother-in-law Charles Fleetwood. The 'Old Protestants'—the heirs of the Elizabethan and Jacobean planters and settlers—were put back into power at the expense of ex-soldiers; Catholics were allowed back into towns and participation in trade; and the army was winnowed of its more aggressive sectaries—the Baptists and Quakers who had sought service there in order to create their own model commonwealth. Nowhere was the conservative swing of the Republic more marked.

The Army and Politics

In August 1647 and December 1648 officers of the New Model, escorted by detachments of troops, purged those they did not like from the Long Parliament. In April 1653 Oliver Cromwell called troops into the Parliament house and dissolved the Rump of the Long Parliament and then turfed out its council of state. The constitutional settlement that resulted in the Nominated Assembly was worked out in closed sessions of the Army Council. When that Nominated Assembly decided that it was too riven to achieve anything worthwhile and fell, metaphorically, on its sword in December 1653, it was the officers who imposed a version of the Instrument of Government upon the Commonwealth of England, Scotland, and Ireland. That Instrument was the brainchild of an army general, John Lambert, and was essentially a digest of army constitutionalist thinking in the years 1647–9. In 1657 Cromwell was inhibited in accepting the revised constitution proposed by the Parliament, the centrepiece of which was the establishment of the House of Cromwell as a restored constitutional monarchy, by intense army pressure against it. It was the army that brought down the Protectorate in 1659 and it was the army leaders who twice put the Rump back into power and twice took away their power. It was General Monck, an army leader, who determined the nature of the elections of 1660 that paved the way for the Restoration. The army was the most important guarantee of political stability and the greatest single source of instability throughout the Interregnum.

And yet, determined though it was to decide who governed and how, the army was shy about undertaking the day-to-day exercise of power. When Cromwell threw out the Rump, he could have established a military junta, but he refused to do so. Although the Council of Officers vetted nominations for the constituent assembly that took up the reins in July, the council resolutely refused to nominate itself; soldiers were almost as invisible as lawyers in the assembly. When the Instrument of Government was imposed in December 1653, there was a similar limited self-denial. Only four of the eighteen members of the Council of State were serving officers, and while four others had held military positions, they were—with one brief exception—in provincial armies long before and had little bearing on their selection.[32] The Instrument also sought a self-imposed limit of 30,000 on the army, which entailed a halving of the numbers in arms at the moment when the decision was made. In the early days of the Protectorate a thorough review and new modelling of the various local commissions took place: less than three per cent of the Justices of the Peace of the Protectorate, less than three per cent of the assessments commissioners (the financial artery of the army), and barely five per cent of the commissioners for ejecting scandalous ministers were serving officers.[33] Although the Major-Generals brought a stronger army presence to the localities, it is important to remember that central to their purpose was to make possible a reduction in the size of the standing army, and that they had to work through deputies, amongst whom were to be found remarkably few current or former officers of the New Model or other 'marching armies'.[34] Even in 1659, after the failure of Richard Cromwell and the collapse of the Protectorate, the army preferred to reinstate the Rump than to attempt to turn the Army Council into a ruling council.

OLIVER CROMWELL

The army thus took upon itself to make and to break all the constitutions of the Interregnum, but to refuse to exercise power directly and *institutionally*. From December 1653, of course, its own leader, Oliver Cromwell, was head of state and it could be argued that that ensured that the army's interests were always uppermost, both because Cromwell encapsulated the mind of the army, and because he was in fact constrained to act within the parameters established by the collective will of the senior officers.

The army in the 1650s was scattered and constantly changing its composition. There was a high turnover of men, regiments were frequently culled to create new units such as those to serve in Flanders, and both in England and Scotland regiments were constantly broken up into companies often serving hundreds of miles apart and being reshuffled. The one element of stability is that while the junior officers and men were on garrison duty or on stand-by, a high proportion of the senior officers were in London and meeting regularly for dinner and sociability. This increased their potential importance as a lobby group, but it also indicates a weakening personal bond between senior officers and the rank and file. This loss of closeness, together with mounting arrears, seems to have bred very low morale. In 1659 the secretary of the army even records one body of soldiers as having said that 'they will not fight, but will make a ring for the officers to fight in'.[35] Cromwell met all the officers currently in London for dinner once a week and the key to the politics of the decade may lie in those informal meetings which have left virtually no trace in the record. The shards of evidence, however, suggest that Cromwell was no one's dupe. He was well able to deal decisively with those officers who opposed him—as he did in the enforced resignation and cashiering of three colonels for petitioning against the Instrument of Government; or in the arrest and incarceration without trial of two even more senior officers on flimsy and unsubstantiated suspicion of plotting against him (Major-Generals Thomas Harrison and Robert Overton, both in the early months of 1655). He did not flinch from cashiering the major and other company commanders in his own regiment in early 1658, again for organizing a petition to the Parliament; and he helped to push into resignation his independently powerful deputy and likely successor John Lambert, when Lambert's dissatisfactions at the substitution of the Humble Petition and Advice for his own Instrument of Government got too much for Oliver. Furthermore, the one recorded account of Cromwell's meetings with the officers—at the height of the kingship crisis in February 1657—shows the lord protector upbraiding them in a ferocious verbal assault, accusing them of serious miscalculations in the past; although his criticism of them for seeking to make him their 'drudge on all occasions' is distinctly double-edged.[36] If 'the army was the constituency Cromwell represented'[37] its influence over him was moral and not physical. If he turned down the crown under army pressure, it was not because the army would have prevented him from taking the crown, but rather that with so many of his oldest friends expressing personal unhappiness at the idea and saying they would rather retire from the army than serve under him as king, he could not bring himself to see it as God's will that he should take what in secular terms made so much sense.[38] Thus Cromwell wanted to believe that he would get better advice from those who worked for the cause of liberty and righteousness God had so much hallowed; and it may be that those Monday evening

Seal

The Scottish seal of Oliver Cromwell, with the battlefield of Dunbar in the background, shows him as lord protector of England, Scotland, and Ireland. It bears a striking resemblance to the seal used by Charles I which highlights the extent to which the Protectorate modelled itself on the monarchy. Protector Cromwell strove to promote stability, to foster unity, and to make his regime acceptable to the political nation. Excoriated as a usurper and hypocrite by his adversaries and venerated as a saviour and hero by his supporters, Cromwell died on 3 September 1658—the anniversary of two of his greatest victories—probably of malaria. Almost as soon as his son Richard took over the reigns of power, his subordinates in Scotland and Ireland began to plot the restoration of the monarchy.

dinners stiffened his resolve to stick by the more visionary aspects of his programme, such as the war with Spain, the readmission of the Jews, the protection
of such religious liberty as had been established in the later 1640s. However, this
did not amount to a military dictatorship.

The Collapse of the Protectorate and Commonwealth

By the time of Cromwell's death (3 September 1658), the prospects of long-term
stability without a restoration were already fading badly. Any free election would
produce a natural majority for a restoration. The attempt of the Protectorate to
keep in creative balance the interests both of the army and of local élites was looking more and more threadbare, and despite some success in winning over prominent figures in the indigenous communities in Scotland and Ireland and a
dramatic reduction in the costs to the English exchequer of maintaining military
control of those countries, the problem of state indebtedness was looking more
and more insoluble: army and navy arrears were mounting to unmanageable
levels with all the threat of disaffection and disloyalty that that implied. In 1649
the problem of arrears had been solved by the confiscation and sale of crown
lands; and in 1653 by the confiscation of Catholic-Irish land. By 1659 there were
no milch cows left; yet the arrears to the army were approaching £1 million and
the arrears of the navy exceeded that sum.

Although many of the devices which from the 1690s gave Britain the most
sophisticated funded national debt in the world were already in place,[39] the brute
fact was that the state was spending at least thirty per cent more each year than it
was generating in income; and that was a situation which made the earlier problems of James VI and I's treasurers seem trivial. In early 1659 large sections of the
army were put back on free quarter for the first time since 1652.

If Oliver Cromwell had been succeeded by John Lambert—the only other
man who could have united the army within itself, and the army and 'country'
opinion (he was more intelligent and better read than Cromwell, with less religious passion and a greater political pragmatism)—Britain might just have
evolved as a liberal gentry republic. However, with Richard Cromwell at the
helm, and arrears mounting, constitutional meltdown became all too predictable.
Only Parliament could secure the taxation that would bring the finances back
into balance and the Parliament seemed determined to ensure civilian control of
the army, seeking to reinstate officers cashiered in earlier years and impeaching
James Boteler for alleged excesses as Major-General in 1656–7. The Council of
the Army retaliated with its own Humble Representation demanding a purge of
backsliders from the Good Old Cause within council and Parliament. Richard
Cromwell responded first by dismissing Parliament and then dismissing himself.
It was probably his only astute political move. The Commonwealth took another
ten months to die a slow, agonizing death from a series of incompetently delivered

self-inflicted wounds. It really was not a question of whether the king would return, but how and when.

The Legacy

It is frequently said that one of the most enduring legacies of the civil-war era was an English fear and distrust of standing armies. It is certainly something one can see in the 1690s as William III struggled to keep together an army after the treaty of Ryswick in 1698 in anticipation of a war to prevent the French from making good their hopes of uniting the French and Spanish thrones on the daily awaited death of Carlos II.[40] It is not so clear that it was an inveterate part of English political rhetoric from the beginning. One specialist intellectual historian has noted that between 1660 and 1698 anti-militarism was not a dominant motif of English political rhetoric—except as an aspect of a deep 'loyalist' loathing of religious sectarianism—and that the belief that it was so is a clear nineteenth-century invention.[41] It was not a standing army that alarmed the Protestant subjects of James II, but an army officered by Catholics and professional mercenaries.

In 1660 a priority had been to demobilize the fractious, unpaid, volatile army that had so long kept the king out. That was achieved by the willingness of the Convention Parliament to grant—and the people to pay—huge taxes to secure that end. Regiments were selected by lot for disbandment as money poured in, General Monck's regiments—for obvious reasons—being kept back till last. However, at no point was it expected that there would be *no* standing army. The rising of the frenzied Fifth Monarchist Thomas Venner at the turn of 1660/1 legitimized the re-enlisting of two guards regiments (including Monck's own, renamed the Coldstream Guards to commemorate the march from Coldstream to London that inaugurated the process that culminated in Restoration).

Monck had left about half of the army based in Scotland behind him when he marched south, but those soldiers were also disbanded, rather later than the regiments in England. Those troops too were replaced by re-enlisted men, constituting a single regiment of horse and one of foot, totalling 1,200, which formed the nucleus of a new standing force. In Ireland, the pattern was slightly different. New senior officers were sent out there, and the junior officers and soldiers were tendered the Oaths of Allegiance and Supremacy: those that took them were kept on and those who refused them were immediately cashiered. Those who were invited to serve on were not regimented, but divided into thirty small troops of horse and sixty-six companies of foot under officers given commissions for life. Most of the officers were former Cromwellians, but they had taken the requisite oaths. Each troop and company was quartered in a different part of the countryside as an independent unit. Dispersed security, not a force in readiness for England, was what the regime had in mind.[42] However, Charles II was determined to

Coldstream Guards *by Peter Tillemans (top)*
George Monck, first duke of Albemarle (1608–70) *by Samuel Cooper (above)*

One of the two New Model Army regiments to survive from the 1650s was the Coldstream Guard, shown here. The regiment, which formed part of Charles II's personal bodyguard was named in commemoration of the march from Coldstream in Berwickshire to London that inaugurated the process that culminated in the Restoration. The regiment was commanded by George Monck, later first duke of Albemarle (1608–70), who had served with distinction in Ireland for much of the 1640s before taking command of the army in Scotland in 1651 and again after 1654. Despite the fact that he had no naval experience he became one of the three generals of the fleet and played a key role in winning the First Anglo-Dutch War. However, he is remembered as the architect of the restoration of Charles II.

have out of sight but not out of mind a substantial standing army ready to meet any emergencies in Britain itself.

Charles also carefully kept the 6,000 men at Dunkirk—the residue of both the Cromwellian brigade that had fought the battle of the Dunes and the royalist army that had fought with the Spaniards—outside the demobilization process, and that force was moved to Tangiers when that became British under the Anglo-Portuguese marriage treaty of 1661. By another clause of that treaty Charles willingly agreed to send a brigade of English veterans to serve with the Portuguese army and at the expense of the Portuguese crown, subject to its recall at will to defend England should Charles deem it necessary. A similar arrangement was made with the Dutch in 1661 and with the French a decade later. As a result Charles always had 10,000 men in battle-readiness at his disposal.[43]

Furthermore, the loyalist Cavalier Parliament was far more fearful of a return to popular anarchy than royal tyranny and so resolved to make explicit in a statute that the right to organize, control, and direct military force lay in the crown: it was unambiguously entitled 'An Act declaring the sole right of the Militia to be in the king'. A succession of refining statutes provided a secure financial basis for a regularly trained militia to supplement the standing forces. More dramatically, Charles took up the Interregnum experiments in creating separate corps of self-supporting volunteers, as great in numbers as the regular militia. Working through the lords lieutenant, Charles created a nationwide army of royalist stalwarts. The number of men enlisted into these corps may have exceeded 100,000 and their role in the events of the 1680s is an important unstudied one.[44]

There was no simple hiatus between the militarization of Britain during the civil wars and the militarization that took place after 1688 with the succession of international and colonial wars that saw British armies in action for sixty-three of the following 125 years. The long shadow cast by the British and Irish Civil Wars was not that of anti-militarism but of military preparedness. There were always significant numbers of men fit and ready for whatever emergency the crown faced; there was an ordnance office able and willing to acquire and shift large quantities of military supplies; there were forms of taxation capable of supplying the sinews of war; and there had even been experiments in funded credit that could be developed and transformed into a national debt that would sustain the most extended and ambitious programme of military and naval expansion. Although eighteenth-century governments enormously expanded the size of the British army, the British navy, and the bureaucracies of war, all the foundations had been laid in the 1640s and the 1650s.

NOTES

Introduction

1. See for example the discussion by J. Pocock, 'The Atlantic Archipelago and the War of the Three Kingdoms', in B. Bradshaw and J. Morrill (eds.), *The British Problem c.1534–1707: State Formation in the Atlantic Archipelago* (London, 1996), 172–191, and J. Morrill, 'The Un-English Civil War', in J. R. Young (eds.), *Celtic Dimensions of the British Civil Wars* (Edinburgh 1997), 1–16.
2. For John Kenyon's willingness to make these parallels with the European General Crisis, see his *The Civil Wars of England* (London, 1988), 5–6.
3. Id., *The Stuart Constitution: Documents and Commentary* (1st edn., Cambridge 1966), 7; (2nd rev. edn., Cambridge, 1986), 7.
4. e.g. id. *Stuart England* (2nd rev. edn., London, 1985), 15–16.
5. Id., *The Stuarts: A Study in English Kingship* (London, 1958), 70.
6. e.g. ibid. 34–5.
7. e.g. ibid. 45.
8. Id., *Stuart Constitution* (1966 edn.), 11; (1986 edn.), 10.
9. Id., *Stuart England*, 54–5.
10. Id., *The Stuarts*, 72.

Chapter 1

John Kenyon left a draft of his introduction which forms the basis for this chapter. Dr Edward Furgol kindly provided the sections on the Bishops' Wars.

1. L. Stone, *Crisis of the Aristocracy* (Oxford, 1965), 223.
2. Quoted in G. M. Frazer, *The Steel Bonnets: The Story of the Anglo-Scottish Border Reviers* (London, 1989), 170.
3. *Register of the Privy Council for Scotland*, 2nd ser., iv. 100.
4. Lord Mountjoy quoted in G. Parker, *The Military Revolution: Military Innovation and the Rise of the West, 1500–1800* (Cambridge, 1988), 53.
5. Quoted ibid. 49.
6. Quoted in J. P. Prendergast, *The Cromwellian Settlement of Ireland* (3rd edn., Dublin, 1922), 87.
7. *A discourse concerning the rebellion . . .* (London, 1642), 22.
8. Quoted in J. Hennig, 'Irish Soldiers', *Journal of the Royal Society of Antiquaries of Ireland*, 81 (1952), 33.

9. Quoted in G. Simpson (ed.), *Scotland and the Low Countries 1124–1994* (Edinburgh, 1996), 113, 114.
10. A. Fowler (ed.), *Seventeenth Century Verse* (Oxford, 1991), 596.
11. Brown to [ ], 18/28 Feb. 1642 (British Library, Additional MSS 12, 184 fo. 63).
12. W. Knowler (ed.), *The earl of Strafforde's letters and despatches with an essay towards his life by Sir George Radcliffe* . . . (2 vols., London, 1739), i. 450.
13. G. Donaldson (ed.), *Scottish Historical Documents* (Edinburgh, 1974), 173.
14. W. C. Dickinson and G. Donaldson (eds.), *A Source Book of Scottish History* (3 vols., Edinburgh, 1961), iii. 261.
15. *Register of the Privy Council of Scotland*, 2nd ser., i. 193.
16. Quoted in D. Stevenson, *King or Covenant? Voices from Civil War* (Edinburgh, 1996), 158.
17. Charles I to Hamilton, 11 June 1638 (Scottish Record Office, Gifts and Deposits, 406/1/10484).
18. Knowler (ed.), *Letters*, ii. 300 and 358.
19. Antrim to [Hamilton], 17 Mar. 1639 (Scottish Record Office, Gifts and Deposits 406/1/1154).
20. Knowler (ed.), *Letters*, ii. 305.
21. Donaldson (ed.), *Historical Documents*, 201.
22. The royal forces failed to take advantage of Dumbarton, because Hamilton, who was responsible for providing transport vessels for the Irish army refused to act. He feared not only for his own estates, but worried about the backlash in England and Scotland against the king's employment of Catholic Irishmen.
23. This and the rest of the account of the plot comes from 'Information of the Marquis of Antrim', in G. Hill, *An Historical Account of the MacDonnells of Antrim* (Belfast, 1873), 448–51. Some historians have argued that Antrim fabricated this account.
24. Ibid. 450.
25. Ibid.
26. *An exact relation of all such occurences* . . . (London, 1642), 1.
27. *Mercurius Hibernicus* (Bristol, 1644), 7.
28. Edward Hyde, earl of Clarendon, *The History of the Rebellion and Civil Wars in England*, ed. W. D. Macray (6 vols., Oxford, 1988; reissued, 1992), vi. 2–3.
29. *The Parliament Scout* . . . (London, 20–7 June 1643), 4.
30. *Two letters of note* (London, 1642), no page.
31. Clarendon, *Rebellion*, ii. 276.
32. *Lord Balmerino's speech in the high court of Parliament* . . . (London, 1641), 3.
33. For all this see Chs. 2 and 3. Also J. Morrill, 'Three Kingdoms and One Commonwealth? The Enigma of Mid Seventeenth-Century Britain and Ireland', in A. Grant and K. J. Stringer (eds.), *Uniting the Kingdom? The Making of British History* (London, 1995), 170–92.
34. Calculated from data in P. Young and R. Holmes, *The English Civil War* (London, 1974). Also see I. Gentles, *The New Model Army* (Oxford, 1992).
35. Extrapolated from P. Young, *Civil War England* (London, 1981), map at p. 6.
36. Ibid. 79.
37. C. Carlton, 'The Impact of the Fighting', in J. Morrill (ed.), *The Impact of the English Civil War* (London, 1991), 17–20.
38. I. Roy, 'England turned Germany? The Aftermath of the Civil War in its European Context', *Transactions of the Royal Historical Society*, 4th ser. 28 (1978), 127–44.

Chapter 2

1. New Register House, Edinburgh, Kirk Session Record Carnock, 24 Sept. 1643.
2. *The letters and Journals of Robert Baillie, Principal of the University of Glasgow, 1637–1662*, ed. D. Laing (3 vols., Bannatyne Club, 72/1–2 and 77; Edinburgh, 1841–2), i. 196.
3. E. M. Furgol, 'Scotland turned Sweden: The Scottish Covenanters and the Military Revolution, 1638–1651', in J. Morrill (ed.), *The Scottish National Covenant, in its British Context 1638–1651* (Edinburgh, 1990), 141.
4. *Articles and ordinances of warre for the present expedition of the Armie of the kingdom of Scotland* (Edinburgh, 1640), 3–4; and *Articles and Ordinances of warre, for the present Expedition of the Armie of Scotland* (London, 1644), 1.
5. *A True Relation of the taking of Mountjoy in the County of Tyrone* (London, 4 Aug. 1642).
6. T. Thomson and C. Innes (eds.), *Acts of the Parliament of Scotland* (Edinburgh, 1814–75), vol. vi, prt. i, p. 44.
7. Edward Hyde, earl of Clarendon, *The Life of Edward, Earl of Clarendon* (3 vols., Oxford, 1827), ii. 80.
8. C. Ó Baoill (ed.), *The Harps' Cry* (Edinburgh, 1994), 111.
9. Clarendon, *Life*, ii. 80–1.
10. *Lords Arglye, Crawford-Lindsay, Despatch on Philiphaugh* (London, 1645).
11. J. T. Gilbert (ed.), *A Contemporary History of Affairs in Ireland (1641–1652)* (3 vols., Irish Archeological and Celtic Society, Dublin 1879), i. 678–9.
12. *Letters*, ed Laing, ii. 377.
13. Quoted in A. I. Macinnes, *Charles I and the Making of the Covenanting Movement* (Edinburgh, 1991), p. ii.
14. *A new declaration set forth by the Lord Ge. Hamilton* (London, 1648), 4.
15. J. Kirk (ed.), *The Records of the Synod of Lothian and Tweeddale, 1589–1596, 1640–1649* (Stair Society, 30; Edinburgh 1977), 267–8.
16. J. Nicoll, *A Diary of Public Transactions* (Bannatyne Club; Edinburgh, 1836), 9.
17. *The Writings and Speeches of Oliver Cromwell*, ed. W. C. Abbott (4 vols., Oxford, 1939; reissued 1988), ii. 320.
18. Ibid. 321, 324.
19. Ó Baoill (ed.), *The Harps' Cry*, 133.
20. Gordon Donaldson (ed.), *Scottish Historical Documents* (Edinburgh, 1974), 200.

Chapter 3

I am grateful to Ian Gentles, John Morrill, and Micheál Ó Siochrú for reading this chapter and for making many helpful comments.

1. *An exact relation of all such occurences . . .* (London, 1642), 1.
2. N. Canny, *Kingdom and Colony: Ireland in the Atlantic World 1560–1800* (Baltimore, 1988), 61.
3. Nicholas Bernard, *The whole proceedings . . .* (London, 1642), 3.
4. A. Clarke, *The Old English in Ireland 1625–1642* (New York, 1966), 218.
5. J. C. Beckett, 'The Confederation of Kilkenny Reviewed', in M. Roberts (ed.), *Historical Studies*, ii (London, 1959), 36.
6. W. K. Sessions, *The First Printers . . .* (York, 1990), 8.
7. G. Hill, *The Stewarts of Ballintoy: With Notices of Other Families of the District in the Seventeenth Century* (Coleraine, 1865; repr. Ballycastle, 1976), 14–15.

8. B. Jennings (ed.), *Wild Geese in Spanish Flanders 1582–1700: Documents relating chiefly to Irish regiments from the Archives Générales du Royaume, Brussels and other Sources* (Irish Manuscripts Commission; Dublin, 1964), 507.

9. *Speciall good news from Ireland* ... (London, 1643[–4]), 2–3.

10. J. T. Gilbert (ed.), *History of the Irish Confederation* (7 vols., Dublin, 1882–91), iv. 93–5.

11. Cited in Clarke, *Old English*, 179–80 and Gilbert (ed.), *Irish Confederation*, vol. i, p. lxv, and vol. ii, p. 85.

12. B. Ó Buachalla, 'James Our True King: The Ideology of Irish Royalism in the Seventeenth Century', in D. G. Boyce, R. Eccleshall, and V. Geoghegan (eds.), *Political Thought in Ireland since the Seventeenth Century* (London, 1993), 23.

13. *Calendar of State Papers relating to Ireland 1633–1647*, 350.

14. For further details see Chapter 7.

15. *Calendar of State Papers relating to Ireland 1633–1647*, 429.

16. L. P. Murray, 'An Irish Diary of the Confederate Wars', *Journal of the County Louth Archaeological Society*, 5:3 (1923), 211.

17. J. T. Gilbert (ed.), *A Contemporary History of Affairs in Ireland (1641 to 1652)* (3 vols., Irish Archaeological and Celtic Society; Dublin, 1879), vol. ii, p. xxxviii.

18. Gilbert (ed.), *Irish Confederation*, vi. 66.

19. T. Carte, *History of the Life of James, First Duke of Ormond* (6 vols., Oxford, 1851), vi. 71.

20. Gilbert (ed.), *Contemporary History*, ii. 350.

21. Ibid. i. 30.

22. Jennings (ed.), *Wild Geese*, 507–8.

23. Sir James Turner, *Memoirs of his own life and times*, ed. Thomas Thomson (Bannatyne Club, 28; Edinburgh, 1829), 26.

24. G. A. Hayes-McCoy, *Irish Battles: A Military History of Ireland* (Belfast, 1989), 184.

25. Gilbert (ed.), *Irish Confederation*, iv. 284.

26. 'State of the kingdom of Ireland, 10 December 1646' by [Arthur] Annesley and Sir William Parsons (British Library, Egerton MSS 917, fos. 25–7).

27. Gilbert (ed.), *Irish Confederation*, vii. 149.

28. Ibid. vi. 216–17, 221–2, 223.

29. Historical Manuscripts Commission, *Fourteenth report. Appendix VII. The Manuscripts of the Marquis of Ormonde, preserved at the Castle, Kilkenny* (2 vols., London, 1895 and 1899), i. 147.

30. For further details on logistics see Chapter 7.

31. Conway to the committee of Irish affairs at Derby House, [1646–7] (Huntington Library, Hastings MSS, Irish papers, box 9/14345).

32. Historical Manuscripts Commission, *MSS of the Marquis of Ormonde*, ii. 86.

33. Bernard, *The whole proceedings*, 50.

34. Gilbert (ed.), *Irish Confederation*, iv. 187.

35. Historical Manuscripts Commission, *MSS of the Marquis of Ormonde*, ii. 121.

36. See Chapter 4 for a general discussion of European and battlefield tactics.

37. P. Lenihan, ' "Celtic" Warfare in the 1640s', in J. R. Young (ed.), *Celtic Dimensions of the British Civil Wars* (Edinburgh, 1997), 116–40.

38. Historical Manuscripts Commission, *Report on the Franciscan manuscripts preserved at the Convent, Merchant's Quay, Dublin* (Dublin, 1906), 239.

39. *Calendar of State Papers relating to Ireland 1633–1647*, 540–1.

40. Gilbert (ed.), *Irish Confederation*, v. 262.

41. *A letter from the . . . Lord Inchiquin* (London, 1644), 6.

42. Carte, *Ormond*, vi. 305.

43. *Letter-Book of the Earl of Clanricarde 1643–1647*, ed. John Lowe (Irish Manuscripts Commission, Dublin, 1983), 41.

44. Ibid.

45. Micheál Ó Siochrú's doctoral thesis 'Confederate Ireland 1642–1649: A Constitutional and Political Analysis' (Trinity College, Dublin, 1997) examines confederate politics in detail.

46. *A letter from Sr Lewis Dyve to the lord marquis of Newcastle . . .* (Hague, 1650), 5.

47. *The Tanner Letters*, ed. C. McNeill (Irish Manuscripts Commission; Dublin, 1943), 361.

48. G. Aiazza (ed.), *The Embassy in Ireland of Monsignor G. B. Rinuccini . . .* trans. Annie Hutton (Dublin, 1873), 326.

49. La Torre to Philip IV, 20/30 April 1647 (Archivo General de Simancas, Estado. 2523 unfol.).

50. Foissotte to Philip IV, 8/18 May 1648 (Archivo General de Simancas, Estado. 2566 unfol.)

51. Paper I, presented by Crelly to parliamentary committee, Dec. 1648 (Archivo General de Simancas, Estado. 2524, fo. 81).

52. R. O'Ferrall and R. O'Connell, *Commentarius Rinuccinianus*, ed. S. Kavanagh (6 vols., Irish Manuscripts Commission, Dublin, 1932–49), iii. 385.

53. Aiazza (ed.), *Embassy*, 441.

54. Quoted in Sessions, *First Printers*, 251.

55. Gilbert (ed.), *Irish Confederation*, vii. 184–211.

56. *The Taking of Wexford. A Letter from an eminent officer in the army, under the command of the Lord Lieutenant of Ireland . . .* (London, 1649), 5.

57. J. R. Powell and E. K. Timmings (eds.), *Documents relating to the Civil War 1642–1648* (London, 1963), 314.

58. Bodleian Library, Oxford, Carte MSS 19 fo. 327.

59. *Perfect Occurrences of Everie Daies Journall . . .* no. 145 (London, 1649), 1342.

60. Edward Hyde, earl of Clarendon, *The History of the Rebellion and Civil Wars in England*, ed. W. D. Macray (6 vols., Oxford, 1988; reissued, 1992), v. 215.

61. *The Writings and Speeches of Oliver Cromwell*, ed. W. C. Abbott (4 vols., Cambridge, Mass, 1947), ii. 124.

62. *A Letter from the Lord Lieutenant* (London, 1649), 6–7.

63. For further details on Clonmel and Limerick, see Chapter 6.

64. Bellièvre to Brienne, 3/13 Nov. 1648 (Archives du Ministère des Affaires Etrangères, Correspondance Politique Angleterre, Côte 57, fos. 314–15).

Chapter 4

1. For details on the recruitment and size of Irish and Scottish armies, see Chapters 2 and 3.

2. I. Roy, 'The Royalist Army in the First Civil War' (D.Phil. thesis, Oxford, 1963), 188.

3. *Lords Journal*, vi. 160.

4. Roy, 'Royalist Army', 3.

5. P. M. Darman, 'Prince Rupert of the Rhine: A Study in generalship, 1642–1646' (M.Phil. thesis, York, 1987), 117.

6. Roy, 'Royalist Army', 146.

7. Ibid. 125, 160; R. Hutton, *The Royalist War Effort 1642–1646* (London, 1982), 123–4, 148; Darman, 'Prince Rupert', 165; P. Newman, *The Old Service: Royalist Regimental Colonels and the Civil War, 1642–1646* (Manchester, 1983), 229.

8. The papers of Commons Speaker William Lenthall preserved in the Bodleian Library, Tanner MSS, are full of complaints from the northern counties about the cruelty and depredations of Scottish troops.

9. B. C. Hacker, 'Women and Military Institutions in Early Modern Europe: A Reconnaissance', *Signs*, 6 (1981), 643.

10. *Pallas Armata. Military Essayes of the Ancient Grecian, Roman, and Modern Art of War. Written in the Years 1670 and 1671* (London, 1683), 277.

11. Quoted in C. H. Firth, *Cromwell's Army* (4th edn., London, 1962), 262.

12. C. Carlton, *Going to the Wars: The Experience of the British Civil Wars 1638–1651* (London, 1994), 204, 210–11.

13. Newman, *Old Service*, 69.

14. A. Woolrych, *Battles of the English Civil War* (London, 1961), 19.

15. *The Writings and Speeches of Oliver Cromwell*, ed. W. C. Abbott (4 vols.; Cambridge, Mass., 1937–47), i. 256.

16. J. Jones, 'The Army of the North, 1642–1645' (Ph.D. thesis, York [Toronto], 1991), 241–2, 248, 254.

17. I. Gentles, 'The New Model Army Officer Corp in 1647: A Collective Portrait', *Social History*, 22 (1997), 128, 133–7; Denzil Holles, *Memoirs* (London, 1699), 149.

18. Quoted in Firth, *Cromwell's Army*, 276–7.

19. For the royalist Articles of War see Bodleian Library, Godwin pamphlet no. 682(3), *Military Orders and Articles Established by His Maiesty, for the Better Ordering and Government of His Majesties Army* (Oxford, 1643). For a valuable discussion of them see Margaret Griffin, 'Regulating Religion and Morality in the King's Armies 1639–46' (Ph.D. thesis, Toronto, 1997). The New Model Army's Articles, which were closely modelled on those of Essex's Army in 1642, are reprinted by Firth in *Cromwell's Army*, 400–12.

20. B. Donagan, 'Atrocity, War Crime, and Treason in the English Civil War', *American Historical Review*, 99 (1994), 1146. In Ireland and Scotland warfare seems to have been more bloody, see Chapters 2 and 3.

21. See, for example, British Library, Harleian MS 6804, fos. 75–6.

22. Quoted in F. M. Richardson, *Fighting Spirit: A Study of Psychological Factors in War* (London, 1978), 1, 3.

23. The phrase was used by the men of Colonel Nathaniel Rich's regiment in the spring of 1647. Worcester College, MS 41 (Clarke Papers), fo. 113.

24. Quoted in Carlton, *Going to the Wars*, 34. For further information see also Chapters 1 and 3.

25. J. Malcolm, 'A King in Search of Soldiers: Charles I in 1642', *Historical Journal*, 21 (1978), 271; P. R. Newman, 'The Royalist Army in Northern England 1642–1645' (Ph.D. thesis, York, 1978), 42.

26. Quoted in J. Adair, *Roundhead General: A Military Biography of Sir William Waller* (London, 1969), 75–6.

27. Quoted in C. Holmes, *The Eastern Association in the English Civil War* (London, 1969), 286 n. 123.

28. Drawings of close to 500 royalist and parliamentarian banners have been preserved. The

two best sources, from which the examples which follow are taken, are Dr Williams's Library (London), Modern MS Folio 7, and British Library, Sloane MS 5247. For an extended analysis of the iconography of the civil war banners see I. Gentles, 'The Iconography of Revolution: England 1642–1649', in I. Gentles, J. Morrill, and B. Worden (eds.), *Writers, Soldiers and Statesmen of the English Revolution* (Cambridge, 1998).

29. Scottish Record Office, Gifts and Deposits 406/1/167 (Hamilton MSS).

30. Codrington Library, All Souls College, Oxford, *The Humble Desires and Proposals of the Private Agitators of Colonel Hewson's Regiment* (London, 1647), pp. 1–2.

31. This is the admittedly controversial argument of W. McNeill, in *Keeping Together in Time: Dance and Drill in Human History* (Cambridge, Mass., 1996). See also the *Times Literary Supplement*, 12 July, and 2, 9, 16, and 23 Aug. 1996.

32. [Anon.], *A Trve Relation of a Victory . . . [at] Nasiby* (1645), unpaginated. [John Rushworth], *An Ordinance . . . for . . . a Day of Thanksgiving . . .* (1645), 3.

33. The leading authority on Edgehill is Peter Young, on whose work the following account is largely based. See his *Edgehill* (Moreton-in-Marsh, Gloucs., 1967), and P. Young and R. Holmes, *The English Civil War: A Military History of the Three Civil Wars 1642–1651* (London, 1974), ch. 4.

34. J. P. Kenyon, *The Civil Wars of England* (London, 1988), 73.

35. G. Donaldson (ed.), *Scottish Historical Documents* (Edinburgh, 1974), 209.

36. Quoted in J. Morrill, *The Nature of the English Revolution* (Harlow, 1993), 343.

37. *The Representations and Consultations of the Generall Councell of the Armie at St. Albans* (1648), quoted in I. Gentles, *The New Model Army in England, Ireland and Scotland, 1645–1653* (Oxford, 1992), 272.

38. S. R. Gardiner (ed.), *Constitutional Documents of the Puritan Revolution, 1625–1660* (3rd edn., Oxford, 1906), 380.

Chapter 5

1. Edward Hyde, earl of Clarendon, *The History of the Rebellion and Civil Wars in England*, ed. W. D. Macray (6 vols., Oxford 1888), ii. 224.

2. Ibid. 219n.

3. Ibid. 218n.

4. J. R. Powell and E. K. Timings (eds.), *Documents relating to the Civil War* (Navy Records Society; London, 1963), 85.

5. Ibid. 61.

6. Ibid. 78.

7. Ibid. 188.

8. Ibid. 203.

9. Ibid. 194, 213–14.

10. J. Ohlmeyer, 'Irish Privateers during the Civil War, 1642–1650', *Mariner's Mirror*, 76 (1990), 123.

11. Ibid. 126–7, 131.

12. *Memorials of Sir William Penn*, ed. G. Penn (2 vols., London, 1833), i. 221–2.

13. Powell and Timings (eds.), *Documents*, 330

14. Ibid. 355.

15. Ibid. 382.

16. Ibid. 382.

17. Ibid.

18. Ibid. 398.
19. Ibid.
20. E. Warburton, *Memorials of Prince Rupert* (London, 1849), iii. 313.

Chapter 6

1. For further details see G. Parker, *The Military Revolution: Military Innovation and the Rise of the West, 1500–1800* (Cambridge, 1988; 3rd edn. 1996). Parker's thesis and conclusions have, however, been subjected to criticism by a number of scholars. For instance J. Black, *A Military Revolution? Military Change and European Society, 1550–1800* (London, 1991) argues that the critical precondition was enhanced state power; while J. A. Lynn, 'The *trace italienne* and the Growth of Armies: The French Case', *Journal of military history*, 55 (1991), 297–330, suggests that army size was the key development. Also see C. J. Rogers (ed.), *The Military Revolution Debate* (Oxford, 1995).
2. Edward Furgol kindly provided these references to Scottish fortifications.
3. Historical Manuscripts Commission, *Report on the Manuscripts of the Duke of Ormonde*, NS (8 vols., London, 1902–20), ii. 33.
4. *The Diary of Henry Townshend of Elmley Lovett*, ed. J. W. Willis Bundi (Worcestershire Historical Society; London, 1920), 134.
5. J. Duncumb, *Collections towards the History and Antiquities of the County of Hereford* (Hereford, 1804), i. 248.
6. *Tracts relating to Military Proceedings in Lancashire*, ed. G. Ormerod (Chetham Society, ii/2; London, 1844), 46.
7. The whole sequence of categories was complicated by frequent use of the term 'drake', which could refer to a distinctive light tapering gun or else to any of the pieces described above, with the barrel cut down to reduce its weight while retaining the firepower.
8. Quoted in R. Loeber and G. Parker, 'The Military Revolution in Seventeenth Century Ireland', in J. Ohlmeyer (ed.), *Ireland from Independence to Occupation* (Cambridge, 1995), 74.
9. For example see R. Norton, *The Gunners Dialogue* (London, 1643), 87.
10. *Memorials of the Civil War in Cheshire*, ed. James Hall (Lancashire and Cheshire Record Society, 1879), 106.
11. J. T. Gilbert (ed.), *History of the Irish Confederation and the War in Ireland, 1641–1643* (7 vols., Dublin, 1882–91), i. 74.
12. B. Jennings (ed.), *Wild Geese in Spanish Flanders, 1582–1700: Documents relating chiefly to Irish Regiments from the Archives Générales du Royaume, Brussels and Other Sources* (Irish Manuscripts Commission, Dublin, 1964), 508–9.
13. Gilbert (ed.), *Irish Confederation*, iv. 284.
14. *The Royalist Ordnance Papers*, ed. I. Roy (Oxfordshire Record Society, 43 and 49; Oxford, 1964 and 1975), i. 53, 155, 226; ii. 255–7, 269, 353.
15. Public Record Office, SP 21/8E, pp. 277–8; Joshua Sprigge, *Anglia Rediviva* (Oxford edn. 1854), 54.
16. Public Record Office, SP 16/501/145.
17. *Royalist Ordnance Papers*, ii. 261–3.
18. Loeber and Parker, 'Military Revolution', 74.
19. *Oliver Cromwell's Letters and Speeches*, ed. T. Carlyle (5 vols., London, 1870), ii. 197.
20. The quotations and several details are from William Lithgow, *The Present Surveigh of London and England's State* (London, 1643).

21. Nottingham University Library, Twentiman MS, mcxv.

22. Richard Franck, *Northern Memoirs* (Edinburgh, 1821), 269–70.

23. Ibid. 271.

24. John Rushworth, *Historical Collections* (8 vols., London, 1721), ii. 1176–1242; Historical Manuscripts Commission, *12th Report, Appendix, Part IX. The Manuscripts of the Duke of Beaufort* (London, 1891), 24–9.

25. Richard Symonds, *Diary of the Marches of the Royal Army*, ed. C. E. Long (Camden Society, 74; London, 1859), 179–80; *A More Exact Relation of the Siege Laid to the Town of Leicester* (London, 1645); *A Narration of the Siege and Taking of the Town of Leicester* (London, 1645).

26. For Oswestry, see *Two Great Victories* (London, 1644).

27. *A True Relation of the Taking of the City, Minster and Castle of Lincoln* (London, 1644).

28. Quoted in C. Carlton, *Going to the Wars: The Experience of the British Civil Wars, 1638–1651* (London, 1994), 159.

29. De Gomme, in *Memoirs of Prince Rupert and the Cavaliers*, ed. E. Warburton (3 vols., London, 1849), ii. 264.

30. Sir John Temple, *The Irish Rebellion . . .* (London, 1646), 51–2.

31. Nicholas Bernard, *The whole proceedings of the siege of Drogheda . . .* (London, 1642), 18.

32. Historical Manuscripts Commission, *Ormond*, i. 53.

33. *Two letters sent from the Lord Inchiqueen . . .* (London, 1647), 3.

34. D. Massari, 'My Irish Campaign', *Catholic Bulletin*, 6 (1916), 221.

35. *The Writings and Speeches of Oliver Cromwell*, ed. W. C. Abbott (4 vols., Cambridge, Mass., 1939), iii. 125–251; *The Memoirs of Edmund Ludlow*, ed. C. H. Firth (2 vols., Oxford, 1894), i. 268–89.

36. P. Lenihan, 'Aerial Photography: A Window on the Past', *History Ireland*, 1/2 (1993), 9–13.

37. Quoted in Loeber and Parker, 'Military Revolution', 83–5.

38. L. Butler, *Sandal Castle, Wakefield* (Wakefield Historical Publications; Wakefield, 1991), 89–104.

39. Since 1974 it has been in Wales.

40. *Memoirs of Ludlow*, i. 70–4.

41. *Memorials of the Civil War in Cheshire*, ed. Hall, 189.

42. Ibid. 91.

43. *Memoirs of Ludlow*, i. 271–3.

44. *A Journal of the Siege of Lathom House* (London, 1644; repr. 1823), 13–53.

45. Quoted in Loeber and Parker, 'Military Revolution', 73.

46. Roger Boyle, earl of Orrery, *A Treatise on the Art of War* (London, 1677), 15.

Chapter 7

Jane Ohlmeyer and Edward Furgol kindly supplied many references to Ireland and Scotland and Ian Gentles to parliamentary and royalist finance which have been incorporated throughout this chapter.

1. Quoted in G. Parker, *The Military Revolution: Military Innovation and the Rise of the West 1500–1800* (Cambridge, 1988), 68.

2. Quoted in P. Young and R. Holmes, *The English Civil War* (London, 1974), 209.

3. Quoted in C. H. Firth, *Cromwell's Army* (London, 1921), 233.

4. Quoted in Parker, *Military Revolution*, 68.

5. Quoted in P. Wenham, *The Siege of York 1644* (York, 1970), 23.

6. Quoted in J. Ohlmeyer (ed.), *Ireland from Independence to Occupation* (Cambridge, 1995), 74.

7. Quoted in I. Roy, 'The Royalist Ordnance Papers 1642–1646', *Oxford Record Society*, 43 (1963–4), 36.

8. *The Letter books of Sir William Brereton*, ed. R. N. Dore, pt. ii (Record Society of Lancashire and Cheshire, 128, Chester, 1990), 380.

9. Historical Manuscripts Commission, *Calendar of the Manuscripts of the Marquess of Ormond* NS (8 vols., London, 1902–20), ii. 76.

10. Public Record Office, State Papers 28/253B fo. 93.

11. Public Record Office, State Papers 28/253B, fo. 75.

12. J. T. Gilbert (ed.), *History of the Irish Confederation and the War in Ireland, 1641–1643* (7 vols., Dublin, 1882–91), ii. 262.

13. S. Groenveld, 'Verlopend Getij: De Nederlandse Republiek en de Engelse Burgerloorlog 1640–1646' (Ph.D. thesis, Leiden University, 1984), 237.

14. *Calendar of State Papers, Domestic 1644*, 320.

15. Historical Manuscripts Commission, *Report on the Franciscan Manuscripts* (Dublin, 1906), 196.

16. I. Roy, 'Royalist Ordnance Papers, II', *Oxford Record Society*, 49 (1971–3), 381.

17. Quoted in Parker, *Military Revolution*, 76.

18. Quoted in C. Holmes, *The Eastern Association in the English Civil War* (Cambridge, 1974), 156.

19. British Library, Additional MSS 18,981, fo. 153^v.

20. Quoted in P. Tennant, *Edgehill and Beyond* (Far Thrupp, Stroud, 1992), 46.

21. J. S. Wheeler, 'English Army Finance and Logistics 1642–1660' (Ph.D. thesis, Berkeley, 1980), 153. Wheeler's thesis provides an indispensable guide to parliamentary war finance during the 1640s and 1650s.

22. J. Engberg, 'Royalist Finances during the English Civil War 1642–1646', *Scandinavian Economic History Review*, 19 (1966), 91.

23. Gilbert (ed.), *Irish Confederation*, iv. 36.

24. Quoted in J. Ohlmeyer, 'The Wars of Religion, 1603–1660', in T. Bartlett and K. Jeffery (eds.), *A Military History of Ireland* (Cambridge, 1996), 177.

25. A. Hughes, *Politics, Society and Civil War in Warwickshire, 1620–1660* (Cambridge, 1987), 210.

26. P. M. Darman, 'Prince Rupert of the Rhine: A study in generalship, 1642–1646' (M.Phil. thesis, York, 1987), 106.

27. Quoted in D. Stevenson, 'The Financing of the cause of the Covenants, 1638–45', *Scottish Historical Review*, 51 (1972), 104.

28. Quoted in J. R. Young (ed.), *Celtic Dimension of the British Civil Wars* (Edinburgh, 1997), 68.

29. Public Record Office, State Papers 28/353, ii, fo. 359.

30. Quoted in Tennant, *Edgehill*, 207.

31. Quoted in J. S. Morrill, *The Revolt of the Provinces* (London, 1976), 55.

32. *The Letter Books 1644–1645 of Sir Samuel Luke*, ed. H. G. Tibbutt (London, 1963), 599.

33. Gilbert (ed.), *Irish Confederation*, vi. 81–2.

34. Ibid. 271.

35. Roy, 'Royalist Army', 344, 350.

36. Historical Manuscripts Commission, *Calendar of Manuscripts of Ormond*, ii. 327.
37. H. Hazlett, 'The Financing of the British Armies in Ireland, 1641–1649', *Irish Historical Studies*, 1 (1938), 41.

Chapter 8

1. Quoted in I. Roy, 'The English Civil War and English Society', in B. Bond and I. Roy (eds.), *War and Society* (London, 1975), 29.
2. C. H. Firth, *Narrative of General Venables* (Camden Society, NS 61; London, 1990), 1.
3. T. Royle, *A Dictionary of Military Quotations* (London, 1990), 36.
4. C. Carlton, *Going to the Wars: The Experience of the British Civil Wars, 1638–1651* (London, 1994), 208–15.
5. Quoted in R. E. Sherwood, *Civil Strife in the Midlands* (London, 1974), 69.
6. G. N. Godwin, *The Civil War in Hampshire* (London, 1908), 309.
7. Fanshawe quoted in P. Slack, *The Impact of Plague in Tudor and Stuart England* (London, 1985), 73. Taylor quoted in R. and T. Kelly, *A City at War: Oxford, 1642–1646* (Cheltenham, 1987), 25–6.
8. R. Baxter, *Religiue Baxterianae* (London, 1696), 55.
9. Historical Monuments Commission, *Newark on Trent: The Civil War Siegeworks* (London, 1964), 23. Quote from E. Broxap, *The Great Civil War in Lancashire* (Manchester, 1910), 154.
10. T. Dekker, 'Dialogue between War, Famine and Pestilence (1604)', in *The Plague Pamphlets of Thomas Dekker*, ed. F. P. Wilson (Oxford, 1925), 25–6.
11. G. Parker, *The Military Revolution: Military Innovation and the Rise of the West, 1500–1800* (Cambridge, 1988), 55. D. Stewart, 'Sickness and Mortality Rates in the English Army until the Twentieth Century' *Journal of the Royal Army Medical Corps*, 91 (1948), 23–35. I. Roy, 'The English Civil War and English Society', *War and Society*, 1 (1977), 31. I am grateful to my colleague William C. Harris for the information on the American Civil War.
12. C. Ó Baoill (ed.), *The Harps' Cry* (Edinburgh, 1994), 111.
13. B. Jennings (ed.), *Wild Geese in Spanish Flanders 1582–1700: Documents relating chiefly to the Irish Regiments from the Archives Générales du Royaume, Brussels and other Sources* (Irish Manuscripts Commission, Dublin, 1964), 507.
14. Quoted in R. Bagwell, *Ireland under the Stuarts* (3 vols., London, 1906–16), ii. 301.
15. Quoted in T. L. Coonan, *The Irish Catholic Confederacy and the Puritan Revolution* (Dublin, 1954), 328.
16. P. J. Corish, 'The Rising of 1641', and 'The Cromwellian Regime', in T. W. Moody, F. X. Martin, and F. J. Byrne (eds.), *A New History of Ireland*, iii: *1534–1691* (Oxford, 1976; repr. 1978), 292 and 357.
17. F. P. and M. M. Verney, *Memoirs of the Verney Family during the Civil War and Commonwealth* (4 vols., London, 1892–9), ii. 136.
18. G. Nugent, *Some Memoirs of John Hampden* (2 vols., London, 1832), ii. 423.
19. Historical Manuscripts Commission, *Fourth Report* (London, 1874), appendix, 259–61.
20. Sir Hugh Cholmley, *The Memoirs of Sir Hugh Cholmley* (London, 1870), 71.
21. Folger Library MSS, L.6. 701.
22. C. Durston, *The Family and the English Civil War* (Oxford, 1988), 140.
23. J. Webb, *Memorials of the Civil War . . . As it affected Hertfordshire* (2 vols., London, 1879), ii. 85.

24. Richard Gough, *The History of Myddle* (Harmondsworth, 1981), 73–4.

25. E. Foord, *Wine and Women* (London, 1646), 27.

26. J. A. Atkinson, *Tracts relating to the Civil War in Cheshire* (Chetham Society, 65; Manchester, 1909), 120.

27. *Writings and Speeches of Oliver Cromwell*, ed. W. C. Abbott (4 vols., Cambridge Mass., 1937–47), i. 333.

28. Quoted in A. Fraser, *The Weaker Vessel* (London, 1985), 220–1.

29. 'The Gallant She-Soldier' (1655), 9.

30. H. Stocks (ed.), *Records of the Borough of Leicester, 1603–1688* (Leicester, 1923), 359.

31. H. Peters, *The Full and Last Relation of all things concerning Basing-House* (London, 1645), 2.

32. J. W. Bund, *The Civil War in Worcestershire, 1642–1646* (Birmingham, 1905), 96.

33. Samuel Butler, *Hubridas*, pt. 2, canto 2.

34. J. T. Gilbert (ed.), *The History of the Irish Confederation and War in Ireland, 1641–1643* (7 vols., Dublin, 1882–91), vol. i, p. xlv.

35. M. Cuffe, *The Siege of Ballyally Castle* (Camden Society, London, 1841), p. viix.

36. R. H. Morris, *The Siege of Chester* (Chester, 1924), 85.

37. Quoted in J. Eales, *Puritans and Roundheads: The Harleys of Brampton and the Outbreak of the English Civil War* (Cambridge, 1990), 3, 150–70.

38. E. Chisenhall, *A Brief Journal of the Siege of Latham Hall, 1644* (London, 1823), 17–74.

39. E. Hyde, *The Life of Edward, Earl of Clarendon* (2 vols., Oxford, 1857), i, 358–9.

40. Quoted in G. R. Quaife, *Wanton Wenches and Waywood Wives* (London, 1979), 49–50.

41. Quoted ibid., 50.

42. A. Thornton, *Autobiography of Mrs. Alice Thornton of East Newton, Co. York* (Surtees Society, 62; Durham, 1875), 44–7.

43. Verney, *Memoirs*, ii. 200.

44. Quoted in Quaife, *Wanton Wenches*, 133.

45. R. Josselin, *Diary* (Oxford, 1976), 51.

46. A. Fanshawe, *Memoirs* (London, 1909), 56.

47. Ibid.

48. She was exceedingly relieved to learn that Sir Richard had been taken prisoner, ibid. 105.

49. R. Polwhele, *Traditions and Recollections* (London, 1826), i. 17.

50. Quoted in Thornton, *Autobiography*, 48–50.

51. *The Widowes' Lamentation for the Absence of the dear children and suitors and for divers of their deaths in these fatal civil wars* (London, 1643), 3.

52. Historical Manuscripts Commission, *Fourth Report*, appendix, 261.

53. The royalist newspaper *Mercurius Aulicus* printed Susan's letter: John Adair, *By the Sword Divided: Eyewitness Accounts of the English Civil War* (London, 1983), 118.

54. Verney, *Memoirs*, i. 297.

55. J. T. Gilbert (ed.), *A Contemporary History of Affairs in Ireland from 1641 to 1652* (3 vols., Dublin, 1897–1880), vol. i, p. lxi.

56. Verney, *Memoirs*, i. 60–78.

57. *Widowes' Lamentation*, 3–4.

58. *The Virgins' Complaint for the Loss of their Sweethearts* (London, 1643), 1–4.

59. *The Humble Petition of the Many Thousands Wives and Matrons of the City and London and Other Parts of this Kingdom* (London, 1643), 7.

60. Bruno Ryves, *Mercurius Rusticus* (London, 1685), 167–8.

61. Quote from G.S., *A true relation of the sad passages of the two armies* (London, 1644), 6–11. B. Donagan, 'Codes and Conduct in the English Civil War', *Past and Present*, 118 (1988), 89–91.

62 Quoted in B. Donagan, 'Prisoners in the English Civil War', *History Today*, 41 (1991), 31.

63. *The Scourge of Civil Warre: the Blessings of Peace* (London, 1645), no page.

64. Durston, *Family*, 147. I cannot accept the conclusion of this excellent book that rape was fairly common during the English Civil Wars.

65. N. Wallington, *Historical Notices of Events occurring chiefly in the Reign of Charles I*, ed. R. Webb (2 vols., London, 1869), ii. 171.

66. Folger Library MSS, Vol. 436, 89.

67. Quoted in H. Simms, 'Violence in County Armagh, 1641', in B. MacCuarta (ed.), *Ulster 1641: Aspects of the Rising* (Belfast, 1993), 136.

68. Quoted in M. O'Dowd, 'Women and War in Ireland in the 1640s', in M. MacCurtain and M. O'Dowd (eds.), *Women in Early Modern Ireland* (Dublin, 1991), 101.

69. Antrim to [Hamilton], 14 July 1639 (Scottish Record Office, Gifts and Deposits 406/1/1165).

70. Robert Douglas, 'Civil War Diary', in J. Maidment (ed.), *Historical Fragments relative to Scottish Affairs* (Edinburgh, 1832), 67.

71. *A Discovery of Many Robberies committed by the late disbanded Troopers chiefly about the City of London since the Disbanding of the Army of the North* (London, 1644), 1–3.

72. E. Melling, *Kentish Sources*, ii. *Kent and the Civil War* (Maidstone, 1960), 17.

73. Suit by Aenas Lord MacDonald and other MacDonalds against Argyll for losses sustained in 1640, 1645, and 1654, 20 Mar. 1661 (Inverary Castle, Argyll muniments, bundle 801).

74. *A bloody fight at Balrvd-Derry in Ireland* . . . (London, 1647), 4.

75. Gilbert (ed.), *Irish Confederation*, iv. 153.

76. N. Wharton, 'The Letters of Sergeant Nehemiah Wharton', *Archaelogia*, 35 (1853), 311–13.

77. Quoted ibid., 313. J. W. Bund, *The Civil War in Winchester* (Birmingham, 1905), 56. R. Sherwood, *Civil Strife in the Midlands* (London, 1974), 17.

78. H. Foulis, *An exact and true relation of a bloody fight . . . before Tadcastle and Selby* (London, 1642), 9.

79. C. V. Wedgwood, 'The Scientists and the English Civil War', in *The Logic of Personal Knowledge: Essays presented to Michael Polanyi* (London, 1961), 62–3.

80. Josselin, *Diary*, 128–9.

81. A. Brome, *Poems*, ed. R. R. Dubinski (2 vols. Toronto, 1982), i. 214.

82. *The Western Husbandman's Lamentation* (1644), quoted in B. Manning, 'Neutrals and Neutralism in the English Civil Wars, 1642–1646' (D.Phil. thesis, Oxford, 1957), 403.

83. Henry Townsend, *Diary* (4 vols., London 1915–20), i. 128.

84. *Letter-book of the earl of Clanrciarde 1643–1647* ed. John Lowe (Irish Manuscripts Commission, Dublin, 1983), 39.

85. J. Webb, 'The Account Book of Mrs Joyce Jeffries', *Archaelogia* (1857), 37, 206.

86. M. Hazell, *Fidelity and Fortitude: Lord Capel and his Regiment and the English Civil War* (Leigh-on-Sea, 1987), 25.

87. D. A. Johnson and D. G. Vaisey, *Staffordshire in the Great Rebellion* (Stafford, 1964), 31.

88. Historical Manuscripts Commission, *Fourth Report*, appendix, 264.

89. R. E. Bell, *Memorials of the Civil Wars . . . the Fairfax Correspondence* (2 vols., London, 1849), ii. 98.

90. Townsend, *Diary*, vol. i, p. lxxx.
91. J. Sprigge, *Anglia Rediva* (London, 1854), 80.
92. *Lords' Journals*, vii. 485–6.
93. Quote from petition adopted by some thousand clubmen at Woodbury Hill, Worcester, 5 Mar. 1645, in Townsend, *Diary*, ii. 221–2.
94. C. M. Thomas, 'The Civil War in Glamorgan', in G. Williams (ed.), *Glamorgan Country History* (6 vols., Cardiff, 1974), iv. 269.
95. Quoted in Oliver Warner, 'The Clubmen and the English Civil War', *Army Quarterly*, 38 (1938), 287–90.
96. *Oliver Cromwell*, ed. Abbott, i. 369.
97. W. H. Blaauw, 'Passages of the Civil War in Sussex from 1642 to 1660', *Sussex Archaeological Collection*, 5 (1852), 64.
98. Verney, Memoirs, ii. 205.
99. B. Whitelocke, *Diary* (London, 1990), 132.
100. Quoted in A. Hughes, *Politics, Society and Civil War in Warwickshire, 1620–1660* (Cambridge, 1987), 300.
101. Verney, *Memoirs*, ii. 205. Quoted in William Blundell, *Crossby Records: A Cavalier's Notebook*, ed. T. Ellinson Gibson (London, 1880), 28.

Postlude

1. I take my figures from Henry Reece, 'The Military Presence in England 1649–1660' (D.Phil. diss., Oxford University, 1981), app. 1.
2. Ibid.
3. W. Prynne, *Eight Military Aphorismes demonstrating the uselessness, unprofitableness, hurtfulness and prodigall expensiveness of all standing English forts* (London, 1658). Prynne had earlier tangled with the army over the issue of free quarter in his *A Legal Vindication of the Liberties of England* (London, 1649), esp. 23–8.
4. The best modern account of Glencairn's revolt and of its suppression is F. Dow, *Cromwellian Scotland 1651–1660* (Edinburgh, 1979), chs. 4–7.
5. Reece, 'Military Presence', 23–6; C. H. Firth and G. Davies, *A Regimental History of Cromwell's Army* (2 vols., Oxford, 1940), chs. 2–7.
6. For a complete list of the regiments that served there 1649–56, see R. Dunlop, *Ireland under the Commonwealth* (3 vols., London, 1913), ii. 638–45; and see the discussion in C. H. Firth and G. Davies, *A Regimental History of Cromwell's Army* (2 vols., Oxford, 1940), chs. 8–10.
7. Firth and Davies, *Regimental History*, ch. 13.
8. C. H. Firth, 'Royalist and Cromwellian Armies in Flanders 1657–1662', *Transactions of the Royal Historical Society*, 17 (1903), at 76–8.
9. I. Gentles, 'The Debentures Market and the Military Purchase of crown Lands 1649–60', (Ph.D. diss., University of London, 1969), chs. 3–5.
10. We possess full lists of signatories to petitions from the regiments of William Goffe and Thomas Pride in 1659 which can be compared with the lists of debentures issued in 1650. These have been analysed by Henry Reece, and show a continuity rate of 20 per cent (80 out of 392) for Goffe's and 12 per cent (85 out of 684) for Pride's men (Reece, 'Military Presence', 27–8).
11. W. F. T. Butler (ed.), *Confiscations in Irish History* (Dublin, 1977 edn.); J. G. Simms, *The Williamite Confiscations in Ireland* (London, 1956), ch. 1; K. Bottigheimer, *English Adventurers and Irish Land* (Oxford, 1971) P. Corish, 'The Cromwellian Regime', in

T. W. Moody, F. X. Martin, and F. J. Byrne (eds.), *A New History of Ireland*, iii. *1534–1691* (Oxford, 1976), 357–74.

12. I believe this is also the conclusion of D. Massarella, 'The Politics of the Army 1647–1660' (D.Phil. diss., University of York, 1977) although I have not been able to consult it and rely on the testimony of those who have and upon the digest of the thesis published as 'The Politics of the Army and the Quest for Settlement', in I. Roots (ed.), *'Into another mould': Aspects of the Interregnum* (Exeter, 1981), 42–70.

13. This section draws heavily on J. G. A. Ive, 'The Local Dimensions of Defence: The Standing Army and the Militia in Norfolk, Suffolk and Essex 1649–1660' (Ph.D diss., University of Cambridge, 1986). The estimate that one-third of Cromwell's army comprised militiamen comes from S. R. Gardiner, *The Commonwealth and Protectorate* (4 vols., London, 1903), ii. 43.

14. S. Barber, 'A Bastard Militia?', in I. Gentles, J. Morrill, and B. Worden (eds.), *Soldiers, Writers and Statesmen of the English Revolution* (Oxford, 1998), ch. 6.

15. T. C. Barnard, 'The Protestant Interest 1641–1660' in J. Ohlmeyer (ed.), *Ireland: From Independence to Occupation 1641–1660* (Cambridge, 1992), 233–4.

16. R. C. Andersen, *Lists of Men-of-War, 1650–1700: part I, English Ships 1649–1702* (London, n.d.), 5–8. See the discussion in B. Capp, *Cromwell's Navy* (Oxford, 1989), 5–7.

17. J. S. Corbett, *England and the Mediterranean* (2 vols., London, 1917), ch. 15; Gardiner, *Commonwealth and Protectorate*, vol.ii, chs. 22–3; vol.iii, chs. 30–1; Capp, *Cromwell's Navy*, 73–87.

18. For this last group, see E. Ó. Ciardha, 'Tories and Moss-Troopers in Scotland and Ireland in the Interregnum: A Political Dimension', in J. Young (ed.), *Celtic Dimensions of the British Civil Wars* (Edinburgh, 1997), 141–62.

19. Ive, 'Local Dimensions', 75–84.

20. A. Woolrych, *Penruddock's Rising* (Historical Association Pamphlet G29, London, 1955); Gardiner, *Commonwealth and Protectorate*, iii. 287–94; D. E. Underdown, *Royalist Conspiracy in England 1649–1660* (New Haven, 1960), ch. 7.

21. R. N. Dore, 'The Cheshire Rising of 1659', *Transactions of the Lancashire and Cheshire Antiquarian Society* 69 (1959), 60–7; Underdown, *Royalist Conspiracy*, ch. 12.

22. T. C. Barnard, *Cromwellian Ireland* (Oxford, 1975), 22, 61, 98–111, 290–302; Corish, 'Cromwellian Regime', 360–6.

23. Dow, *Cromwellian Scotland 1651–1660*, chs. 4–7.

24. There is a graphic account in Gardiner, *Commonwealth and Protectorate*, iv. 120–45, surpassed only by the self-serving *Narrative of General Venables*, ed. C. H. Firth (Camden Society, NS 61; London, 1900) which has an excellent introduction and an appendix containing other recriminatory accounts. For Cromwell's mawkish reaction and its consequences, see A. B. Worden, 'Oliver Cromwell and the Sin of Achan', in D. Beales and D. Best (eds.), *History, Society and the Churches* (Cambridge, 1983), 125–46.

25. I have relied heavily here on the vivid reconstructions by C. H. Firth in his *Last Years of the Protectorate* (2 vols., Oxford, 1909), i. 42–56, 268–300; ii. 177–222.

26. J. Lilburne, *A just reproof to Haberdasher's Hall* (London, 1651), 9.

27. Reece, 'Military Presence', 201–10.

28. John Evelyn gives a graphic account of one such incident on Christmas Day 1657, cited in Morrill, *The Nature of the English Revolution* (London, 1992), 174–5.

29. This and the previous paragraph draw very extensively on Reece 'Military Presence', 177–210.

30. Dow, *Cromwellian Scotland*, chs. 7, 8, 10 (quotation is from p. 223); L. M. Smith, 'Scotland and Cromwell: A Study in Early Modern Government' (D.Phil. diss., University of Oxford, 1979), chs. 2, 3, 7.
31. K. McKenny, 'The Seventeenth-Century Land Settlement in Ireland', in Ohlmeyer (ed.), *Ireland: From Independence to Occupation*, 181–200.
32. A. Woolrych, *Commonwealth to Protectorate* (Oxford, 1982), 379–80.
33. Id., 'The Cromwellian Protectorate: A Military Dictatorship?' *History*, 244 (1990), 216–19.
34. The best case study is J. Sutton, 'Cromwell's Commissioners for preserving the Peace of the Commonwealth: A Staffordshire Case study', in Gentles, Morrill, and Worden (eds.), *Soldiers, Writers and Statesmen*. See also the comments in Woolrych, 'Military Dictatorship?', 222–4.
35. C. H. Firth (ed.), *The Clarke Papers* (4 vols., Camden Society, NS 49, 54, 60, 62; London, 1891–1901), iv. 200.
36. *The Writings and Speeches of Oliver Cromwell*, ed. W. C. Abbott, (Cambridge, Mass., 4 vols., 1934–44), iv. 412–19.
37. C. H. Firth, *The Last Years of the Protectorate* (2 vols., Oxford, 1909), i. 384.
38. The fullest analysis of Cromwell's thoughts during the Kingship crisis remains id., 'Cromwell and the Kingship', *English Historical Review*, 17 (1902), 429–42 and 18 (1903), 52–80. See also J. S. Morrill, 'King Oliver?', *Cromwelliana* (1981–2), 20–30.
39. J. S. Wheeler, 'Navy Finance 1649–1660', *Historical Journal* 39/2 (1996), 457–66; M. J. Braddick, 'An English Military Revolution', *Historical Journal*, 36:4 (1993), 965–75.
40. L. Schwoerer, *No Standing Armies!* (Baltimore, 1973), esp. chs. 6 and 8.
41. J. G. A. Pocock, *Politics, Language and Time* (London, 1972), 121; Gardiner, *Commonwealth and Protectorate*, iii. 346ff.
42. J. Childs, *The Army of Charles II* (London, 1976), chs. 1 and 11.
43. Ibid. 7–19.
44. J. Malcolm, *To Keep and Bear Arms: The Origins of an Anglo-American Right* (Cambridge, Mass., 1996), 36–40.

SELECT BIBLIOGRAPHY

The Principal Publications of John Philipps Kenyon

Books

Robert Spencer, Earl of Sunderland 1641–1702 (Longman, 1958; repr. 1975 and 1992).

The Stuarts: A Study in English Kingship (London, 1958).

The Stuart Constitution: Documents and Commentary (Cambridge, 1966; 2nd (rev.) edn., 1986).

The Popish Plot (London, 1972; paperback edn. 1973; 2nd edn. 1984).

Revolution Principles: The Politics of Party 1689–1720 (Cambridge, 1977; rev. edn. (paperback), 1990).

Stuart England (London, 1978; 2nd (rev.) edn., 1985).

The History Men: The Historical Profession in England since the Renaissance (London, 1983; 2nd (rev.) edn., 1993).

The Civil Wars of England, (London, 1988; Phoenix paperback edn. 1996).

Articles

'The Earl of Sunderland and the Revolution of 1688', *Cambridge Historical Journal*, 11 (1955).

'The Earl of Sunderland and the King's Administration 1693–1695', *English Historical Review*, 71 (1956).

'Charles II and William of Orange in 1680', *Bulletin of the Institute of Historical Research*, 30 (1957).

'The Acquittal of Sir George Wakeman', *Historical Journal*, 14 (1971).

'The Revolution of 1688: resistance and contract', in N. McKendrick, ed., *Historical Perspectives* (Cambridge, 1974), pp. 43–69.

'Sir Charles Firth and the Oxford School of Modern History 1892–1925', in A. C. Duke and C. A. Tamse (eds.), *Clio's Mirror: Britain and the Netherlands VIII* (Zutphen, 1985).

'The Commission for Ecclesiastical Causes 1686–1688', *Historical Journal*, 34 (1991).

Review Articles

'The Reign of Charles II', *Cambridge Historical Journal*, 13 (1957).

'Revisionism and Post-Revisionism in Early Stuart History', *Journal of Modern History*, 64 (1992).

Chapter 1: The Background to the Civil Wars in the Stuart Kingdoms

Recently Conrad Russell, *The Causes of the English Civil War* (Oxford, 1990), *The Fall of the British Monarchies* (Oxford, 1991), and *Unrevolutionary England, 1603–1642* (London, 1990); J. Morrill (ed.), *The Scottish National Covenant in its British Context 1638–1651* (Edinburgh, 1990); and R. Asch (ed.), *Three Nations—A Common History? England, Scotland, Ireland and British History c. 1600–1920* (Arbeitskreis Deutsche England-Forschung, 23; Bochum, 1993), have drawn attention to the British and Irish context of the origins of the Wars of the Three Kingdoms. For a detailed analysis of the Bishops' Wars see P. Donald, *An Uncounselled King: Charles I and the Scottish Troubles 1637–1641* (Cambridge, 1990) and M. Fissell, *The Bishops' Wars: Charles I's Campaigns against Scotland 1638–1640* (Cambridge, 1994). For the origins of the Irish rebellion see H. Kearney, *Strafford in Ireland 1633–1641: A Study in Absolutism* (Cambridge, 2nd edn., 1989); B. MacCuarta (ed.), *Ulster 1641: Aspects of the Rising* (Belfast, 1993); and M. Perceval-Maxwell, *The Outbreak of the Irish Rebellion of 1641* (Dublin, 1994).

For an integrated account of the Wars of the Three Kingdoms see S. R. Gardiner, *History of the Great Civil War, 1642–1649* (new edn., 4 vols., London, 1893; repr. 1987) and M. Bennett, *The Civil Wars in Britain and Ireland 1638–1651* (Oxford, 1997). The close interconnections between the Stuart kingdoms are also discussed in J. Ohlmeyer, *Civil War and Restoration in the Three Stuart Kingdoms: The Career of Randal MacDonnell, earl of Antrim* (Cambridge, 1993); D. Stevenson, *Scottish Covenanters and Irish Confederates: Scottish-Irish Relations in the Mid-Seventeenth Century* (Belfast, 1981) and *Alasdair MacColla and the Highland Problem in the 17th Century* (Edinburgh, 1980); and J. R. Young (ed.), *Celtic Dimensions of the British Civil Wars* (Edinburgh, 1997). For astute contemporary comments on the course of the wars in—and between—the Stuart monarchies see Edward Hyde, earl of Clarendon, *The History of the Rebellion and Civil War in England*, ed. W. D. Macray (6 vols., Oxford, 1888; reissued, 1992).

Chapter 2: Civil War in Scotland

The principal sources for the study of covenanting Scotland include T. Thomson and C. Innes (eds.), *The Acts of the Parliament of Scotland* (12 vols., Edinburgh, 1814–75); C. S. Terry (ed.), *The Army of the Covenant* (2 vols., Scottish History Society, 2nd ser. 16–17; Edinburgh, 1917); H. W. Meikle (ed.), *Correspondence of Scots Commissioners in London, 1644–1646* (Roxburghe Club, 160; Edinburgh, 1917); *The Letters and Journals of Robert Baillie: Principal of the University of Glasgow, 1637–1662*, ed. D. Laing (3 vols., Bannatyne Club, 72/1–2, 77; Edinburgh, 1841–2); and J. Spalding, *Memorialls of the Trubles in Scotland and England, 1624–1645*, ed. J. Stuart (2 vols., Spalding Club, 21–2; Aberdeen 1850–1).

For a general overview of these years see D. Stevenson, *The Scottish Revolution, 1637–1644* (Newton Abbot, 1973) and *Revolution and Counter-Revolution in Scotland, 1644–1651* (London, 1977). For detailed military histories see E. M. Furgol, *A Regimental History of the Covenanting Armies, 1639–1651* (Edinburgh, 1990) and S. Reid, *Scots Armies of the Civil War 1639–1651* (Norwich, 1982). For the Scottish Army in Ulster see H. Hazlett, 'The Recruitment and Organisation of the Scottish Army in Ulster, 1642–1649' in H. A. Cronne, T. W. Moody, and D. B. Quinn (eds.), *Essays in British and Irish History in Honour of James Eadie Todd* (London, 1949), 107–33, and D. Stevenson,

Scottish Covenanters and Irish Confederates: Scottish-Irish Relations in the Mid-Seventeenth Century (Belfast, 1981). The royalist war-effort in Scotland is analysed in E. J. Cowan, *Montrose for Covenant and King* (London, 1977) and D. Stevenson, *Alasdair MacColla and the Highland Problem in the 17th Century* (Edinburgh, 1980). Also see *Memorials of Montrose and his Times*, ed. M. Napier (2 vols., Maitland Club, 66/1–2; Edinburgh, 1848–50) and G. Wishart, *The Memoirs of James, Marquis of Montrose, 1639–1650*, ed. A. D. Murdoch and H. F. M. Simpson (London, 1893). For the Cromwellian conquest see W. S. Douglas, *Cromwell's Scotch Campaigns: 1650–1651* (London, 1898) and C. H. Firth (ed.), *Scotland and the Commonwealth*, (Scottish History Society, 1st ser. 18; Edinburgh, 1895).

Chapter 3: Civil War in Ireland

Many of the seminal documents relating to the Irish Civil Wars have been reprinted in J. T. Gilbert (ed.), *A Contemporary History of Affairs in Ireland (1641–1652) Containing the . . . Narrative entitled an 'Aphorismical discovery of treasonable faction'* (3 vols., Irish Archaeological and Celtic Society; Dublin, 1879); J. T. Gilbert (ed.), *History of the Irish Confederation and the War in Ireland, 1641–1643* . . . (7 vols., Dublin 1882–91); Giuseppe Aiazza (ed.), *The Embassy in Ireland of Monsignor G. B. Rinuccinni, archbishop of Fermo, in the years 1645–1649* . . ., trans. A. Hutton (Dublin, 1873); and T. Carte, *History of the life of James, first duke of Ormonde* (2nd edn., 6 vols., Oxford, 1851).

The relevant chapters in T. W. Moody, F. X. Martin, and F. J. Byrne (eds.), *A New History of Ireland*, iii. *1534–1691* (Oxford, 1976) remain the most authoritative introduction to this period. The military aspects of the war are discussed in G. A. Hayes-McCoy, *Irish Battles: A Military History of Ireland* (Belfast, 1989); J. Ohlmeyer (ed.), *Ireland from Independence to Occupation 1638–1660* (Cambridge, 1995); J. Ohlmeyer, 'The Wars of Religion, 1603–1660', in T. Bartlett and K. Jeffery (eds.), *A Military History of Ireland* (Cambridge, 1996); P. Lenihan, ' "Celtic" Warfare in the 1640s', in J. R. Young (ed.), *Celtic Dimensions of the British Civil Wars* (Edinburgh, 1997); J. Casway, *Owen Roe O'Neill and the Struggle for Catholic Ireland* (Philadelphia, 1984); and J. Lowe, 'Some Aspects of the War in Ireland, 1641–1649', *Irish Sword*, 4 (winter, 1959). For the confederation of Kilkenny see D. F. Cregan, 'The Confederation of Kilkenny', in B. Farrell (ed.), *Irish Parliamentary Tradition* (Dublin, 1973) and 'The Personnel of the Confederation of Kilkenny', *Irish Historical Studies*, 39 (1995). For the relations between Charles and the confederates see J. Lowe, 'Charles I and the Confederation of Kilkenny, 1643–1649', *Irish Historical Studies*, 14 (1964) and 'The Glamorgan Mission to Ireland 1645–1646', *Studia Hibernica*, 4 (1964).

Chapter 4: Civil Wars in England

The best general military histories of the civil wars in England are A. Woolrych, *Battles of the English Civil War* (London, 1961; repr. 1991), P. Young and R. Holmes, *The English Civil War: A Military History of the Three Civil Wars 1641–1651* (London, 1974), and J. P. Kenyan, *The Civil Wars of England* (London, 1988). Briefer but useful studies are P. R. Newman, *Atlas of the English Civil War* (London, 1985), which consists of fifty-six maps accompanied by one-page descriptions of military movements and engagements, and P. Haythornthwaite, *The English Civil War 1642–1651: An Illustrated Military History*

(London, 1994), which is profusely illustrated in colour and black and white. For an interesting local study see P. Tennant, *Edgehill and Beyond: The People's War in the South Midlands 1642–1645* (London, 1992). C. Carlton, *Going to the Wars: The Experience of the British Civil Wars, 1638–1651* (London, 1994) presents a vivid account of what the war was like for those who participated in it, and attempts a calculation of its material and human cost. For an intelligent, finely written narrative that interweaves military and political themes one cannot do better than C. V. Wedgwood's *The King's War 1641–1647* (London, 1958). Much of the work on individual armies remains largely inaccessible in unpublished theses. For Parliament C. H. Firth's often reprinted *Cromwell's Army* (London, 1902) is an indispensable study of the army's institutional structure. M. Kishlansky, *The Rise of the New Model Army* (Cambridge, 1979) treats the army's founding and its political activities between 1645 and 1647, while I. Gentles, *The New Model Army in England, Ireland and Scotland, 1645–1653* (Oxford, 1992) combines institutional history with a connected military and political narrative. C. Holmes, *The Eastern Association in the English Civil War* (London, 1974) is very informative about the earl of Manchester's army; while J. Adair, *Roundhead General: A Military Biography of Sir William Waller* (London, 1969) provides an excellent account of Waller's army. The earl of Essex's army awaits its historian. Ronald Hutton presents the fruits of much new research on the king's army in the west in *The Royalist War Effort 1642–1646* (London, 1982), but says nothing about Newcastle's army in the north.

Chapter 5: Naval Operations

The standard work on the navy in the civil wars remains J. R. Powell's pioneering *The Navy in the English Civil War* (London, 1962), though it shows the trees more clearly than the wood. J. R. Powell and E. K. Timings (eds.), *Documents relating to the Civil War 1642–1648* (Navy Records Society; London, 1963), prints a wide range of contemporary source-materials which give a vivid impression of the war at sea. For the later part of the period, B. Capp, *Cromwell's Navy: The Fleet and the English Revolution, 1648–1660* (Oxford, 1989; paperback edn., 1992), places naval history from the Revolt of 1648 to the Restoration against the political background. There has been considerable recent work on the navy of the 1630s, including B. Quintrell, 'Charles I and his Navy', *Seventeenth Century*, 3 (1988), and K. R. Andrews, *Ships, Money & Politics: Seafaring and Naval Enterprise in the Reign of Charles I* (Cambridge, 1991). Changes in the officer corps, which help to explain what happened in 1642, are well covered by D. E. Kennedy, 'Naval Captains at the Outbreak of the English Civil War', *Mariner's Mirror* (henceforth *MM*), 46 (1960). The seizure of the fleet has recently been re-examined by S. J. Greenberg in 'Seizing the Fleet in 1642: Parliament, the Navy and the Printing Press', *MM* 77 (1991), an account rebutted in part by M. L. Baumber, 'Seizing the Fleet in 1642', *MM* 78 (1992). Naval operations in the Irish Sea and their significance for the war on land are treated by M. L. Baumber, 'The Navy and the Civil War in Ireland, 1643–1646,' *MM* 75 (1989), while the operations of the Irish and Flemish privateers have been examined in depth by Jane Ohlmeyer in 'Irish Privateers during the Civil War, 1642–1650', *MM* 76 (1990). The first volume of *Memorials of Sir William Penn*, ed. G. Penn (2 vols., London, 1833), includes Penn's journals from the 1640s, when he was a young commander in Parliament's Irish guard, and gives a good picture of operations afloat and ashore in this theatre, as well as fascinating glimpses of social relations on board ship. D. E. Kennedy, 'The English Naval Revolt of 1648', *English Historical Review*, 77 (1962) gives a good account of the crisis. For a detailed account of royalist operations under the prince of Wales and Rupert see R. C. Anderson, 'The Royalists at Sea in 1648', *MM* 9 (1928), and his subsequent articles on 1649 (*MM* 14 (1928)), 1650 (*MM* 1/ (1931)), and 1651–3 (*MM* 21 (1935)), and for contemporary accounts E. Warburton, *Memoirs of Prince Rupert* (London, 1849). There are several good biographies of Blake, including M. L. Baumber, *General-at-Sea: Robert Blake* (London, 1989) and J. R. Powell, *Robert Blake: General at Sea* (London, 1972). *The Letters of Robert Blake*, ed. J. R. Powell, (Navy Records Society; London, 1937), shows us the man in his own words. M. Oppenheim, *A History of the Administration of the Royal Navy . . . from 1509 to 1660* (London, 1896; reissued 1988) remains a valuable overview. For naval administration in this period see A. C. Dewar, 'The Naval Administration of the Interregnum, 1641–1659', *MM* 12 (1926); G. E. Aylmer, *The State's Servants* (London, 1973); and V. A. Rowe, *Sir Henry Vane the Younger* (London, 1970).

Chapter 6: Sieges and Fortifications

General introductions to the European and British military contexts, usually with some helpful specific information upon the British and Irish Civil Wars, can be found in B. H. St J. O'Neil, *Castles and Cannon* (Oxford, 1960); G. Parker, *The Army of Flanders and the Spanish Road 1567–1659* (London, 1972) and *The Military Revolution: Military Innovation and the Rise of the West, 1500–1800* (London, 1988, 3rd edn. 1996); C. Duffy, *Siege Warfare: The Fortress in the Early Modern World 1494–1660* (London, 1979); and S. Porter, *Destruction in the English Civil Wars* (London, 1994). Insights are also furnished by J. Kenyon, *The Civil Wars of England* (London, 1988) and C. Carlton, *Going to the Wars: The Experience of the British Civil Wars, 1638–1651* (London, 1994), and accounts of some major sieges, often with a full reprinting of contemporary sources, occur in J. W. Willis-Bund, *The Civil War in Worcestershire* (London, 1905); A. R. Bayley, *The Civil War in Dorset 1642–1660* (London, 1910); J. Webb and T. W. Webb, *Memorials of the Civil War . . . as it Affected Herefordshire* (London, 1879); M. Coate, *Cornwall in the Great Civil War* (London, 1933); and G. N. Godwin, *The Civil War in Hampshire* (London, 1904).

The principal military manuals referred to in the text (apart from the excellent Robert Norton) were Henry Hexham, *The Principles of the Art Military* (3 pts., London, 1642–3); William Bourne, *The Arte of Shooting in Great Ordnance* (London, 1643); *Enchridion of Fortification* (London, 1645); and William Eldred, *The Gunners Glasse* (London, 1646). A number of famous accounts of sieges have also been published: Isaac Tullie, *A Narrative of the Siege of Carlisle*, ed. S. Jefferson (Carlisle, 1840); C. H. Firth, 'Sir Hugh Cholmley's Narrative of the Siege of Scarborough, 1644–1645', *English Historical Review*, 32 (1917); Nathan Drake, *A Journal of the First and Second Sieges of Pontefract Castle 1644–1645*, ed. W. H. D. Longstaffe (Surtees Society, 37; London, 1860); *A Journal of the Siege of Lathom House* (London, 1644; repr. 1823); *The Siege of Chester: Nathaniel Lancaster's Narrative*, ed. John Lewis (London, 1987); and 'John Byron's Account of the Siege of Chester', *Cheshire Sheaf*, 4th ser. 6. Also see W. G. Ross, *Military Engineering during the Great Civil War 1642–1649* (Royal Engineers' Institute

Occasional Papers, 13; 1887); the study of ordnance is dealt with by D. E. Lewis, 'The Use of Ordnance in the English Civil War 1642–1649' (MA thesis, Manchester, 1971), and P. Young and W. Emberton, *Sieges of the Great Civil War* (London, 1978).

The recent contributions to the subject by archaeologists are best represented by H. Clayton, *Loyal and Ancient City: Lichfield in the Civil Wars* (Derby, n.d.); D. Sturdy, 'The Civil War Defences of London', *London Archaeologist*, 7 (1975), 334–8; S. Ward, *Excavations at Chester: The Civil War Siegeworks* (Chester, 1987); M. Stoyle, *Exeter City Defences Project* (Exeter Museums Archaeological Unit, Exeter, 1988) and *The Civil War Defences of Exeter and the Great Parliamentary Siege of 1645–1646* (Exeter Museums Archaeological Unit, Exeter, 1990); T. Warner, *Newark: The Civil War Siegeworks* (Nottingham County Council, Nottingham, 1992); L. Butler, *Sandal Castle, Wakefield* (Wakefield Historical Publications Wakefield, 1991); and M. Atkin and W. Laughlin, *Gloucester and the Civil War* (London, 1992).

Other valuable studies of sieges which occurred during the English Civil Wars, drawing more heavily upon documentary sources, are E. Green, 'The Siege and Defence of Taunton, 1644–1645', *Somerset Archaeological and Natural History Society Proceedings*, 25 (1879); F. J. Varley, *The Siege of Oxford* (London, 1932); P. Wenham, *The Great and Close Siege of York, 1644* (London, 1970); and P. McGrath, *Bristol and the Civil War* (Bristol Branch of the Historical Association; Bristol, 1981). The Varley book should be read in conjunction with R. Lattey, E. Parsons, and I. G. Philip, 'A Contemporary Map of the Defences of Oxford in 1644', *Oxoniensa*, 1 (1936).

Three recent publications have immensely improved knowledge of the subject during the civil wars in Ireland: P. M. Kerrigan, *Castles and Fortifications in Ireland 1485–1945* (London, 1995); R. Loeber and G. Parker, 'The Military Revolution in Seventeenth-Century Ireland', in J. Ohlmeyer (ed.), *Ireland from Independence to Occupation 1641–1660* (Cambridge, 1995); and P. Lenihan, 'Galway and the "New" System of Fortifications, 1643–1650', *Galway Archaeological and Historical Society Journal*, 48 (1996). There appears to be no comparable body of scholarship for Scotland.

Chapter 7: Logistics and Supply

The sources dealing with supply in the English Civil Wars are disparate and include *The Letter Books of Sir William Brereton*, ed. R. N. Dore, (2 pts., Record Society of Lancashire and Cheshire, 123 and 128; Chester, 1984 and 1990); C. H. Firth and R. S. Rait (eds.), *Acts and Ordinances of the Interregnum, 1642–1660* (London, 1911); G. I. Mungeam (ed.), 'Contracts for the Supply of Equipment to the "New Model" Army in 1645', *Journal of the Arms and Armour Society*, 6 (1968–70); and I. Roy, 'The Royalist Ordnance Papers', *Oxfordshire Records Society*, 43 (1963–4) and 49 (1971–3). For details on how the covenanters secured supplies from the continent see *The Journal of Thomas Cunningham of Campvere 1640–1654*, ed. E. J. Courthope (Edinburgh, 1928).

The history of supply to the various armies serving throughout the three kingdoms remains to be written. Useful starting-points include R. Brenner, *Merchants and Revolution* (Cambridge, 1993); C. H. Firth, *Cromwell's Army* (London, 1962 edn.); I. Gentles, *The New Model Army* (Oxford, 1992); C. Holmes, *The Eastern Association in the English Civil War* (Cambridge, 1974); R. Hutton, *The Royalist War Effort 1642–1646* (New York, 1982); J. Morrill, *The Revolt of the Provinces* (London, 1976); and J. De L.

Mann, *The Cloth Industry in the West of England from 1640 to 1880* (Gloucester, 1987). Also see the numerous regional studies which analyse the war in England at a local level. These include E. A. Andriette, *Devon and Exeter in the Civil War* (Newton Abbot, 1971); M. Atkin and W. Laughlin, *Gloucester and the Civil War* (Stroud, 1992); A. M. Everitt, *The Community of Kent and the Great Rebellion 1640–1660* (Leicester, 1973); A. Hughes, *Politics, Society and Civil War in Warwickshire, 1620–1660* (Cambridge, 1987); J. Wroughton, *A Community at War: The Civil War in Bath and North Somerset, 1642–1650* (Bath, 1992); and D. Underdown, *Somerset in the Civil War and Interregnum* (Newton Abbot, 1973). On the arms industry see W. H. B. Court, *The Rise of Midland Industries 1600–1838* (London, 1938); G. and A. Crocker, 'Gunpowder Mills of Surrey', *Surrey History*, 4/3 (1990); P. Edwards, 'Gunpowder and the English Civil War', *Journal of the Arms & Armour Society*, 15/2 (1995); and C. Foulkes, *The Gun-Founders of England* (Cambridge, 1937). Taxation and the financing of the war-efforts in England are discussed in M. Bennett, 'Contribution and Assessment: Financial Exactions in the English Civil War, 1642–1646', *War and Society*, 4 (1986), and J. Engberg, Royalist Finances during the English Civil War, *Scandinavian Economic History Review*, 14 (1966).

For material relating to logistics in the Irish and Scottish Civil Wars see the titles listed under Chapters 2 and 3, above. In addition see D. Stevenson, 'The Financing of the Cause of the Covenants, 1638–45', *Scottish Historical Review*, 51 (1972); J. S. Wheeler, 'The Logistics of the Cromwellian Conquest of Scotland 1650–1651', *War and Society*, 10 (1992); and H. Hazlett, 'The Financing of the British Armies in Ireland, 1641–1649', *Irish Historical Studies*, 1 (Mar., 1938).

Chapter 8: Civilians

While there are no books written specifically on civilians during the British and Irish Civil Wars, I. Roy, 'The English Civil War and English Society', in B. Bond and I. Roy (eds.), *War and Society* (London, 1975), and C. Durston, *The Family and the English Civil War* (Oxford, 1988), are excellent introductions. C. Carlton, *Going to the Wars: The Experience of the British Civil Wars, 1638–1651* (London, 1994) deals with civilians and soldiers alike. Richard Gough, *The History of Myddle* (Harmondsworth, 1981) is an excellent contemporary record of the effects of the war on a single village. J. Adair, *By the Sword Divided: Eyewitness accounts of the English Civil War* (London, 1983) is a useful collection, while F. P. and M. M. Verney, *Memoirs of the Verney Family during the Civil War and Commonwealth* (4 vols., London, 1892–9) is a fascinating source for a single family. In *The Weaker Vessel* (London, 1985), Antonia Fraser describes the experience of women with her usual skill and style, while Anne Fanshawe's *Memoirs* (London, 1909) are a moving record of one woman's ordeals. B. Donagan, 'Codes and Conduct in the English Civil War', *Past and Present*, 118 (1988) is a splendid appetizer for her forthcoming book. B. Manning, 'Neutrals and Neutralism in the English Civil War' (D.Phil., Oxford University, 1957), and J. T. Zeller, 'Anti-War Sentiment during the English Civil War', (Ph.D., University of Minnesota, 1974), stress the importance of economics as opposed to violence in motivating the clubmen. See also O. Warner, 'The Clubmen and the English Civil War', *Army Quarterly*, 38 (1936); J. Morrill, *The Revolt of the Provinces* (London, 1976); R. Hutton, *The Royalist War Effort* (London, 1983); and A. Fletcher, *A County Community in Peace and War: Sussex, 1600–1660* (London, 1975).

Postlude: Between War and Peace 1651–1662

There has been little detailed study of the army of the 1650s, all the leading studies of the New Model ending with the initial conquests of Scotland and Ireland. There is, however, a superb study *Cromwell's Navy* by Bernard Capp (Oxford, 1989). The campaign histories of the 1650s were expertly put together and woven into the fabric of the authoritative narratives of the Interregnum published a century ago by S. R. Gardiner, *The Commonwealth and Protectorate* (4 vols., London, 1892), and C. H. Firth, *The Last Years of the Protectorate* (2 vols., Oxford, 1911). Subsequent work adds little, although H. C. B. Rogers, *Generals at Sea* (London, 1992), and R. Ollard, *Cromwell's Earl* (London, 1990) contain gripping narratives. The fundamental analytical work on the army is a sadly unpublished thesis: H. Reece, 'The Military Presence in England 1649–1660' (D.Phil. thesis, University of Oxford, 1981), which looks at every aspect of its organization, deployment, and military, administrative, and political role and which also contains an important narrative of the military activity in the dying months of the Interregnum. Two other theses are important supplements: D. Massarella, 'The Politics of the Army 1647–1660' (D.Phil. thesis, University of York, 1977)—the argument of which is abstracted in an essay in I. Roots (ed.), *'Into another mould': Aspects of the Interregnum* (Exeter, 1981) and J. G. A. Ive, 'The Local Dimensions of Defence: The Standing Army and the Militia in Norfolk, Suffolk and Essex 1646–1660' (Ph.D. thesis, University of Cambridge, 1986). C. H. Firth and G. Davies, *A Regimental History of Cromwell's Army* (2 vols., Oxford, 1940) is in essence an annotated officer list with campaign notes. There is much of interest for the 1650s in P. R. Newman's *Royalist Officers in England and Wales 1641–1660: A Biographical Dictionary* (New York, 1981). The role of the army in Scotland is best described by Frances Dow, *Cromwellian Scotland* (Edinburgh, 1979) although there is much of interest in C. H. Firth (ed.), *Scotland and the Commonwealth* (Scottish History Society, 1st ser. 18; Edinburgh 1895); C. H. Firth (ed.) *Scotland and the Protectorate* (Scottish History Society 1st ser. 31; Edinburgh, 1899); and C. S. Terry (ed.), *The Cromwellian Union* (Scottish History Society, 1st ser. 40; Edinburgh, 1902). The role of the army in Ireland is traced in T. C. Barnard, *Cromwellian Ireland* (Oxford, 1975), but is more fully explored in older works such as J. P. Prendergast, *The Cromwellian Settlement of Ireland* (1865) and more particularly R. Dunlop, *Ireland under the Commonwealth* (3 vols., London, 1913).

CHRONOLOGY

(Major military encounters are indicated in bold)

Year	England and Wales	Scotland	Ireland	The Continent
1639		Feb: Covenanters seize Inverness		
		21 Mar: Edinburgh Castle falls to covenanters		
		26 Mar: Covenanters capture Dumbarton Castle		
	30 Mar: King reaches York	30 Mar: Montrose occupies Aberdeen for covenanters		
		May–June: First Bishops' War (ended by Treaty of Berwick, 18 June)		
		14 May: Trot of Turriff, a royalist victory		
		14 May: Royalists briefly occupy Aberdeen	21 May: Proclamation of the 'black oath', requiring all Scots in Ulster to take an oath of loyalty to the king	
	30 May: King reaches Newcastle	18 June: Treaty of Berwick, return to the *status quo ante bellum*		
		18-19 June: battle of Brig of Dee—covenanters occupy Aberdeen		
		20 June: Leslie's army disbands		
		30 Aug–14 Nov: First session of Charles I's Second Scottish Parliament		Oct: **Dutch destroy Spanish fleet at battle of the Downs**
				Dec: c.1300 Irish troops serving in Flanders (under Owen Roe O'Neil)
1640			Aug: Poor harvests (since 1636)	
			Mar 1640; Wentworth prepares to raise 9,000 for king's service	Feb: Stafford asks Spain for assistance

The Chronology is based on material in the preceding chapters. The following have also been consulted: T. W. Moody, F. X. Martin, and F. J. Byrne (eds.), *A New History of Ireland*, viii. *A Chronology of Irish History to 1976* (Oxford, 1982); P. R. Newman, *Atlas of the English Civil War* (Beckenham, Kent, 1985); and Peter Grant, *The Cromwellian Gazetteer* (Gloucester, 1987).

The Europeans dated according to New (Gregorian) Style which was ten days ahead of the Old Style (Julian) Calender. Where two dates appear in the form '10/20 November' for example, '10' refers to Old Style and '20' to New Style

Year	England and Wales	Scotland	Ireland	The Continent
	13 April–5 May: Short Parliament in England	5–8 May: Marischal's occupation of Aberdeen	16 Mar–17 June: First session of Charles I's Second Irish Parliament	May: Revolt of Catalonia (until 1652)
		Late May: Siege of Edinburgh (surrenders 19 Sept)	1 April: Irish Parliament adjourns to 1 June	
	June: Alonso de Cárdenas becomes Spanish ambassador in London (until Oct 1655)	28 May–12 Sept: Munro's north-eastern campaign		June–Aug: Owen Roe O'Neil defends Arras against the French
		2–11 June: Second session of Charles I's Second Scottish Parliament		
		18 June–1 Aug: Argyll's campaign against Highland royalists		July: Olivares offers Charles I financial assistance
		15 July–Nov 1641: Third session of Charles I's Second Scottish Parliament	July: Wentworth's 'New Army' assembles at Carrickfergus	
		20–30 Aug: Leslie's campaigns in the north-east of England		
	20 Aug: King leaves London for north	20 Aug: Scottish army crosses the Tweed; beginning of Second Bishops' War		
		27 Aug: Covenanters capture Dumbarton Castle after siege		
	28 Aug: Covenanter victory at Newburn			
	30 Aug: Covenanters take Newcastle	19 Sept: Edinburgh Castle surrenders		
	24 Sept: King summons Great Council to York	Sept: Caerlaverock and Threave Castles surrender after sieges	1 Oct–12 Nov: Second session of Charles I's Second Irish Parliament	
		16 and 26 Oct: Treaties of Ripon		
	3 Nov: Meeting of the 'Long Parliament'			

1641

11 Nov: Strafford impeached
11 Dec: Root and Branch petition

30 Jan: Articles of impeachment against Strafford sent to House of Lords
15 Feb: Triennial Act
22 Mar: Beginning of Strafford's trial
End Apr–mid-May: Charles I instructs Antrim to continue the 'New Army'
8 May: Charles I orders 'New Army' to disband
11 May: Act 'against the dissolving of Parliament without its own consent'
12 May: Strafford executed; unsuccessful plans for use of force against Parliament
24 June: Ten Propositions

5 July: Abolition of Courts of Star Chamber and High Commission
Aug: Charles I leaves London for Edinburgh and orders Antrim to remuster the 'New Army' which is to 'declare for him [the king] against the parliament in England'

May: Montrose calls for a more conciliatory policy towards the king

June: Treaty of London concluded

26 Jan–5 Mar: Third session of Charles I's Second Irish Parliament
Feb: O'More–Maguire plot resulted in the outbreak of the Ulster rebellion

11 May–17 Nov: Fourth session of Charles I's Second Irish Parliament

Dec: Revolt of Portugal (until 1668)
Gennep (governor Thomas Preston) surrenders to Dutch after a bitter struggle during which the Irish troops distinguished themselves
Francisco de Melo becomes governor of the Spanish Netherlands
Jan: Catalonia accepts French protection

May: Mary Stuart marries William, prince of Orange

June: Portugal and France sign a mutual aid treaty
Portugal and Netherlands sign ten-year truce
Treaty of Hamburg between France and Sweden
July: Soissons conspiracy in France

Year	England and Wales	Scotland	Ireland	The Continent
		21 Aug: Leslie's army leaves Newcastle; covenanters begin to disband their armies		
		21 Oct: The Incident—Charles backs attempts to seize covenanting leaders in Scottish Parliament		
		28 Oct: Scottish Parliament offers to send an army of 10,000 to crush the Ulster rising	22 Oct: **Outbreak of the Ulster rebellion**	
			23 Oct: Alleged attempt to seize Dublin thwarted	
			26 Oct: Sir Phelim O'Neill captures Armagh	
			4 Nov: Sir Phelim O'Neill issues commission purporting to be from king	
			11 Nov: Ormond appointed lieutenant-general of the king's army	
			16–17 Nov: Brief meeting of Irish Parliament	
			21 Nov: Insurgents attack and plunder Lord Moore's residence at Mellifont	
	22 Nov: Publication of Grand Remonstrance		21 Nov: **Insurgents begin siege of Drogheda (raised in Mar 1642)**	
			28 Nov: Insurgent attack on Lisburn repulsed	
			29 Nov: Army, sent to relieve Drogheda, defeated at Julianstown, Co. Meath; Irish insurgents open negotiations with Old English	
			End Nov: Sir Charles Coote garrisons Newcastle, Co.	

1 Dec: Charles I presented with Grand Remonstrance

3 Dec: Negotiations with Charles I regarding sending an army to Ireland

Wicklow, and relieves Wicklow Castle

Early Dec: Meetings at Knockcrofty and Hill of Tara leads to an alliance between Ulster Irish and leadership in the Pale

1 Dec: Coote skirmishes with insurgents at Kilcoole, Co. Wicklow, before returning to Dublin

3 Dec: Antrim and lords of the Pale summoned to a conference in Dublin on 8 Dec: they refuse

15 Dec: Coote attacks Santry and Clontarf

30 Dec: Sir Simon Harcourt and 1,100 foot arrive in Dublin from England

Dec: Alliance between Old English and Ulster insurgents; Cos. Roscommon, Mayo, Sligo, Kilkenny, and Tipperary join the rising

Jan: England unofficially recognizes Portugal's independence

Jan: Attempt to arrest the Five Members; Charles I leaves London

Publication of Henry Jones, *A Remonstrance of Divers Remarkable Passages concerning the Church and Kingdom of Ireland* (London); c.22,000–37,000 and c.11,000–23,000 Catholic troops in arms

Jan: Catholics in Cos. Antrim, Limerick, and Clare join the rising

Early Jan: Coote routs insurgent forces at Swords

11 Jan: O'Neill's attempt to take Drogheda fails

1642

Year	England and Wales	Scotland	Ireland	The Continent
			11 Jan–9 Feb 1647: Fifth session of Charles I's Second Irish Parliament	Feb: Henrietta Maria travels to Dutch Republic for assistance
			1–3 Feb: Ormond burns Newcastle and takes Naas, Co. Kildare	
			12 Feb: Lord Lambert defeats insurgents in Wicklow and clears Dublin of insurgents	
			Mid-Feb: Rebellion spreads to Co. Kerry	
			20 Feb: 1,500 foot under Col. Monck arrive in Dublin from England	
			End Feb: Viscount Muskerry and Co. Cork Catholics join the insurrection; a further assault on Drogheda fails	
			Mar: Siege of Drogheda raised	
			16 Mar: Lords justices later allege that by this date 154,000 Protestants have been killed by 'rebels' (more realistic figure is c.4,000)	
	5 Mar: Militia Ordnance	13 Mar: Three standing regiments sail for Ulster	19 Mar: Town of Galway declares for the insurgents and then comes to an agreement with Clanricard	
	18 Mar: King arrives in York and establishes his court		22: Mar: Catholic bishops and vicars of the province of Armagh meet at Kells	
	19 Mar: 'Adventurers' Act' pledging Irish land to those who invest in the army raised to suppress the rebellion		End Mar: Henry Tichborne retakes Ardee and Dundalk	
			Apr: Mayor of Galway informs Clanricard of the town's intention to joint the confederates and besieges Galway fort (until June 1643)	
	Apr: Gates of Hull shut against the king		2 Apr: Ormond campaigns in Co. Kildare and relieves Borris, Birr, and Knockmenease	

May: Spanish Army of Flanders defeats the French at Honnecourt

3 Apr: A Scottish army under Munro lands at Carrickfergus

15 Apr: Ormond defeats insurgents at Kilrush

27 Apr–12 May: Munro campaigns in Armagh, Newry, and Down

29 Apr: Skirmish between Scots and forces of Sir Phelim O'Neill's at Kilwarlin Wood, near Lisburn, Co. Down

End Apr: Siege of Cork raised; Muskerry besieges Limerick Castle; Coote relieves Castlegeasal of Castlejordan and captures Philipstown and Trim

May: Argyll takes Rathlin Island, massacring the inhabitants

Early May: Tichborne seizes Carlingford

7 May: Insurgents fail to recapture Trim but Coote 'received his ticket to hell'

10–13 May: Meetings of Catholic clergy at Kilkenny; laity invited to attend

13 May: Munro's expedition to Armagh, Newry and Co. Down

24 May–6 June: Munro's expedition through Bannside and Glens of Antrim

End May: Government offensive grinds to a standstill for want of victuals and supplies; two English regiments arrive in Munster

June: Confederate Oath of Association drawn up and provisional Supreme Council nominated; Scots march on Lisnagarvey and Newry and

1 June: Charles I presented with Nineteen Propositions

18 June: Charles I rejects Nineteen Propositions

Year	England and Wales	Scotland	Ireland	The Continent
			Armagh; insurgents besiege Limerick; alleged massacre of Protestants at Kilmore	
			10 June: First meeting of presbytery of the Scottish Army at Carrickfergus	
	2–3 July: Fleet in Downs declares for Parliament with Warwick as commander-in-chief		July: Owen Roe O'Neill and some veterans from Flanders land at Doe Castle, Co. Donegal; 10,000 Scots now in Ulster; Munro marches on Charlemont and raids creaghts from Newry	
	15–27 July: King besieges Hull		July–Aug: Thomas Preston lands at Wexford	
	2 Aug: Goring delivers Portsmouth to king		25 Aug: Inchiquin's victory at Liscarroll, Co. Cork	Aug: French take Perpignan (Catalonia) from Spain
	21 Aug: Parliament takes Dover Castle		Aug: Good local harvests; Leven takes Duncannon, Co. Tyrone and campaigns in Newry and Down	
	22 Aug: King raises his standard at Nottingham; outbreak of First English Civil War			
	4 Sept: Storming of Southsea Castle by Parliament			
	23 Sept: Rupert's victory at Powick Bridge, near Worcester			
	Oct: King makes Oxford his headquarters		5 Oct: Preston routs Monck near Timahoe, Queens County	
	23 Oct: Battle of Edgehill (royalist victory)		24 Oct–21 Nov: First confederate General Assembly	
	12 Nov: Rupert storms and takes Brentford		Nov: Dublin administration and confederates strike coinages; Inchiquin wins battle of Bandonbridge; Leven leaves Ulster	24 Nov/4 Dec: Cardinal Richelieu dies; succeeded by Mazarin as French chief minister (until 1661)
	13 Nov: King retreats to winter quarters in Reading			
	13 Dec: Waller storms Manchester			Dec: Confederates appoint representatives in Spanish Netherlands (Bourke); Paris (O'Hartegan); Rome (Wadding); Madrid (Magennis and Talbot)

1643

20 Dec: Eastern Association formed

19 Jan: Cornwall secured for king at battle of Braddock Down
23 Jan: Fairfax takes Leeds
Feb: Queen arrives with arms off Bridlington, Yorkshire
1 Feb: Oxford Propositions
2 Feb: Rupert takes Cirencester
9 Feb: Parliament attacks Preston
11 Feb: Western Association formed
24 Feb: Ordinance for the Assessment
Feb-6 Mar: Siege of Lichfield Cathedral Close by Parliament
19 Mar: Royalist victory at Hopton Heath
27 Mar: Sequestration Ordinance
Apr: Lancashire falls to Parliament (except Lathom House)
3 Apr: Storming of Birmingham by royalists
7-21 Apr: Siege of Lichfield Cathedral Close by royalists
24 Apr: Capture of Hereford by Parliament
25 Apr: Essex captures Reading

c.27,000-35,000 Protestant and c.14,000-22,000 Catholic troops in arms
20 Jan: Preston takes Birr Castle
Feb: Preston takes Barre
17 Feb: Catholic remonstrance presented to royalists at Trim
18 Mar: Ormond, after failing to take New Ross, defeats Preston near Old Ross
4-6 Apr: Scottish and British settler regiments burn Clandeboy's woods
23 Apr: King orders Ormond to treat with the confederates

Dec-Feb 1643: Confederate agents issue c.20 letters of marque; by end of 1642 the confederate navy allegedly comprised c. thirty ships, rising to c.40-50 warships by the mid-1640s.

French agents disseminate anti-Spanish propaganda in Naples

Jan: Fall of Olivares

4/14 May: Louis XIII of France dies; succeeded by Louis XIV (until 1715)

Year	England and Wales	Scotland	Ireland	The Continent
				9/19 May: Habsburg defeat at battle of Rocroi
			May: Ormond's troops mutiny in Dublin	
			14 May: Scots and Irish skirmish near Loughgall, Co. Armagh; Scots burn all houses between Armagh and Charlemont	
			18 May: Newcastle surrenders to Munro after siege	
			20 May–19 June: Second confederate General Assembly	
			13 June: Owen Roe O'Neill defeated by Sir Robert Stewart at Clones, Co. Monaghan	
			20 June: Fort of Galway surrenders to confederates	
			24 June: Truce negotiations between Ormond and the confederates begin	
			July: Papal agent, Pier Francesco Scarampi, arrives at Kilkenny; Owen Roe O'Neill's forces defeat English at Trim; Munro's Dungannon expedition	
		22 June–26 Aug: First session of Convention of Estates		
	12 June: Ordinance setting up Westminster Assembly			
	29 June: Royalists control York after battle of Adwalton Moor			
	1 July: Westminster Assembly (sat until 1649)			
	5–13 July: Royalist victories in the west, especially at Roundway Down (13th)			
	14 July: 'Doubling Ordinance' passed by Parliament promises land to all who double previous loans to help secure victory in Ireland			
	17 July: Royal Proclamation ordering naval officers and seamen to carry their ships into Falmouth			
	22 July: Excise Ordinance			
	26 July: Royalists capture Bristol,			

leading to establishment of a royalist squadron in River Severn

5 Aug: Royalist capture Portland Castle

6 Aug–4 Sept: Royalists besiege Gloucester and fail to take it

2 Sept: Second siege of Hull begins (abandoned Oct)

4 Sept: Royalists capture Exeter

20 Sept: Covenanters occupy Berwick

20 Sept: Indecisive 1st battle of Newbury

24 Sept–2 Oct: Royalists besiege Manchester

Oct: Royalists capture Dartmouth

11 Oct: Royalists defeated at Winceby; Lincoln falls to Parliament

Nov: First series of attacks by parliamentarians on Basing House

7 Dec: Warwick appointed Lord High Admiral

13 Dec: Royalists capture Beeston Castle, Cheshire

---

7 Aug: English parliamentarian commissioners arrive in Edinburgh

17 Aug: Convention of Estates and General Assembly agree to Solemn League and Covenant

18 Aug: All fencible men placed on 48-hour standby

25 Sept: Solemn League and Covenant between the English Parliament and the Covenanters

16 Sept: First new levies rendezvous at Leith Links

Nov: Alasdair MacColla raids Western Isles and takes Colonsay

29 Nov: Military treaty with Parliament

Mid-Dec: Scottish levies march into southern Lowlands

Aug: Scots/British forces besiege Charlemont and raid Irish territory (until 16 Sept)

Aug: Disastrous harvests

15 Sept: One-year cease-fire concluded between the royalists and confederates

7 Nov–1 Dec: Third confederate General Assembly

13 Nov: Ormond appointed lord lieutenant by Charles I

19 Nov: Confederates nominate seven delegates to meet Charles I at Oxford

---

Aug: Negotiations at Westphalia to end the Thirty Years War begin (until 1648)

Year	England and Wales	Scotland	Ireland	The Continent
	Dec–26 Jan: Siege of Nantwich by royalists Dec–18 Mar 1644: Royalists besiege Wardour Castle			
1644	19 Jan: Scots army invades England 25 Jan: Royalist defeat at battle of Nantwich	Plague and poor harvests 1 Jan: Army of the Solemn League and Covenant rendezvous at Harlaw 3 Jan–3 June: Second session of the Convention of Estates 19 Jan: Scottish army invades England	c.19,000–25,000 Protestant and c.18,000–24,000 Catholic troops in arms Jan: Charles I authorizes Antrim to request arms men and supplies from the confederates; Foissotte (Spanish agent, until early 1652) and de la Monnerie (French agent, until Feb 1646) arrive	Opening of peace talks with French in Munster; marquis of Castel Rodrigo becomes governor of Spanish Netherlands; c.1,230 Irish mercenaries arrive for service in Spain; by 1652 c.22,200 had left Ireland for Spanish service; and by 1649 c.7,000 more had left for service in France
	19 Feb: Covenanting cavalry skirmish at Corbridge 29 Feb–21 Mar: Parliamentarians besiege Newark 27 Feb–27 Mar: Parliamentarians besiege Lathom House 7–8 May: Covenanters skirmish with royalists at Bolden Hills 20 Mar: Covenanters storm South Shields Fort 21 Mar: Royalists raise siege of Newark 24 Mar: Confederate agents arrive at Oxford to negotiate with Charles 24–5 Mar: Covenanters skirmish with royalists at Hilton 29 Mar: Waller defeats royalists at battle of Cheriton, Surrey	3 Feb: Scottish army reaches Newcastle Mar–Apr: Scottish royalists rise along Deeside	Feb–Mar: 3 Scottish regiments evacuate Ulster and hand Newry over to Ormond	

Apr: Inchiquin visits the king in Oxford; denied the lord presidency of Munster
1 Apr: Charles I grants plenary powers to Glamorgan
17 Apr: Protestant delegation from Ireland arrive in Oxford to negotiate with Charles
20 Apr–15 June: Royalists besiege Lyme
22 Apr: Siege of York begins (lifted 2 July)

Apr–May: Irish chased from Western Isles
15 Apr: Aboyne and Montrose capture Dumfries
16 Apr: New levy appointed to reinforce Scots in England; Callendar made commander in Scotland
17 Apr–1 July: Argyll campaigns against north-eastern royalists
21 Apr: Huntly's forces capture Montrose
1 May: Huntly disbands

4 Apr–25 May: Solemn League and Covenant sworn in Ulster

May–June: Montrose takes Morpeth and Lumley Castles, South Shields Fort, Stockton and Hartlepool for royalists
5 June: Unsuccessful allied attack on York
23 June: Parliamentarians capture Oswestry, Shropshire
June 29: Royalist victory at Cropredy Bridge, Oxfordshire
June–20 Nov: Parliamentarians besiege Basing House

4 June–29 July: First session of First Triennial Parliament

14 May: Munro seizes Belfast

June: Confederates allow French and Spanish to recruit 2,000 Irish troops
24 June: Ormond instructed to continue negotiations with the confederates
27 June: Antrim sends c.2,000 Irish troops to fight in Scotland with Montrose
27 June–15 July: Munro campaigns in Cos. Down, Cavan, and Monaghan
17 July: Inchiquin abandons royalists cause and declares for Parliament; many of the Protestants in Munster follow him
20 July–31 Aug: Fourth confederate General Assembly

June: Dutch unofficially 'recognize' Parliament

2 July: Rupert defeated at Marston Moor
16 July: York falls
21 July–3 Aug: King defeats Essex at Lostwithiel: Parliament lose forty heavy guns

22 July–2 Sept: Argyll campaigns in the Western Isles against Alasdair MacColla

July: Innocent X succeeds Urban VIII as pope

Year	England and Wales	Scotland	Ireland	The Continent
	28 July: Siege of Newcastle begins (surrenders 22 Oct)		End July: Earl of Castlehaven's confederate army reaches Armagh July–Oct: O'Neill and Castlehaven campaign in Ulster against Munro and British regiments; stalemate at Charlemont	Aug: French occupy Alsace; c.600 Irish troops serving in Flanders (under Patrick O'Neil)
	2–10 Aug: Parliamentarians besiege Sheffield Castle	8 Aug: Sieges of Mingary and Kinlochaline Castles commence (lifted 6 Oct)	Aug: Inchiquin strikes a coinage (further issues in Cork, 1645 and 1646) and expels Catholics from Cork	
	26 Aug: Parliamentarians capture Wingfield manor	9 Aug: Covenanters abandon Blair Atholl		
	Sept–25 June 1645: Scots and parliamentarians besiege Carlisle	1 Sept: **Montrose's victory at Tippermuir, near Perth—1,300 killed and 800 captured**		
		1 Sept: Montrose capture Perth		
		11 Sept–14 Nov: Argyll's inconclusive campaign against Montrose	Sept: Confederates abandon siege of Youghal	
		13 Sept: Battle of Aberdeen—800 killed, Montrose sacks Aberdeen		
	22 Oct: Newcastle falls to Covenanters	28–9 Oct: Skirmish at Fyvie Castle near Aberdeen		
	24 Oct: English Parliament's 'no-quarter' ordinance for Irishmen captured in England or Wales			
	27 Oct: North Shields and Tynemouth Castle surrender	Late Nov: Baillie appointed commander-in-chief		Nov: Henrietta Maria arrives in Paris
	24 Nov: Uxbridge Propositions			31 Dec: Richard Belling seeks continental aid for the confederates
	19 Dec: Self-Denying Ordinance (leads to creation of New Model Army in April)	Early Dec: Montrose and MacColla capture Inverary and plunder Argyll—900 Campbell deaths		
	Dec–19 July 1645: Parliamentarians and covenanters besiege Pontefract Castle			

1645				
Jan: Parliament appoints Inchiquin as lord president of Munster	Plague and poor harvests in Scotland—one-fifth of population of Edinburgh die	c.18,000–25,000 Protestant and c.14,000–20,000 Catholic troops in arms	20,000 French capture ten towns in the Spanish Netherlands; Publication of Conor O'Mahony, *Disputatio Apologetica* (Lisbon)	
Jan–Mar: Clubmen risings in Shropshire, Worcestershire, Herefordshire	7 Jan–8 Mar: Second session of First Triennial Parliament	**20 Jan: Preston invests Duncannon fort (taken 19 Mar)**		
Jan–22 July: Parliamentarians besiege Scarborough Castle	**2 Feb: Montrose's victory at Inverlochy—1,500 covenanters killed**			
22 Feb: Parliamentarians storm Shrewsbury	9 Mar: Montrose occupies Aberdeen		**Mar: Edward Tirrell replaces O'Hartegan as confederate agent in Paris; Habsburg defeat at battle of Jankov makes German peace more likely**	
	15–16 Mar: Covenanters seize Aberdeen			
Apr: Formation of New Model Army	4 Apr: Montrose storms Dundee and pillages the burgh	Apr: 1,400 Scottish foot leave for Scotland		
10 Apr: Warwick lays down his commission under Self-Denying Ordinance; succeeded by Batten				
26 May: Parliamentarians storm Evesham	**9 May: Montrose's victory at Auldearn, near Nairn—2,000 killed**	15 May–31 Aug: Fifth confederate General Assembly		
31 May: Royalists capture Leicester	23 May: Highland royalists beat north-eastern covenanters at battle of Strathdon			
May–June: Clubmen risings in Wiltshire, Dorset, and Somerset				
May–15 Nov: Parliament besieges Beeston Castle, Cheshire		End June: Glamorgan arrives in Ireland	June: Turks besiege Crete leading to war with Venice (until 1664)	
14 June: Charles I defeated at Naseby (Northants)				
17 June: Fairfax retakes Leicester	**2 July: Montrose's victory at Alford—700 covenanters killed**	8 July: A parliamentary force under Sir Charles Coote takes Sligo		
10 July: New Model Army defeats Western royalists at battle of Langport	8–11 July: Third session of First Triennial Parliament	July: Munro campaigns in Cos. Down, Fermanagh, and Armagh		
30 July: Unsuccessful covenanting siege of Hereford begins (lifted 27 Aug)	24 July–7 Aug: Fourth session of First Triennial Parliament			
July–1 Oct: Parliamentarians besiege Sandal Castle				

Year	England and Wales	Scotland	Ireland	The Continent
	1-16 Aug: Parliamentarians besiege Sherborne Castle	15 Aug: Montrose's victory at Kilsyth—3,000 covenanters killed	25 Aug: Secret treaty between Glamorgan and the confederates	Aug: French victory at Alerheim
	Aug-14 Oct: Final siege of Basing House by parliamentarians	17 Aug: Montrose takes Glasgow; Leith also falls	Late Aug: Munro campaigns in Cos. Armagh and Monaghan, Longford and Cavan	
	10 Sept: Fairfax takes Bristol	13 Sept: Montrose defeated at Philiphaugh and flees to the north-east		
	19 Sept-3 Feb 1646: Siege of Chester by parliamentarians			
	Sept-Nov: Clubmen risings in Berkshire, Sussex, Hampshire, South Wales, and Welsh Borders			
	24 Sept: King defeated at battle of Rowton Moor (Chester)		12 Oct: Papal nuncio, Rinuccini, arrives in Co. Kerry	
	21 Oct: Battle of Annan Moor—defeat of royalist horse		Late Oct: Archbishop O'Queely of Tuam killed in a skirmish near Sligo—he was carrying a copy of the secret agreement reached between Glamorgan and the confederates which the parliamentarians captured and then published in London.	
	28 Oct-9 Apr 1646: Siege of Exeter by parliamentarians			
		26 Nov-4 Feb 1646: Fifth session of First Triennial Parliament		10/20 Nov: Treaty between Innocent X and Sir Kenelm Digby signed at Rome
	15 Nov-6 May 1646: Siege of Newark by parliamentarians and covenanters			
	29 Nov: Battle of Muskham Bridge, near Newark	Dec: Most of cavalry which Leslie had brought to Scotland return to England	20 Dec: Second secret treaty, dictated by Rinuccini, between Glamorgan and the confederates	
	18 Dec: Parliamentarians capture Hereford	Dec-2 Apr 1646: Montrose begins siege of Inverness	26 Dec: Ormond arrests Glamorgan (released 22 Jan 1646)	
			c.16,000-25,000 Protestant and c.15,000-23,000 Catholic troops	c.140 Irish mercenaries arrive for service in Spain
1646				

17 Jan: Army of Solemn League and Covenant (9 regiments of foot, 10 of horse, 2 companies of dragoons, and 13 troops of horse) mustered near Newark

26 Jan: Parliament appoints Philip Sidney, Viscount Lisle as commander-in-chief for projected Irish campaign

3 Feb: Chester falls to Parliament

27 Feb: Parliament captures Corfe Castle, Dorset

17 Mar–17 Aug: Parliamentarians besiege Pendennis Castle, Cornwall

21 Mar: Last royalist army surrenders at Stow-on-the-Wold, Gloucestershire

15 Apr: Parliament appoints Philip Sidney as lord lieutenant of Ireland for one year

3 May–25 June: Parliamentarians besiege Oxford

5 May: Charles I surrenders to Scots near Newark

6 May: Newark surrenders

21 May–19 July: Parliamentarians besiege Worcester

May–19 Aug: Parliamentarians

---

3 Jan: Covenanters reoccupy Aberdeen

13 Feb: Covenanter defeat at battle of Callender

Spring–summer: Alasdair MacColla unsuccessfully besieges Kilbeny and Craignish castles; victory over the Campbells at Lagganmore

Apr: Montrose lifts siege of Inverness at approach of relieving army

29 Apr: Covenanters capture Fyvie Castle, near Aberdeen

14 May: Huntly storms Aberdeen

---

in arms; publication of Sir John Temple's *The Irish rebellion* (London); Ormond strikes a gold coinage in Dublin

Jan: De la Torre (Spanish agent) arrives (until late 1649)

5 Feb–4 Mar: Sixth confederate General Assembly

19 Feb: Confederates prolong truce with king to 1 May

Late Feb: Dumolin (French agent) arrives

28 Mar: Peace signed between confederates and Ormond

Apr–May: Argyll's Ulster foot unsuccessfully invade Islay

Jan: Dutch Republic's negotiators arrive in Munster

Year	England and Wales	Scotland	Ireland	The Continent
	besiege Raglan Castle, Glamorgan	3 June: Huntly disbands	June: Roscommon surrenders to Preston but he fails to move against Sligo	July: Congress of Münster; provisional peace articles signed by Dutch and Spaniards
	25 June: Oxford surrenders		**5 June: Confederate victory over the Scots at Benburb, Co. Tyrone; c.2,000–3,000 Scots and British settlers killed**	
	June–31 July: Parliamentarians besiege Goodrich Castle, Herefordshire	30 July: Montrose's forces disband	14 July: Capture of Bunratty Castle, Co. Clare, by confederates	
	July: Charles I rejects the Newcastle Propositions	Late July: Maccolla lifts siege of Skipness Castle	30 July: Proclamation of the 'First Ormond Peace' in Dublin (3 Aug in Kilkenny)	Summer 1646: c.2,200 Irish troops serving in Army of Flanders (under Patrick O'Neil)
	July: Brothers Bellièvre appointed by France to mediate between the king and Parliament (until Apr 1649)	Aug: Covenanters take Blair Atholl	12 Aug: Rinuccini's legatine synod declares confederates adhering to the Ormond Peace to have broken the Oath of Association	Sept: Franco-Imperial preliminary peace
		3 Sept: Montrose leaves for Norway	Sept: Ormond announces his intention of surrendering Dublin to Parliament	
		Sept: Inverary area under covenanter control and Huntly rises	1 Sept: Rinuccini's synod excommunicates all who favour the Ormond Peace	
			18 Sept: Rinuccini returns to Kilkenny to dictate terms to the Supreme Council	
			26 Sept: New Council nominated under presidency of Rinuccini	
			Sept–Nov: confederate offensive	

	England	Scotland	Ireland	Europe
1647	26 Nov: Completion of Westminster Assembly's confession of faith	3 Nov–27 Mar: Sixth session of First Triennial Parliament	against Dublin (8,000–10,000 confederates versus 3,000–4,000 royalists) fails to take the city	Oct: French take Dunkirk
		30 Dec: Huntly occupies Banff	Oct: Publication of *Ormonds curtain drawn* (London)	Dec: Peace of Vienna between Habsburgs and Transylvania
			Late 1646: Confederates allow Spain to recruit two regiments and France one	500 Irish mercenaries arrive for service in Spain; c.1,147 Irish troops serving in Flanders (largely under Patrick O'Neil and John Murphy)
			c.18,000–26,500 Protestant and c.20,000–30,000 Catholic troops in arms	Jan: Spanish–Dutch truce (until 1648)
	30 Jan: Scots hand Charles I over to parliament and receive £100,000 to leave Newcastle	1 Jan: Middleton campaigns against the Gordons	Early 1647: La Monnerie returns (until Jan 1649) with Du Talon	
			10 Jan–4 Apr: Seventh confederate General Assembly	
	3 Feb: Further payment of £100,000 to covenanting Scots army	Feb: Covenanter regiments begin to disband	Feb: Lisle arrives in Munster	
	12 Feb: Last regiments of covenanters leave England		2 Feb: Declaration of the confederate General Assembly against the First Ormond Peace	
	12 Mar: Parliament refuses to pay Scottish army in Ulster	20 Mar: Successful campaign against north-eastern royalists	Mar: New Oath of Association adopted by the confederate assembly	
	Mar: Parliament dismisses Lisle			
	1 May: Clash with Swedish Fleet off Isle of Wight	17 May–7 Sept: Covenanters retake the Western Isles	May: Dungarvan falls to Inchiquin	Apr: Archduke Leopold becomes governor of the Spanish Netherlands
		31 May: Siege of Dunaverty Castle, Kintyre; 300 defenders massacred		May: Revolt of Sicily against Spain (until Apr. 1648)
	4 June: Charles I seized by parliamentary army at Holmby, Northants		7 June: Parliamentary force of 2,000 under Colonel Michael Jones lands near Dublin	
	14 June: Declaration of the Army		19 June: Ormond surrenders Dublin to Parliament	

Year	England and Wales	Scotland	Ireland	The Continent
			End June: Parliamentary commissioners recommend that the Dublin clergy replace the Book of Common Prayer with the Directory of Worship	July: Revolt of Naples against Spain
		4 July: Dunyveg Castle surrenders	28 July: Ormond withdraws to England	
	1 Aug: Heads of the Proposals		**8 Aug: Jones defeats Preston at Dungan's Hill, near Trim**	
	6 Aug: New Model Army occupies Westminster		Aug: O'Neill's army fails to take Sligo then mutinies	
	Aug: Ormond confers with king at Hampton Court		Late Aug–Nov: O'Neill summoned to Leinster by Supreme Council and carries out scorched earth policies to outskirts of Dublin	
	17 Sept: Batten lays down commission	Sept: Loch Gorm Castle surrenders	14 Sept: Inchiquin sacks Cashel, Co. Tipperary	Oct: Spain declares bankruptcy
	Late Oct–early Nov: Putney debates		Oct: Jones campaigns against O'Neill and clears northern Leinster of confederate strongholds	
	28 Oct: Agreement of the People		Nov: O'Neill campaigns in Leinster; withdraws when Jones pursues	
	11 Nov: King escapes from army	Nov: Huntly captured	Nov: O'Neill fails to recapture lost garrisons and to take Dublin	
	15 Nov: Leveller-inspired mutiny in army suppressed		12 Nov–24 Dec: Eighth confederate General Assembly	
			13 Nov: Inchiquin defeats confederate army of Munster at Knocknanuss, near Mallow (Co. Cork) and captures major towns in Munster (except Limerick, Clonmel, and Waterford)	
	14 Dec: Four Bills			Dec: French fleet arrives to help Neapolitans (until Jan 1648)
	26 Dec: King and Scots sign an 'Engagement' on Isle of Wight			

1648			
Jan: Parliament breaks off negotiations with king	Severe famine in Scotland	c.14,000–38,000 Protestant and c.18,000–24,000 Catholic troops in arms; outbreaks of smallpox and dysentery	20/30 Jan: Peace of Munster between Dutch Republic and Spain (ratified 5/15 May)
1 Jan: Rainborough ordered to assume command of navy		Spring: Talks between parliamentarians and Nuncio's followers begin; Nuncio favours dealing with the Scots	
		Late Jan: Confederate delegations leave for Rome and Paris	Feb: Confederate envoys sent to France and Rome
Mar: Revolt in south Wales	2 Mar: Estates convene and accept Engagement	Feb: Inchiquin begins negotiations with confederates	
	2 Mar–to Mar: First session of Second Triennial Parliament		
28 Apr: English royalists take Berwick		3 Apr: Inchiquin declares for the king	
29 Apr: English royalists take Carlisle		4 Apr: Ulster Council of War accepts the Engagement	
May: Revolt in Kent	4 May: Levy of Engager Army	20 May: Declaration of truce between Inchiquin and confederates	May: Outbreak of Fronde in France
May–11 July: Parliamentarians besiege Pembroke		27 May: Rinuccini excommunicates supporters of 'Inchiquin Truce'	19/29 May: French take Ypres
27 May: Naval revolt in Downs—mutineers expel Rainborough and declare for the king		31 May: Supreme Council appeals to Rome against the excommunication	
29 May: Rainborough dismissed; Warwick reinstated as Lord High Admiral			
May–Aug: Second English Civil War			
10–11 June: revolted fleet leaves Downs and sails for Holland	June: Scottish Committee of Estates prepared to make common cause with Inchiquin and confederates	11 June: Owen Roe and Catholic hardliners declare 'war' on confederate supreme council	
27 June: Publication of			

Year	England and Wales	Scotland	Ireland	The Continent
	Westminster Confession of Faith	12 June: Engagers win battle of Mauchline Moor against Kirk Party rebels		
	June–28 Aug: Parliamentarians besiege Colchester			
	July–17 Mar 1649: Second siege of Pontefract Castle by Parliamentarians	Late July: Major-General George Munro reaches Scotland with 1,900 troops from Ulster		
	17 July: Revolted fleet, now under Prince of Wales, returns to Downs			
	17 Aug: Oliver Cromwell defeats 4,000 Scots and an English force at Preston, Lancashire	8 Aug: Hamilton, with 9,000 Scottish Engagers, crosses into Cumberland	Aug: Owen Roe O'Neill in direct contact with Michael Jones	10/12 Aug: French defeat Spain at battle of Lens
	19 Aug: Scots defeated at Winwick, Lancashire 1,000 killed; 2,000 captured; further 2,600 surrender at Warrington	Late Aug: Whiggamores take field in south-west Lowlands		Aug: Chmielnicki's revolt in Ukraine (until 1654)
	25 Aug: Hamilton captured			
	29–31 Aug: Confrontation of prince of Wales and Warwick in mouth of Thames; royalists retire to Helvoetsluys			
	19 Sept: Warwick arrives at Helvoetsluys to challenge royalists	5 Sept: Whiggamores take Edinburgh Castle	Sept: Belfast and Coleraine surrender; Monck takes Carrickfergus; Scottish Ulster Army ceases to exist	
		11 Sept: Engager victory at Linlithgow skirmish	4 Sept–17 Jan 1649: Ninth and final confederate General Assembly	
		27 Sept: Treaty of Stirling and Edinburgh ends Engager dominance in Scotland	30 Sept: Ormond lands at Cork	
		12 Sept: Engagers defeat Argyll at Stirling		
			8 Oct: Antrim leads a rebellion against Ormond; quickly crushed	14/24 Oct: Peace of Westphalia ends war in Germany (began 1618)
	8–10 Nov: Surrender of several royalist ships; remainder escape	22 Nov: Western Association established	21 Nov: Confederate envoys return from Rome	

16 Nov: Remonstrance of the Army	Severe famine	End 1648: Confederation virtually bankrupt	Spain recovers Ypres; c.2,200 Irish mercenaries arrive in Spain
21 Nov: Warwick's fleet sails for England			Jan: French court leaves Paris for St Germain
2 Dec: Army occupies Westminster			Jan: Dutch delegates sent to London to plead for King's life
6 Dec: Colonel Pride's purge of Parliament			
Mid-Dec: Negotiations between Independents and Old Irish begin in London (until Aug 1649)			
1649			
4 Jan: Parliament's 'Three Resolutions'	Jan: Second Act of Classes enacted	c.25,000–38,000 Protestant and c.18,000–28,000 Catholic troops in arms	
20 Jan: Trial of Charles begins	4 Jan–16 Mar: Second session of Second Triennial Parliament	Early 1649: Count of Berehaven (Spanish agent) arrives	
21 Jan: Prince Rupert leads royalist squadron to sea		17 Jan: Declaration of 'Second Ormond Peace'; confederates to raise 18,000 troops	
30 Jan: Charles I executed		Late Jan: Rupert and twelve royalist warships arrive at Kinsale	
6 Feb: Abolition of House of Lords	5 Feb: Charles II proclaimed king by Scots	23 Feb: Rinuccini leaves for continent	
7 Feb: Abolition of monarchy	9 Feb: Act of Levy		
13 Feb: Council of State appointed	22 Feb: Royalists take Inverness		
23–4 Feb: Warwick dismissed; Popham, Blake, and Deane appointed Generals at Sea	Feb: Lord Reay's rebellion		
30 Mar: Cromwell approved as commander-in-chief in Ireland	27 Mar–19 May: Negotiations in Netherlands with Charles II		Mar: Treaty of Rueil and temporary end to Fronde; French court returns to Paris
	1 Mar: Mutinies in two covenanter regiments.		
	Mid-Apr–early May: Northern royalists rise and Huntly joins them	1 Apr–8 Aug: Derry besieged by Ulster Scots; relieved by Owen Roe O'Neill	Apr: Imperial cities admit religious parity
14 May: Defeat of Leveller mutineers at Burford	9 May: Battle of Balvenie—royalist army destroyed	May–June: Jones reinforced from England	
19 May: England declared a 'Commonwealth'	23 May–7 Aug: Third session of Second Triennial Parliament	8 May: truce concluded between Monck and O'Neill	

Year	England and Wales	Scotland	Ireland	The Continent
	May: Publication of John Milton, *Observations* (London) 5 June: Parliamentary army ordered to leave for Ireland 10 June: Cromwell leaves London for Ireland	Mid-May–June: Covenanter garrisons established in north 21 June: Act for purging the army 6 Aug: Act of Levy 5 Sept: Advance party of Montrose's army from the continent lands in Orkney	June–July: Confederates advance on Dublin July: Plague reaches Galway from continent (until 1652) 2 Aug: **Ormond's army defeated by Jones at Rathmines** 15 Aug: Cromwell lands near Dublin 11 Sept: **Fall of Drogheda** 11 Oct: **Fall of Wexford** 19 Oct: Surrender of New Ross 20 Oct: Treaty between Ormond and Owen Roe O'Neill 20 Oct: Rupert escapes from Kinsale; sails for Tagus 2 Nov: Scots surrender Carrickfergus to Parliament 6 Nov: Death of Owen Roe O'Neill 20 Nov: Fall of Carrick-on-Suir 24 Nov: **Waterford invested (siege raised 2 Dec)** Late 1649–1652: c.13,000 Irish soldiers leave for service in the Habsburg armies	Nov: Prince Rupert and royalist fleet take refuge off Lisbon
1650	7–8 Mar: Fourth session of Second Triennial Parliament Mid-Mar: Montrose arrives in Orkney with 1,200 continental mercenaries Early Apr: Montrose lands in Caithness 27 Apr: Battle of Carbisdale—600–700 royalists killed and 450 captured		3 Feb: Fethard, Co. Tipperary surrenders 24 Feb: Cahir surrenders 18 Mar: Heber MacMahon succeeds Owen Roe O'Neill 27 Mar: Kilkenny surrenders 10 Apr: **Parliamentary victory at battle of Macroom, Co. Cork**	1650: Fronde flares up again Mar: Robert Blake and Commonwealth navy blockade royalist fleet off Lisbon 19 Mar–2 May: Negotiations with Charles II and Treaty of Breda

June: Cromwell returns from Ireland; beginning of the 'Third Civil War' in Britain

1 May: Treaty of Breda between Kirk party and Charles II
15–25 May: Fifth session of Second Triennial Parliament

12 May: Remnants of the Leinster forces surrender
18 May: New Model Army takes Clonmel but only after suffering very heavy casualties
26 May: Cromwell leaves Ireland; replaced by Henry Ireton

May: Montrose executed; last royalist stronghold in Scotland (Westray in Orkney) falls to Parliament
24 June: Charles II lands at Garmouth
25 June: Act of Levy

21 June: Parliamentary victory at battle of Scarrifhollis, Co. Donegal, destroys Army of Ulster
22 June: Muskerry and Munster forces surrender at Ross Castle
24 July: Carlow surrenders

July: Cromwell leads army into Scotland with 16,000 horse and foot
30–1 July: Musselburgh skirmish

6 Aug: Waterford surrenders
12 Aug: Ormond repudiated by Catholic bishops
14 Aug: Charlemont fort surrenders
17 Aug: Duncannon surrenders
15 Sept: Catholic bishops excommunicate supporters of Ormond

3 Sept: Scots defeated by Cromwell at battle of Dunbar—3,000–4,000 Scots dead and 10,000 captured

12 Oct: Rupert escape Tagus and sails for Mediterranean
3 Nov: Blake destroys most of Rupert's squadron

26 Nov: Assembly of the Catholic laity at Loughrea, Co. Galway

4 Nov: Treaty of Strathbogie—royalists submit and disband
26–30 Dec: Sixth session of Second Triennial Parliament
1 Dec: Battle of Hamilton—Western Association Army routed

6 Dec: Ormond appoints the marquis of Clanricard as his deputy

Dec: Philip IV of Spain recognizes the English Commonwealth

Year	England and Wales	Scotland	Ireland	The Continent
1651		24 Dec Edinburgh Castle surrenders after three-month siege	11 Dec: Ormond leaves Ireland for France	1651/.12: c.1,120 Irish mercenaries arrive in Spain
		1 Jan: Charles II crowned at Scone	Jan–June: Efforts by Protestant clergy to preach in Irish	Feb: Mazarin goes into temporary exile
			26 Feb: Stephen de Henin, ambassador of Charles, duke of Lorraine arrives to treat with confederates	
				May: Anthony Ascham murdered in Madrid by royalists
		13–31 Mar: Seventh session of Second Triennial Parliament		
		23 May–6 June: Eighth session of Second Triennial Parliament		
		4 June: Act of Classes repealed	4 June: Limerick invested (surrenders 27 Oct)	
		20 July: Battle of Inverkeithing—2,000 Scots killed		
		2 Aug: Perth falls to Cromwell	Aug–12 Apr: Parliamentarians blockade Galway	
		14–15 Aug: Stirling Castle surrenders		
		30 Aug: St Andrews surrenders		
		Aug: English fail to take Burntisland		
		Late Aug: South-west Lowlands cleared of Scottish troops		
	Aug: Charles II and 13,000 army marches south via Cumbria, Nantwich and Newport reaching Worcester on 22nd	1 Sept: English storm Dundee–800 Scots killed and burgh pillaged		
		6 Sept: Montrose falls to English		
		7 Sept: English occupy Aberdeen		
	3 Sept: Defeat of Charles II at Worcester ends 'Wars of the Three Kingdoms'; 2,000 Scots killed and 10,000 captured			
		Mid-Nov–Dec: Highland clans in field against English	26 Nov: Ireton dies; replaced by Edmund Ludlow	
	9 Oct: First Navigation Act			

1652	3 Dec: Last regular Scots forces surrender 29 Dec: Dumbarton Castle surrenders following a siege 31 Dec: English control all of eastern Scotland to Caithness and south-western Lowlands	Publication of Gerard Boate, *Ireland's Naturall history* (London) Feb: Act of Indemnity and Oblivion	English standing army of c.30,000 stationed in Ireland	c.4,500 Irish mercenaries arrive in Spain
	28 Jan: English invade and occupy Orkney		12 Apr: Galway surrenders	
	Apr–24 May: Last Lowland strongholds surrender to English 24 May: Dunnottar Castle, near Aberdeen, surrenders after siege Late June: Monck's highland campaign begins		28 June: Clanricard surrenders July: Lorraine sends pinnace to Innishbofin Island	
		8 July: Outbreak of First Anglo-Dutch war (ends 5 Apr 1654) 9 July: Charles Fleetwood appointed commander-in-chief in Ireland (arrived in Sept) 12 Aug: Act for Settlement of Ireland passed		
	Aug–Oct: Argyll submits to England			
1653		27 July: Last formal capitulation by Philip O'Reilly at Cloghoughter; only bands of 'tories' remain		Sept: Blake destroys French squadron off Dunkirk; surrender of Dunkirk follows; France recognizes the Commonwealth Oct: Barcelona submits to Philip IV Nov: Dutch Admiral Tromp defeats Blake

INDEX

Page numbers in *italics* indicate an illustration.

ACKNOWLEDGEMENTS

The publishers gratefully acknowledge the following for their help in supplying black and white illustrative material and for giving their permission to reproduce it.

frontispiece The Royal Collection © Her Majesty Queen Elizabeth II
1 Mary Evans Picture Library
18 Viscount Dunluce
27 Mary Evans Picture Library
33 The British Library (E 115(4))
39 The British Library (669 f. 12 (88))
43 The Trustees of the National Library of Scotland
47 Scottish National Portrait Gallery
52 James Graham, Marquis of Montrose attributed to W. van Honthorst, Scottish National Portrait Gallery
67 Fotomas Index
68 Ashmolean Museum, Oxford
71 Mary Evans Picture Library
76 Claydon House Trust, photo © The Royal Academy
79 By permission of the Syndics of Cambridge University Library, Sir J. T. Gilbert (ed), *History of the Irish Confederation* 1882–91, vol. 2
85 Fotomas Index
92 Ashmolean Museum, Oxford
109 Ashmolean Museum, Oxford
114 The British Library (E1185(5))
117 (*bottom*) G. A. Hayes-McCoy, *A History of Irish Flags*, Academy Press, 1979
122 By courtesy of the Earl of Dartmouth
125 York City Art Gallery
129 By permission of the Syndics of Cambridge University Library, Francis Grose, *Military Antiquities* vol. 2
142 Ioshua Sprigge, *Anglia Rediviva* 1647
146 The British Library (669 f. 10 (107))
149 The British Library ((E409 (25))
155 The Bodleian Library, University of Oxford (Rawl. Prints. a.7 (52))
159 Fotomas Index

181 National Maritime Museum, London (VV7)
188 (*top*) National Maritime Museum, London (1375) (*bottom*) Archaeological Diving Unit, St Andrews University
206 Hereford City Museum and Art Gallery
211 By permission of the Syndics of Cambridge University Library, William Maitland, *History of London* 1756, vol. 1
213 Ashmolean Museum, Oxford
214 RCHME © Crown copyright (SK7953/1)
222 Cambridge University Collection of Air Photographs: copyright reserved
223 By courtesy of Edinburgh City Libraries
229 © British Museum
235 The British Library (61.h.18 part 2)
237 The British Library (C 12214)
247 Oxfordshire City Archives (E4. 5)
249 The Board of Trustees of the Armouries (II.231)
253 © Dept of Archaeology, City of Bristol Museum & Art Gallery
262 Ashmolean Museum, Oxford
274 Oxfordshire Archives (MSS D.D.Par. Banbury C.1)
279 The British Library (669 f.11(4))
293 'Pillage d'un village' Louvre © photo RMN
296 The British Library (669 f.6(12))
299 D. Eddershaw
302 The British Library (E 138 (30))
307 Ashmolean Museum, Oxford
314 Conway Library, Courtauld Institute of Art
317 © British Museum
318 Fotomas Index
324 Scottish Record Office
327 (*top*) His Grace the Duke of Roxburghe (*bottom*) The Royal Collection © Her Majesty Queen Elizabeth II

Picture research by Sandra Assersohn

{ 391 }